——————— Partly Colored ———

# Partly Colored

*Asian Americans and Racial*

*Anomaly in the Segregated South*

———— Leslie Bow ————————————————

NEW YORK UNIVERSITY PRESS

*New York and London*

NEW YORK UNIVERSITY PRESS
New York and London
www.nyupress.org

© 2010 by New York University

Library of Congress Cataloging-in-Publication Data

Bow, Leslie, 1962–
Partly colored : Asian Americans and racial anomaly in the segregated South / Leslie Bow.
p. cm.
Includes bibliographical references and index.
ISBN-13: 978-0-8147-9132-5 (cl : alk. paper)
ISBN-10: 0-8147-9132-8 (cl : alk. paper)
ISBN-13: 978-0-8147-9133-2 (pb : alk. paper)
ISBN-10: 0-8147-9133-6 (pb : alk. paper)
1. Asian Americans—Southern States. 2. Asian Americans—Race identity—
Southern States. 3. Segregation—Southern States. 4. Southern States—Race relations.
I. Title.
 F220.A75B69     2010
 305.895'073075—dc22          2009048943

New York University Press books are printed on acid-free paper,
and their binding materials are chosen for strength and durability.
We strive to use environmentally responsible suppliers and materials
to the greatest extent possible in publishing our books.

Manufactured in the United States of America
c  10 9 8 7 6 5 4 3 2 1
p  10 9 8 7 6 5 4 3 2 1

# Contents

Acknowledgments ix

Introduction: Thinking Interstitially 1

1 Coloring between the Lines: 23
  Historiographies of Southern Anomaly

2 The Interstitial Indian: 57
  The Lumbee and Segregation's Middle Caste

3 White Is and White Ain't: 91
  Failed Approximation and Eruptions of Funk in
  Representations of the Chinese in the South

4 Anxieties of the 'Partly Colored' 123

5 Productive Estrangement: 159
  Racial-Sexual Continuums in Asian
  American as Southern Literature

6 Transracial/Transgender: 197
  Analogies of Difference in *Mai's America*

Afterword: Continuums, Mobility, Places on the Train 229

Notes 239

Works Cited 261

Index 273

About the Author 285

*For Willie and Sue Mae Bow*
    *and*
*for Maya and Julian*

# Acknowledgments

I originally undertook this project in order to explore an omission.

My Chinese American parents were raised in Arkansas during the Jim Crow era. How they negotiated the color line—not being invited into their white classmates' homes, not attending high school dances, for example—is not something they often talk about, nor is it a history readily conceivable in this now purportedly post-racial moment. I tried to explain this prohibition of intimacy to a Midwesterner who questioned, "Your mother *couldn't* go to her high school dances?" in tones that conveyed incredulity. "Couldn't" conjures up the image of Elizabeth Eckford forcibly turned away from Little Rock Central High, a racist mob behind her.

"I don't mean that if she had shown up the National Guard would have been called out," I countered, feeling the enormity of filling a historical void. To complicate matters, my mother remembers her absence differently: she *chose* not to attend.

In what follows, I place perhaps undue significance on mere subtleties, those moments in segregation-era culture that can be read in a dual register. From the half-told stories of my parents, the ones that do not make an appearance in the iconography of American race relations, I began an exploration into, in part, what it means to survive within a (partially) hostile culture with dignity intact. This book is thus dedicated to Willie and Sue Mae Bow, whose example infuses the pages of this book and whose presence personalized its writing. I thank Nancy Low, Steven Bow, Lori Carson, and Melissa Deponte for sharing this legacy with me.

I am exceedingly fortunate to have been assisted in this project by colleagues in multiple academic communities—Asian American Studies, New Southern Studies, Whiteness Studies, and American literature. I am indebted to Anne Anlin Cheng, Daniel Y. Kim, and David Roediger for their encouraging and productive feedback on this manuscript. Their acute commentary and attention have substantially enriched this work.

I am especially grateful for the support of Elena Tajima Creef, Malini Schueller, and Victor Jew, who helped see this project through at crucial moments. Their expertise and critical reading over the long haul were key to my own continued faith.

Victor Bascara, Shilpa Davé, Lisa Nakamura, Grace Hong, and Michael Peterson were enormously generous in reading the earliest fragments of what would become this book; their own writing continues to inspire me. Numerous colleagues enlarged my thinking along the way or offered strategic support, advice, and encouragement: Cindy I-Fen Cheng, Jigna Desai, Susan Stanford Friedman, Khyati Y. Joshi, John Jung, Josephine Lee, Stacey Lee, Carolyn Levine, Brian Locke, the late Nellie McKay, Jan Miyasaki, Gary Okihiro, Jeff Steele, and Morris Young. Thanks go to Jennifer Ho, Bobby Moon, Junaid Rana, and Steve Kantowitz for references they shared with me, and to Miranda Outman-Kramer and Karen Alexander for their sharp editorial eyes. I would like to acknowledge Jessica Peña, Nmachi Nwokeabia, Lisa Bu, and Atsushi Tajima for providing much needed research support.

My writing has deepened with the feedback of diverse audiences. I am especially indebted to Kent Ono, Tina Chen, Cindy Wu, Jon Smith, Katherine Henninger, Lauren Rabinovitz, and Yoonmee Chang for sharing their ideas and communities with me. I would also like to acknowledge the generosity of Marlo Poras, Louise Gee, Thomas Gregersen, Judy Yung, and Mai Nguyen.

This book has come together under the auspices of the National Endowment for the Humanities, the Max Orovitz Research Awards, the Wisconsin Alumni Research Foundation, and the Vice Provost's Office, the College of Arts and Sciences, English Department, and Asian American Studies Program at the University of Wisconsin. Special thanks go to Lynet Uttal, Hemant Shah, Phil Certain, Steve J. Stern, Michael Bernard-Donals, and Tom Schaub for their support of this work.

I am grateful for the editorial expertise of Bret Lott, the *Southern Review*; Tony Peffer, *Journal of Asian American Studies*; Gordon Hutner, *American Literary History*; and Mary Hawkesworth, *Signs: A Journal of Women in Culture and Society*. I thank these editors and journals for permission to reprint previously published text that appears here in revised form.

Eric Zinner and Ciara McLaughlin at NYU Press are extraordinary editors noteworthy for their professionalism and expertise; they deserve the credit for shepherding this work into being.

Finally, my greatest appreciation goes to Russ, Julian, and Maya, who have been enormously energizing, entertaining, and unfailingly present. They continue to make the often lonely vocation of scholarly writing worthwhile.

# Introduction

*Thinking Interstitially*

The Jim Crow era has produced a powerful visual iconography. Photographs of signs on public facilities demarcating the separation between "white" and "colored" enter our collective memory as potent reminders of past injustice. These signs of racial division in the Deep South make visible the contradictions embedded within democracy, the philosophical commitment to equality against its actuality.[1] The dismantling of the color line in the landmark decision, *Brown v. Board of Education*, became the putative boundary that separated our benighted past from an enlightened future, symbolically dividing past from present, then from now. For better or worse, we have granted the 1954 ruling iconic status as the "Holy Grail of racial justice" (Bell 2004, 3).

Yet that status and the historical periodization that supports it—pre- versus post-1954—nevertheless obscures the ways in which race continues to have force within American culture. It reveals the ways in which the legacy of segregation has come to frame race relations in the United States: first, as the struggle between differential access to rights, and second, as the struggle between black and white. Both, I would argue, have come to constrict our views of what racial difference means. In the first instance, race only becomes intelligible as a problem to be remedied by the state—it is only visible through acts of discrimination antithetical to our notions of democratic universalism. The second struggle frames this book.

The legacy of segregation has come to define the terms of racial meaning in the United States. To wit: the conflation between "black" and "colored." It is a logical slippage; nevertheless, this book is concerned with what becomes elided in that conflation: how did Jim Crow accommodate a supposed "third" race, those individuals and communities who did not fit into a cultural and legal system predicated on the binary distinction between black and white? Put another way, where did the Asian sit on the segregated bus?

Interned with other Japanese Americans in Arkansas during World War II, Mary Tsukamoto recounts her first trip out of camp to attend a YWCA leadership training conference. The bus ride to Jackson, Mississippi in 1943, she writes, "was shocking."

> What an eye opening experience it was for us, victims of racial discrimination, to travel far into the deep South. We learned first hand about two centuries of degradation of blacks that was still taking place in wartime America of 1943. . . . We could not believe the bus driver's tone of voice as he ordered black passengers to stand at the back of the bus, even though there were many unoccupied seats in the front. We wondered what he would do with us, but he smiled and told us to sit in the seat behind him. We were relieved but had strange feelings; apparently we were not "colored." (Tsukamoto and Pinkerton 1987, 176–177)

But what exactly is "not colored"? To say that Tsukamoto's experience simply ratifies Japanese Americans as honorary whites would erase the complexity of being situated in between racial categories. In her speculation, "we wondered what he would do with us," she recognizes that she is required to submit to this representative of white authority who must, both literally and figuratively, put her in "her place." While her interpretation of the driver's friendliness implies that the invitation to "sit in the seat behind him" represents a sign of favor, it also ironically affords him the greatest possibility for surveillance, not a trivial point for a prisoner of war on a temporary furlough. Her apparent privilege is offset by the fact that she is subject to the hyper-segregation of the internment camp. Racial separation in this case was in the name of national security: deciding her place in southern culture would be a moot point if she, an "enemy alien," was to have no place in the national bus, front or back. A straightforward reading of her favored status obscures the multiple axes around which status turns.

Tsukamoto's front-or-back dilemma and "strange feelings" go unseen in the story of America's segregated past. W.E.B. Du Bois's famous pronouncement that "the problem of the Twentieth Century is the problem of the color-line" could not prognosticate on which side of the line an Asian might fall (1965, 239). This very metaphor, the color line, admits no middle space and therefore no straddling that imagined border that defines not just social conduct but, in the process, racial identity itself. How could a buffer, a demilitarized zone of indeterminate race relations, exist within a context where it was said that even days of the week were segregated?[2] Unlike apartheid in South

Africa, segregation in the American South made few provisions for gradations of color. *Partly Colored* is interested in those individuals and communities who came to represent a supposed third caste within a caste system predicated on the distinction between black and white. How were Asians, American Indians, or *mestizos* understood within segregation's racial logic? In other words, what became of *other* "colored people"?

In his informal ethnography of tri-racial peoples in the South, Brewton Berry speculates that a mixed-blood Indian's racial status under segregation "falls somewhere along a continuum, between nearly white on the one hand and nearly Negro on the other" (1963, 47). The uncertain position of these "neither fish nor fowl, neither white, nor black, nor red, nor brown" peoples, the so-called Brass Ankles in South Carolina, Melungeons of Tennessee and Kentucky, and Croatans of North and South Carolina, would seem to mark them outside social relations dictated by Jim Crow. As one informant surmises about mixed-blood Indians in his home county, "My opinion is these Croatans don't want to mix with colored people, and they don't know how to mix with white people. I don't think white people would let'em. That's how come they keep to themselves" (cited in Berry 1963, 68). This social limbo, a segregation from segregation, would appear to support such groups' characterization as racial "isolates" whose distance from dominant culture would render their existence inconsequential to racial hierarchy in the South. But however a people "keep to themselves," there is no outside to social structure even as the history of removal contributes to the romanticized perception of American Indians living beyond the boundaries of civilization.[3] The image of the native living at a remove from American society has its analogue in the figure of the Asian as foreigner. Extending a rare dinner invitation to a Korean anthropologist doing fieldwork in the South in the 1970s, a black manager explains, "If you were a white, I don't think you'd come in my house for a meal. And if you were a black, frankly I'd be more cautious about invitin' you to my place. You're a foreigner. I figure you don' care for local gossip or anythin' like that" (cited in Kim 1977, 59–60). Situated as aloof from or inconsequential to the workings of racial hierarchy in the region, neither Asian nor Indian appears to be easily reconciled to black or white association. This misperception impacts scholarship as well; as John H. Peterson, Jr. notes about the Mississippi Band of Choctaw, "Far too many studies of historic Southern Indians have erroneously assumed that they were socio-cultural isolates, existing outside a complex, stratified society" (1971, 116). Whether characterized as sojourner, foreigner, or "cultural isolate," those who could not be placed as either white or black were not exempt from the complex social formations of the American South.

Nor were they necessarily central to it. Jim Crow culture's treatment of Asians, American Indians, or mestizos does not fundamentally alter our historical understanding of segregation; they may simply be positioned as anomalies to the overall functioning of white supremacy in the South.[4] Moreover, the cultural record of "other" nonwhites in the South during the rise of segregation is sparse, eclectic, quirky, and partial. Consequently, one could say that it can yield only a partial truth.

Nevertheless, I pose the question, "What became of other 'colored people'?" not to add another piece to the puzzle of disenfranchisement in a region often mythologized as unrepentantly racist. Rather, anomaly is a productive site for understanding the investments that underlie a given system of relations; what is unaccommodated becomes a site of contested interpretation. Postcolonial theorist Homi Bhabha conceptualizes the interstitial as the "passage between fixed identifications [that] opens up the possibility of a cultural hybridity that entertains difference without an assumed or imposed hierarchy" (1994, 4). The interstices between black and white forces established perspectives and definitions into disorientation. The racially interstitial can represent the physical manifestation of the law's instability, its epistemological limit, the point of interpellation's excess. Yet it may also be the site of cultural reinscription, the place where difference is made to conform to social norms. *Partly Colored* thus investigates the anomalous subjects and communities that must be brought to heel within a prevailing cultural logic—whether by exclusion, erasure, or incorporation. At one level, their presence could be said to introduce a complicating dissonance to a system of governance and cultural practice that could not perceive gradations of color. Conversely, treatment of nonblack, nonwhite peoples confirmed the flexibility and resourcefulness of white supremacy's apparatus. What is eccentric to race relations serves both to suture and to disrupt.

Interstitial populations unveil the mechanisms, political processes, and stakes behind the making of status. Looking at individuals and communities on the black/white continuum has turned up multiple and varied stories about how status is affirmed, conferred, or denied within the intersection of regionalism, governmentality, and economic privilege. Thus, to ask, "How did the system of segregation accommodate a supposed 'third' race when faced with those who were neither-nor?" is to question the logic of racial classification and to foreground the mutually constitutive nature of racial construction. But in situating this as a cultural problematic, I do not primarily seek to offer an ethnographic or empirical account of American Indians, mestizos, or, in particular, Asians in the South. I am interested in how color lines are drawn and what racial identity segregation demanded of those who seemed to stand outside—or rather, *between*—its structural logics. In taking interstitiality as a conceptual lens, I explore how subjects are made within the space between abjection and normative invisibility as revealed by government documents, sociology, anthropology, history, autobiography, visual culture, and fiction. The pressures of racial polarity challenged the assertion of other racial identities both during the Jim Crow era and afterward, producing narratives that only uneasily resolve ambiguity. While such a lens may appear to reify the black-white binary that is part of segregation's legacy, I also want to understand how status—racial or otherwise—arises out of multiple axes of differentiation: concepts of class, foreignness, sexuality, gender—what lies between the divisions we draw between rich and poor, citizen and alien, ability and disability, illness and wellness, heterosexual and homosexual, male and female. Thinking interstitially is a matter of turning one's gaze toward the space of the in-between to envision alternative connections and affiliations that complicate black and white.

Sociologist Max Handman noted that American society "has no social technique for handling partly colored races. We have a place for the Negro and a place for the white man: the Mexican is not a Negro, and the white man refuses him an equal status" (1930, 609–610).[5] What is the fallout of a failure to be socially "handled"? How does being neither-nor translate into a mindset, a psychology? *Partly Colored* traces narratives that attempt to reconcile Asian or American Indian communities and individuals to the seemingly uncompromising distinction between black and white. Or, conversely, those that refuse reconciliation, highlighting the very contradictions and irrationalities at the heart of white supremacist thought. In this sense, the "partly colored" subject thus represents, as in Mae Ngai's conception of the illegal alien, an "impossible subject," "a person who cannot be and a problem that cannot be solved" (2004, 5). In exploring the repressed stories of southern segregation, I consider what theorizing racial interstitiality might contribute to Asian American Studies, American Studies, New Southern Studies, and comparative race studies, and what the exaggerated context of southern race relations tells us about the cultural anxieties that frame the space of the in-between.

## Segregation's Interpretive Necessity

Since their arrival in 1870, the presence of Chinese immigrants in Arkansas and Mississippi offered a challenge to a society polarized by color. With no formal statutes on how the Chinese were to be treated, their presence called for creative interpretations of Jim Crow etiquette that made for ironic, if not humorous accounts of segregationist logic. David Cohn's memoir-cum-sociological treatise on life in the Mississippi Delta in 1935, *And God Shakes Creation*, depicts just this sort of inconsistency. He recounts an instance in which a Chinese man in need of emergency surgery is denied admission to a hospital for whites, one to which his father has donated money. On being admitted to a hospital for African Americans, he is yet attended by a white surgeon and "assigned a private room so that he would not have to share quarters with a Negro" (1948, 235). When his white wife gives birth to his child in a hospital for whites, he is not permitted entrance. This story of moving between locations illustrates the middle status accorded the Chinese within a binary caste system: the Asian is not quite white but granted privileges above that of the lowest caste. What goes unmarked in the testimony, however, are the taboos already transgressed and racial accommodations already presumed or negotiated by the Chinese: the man sought treatment at the white hospital first, he had (unlawfully) married a white woman in Mississippi, and his father had strategically donated to a White's Only institution from which he himself is barred.

Such instances reveal the system's ready but inconsistent accommodation of ambiguity. Incorporating others into segregation's caste system required on-the-spot interpretation that could not rely on the conventions of custom or history or on legal statutes. Like those contradictions already repressed in Jim Crow treatment of African Americans, the illogical and uneven treatment of Asians stretched the plausibility of the system itself. As Cohn notes regarding the difference between institutions of worship and those of education:

> The minds of the Delta Chinese, already confused by the complexities and contradictions of the alien civilization in which they live, are thrown into utter confusion by the fact that their children who are denied access to the white schools are eagerly received by the white churches. The public-school superintendent views them with a fishy eye but the Sunday school leader welcomes them warmly. They stand before God in equality with white children on Sunday, but on Monday they cannot stand together before the same blackboard. (1948, 156)

Cohn points out the irony of the disjunction between institutions charged with racial uplift: education and religion. While Mississippi deemed it permissible to inculcate the Chinese with the spiritual beliefs that would integrate them into community, it nonetheless barred integration by enforcing the link between race and educational opportunity as it did for African Americans. That one might stand in equality before God was never incompatible with standing in inequality before the state.

Uncertainties about where the color line was drawn and for whom take on both spatial and temporal dimensions. Documenting the tenuousness of Asian placement in southern culture, ethnographer Maxine Fisher recounts an instance in which South Asians driving through the South in the 1960s were denied motel lodging "because the manager saw them as 'Black'":

> He did, however, provide them with the name and address of a place where he was sure they could stay. They arrived, exhausted, at a Black establishment only to be turned away on the grounds that they weren't Black. Their solution finally lay in contacting the nearest university several hours drive away where they finally received accommodation. (1980, 124)

The travelers are perceived to have no place to go; the fact that they are accommodated at a distant university implies that only at a site of liberal education and at some remove can they be acknowledged in their cultural specificity. Nevertheless, it is precisely where "Asian" assumes uncertain content that the historical investments and work of social classification become visible. Similarly, as Berry notes, segregation's etiquette involves negotiation; he finds that whites and American Indians came to a tacit agreement about the shared use of a prime swimming hole in North Carolina: "If some white children went out there to go swimming and found some Croatans swimming there, they would either go away or wait until the Croatans came out. They don't object to swimming in the same place, but not at the same time" (1963, 79).

If segregation was a system that required interpretation and negotiation, the contradictory nature of those deliberations produced obvious ironies. The disjunction between culture's enforcement of racial hierarchies and the Fourteenth Amendment's provisions for due process are evident, for example, in *Hernandez v. Texas* (1954) in which a state court decided against a Mexican American plaintiff who hoped to reverse his conviction for murder on the basis that Mexican Americans had been excluded from the jury. The court ruled that Mexican Americans were white for the purposes of the

Fourteenth Amendment and therefore had not been excluded from a jury comprised of whites. As Ian Haney Lopez points out, the ruling took place within a courthouse with segregated restrooms—one unmarked and the other bearing two inscriptions: "Colored Men" and "Hombres Aqui" ("Men Here") (2003, 77).[6] Instances such as these recover from historical amnesia what the iconography of both segregation and the Civil Rights Movement have hidden from view, that Jim Crow created other "colored" people as well. My intent is not simply to establish that this derogatory appellation applied to groups other than African Americans. These anecdotes signal the irrational nature of white supremacy, those moments in which its requirements stand out in heightened, but ambiguous relief. To look at the "partly colored" is to look at the points at which Jim Crow became subject to interpretation, the instances before it enters into common sense as invisibly normative. While these incongruous moments and the narratives they spawned do not fundamentally change traditionally conceived understanding of southern race relations, I am nevertheless interested in the nuances of comparative race relations and the ways in which comparison challenges or confirms our sense of both the objects of racial hatred and the subjects of racial grievance. What lies outside the frame of historical memory reveals the subtle—and at times not so subtle—workings of southern culture. Moreover, what is forgotten, buried, or repressed for the smooth functioning of racial hierarchy can complicate the ways in which the Jim Crow era is itself rendered as history.

## *Theorizing Racial Interstitiality*

The "partly colored" pose not only historical and cultural questions—were they or weren't they—but a theoretical one as well. The schematic imposed by the law invites an examination of what lies between, as well as a critical lens on the ways in which the legacy of segregation has both informed and constricted our vision. To explore the uses of a spatial metaphor to talk about relations of power and status, I turn to the iconography of segregation itself.

What does it mean to represent between these legislated identities? For the Asian, Indian, or mestizo under segregation, racial meaning is created through the interplay between two signs, "colored" and white, and rests uneasily in ever-increasing or ever-decreasing proximity to either. How the individual comes to drink from either fountain is a matter of both identification and coercion, the affective associations of individual subjects as well as the state's imposition of legal identities.

COLORED                                    WHITE

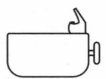

Illustration, courtesy of Wisconsin Union Graphics, 2006.


In this sense, the subject formation of the "partly colored" does not depend upon an epistemological certainty—I know that I am "really" Chinese, for example—but upon submitting to a disciplining social field governed by historically naturalized norms. Theories of multiracialism and passing have likewise exposed the fiction of naturalized racial identity; however, I am not interested in simply unveiling that ficticity. All ethnic identifications ("Chinese" or "Choctaw"), national affiliations ("Mexican" or "American"), or racial identities ("Indian" or "Asian") are no less socially derived than those imposed by Jim Crow culture. Nevertheless, the drinking fountain binary makes obvious what Judith Butler has theorized regarding gender, that all subjects are essentially failed approximations of an idealized norm. Introducing a spatial metaphor into that process, the historical schematic foregrounds not only the process of identification that goes into the formation of the subject, but its inverse—disavowal. The oscillation between two unstable categories reveals not only the individual processes of racial and class subject formation, but community self-conception and political visibility as well. Within this movement between black abjection and white normativity I want to locate a particularly American dynamic enabled by the southern context: that of racial interstitiality.

African American letters have continually asserted that black repudiation lies at the foundation of national community. Jamaica Kincaid writes, "Everyone in every place needs a boundary; in America the boundary is the phrase 'I am not black'" (1997, 73). In other words, the costs of immigrant self-definition and assimilation are disproportionately borne by African Americans. The emergent status of immigrant groups is negotiated not merely through the dominant, but through the apprehension—and rejection—of those who lack social power. A black resident of Miami claims about newly triangulated race relations in the 1960s, "Many Cubans are so eager to Americanize that they take on the worst habits of the white Americans"—the "worst" habits being a mimicry of whites' treatment of "Negroes."[7] Charting this genealogy highlights a comparative script, but with essentially two players: ethnic acculturation and national incorporation are predicated upon a group's inculcation to racial norms. "A hostile posture toward resident blacks must be struck at the Americanizing door before it will open," Toni Morrison argues. "The public is asked to accept American blacks as the common denominator in each conflict between an immigrant and a job or between a wannabe and status" (1994, 98).[8] This is the schema posited by Critical White Studies: identity negatively derived out of self-differentiation from blackness, an identification with "whiteness" that erases ethnic particularism as a condition of national belonging. Critical White Studies has highlighted the very processes that I look at here, those of identification and disavowal. As numerous scholars have suggested, European immigrant acculturation does not merely take place through the apprehension that one's ethnic difference must be erased, but through the apprehension of a more reviled Other who must be repudiated as a condition of entry. The immigrant will to incorporation, they suggest, manifests itself as a learned racism against the African American, the performance of which is not primarily addressed to its abjected object, but to power. In *Colored White: Transcending the Racial Past* (2002), a study that follows upon his influential work, *The Wages of Whiteness: Race and the Making of the American Working Class* (1991), David Roediger includes a chapter entitled, "Inbetween Peoples: Race, Nationality, and the 'New-immigrant' Working Class" that uncovers the "not quite white" status of eastern and southern European immigrants in the beginning of the 20th century. He asks, "What . . . did it mean to live 'inbetween'?"—in this case, between the African American and the Anglo Protestant (2002, 139). The answer, as numerous scholars have revealed, is that there are degrees of whiteness or, as historian Matthew Frye Jacobson notes about Leo Frank, a Jewish man lynched in Atlanta in 1915, those who represent as "inconclusively white" (1998, 65). It is in the spirit of this questioning that I likewise explore the black-white binary with an eye to uncovering the comparative processes of racial formation and the ways in which the boundary, "I am not black" was both literally and figuratively enacted. But I would also like to put those processes into greater relief by taking that body of work in another direction.

## Interstitial Narratives

If the Irish, Italians, or Jews, for example, represent the "success" of white identification as it translates into state and cultural recognition, what of those who failed? By "failed" I mean those who remain within the gap between white identification and black disavowal, who may have taken on the prejudices of the elite without ever gaining entry into their society. In other words, this work is interested in those who bear an asymptotic relationship to the normative, abstract subjectivity coded—and what Jim Crow made manifest—as whiteness, and whose "colored" status was likewise, to echo Jacobson, inconclusive. Moreover, in what ways does the racial continuum enforced by segregation's dichotomy intersect with or parallel the gender and sexual continuums that also define communal belonging and degrees of, to invoke the historically laden term, integration?

Jim Crow's racial continuum underscored the interplay between likeness and difference inherent to subject formation and set the terms by which communities became visible to the state. James Loewen's excellent study, *The Mississippi Chinese: Between Black and White* (1972), represents the definitive ethnography of what I am calling racial interstitiality in the South. The Chinese in Mississippi, he shows, did not accept their designation as "colored," a designation formally established in the 1927 Supreme Court ruling, *Gong Lum v. Rice*. Loewen's study reveals what transpired between the years 1941 and 1966 as the community engineered a "transition from near-black to near-white" (1988, 135). His study of caste shift develops a significant lens for comparative racialization: racial meaning becomes resolved for these Asian Americans through degrees of distance or proximity along a black-white axis. To focus on the interstitial is to focus on the space between normative structures of power—but also, I would emphasize in excess of Loewen's work and its unacknowledged inauguration of Critical White Studies, its incompletion and irresolution. That is, what anomaly reveals is not merely a more nuanced account of racialization, but the counter-narratives that interrupt the work of the dominant, the partial stories that characterize the *unevenly* oppressed.

Interstitial populations reflect the cultural ambiguity of what anthropologist Victor Turner has theorized as "liminal *personae*," initiates who are temporarily shorn of social status prior to undergoing ritual transformation. His work suggests both a spatial and temporal understanding of status transition, most usually, social elevation. Following the work of Arnold van Gennep on rites of passage, Turner conceives of the period of liminality as one in which the ritual subject "passes through a culture realm that has few or none of the attributes of the past or coming state" in symbolic preparation for assuming a new social position (1967, 94). During this phase, these "transitional-beings" temporarily "fall in the intercises of social structure":

> The attributes of liminality or of the liminal *personae* ("threshold people") are necessarily ambiguous, since this condition and these persons elude or slip through the network of classifications that normally locate status and positions in cultural space. Liminal entities are neither here nor there; they are betwixt and between the positions assigned and arrayed by law, custom, convention, and [ceremony]. (1969, 95)

"Liminal *personae*" may be seen not merely as initiates en route to heightening their social status, but as sites of interpretive necessity: they must be read differently as a result of their symbolic spatial placement. In drawing an analogy to interstitial communities or individuals under segregation, I am not suggesting a ritual shearing of status—rank, kinship position, sex, or property. Rather, the "liminal *personae*" of this book are obliged to struggle with the destabilization of established social categories—caste being primary but not singular—until some moment (if ever) of presumed stasis. These transitional moments may also refuse resolution; in other words, they precipitate moments in which indeterminate status is forced into conflict. For Turner, the "phenomena and processes of mid-transition" is both a "moment in and out of time" and one "in and out of secular social structure" (1969, 96). One cannot actually "elude or slip through" the classifications that inform one's position in culture; nevertheless, positing an outside to them, however illusory, forces into visibility the processes and values that underlie both reincorporation and rejection, or more subtly, contingent incorporation and partial rejection.

One can say along with Turner that the promise of looking interstitially lies in the exposure of terms of inclusion or, in this case, integration. What intrigues me, then, about the cultural question to be posed about Jim Crow's anomalies is the larger vision that such a question implies. To what extent does racial, class, gender, or sexual intermediacy reproduce hierarchies of status? Or conversely, to what extent does the existence of intermediacy need to be repressed for the smooth functioning of those hierarchies?

The first part of this book explores instances of disavowal—repudiating likeness to African Americans—as key to the status elevation of ambiguous communities over time, but also within the individual's narration of the self. Whether overt or lingering on the borders of discourse, this disavowal nevertheless produces an interruption, what cannot be reconciled to segregationist logic or the "successful" establishment of a third space within it. In contrast, the second part of the book foregrounds literature, autobiography, and film produced in a post-segregationist moment, texts which either deliberately engage an earlier period in southern culture or mark segregation's continuing legacy. From the perspective of the outsider and with an emphasis on sexuality and gender, the texts in chapters 5 and 6 shift the political valence of interstitiality by exploring alternative ways of thinking through the South's—and the nation's—centering of a black-white frame. Beyond feminist critic Elizabeth Abel's recognition that, as a denigrated term, "colored" "occupies the place of the feminine" (1999, 453), I establish that the forced or veiled assertion of identity around the color line intersects with questions of gender and sexuality in ways that suggest parallel continuums. Whether engaging anti-miscegenation law, women's "assimilation," southern "perversity," analogies to gay migration, or gender ambiguity, the archive surrounding the "partly colored" in the South is one that invites intersectional analysis of, I would claim, a palimpsest of caste systems.

In spite of institutional memory, Jim Crow did encode other subjects of segregationist prohibition and in doing so, created other "colored" subjects. Chapter 1 thus examines 19th-century and 20th-century representations of Asians, American Indians, and mestizos in southern culture. Situating the "partly colored" as interpretive occasions, the chapter witnesses segregation-era attempts to force subjects into recognizable roles, focusing on the ways in which "Asianness" in particular became articulated in terms of its proximity to the "Negro." Moreover, chapter 1 looks at one arena in which the administration of segregation simultaneously acknowledged and erased gradations of color: anti-miscegenation law. In recalling the ways in which state laws prohibiting marriage between "Negroes" and whites implicated and created other "colored" subjects, the chapter argues that such erasures have specific consequences for conceiving African Americans as the proper subjects of grievance in the post–*Brown v. Board of Education* moment. At stake is not so much a new conception of white supremacy, but an understanding of the ways in which American racism becomes narrated.

Chapters 2 and 3 focus on two southern communities that have been the subject of intense cultural, governmental, and academic speculation: the Lumbee Indians of North Carolina and the Chinese in the Mississippi Delta. As case studies of the forced assertion of identity, both these ethnic enclaves have generated voluminous records: they are widely recognized to be "successes" in that, even after being subject to forcible reincorporation into southern culture and its racial norms, they were seemingly able to achieve collective caste elevation during the Jim Crow era. In both chapters, my question is not "Are they or aren't they" but, "How is the space of intermediacy created and how is it maintained?" Taking the oscillation between white normativity and black abjection as an ordering lens, both chapters explore the representation of interstitial communities and the ways in which their ambiguity found uneasy resolution.

Chapter 2 explores one arena in which segregation forced the question of color and status: when faced with the pressures of white or black association, the Lumbee of North Carolina became, ironically, Indian. As late as 1980, anthropologist Robert Thomas noted about the community that some whites "think Lumbees are really a mixture between black and white. They use the word Indian, but they use it to mean a middle ground status position" (1980, 55). This chapter traces the ways in which that position was fought for and won. Following the rise of Jim Crow, school segregation compelled the assertion of their Indian identity in ways that prefigured ongoing arguments for tribal federal recognition. Crucial to this process was the discourse of blood: differentiating from blacks had to be visually inscribed while claims to whiteness—the oral lore of being descended from Raleigh's Lost Colony—ironically contributed to Lumbee claims of Indian specificity. The chapter engages legislative documents, community-generated petitions, popular cultural histories, and visual culture in order to consider the ways in which "Indian" emerged out of differentiation and racial latency surrounding the discourses of class and racial uplift. The chapter suggests that segregationist commitments to the theory of hypo-descent eventually clashed with blood quantum-level requirements and fears of progressive whitening in contemporary determinations of Indianness and sovereignty at the end of the 20th century.

Chapter 3 focuses on narratives articulating Chinese caste elevation in the Mississippi Delta within academic studies, popular culture, film, and memoir. James Loewen's aforementioned study, *The Mississippi Chinese*, argues that when faced with a binary racial system that had no accommodation for a third race, the Chinese engineered a shift in status from "colored" to white in the course of one generation. My interest here lies not in how the shift occurred, but in what becomes repressed in positing racial uplift in response to intermediate status. In contrast to European immigrant groups, the Asian's supposed caste rise can only be characterized as a registered incompletion, as near-whiteness. I suggest that this incompletion is likewise reflected in the discourses that have sought to represent such status, the scholarship surrounding and generated by Loewen's thesis, including the 1982 documentary film, *Mississippi Triangle*. Chapter 3 thus focuses on what discursive contradictions were generated in the incomplete attempts to convince of African American disassociation, specifically, the repression of Chinese-black intimacy. While caste elevation is dependent upon repressing this history, figures of Chinese-black amalgamation are never wholly buried or repressed, interrupting assertions of this southern Chinese community's approximate whiteness. The space of the interstitial is thus not necessarily an alternative "third space," but the crucible of both race and class differentiation and normalization.

While chapters 2 and 3 engage academic, governmental, and popular cultural discourses surrounding interstitial communities, chapter 4 turns to the question of the individual to investigate how intermediacy might be reconciled—or fail to be reconciled—by the subject. Highlighting the ways in which the figure of the Asian "stranger" becomes implicated in southern racial hierarchy, I examine two Asian American southern memoirs—Choong Soon Kim's 1977 work, *An Asian Anthropologist in the South: Field Experiences with Blacks, Indians, and Whites*, a personal narrative about the ways in which his role as "foreigner" impacts his data collection, and Ved Mehta's *Sound-Shadows of the New World*, his 1985 autobiography depicting his tenure as a student at the Arkansas School for the Blind in the 1950s. Both contribute to our understanding of how Asian self-awareness becomes mediated between "not black" and "not white": in Kim's text, the individual's response to his uneven cultural assignment exerts curious pressure upon the text's overt commentary on race relations. In Mehta's southern engagement, race becomes legible through an analogy to attempted integration, that of the blind among the sighted. For this transplanted South Asian writer, caste takes on a double meaning, one that remains largely unseen within the work. The individual's anxiety about social demotion surfaces within narrative traces.

Yet the space of the interstitial where culture is consciously interpreted—whether minutely, forcibly, or over an extended period of time—can be a site where the terms of culture not only become visible but are subject to potential reenvisioning. Homi Bhabha signals this reorientation in theorizing the radical potential of culturally hybrid art and critique. The "in-between" spaces, he writes,

> provide the terrain for elaborating strategies of selfhood—singular or communal—that initiate new signs of identity, and innovative sites of collaboration, and contestation, in the act of defining the idea of society itself.

It is in the emergence of the interstices—the overlap and displacement of domains of difference—that the intersubjective and collective experiences of *nationness*, community interest, or cultural value are negotiated. How are subjects formed "in-between," or in excess of, the sum of the "parts" of difference? (1994, 1–2)

The poles that define the space of the interstitial are multiple; in Bhabha's account, it is not merely the division between black and white that defines culture, but that between the past and future, the home and the world, signifier and signified, theory and activism, history and literature. The collapse of such divisions enables a potential re-ordering: "Private and public, past and present, the psyche and the social develop an interstitial intimacy. It is an intimacy that questions binary divisions through which such spheres of social experience are often spatially opposed" (13).

Thus, at the same time that I read the signs of cultural reinvestment in those oppositions, I want to keep open the possibility of the interstitial's deconstructive reorientation; chapters 5 and 6 engage this promise, marking an alternative political valence. What is queer to Jim Crow, what is unevenly accommodated within the racial schematic it imposed, may not only reveal the investments that uphold white supremacy and its underlying cultural norms, but also a means of rethinking those investments as post–*Brown v. Board of Education* writers and filmmakers gesture beyond the race-based forms of communalism to envision other forms of affiliation. The Asian in the South, for example, represents not merely a space of putatively disinvested race liberalism born of intermediacy, but a reorienting lens; the postcolonial Asian brings with her a "worlding" perspective that exposes the South as what is repressed in the U.S. imaginary, Third World within. Moreover, the figure of the foreigner, the outsider, may be a site of productive estrangement. Chapters 5 and 6 suggest that Asian American literature and film contribute to New Southern Studies not merely as proof of a new diversity. Rather, they engage the very dynamics at the heart of the southern canon, relations between blacks and whites, in perhaps surprising ways. The presumed objectivity or innocence of the foreigner serves as the platform not only for post–1954 race liberalism, but for rethinking embedded forms of alliance or communal belonging. "When we consider cultural institutions," Turner writes, "we have to look in the interstices, niches, intervals, and on the peripheries of the social structure" in order to find forms of *communitas* or comradeship that realign those traditionally conceived (1974, 268). My turn to the ongoing legacy of segregation in chapters 5 and 6 shifts away from understanding the processes of state and cultural legitimacy toward an understanding of how segregation continues to impact our ability to recognize each other beyond and across the racial schematic imposed by history.

In turning to Asian American southern literature in the context of feminist theorist Gayle Rubin's continuum of erotic practices, chapter 5 situates the Asian outsider as a figure of productive alienation and imperfect correspondence, one who questions the ways in which lines of affiliation and connection become drawn and policed. In both Susan Choi's 1998 novel, *The Foreign Student* and Abraham Verghese's 1994 memoir, *My Own Country: A Doctor's Story of a Town and Its People in the Age of AIDS*, embracing "foreignness" from the position of postcolonial exile can be read as a means of suspending loyalty to stratified social structures, both racial and sexual. In both texts, sexual transgression precipitates a renewed understanding of not only the ways in which color lines are drawn, but how points of human division and intimacy, of home and belonging, might be reconfigured. In looking at these two narratives that center on the latency of racism "outed" by proximity to sexual "perversity," the chapter suggests that Asian American literature does not merely add diversity to a now integrated southern canon, but provides a conceptual frame for highlighting other lines that divide and connect.

Chapter 6 returns to the question, "What does it mean to represent between categories of state-enforced identity?" in order to draw an analogy between the "transracial" and "transgendered." In thinking about how transgenderism contributes to a deeper understanding of segregation's legacy, my interest lies beyond the focus on transgender civil rights that is nonetheless a compelling and continuing struggle waged within law and public policy. In advocating for the importance of analogy to the project of social justice, I highlight the interstitial as a means of making visible social structure while seeking another language to describe intermediacy without recourse to the historically denigrating term invoked by my title. Like feminist theorists of transgenderism, I am interested in the conceptual challenge that interstitial individuals and systems of representation might pose to gender binarism and the hierarchy it supports—not incoincidentally, a mirror to my interests in the legacy of southern race relations. The chapter focuses on the depiction of a relationship between a Vietnamese exchange student from Hanoi and a cross-dressing white Mississippian in Marlo Poras's documentary film, *Mai's America* (2002). As the film situates both its protagonists as occasions for interpretation and targets of forced conformity, it suggests an alternate lens for conceiving collectivities beyond those inscribed by identity—"trans" status enables the formation of other concepts of community, of alliances that contest those sedimented by nationality, belief in biological inevitability, and southern history. My interest in twinning the terms "transgender" and "transracial" lies in understanding both interstitial subjects with rights and the abstract nature of intermediacy, the political valence of representing between dominant symbolics.

With the exception of chapter 2, I focus primarily on Asian Americans not only because of the surprising richness of what at first may appear to be an eclectic and undercontextualized archive, but because of the very ways in which the context of southern regionalism exaggerates Asian placement in the United States. As Lisa Lowe has noted, "Throughout the twentieth century, the figure of the Asian immigrant has served as a 'screen,' a phantasmatic site, on which the nation projects a series of condensed, complicated anxieties regarding external and internal threats to the mutable coherence of the national body" (1996, 18). Asian Americans are already situated as the national in-between; they do not merely triangulate relations between citizen/ noncitizen or black/white, they invoke cultural anxiety as American but not quite; as middle class—almost; as minority but not one of "those" minorities; as like us but not really. This conundrum of place is likewise reflected in the history of the Lumbee Indians; in the absence of removal, their history marks them as somewhat anomalous to that of other American Indians. Portrayed as, to invoke sociologist Edna Bonacich's term, "middleman minorities," both the Indians of North Carolina and the Chinese in Mississippi occupy an uneasy place between the dominant and the minor. Thus, this work does not attempt to replicate ethnographic and community studies exploring the tri-part structure of race relations in the United States among them, studies such as Neil Foley's *The White Scourge: Mexicans, Blacks, and Poor Whites in Texas Cotton Culture* (1997) and Claire Jean Kim's *Bitter Fruit: the Politics of Black-Korean Conflict in New York City* (2000). In contrast, drawing upon literary methodology, I seek in this subject matter not necessarily the definitive answer to the question, "are they or aren't they," but an extension of Toni Morrison's recognition that the "Africanist presence" infuses our American imaginary (1992). I want to examine that "thunderous, theatrical presence of black surrogacy" not in regard to the history of the victors, in this case, the canon of American literature, but elsewhere. I want to see where such a presence shadows the admittedly quirky archive of the minor. In the context of southern segregation, everywhere within the narratives produced by and about Asian Americans and others of uncertain belonging one sees the signs of the Africanist presence that "hovers in implication, in sign, in line of demarcation" (1992, 45). Morrison's emphasis on the metaphoric uses of difference offers a potent critical methodology; likewise, I highlight what is hidden, repressed, and partial—and what lies outside the frame of historical imagining.

It is thus that Jane Gallop's commentary on Jacques Lacan resonates with my reading practices here: "The psychoanalyst learns to listen not so much to her patient's main point as to odd marginal moments, slips of the tongue, unintended disclosures. Freud formulated this psychoanalytic method, but Lacan has generalized it into a way of receiving all discourse, not just the analysand's" (1985, 22). Reading the unintended disclosures within discourse ironically parallels my study, the anomaly of the "partly colored." That is, the subject matter occasions a parallel critical methodology, reading anomalously for the signs of both racial and racist latency. Moreover, as a literary scholar invested in fiction as well as legal, visual, anthropological, governmental, popular cultural, sociological, historical, and theoretical discourses, I focus not on the events that have traditionally established race's relevance to the panorama of the nation—genocide, lynching, unionization, armed resistance, collective protest. Rather, I highlight the nuances of racialization, what falls in between the gaps of history, in order to scrutinize the overlooked, what Foucault calls the outer limits of power, "the point where it becomes capillary" (2003, 27).[9] The Asian's uneasy relationship to power in the South is reflected in the uneasiness of the narratives that seek to convey it. For the "partly colored," such ambivalence surfaces not only as an anxiety *about* status, but as an anxiety within discourse itself.

## The Southern Anomaly, the Anomaly to the South

For Asian Americans in the South, the period of legally enforced segregation reveals the literal stakes behind historian Gary Okihiro's question, "Is yellow black or white?" (1994, 34). Mary Tsukamoto's experience on a segregated bus might offer empirical evidence as to one answer, but for the nagging question of how she, a Japanese American, came to be riding a bus in the Deep South in the first place. Posing that question and looking at the space of intermediacy might disrupt easy associations between mobility and racial privilege, front and back, that the legal symmetry of segregation has asked us to draw. My goal, then, is not to seek a more accurate or pluralist understanding of southern race relations by restoring lost histories to memory or expanding an archive to supplement demographers' data. The claim that one in ten inhabitants of Atlanta is now either Latino or Asian is deliberately unsettling, designed to signal that a different, "multicultural" South is emerging. This is the intention behind writer Richard Rodriguez's musing, "You go to these small little towns in South Carolina and there's all these Mexicans, and they're painting their houses Mexican orange and Mexican red. It's like this advancing army" (cited in Torres 2003, 182).[10] This "New South's" racial dimension is suspiciously like that of the nation's: we are colorful, now what?

But that narrative is limiting if it begins and ends with a plea for inclusion or pluralist additions to a scholarly canon. Rather than document this shift from Old South to New in terms of demography, I seek to complicate what we think we know about discrimination during an era that rendered it in black and white terms. My intent is not to restore diversity to a southern (or national) archive (to establish, for example, Susan Choi or Abraham Verghese as southern authors), but to witness what pressures a repressed history poses to traditionally conceived narratives about power and disempowerment. In exploring how racially interstitial communities became visible to the state and on what terms, this project involves establishing not only a more complex understanding of white supremacy and the communal values that undergird it, but a critical relation to how Jim Crow is remembered. The era of segregation is often relegated to the past in ways that belie its conceptual legacy. Yet the era that formalized a racial schematic that continues to resonate today is not itself an anomaly to history; thus, throughout this work, each chapter engages both the period of legal segregation and its aftermath in order to establish a continuity between historical periodizations, pre– and post–*Brown v. Board of Education*.

Nor is the South—contrary to its representation as the rural backwater against which a progressive, modern, and liberal North sought to define itself—a regional anomaly. The period of legally enforced segregation only exaggerated and codified the racial hierarchy existing elsewhere within the nation and outside it; in this sense, southern regionalism is not an aberration to the nation, but a site where the implications of racial classification played out in heightened relief (Gray 2000). In eccentricity one can find the nation writ large. In this sense, the South itself might be situated not as the "abjected regional Other" enabling American cohesion, but, in effect, as a microcosm of the national even as "the South" itself resists homogeneity (Baker and Nelson 2001, 236). Looking at the "partly colored races" under segregation does not fundamentally challenge the South's historically embedded investment in a black-white binary, nor does it simply offer a pluralist corrective that prefigures the emergence of a more multicultural South. This project contributes to Baker and Nelson's 2001 call for a new Southern studies and echoed in Smith's and Cohn's *Look Away!: The U.S. South in New World Studies*—one that resurrects a "civilly disappeared history, the history of indigenous, black, Latino, and Asian laborers and their families" (Baker and Nelson 2001, 236). In focusing on race relations in the South, one of the "old categories" of traditional Southern literary studies (Kreyling 2001, 385), I situate "aberrant" groups as sites revealing the epistemological instability—or retrenchment—of Jim Crow itself, with particular relevance for the ways in which race in the United States continues to be read along a black-white continuum. In this, the South renders the nation's normative racial organization in exaggeration and hyper-relief. How does the South contribute to Asian American comparative ethnic studies not in spite of, but because of, its investment in the black-white paradigm?

A Chinese American grocery store owner once articulated his place in the South thusly:

> We stick together, work, and don't bother nobody. We don't mix with nobody, we keep our mouth shut, no talk, just work. . . .We don't want to become *Bok Guey* [whites] and we sure don't want to become "colored" like the *Hok Guey* [blacks], no sir, those people were treated worse than dogs. We don't want that to happen to us anyhow, anywhere, anyway. We just want to be ourselves, *Hon Yen* [Chinese]. (cited in Quan 1982, 43–44)

The grocer's wistful hope projects a desire for a hypothetical third space. But is it possible "to be oneself" in a context in which there is really no segregation from segregation? Looking at the ways in which the color line was drawn here does not so much affirm the existence or denial of such a space as it foregrounds a genealogy of repressed dissonance. The interstitial is the site of multiple forms of cultural anxiety, as well as a place where status hierarchies are publicly interpreted and subject to evaluation and discipline. Bhabha notes that "it is the 'inter'—the cutting edge of translation and negotiation, the in-between space –that carries the burden of the meaning of culture" (1994, 38). My hope is that *Partly Colored* will uncover where and how that burden falls within the narration of American race relations.

"Drinking Fountains in a Tobacco Warehouse" by Esther Bubley, 1946. Standard Oil (NJ), 1946 courtesy of Special Collections, Ekstrom Library, University of Louisville.

# Coloring between the Lines

*Historiographies of Southern Anomaly*

My old man died in a fine big house.
My ma died in a shack,
I wonder where I'm gonna die,
Being white nor black?
                              —Langston Hughes, "Cross"

Images of segregation have become part of our historical conscience. They are reminders of past intolerance even as de facto segregation continues to permeate society. For better or worse, such images have also fixed our vision; we readily identify the "colored" signs over restroom doors or waiting rooms as literal signs of inequality. We also understand who they implicate; that is to say, we read the signs in black and white.

But in what ways do these assumptions foreclose a complex understanding of the work of white supremacy, its scope, influence, or nuance? A case in point: how do we read the image of divided drinking fountains? Photojournalist Esther Bubley's iconic 1946 photograph represents an apparently straightforward image of racial segregation.

Taken when Bubley worked as a documentary photographer for Standard Oil, the photograph depicts a man and a boy leaning over side-by-side drinking fountains at a tobacco warehouse in Lumberton, North Carolina; one fountain is marked "colored" and the other, "white." Bubley's photograph depicts a scene readily understood in the contemporary moment, an understanding conveyed in historian Grace Elizabeth Hale's assessment, "the black man and the white boy drinking indicate their racial identities even as they refresh their thirsts" (2000, 174). Critic Elizabeth Abel's interpretation of this image highlights additional axes of difference: age, gender, and class (1999). What one sees, writes Abel, is the photographer's staging of racial fraternity in spite of the subjects' formally separate status. They become united not only through their mutual submission as laborers, she suggests, but through the image that floats above them: a post-war advertisement showing a half-naked pinup girl offering the viewer Camel cigarettes. Abel argues that the image of the white woman secures the homoso-cial bond between black and white (men); sexual difference partially reconciles the scene of racial separation. The feminist critic triangulates the "colored"/white dichotomy by introducing gender as a point of mediation; in her reading, the introduction of a third space above the photograph's focal point generates an alternative account of the image that complicates its portrayal of racial division. Her reading exemplifies the complexity of intersectional analysis in its account of the interplay between race, class, and gender, youth and maturity.

In order to gesture to another third space, I would pose this question: what if the figure drinking from the "colored" fountain was not black?

It happens that the town of Lumberton lies in Robeson County, North Caro-lina, where the population was distinctly divided, not in half, but in three parts: white, black, and, according to the census at the time, "other races." This anony-mous figure drinking from the segregated fountain and made to bear the weight of Jim Crow's symbolic abjection could, in fact, identify as American Indian. How does this uncertainty change the meaning we take from the photograph or the dehumanizing history it evokes? What difference would it make?

The rise of segregation at the turn of the century forced the question of color and status in case of the Lumbee Indians of Robeson County. As I dis-cuss in the next chapter, when faced with the pressures of white or black association, the Lumbee became, ironically, Indian. Following the rise of Jim Crow, school segregation forced the assertion of the community's iden-tity in ways that prefigured on-going arguments for tribal federal recogni-tion. Crucial to this process was the discourse of blood: differentiating from blacks had to be visually inscribed, while claims to whiteness—the oral lore of being descended from Raleigh's Lost Colony—contributed to the Lum-bee claim to indigenous specificity. "Indian" became intelligible through approximation—as like black or white—in ways that gesture to a context that lies beyond the photograph's contemporary framing.

Yet Hale's and Abel's assumptions about this faceless man are also our own. As Charles Chesnutt writes in the 1920s, "The term 'colored' as applied to people partly or entirely of Negro descent is used the world over, and in the United States its meaning is not surrounded by doubt or uncertainty. No one refers to Chinamen or Japanese or Indians as 'colored'" (1999, 566). The seemingly unequivocal association between "colored" and black indi-cates the power of a seamless account of history to structure the terms of our comprehension, in this case, of segregation and the subject upon whose back white supremacy rested, as well as, I would argue, the proper subject of racial grievance. Thinking of American Indians as "colored" requires thinking outside segregation's frame and the symbolic significance that frame assumes in the post–Civil Rights moment. The "colored" man's identity as nonblack becomes inconceivable. If this ambiguity was repressed for the sake of the law in the context of Robeson County, North Carolina in 1946, half a century later, it could simply be forgotten. Yet the feminist critic's generative methodology can apply to her own reading: what lies on the borders of the frame establishes meaning and serves to reveal culture's investments. If "Indian" is rendered unintelligible in our national staging of racial injustice in the South, the stakes are high: the liberal frame of political representation in the United States is based on visibility to the state, in Charles Taylor's words, the politics of recognition. Moreover, it could be said that relations between black and white become sutured precisely through the erasure of complicating ambiguity—both in the context of segregation *and* in the way we remember it.

This forgetfulness of Jim Crow's unevenness is perhaps not so much a question of historical amnesia as of historical framing: American race relations center around a black-white axis. In *Colored White* (2002), a study that follows upon his influential work, *The Wages of Whiteness* (1991), David Roediger includes a chapter entitled "Inbetween Peoples: Race, Nationality, and the 'New-immigrant' Working Class" that uncovers the "not quite white" status of eastern and southern European immigrants in the beginning of the 20th century. He asks, "What . . . did it mean to live 'inbetween'?"—in this case, between the African American and the Anglo Protestant (2002, 139). In discussing why her work on Cold War civil rights focuses exclusively on the rights of African Americans, Mary L. Dudziak notes that although the "full story of civil rights reform in U.S. history cuts across racial groups," the American policymakers of her late 20th-century inquiry nevertheless

saw American race relations through the lens of a black/white paradigm. To them, race in America was quintessentially about "the Negro problem." Foreign observers as well remarked that the status of "the Negro" was the paradigm for exploring race in America. . . . As a result, [*Cold War Civil Rights*] works within that narrowed conception of American race relations—not because race in America is a black/white issue, but because [it] seeks to capture the way race politics were understood at a time when "the Negro problem" was at the center of the discourse on race in America (2000, 14).[1]

It was and continues to be. As Derrick Bell observes, the segregated South assumes heightened significance in the staging of American race relations: "Segregation was not merely an oppressive legal regime, it consolidated the imaginative lens through which Americans would now conceive race. It also reaffirmed the binary system through which we Americans tend to think of race—i.e., 'black' and 'white'" (2004, 82). Shifting the gaze to segregation's anomaly, to American Indians, mestizos, or Asian Americans, reveals how enduring and significant that lens remains. Numerous scholars in Asian American Studies, for example, have attested to its power as well as its mythos; Harry Kitano, Eugene Wong, Gary Okihiro, Pawan H. Dhingra, Claire Jean Kim, and Daniel Y. Kim have all affirmed the significance of the black-white paradigm for locating Asian American racialization.[2] In 1969, Alan Nishio borrowed sociologist Edna Bonacich's terminology for his title, "The Oriental as a 'Middleman Minority'": "Orientals," he asserted, "act as the 'well-fed' houseboys of the Establishment, defending the plantation from the 'lowly' field slaves" (1969, n.p.). What becomes lost in this metaphor is its more literal referent, the effort to recruit plantation labor from Asia to the post-bellum South.

This chapter thus begins with a restorative project highlighting segregation's inconsistencies regarding white-black social separation and documenting oscillating southern representations of Asians in particular in terms of their proximity to the "Negro." These comparisons are both overt—as in their representation as alternative labor to supplant the newly freedmen—and subtle—as Asians become the objects of white patronage and paternalism. Multiply situated within segregation's racial etiquette and its class structures, they nonetheless became subject to hostility at both ends of the social spectrum, hostility well-documented in popular cultural representations authored by white and black southerners alike. Mindful of the third space of Abel's reading, I then turn to sexuality's intersection with this specifically American and regional racial continuum, engaging sites where sexual transgression comes to define and mediate social standing. In the most documented account of Asians in the segregated South, the case of Chang and Eng Bunker, race was the least remarkable of their differences. How were race, sex, and class mediated in cultural understanding of these celebrated Siamese twins? As Cindy Wu has noted, Chang and Eng's standing as individuals "who benefited from enslaved labor" becomes elided in their past and present circulation in popular culture (2008, 34). The chapter goes on to look at one arena in which the administration of segregation specifically recognized gradations of color: anti-miscegenation law. Engaging specific state laws in the South, I explore the ways in which the law created other "colored" subjects and their consequences for our understanding of the proper subject of racial redress as Jim Crow restrictions began to be dismantled.

The space of the in-between is one marked by surveillance and interpretation. At stake is not so much a new conception of white supremacy, but an understanding of the ways in which the narration of American racism has erased from view its ambiguity and nuance. As these interventions reveal, the interstitial is the site of both social vulnerability and rhetorical convenience.

## The Etiquette of Racism or "Come on, see the Chinaman"

As the South's *second* peculiar institution, segregation intended to secure black racial inferiority, a job that the legal distinction between slave and free previously achieved. In obeisance to a prior social order based on slavery, it worked to maintain a tractable labor force as both the state and vigilante threats legislated restrictions on public access, education, the exercise of citizenship, and intimate relations between individuals. It did not merely separate white from black through a series of prohibitions but created racial identity: for blacks, intending to instill what was a psychology of inferiority and for whites, providing the figures of abjection necessary to the working of alterity and self-definition. Through this system of apartheid, the state produced legal identities that exceeded their formal classification; Jim Crow made both southern blackness and whiteness, a point that Faulkner recognized in the form of Quentin Compson's musing, "[A] nigger is not a person so much as a form of behavior; a sort of obverse reflection of the white people he lives among" (1984, 86). In defining and delimiting participation in the public sphere to obviate the concept of equal citizenship, segregation established a caste system in a country whose democratic principles are, in theory, antithetical to the notion of caste. Race hierarchy was, as Gunnar Myrdal noted, an "American Dilemma" (1962).

Beyond this ponderous but by no means uniform legal apparatus, what made segregation in the South distinctive was its inscription as an etiquette, a highly refined but variable system of ritualized social conduct. The separation between races specified a series of taboos enforced not only by the law and by vigilantism but by social convention. Statutory regulations might govern the most significant aspects of black life—one's sexual partner, livelihood, social mobility, and the very exercise of citizenship—but the ceremonial requirements of living Jim Crow also manifested themselves in a series of minutely negotiated ways of being: Hat on or off? Front door or back? What mode of address? Which railway coach, elevator, doctor's office, or diner? In the post-bellum South, social ritual contributed to the maintenance of inequality after the primary means of distinguishing between black and white—slave or free—no longer existed. Essential to this system of manners was a particularly regional sense of belonging signaled by and potentially internalized as "knowing one's place." For African Americans, to forget that place was to face potentially violent repercussions and the disapprobation of white and, potentially, black. Illogical to democratic principles, segregation was also a system that functioned smoothly even within the presence of barely repressed contradiction. In documenting forms of segregation by region and context, Charles S. Johnson's 1943 *Patterns of Negro Segregation* reveals that Jim Crow codes were not uniform but fluid, and often so unevenly applied as to defy rationality. On the taboo of interracial dining, a black insurance agent noted, "[White people] seem to think it would make the food poison if a Negro ate with them. They don't say anything about what is the case when the Negro woman in the kitchen fixes the food" (cited in Johnson 1943, 144). Such contradictions highlight the artificiality of social taboos placed on physical and social intimacy. Johnson likewise noted that office buildings in Atlanta had separate elevators for African Americans subject to additional requirements of uncertain expectation: "All Negroes must ride up in this elevator," he writes, "but all of the cars will take Negroes down" (42).

But to say that specific counties, towns, or even buildings had their own interpretations of segregationist mores does not imply that one was therefore exempt from knowing them. To be ignorant of one's place was to risk not only public humiliation but physical assault, especially given that the degree of one's alleged offense did not necessarily prefigure that severity of mob response. In 1908, among reasons for lynching, Ray Stannard Baker listed these: "For being father of boy who jostled white women," "Stealing seventy-five cents," "Expressing sympathy for mob's victim" (1964, 176–177). Nevertheless, the color line between black and white was itself not always clearly demarcated. The following sign posted in an Atlanta streetcar, for example, specified, in logical and orderly fashion, how blacks and whites were to comply with Jim Crow requirements:

WHITE PEOPLE WILL SEAT FROM THE FRONT OF CAR TOWARD
THE BACK AND COLORED PEOPLE FROM REAR TOWARD FRONT

Witnessing this sign and the friction caused by asking both black and white patrons to move in compliance compelled Baker to comment, "This very absence of a clear demarcation is significant of many relationships in the South. The colour line is drawn, but neither race knows just where it is" (1964, 31).

If neither blacks nor whites knew just where the line was drawn, such a directive could hardly be clear to those whose very classification was contested. Langston Hughes's poem, "Cross," speaks to the ambiguous position of biracial individuals: being both white and black, where did they fit in a racially stratified and segregated society? Jim Crow had a ready answer thanks to the "one drop" rule of hypodescent: they were black. Nevertheless, the figure of the "mulatto" is a site of cultural anxiety as a reminder of the color line's permeability. Thus, incidents of passing are significant sites for cultural critique precisely because they disrupt segregation's easy racial epistemology, revealing less about the intrinsic nature of racial identity than the irrationality underlying the South's ordering binary. My subject here redirects Hughes's question by suggesting an alternative intermediacy, one no less a question of epistemology, but avoiding the questions of authenticity implied by concepts of closeting, imposture, or biological descent.

The era of segregation is scarcely remembered as one fraught with inconsistency or contingency; rather, the period has come to signify the very blatant nature of racial discrimination, dehumanization, and violence. Yet segregation was a cultural system that called for interpretation not despite but because of the simple schematic it drew between groups of people. One of the themes that runs throughout Richard Wright's coming of age memoir, *Black Boy*, is the interpretive imperative of living Jim Crow. Richard confesses his inability to read southern codes of behavior:

> The words and actions of white people were baffling signs to me. . . . Misreading the reactions of whites around me made me say and do the wrong things. In my dealing with whites I was conscious of the entirety of my relations with them, and they were conscious only of what was happening at a given moment. I had to keep remembering what others took for granted; I had to think out what others felt. (1993, 231)

Richard's failure to internalize the etiquette of racism reveals both the artificiality and complexity of its rules, the knowledge of which is essential to his survival, and the rejection of which is essential to his humanity. His autobiography provides a significant record of what racial performance segregation required, even as scholars have pointed out the rhetorical embellishments or omissions that figured into its making.[3] In pointed correction, James Baldwin famously wrote, "It is the etiquette which is baffling, not the spirit" (1961, 108). It is that spirit—the straightforward hatred that underlies white supremacy's legal regime—that has come to frame the era. Yet looking at American Indians, mestizos, and, in particular, Asian Americans within that regime recalls Richard Wright's experience as one intimately connected to segregation's interpretive necessity. If the South's enduring iconography conveys with succinct clarity the dehumanizing force of segregation, what of segregation's subtle but no less insidious work?

The "partly colored" provided a conceptual ambiguity that required reading within an established epistemological frame, a frame that necessitated flexibility as well as the heightened surveillance of temporarily suspended judgment. As one Chinese American woman in the Mississippi Delta put it: "Delta whites think there are only two races in the world and do not know what to do with the Chinese" (cited in Loewen 1972, 182). In tracing her father's genealogy in North Carolina's Outer Banks, Elena Tajima Creef notes:

> In this part of the South, the color line that has been in place for hundreds of years is still fairly well established. Just exactly where half-Japanese daughters fit into the local racial hierarchy is ambiguous at best. Folks down here are either far too polite or far too confused to tell me to my face exactly where I should stand in a region where yellow is neither black nor white. (2005, 77)

Part of the consequence of being "outside" the frame of racial reference is being the object of scrutiny—veiled or no—that passes as interest or curiosity. The child protagonist of Cynthia Kadohata's novel, *kira-kira* innocently reports that upon the birth of her brother in Georgia in the 1960s, "All the nurses at the hospital took turns coming to see him . . . . they had never seen a Japanese baby before. . . . It was funny how so many people ignored my mother, but they were all fascinated by this little Japanese baby" (2004, 56). The Asian's simultaneous invisibility and hypervisibility are conveyed in an anecdote that Korean anthropologist Choong Soon Kim tells about arriving in a white neighborhood in Georgia in the 1970s to speak to one of his "native" informants. The neighbors "came out, one by one" to witness him cornered by his informant's aggressive dogs: "Seeing a total stranger, they stood still and gazed at me with obvious surprise and suspicion. Children shouted, 'Come on, see the Chinaman,' calling to their peers" (1977, 33). Their attention recalls that famous hailing, "Look, a Negro!" that accompanies Franz Fanon's recognition of his racial abjection, that sudden awareness of the disjunction between his own self-conception and how he has been made to be a black man (1991, 111). "Come on, see the Chinaman" at first seems to lack the force of Fanon's recognition; Kim has become the racialized object not of threat, but of amusement, contempt, and, then, indifference. The anecdote is not an apocryphal moment, one redolent of Fanon's recognition of the "dialectic between [his] body and the world" (111) that challenges the foundations of self-knowledge and identity; as an obvious misrecognition (Kim is Korean), it can remain for him just that, an anecdote. Nevertheless, the Asian's proximity to the black man here is conveyed not in the anecdote's content but in its structure: "Look, *there's one!*" What "one" is within Jim Crow's binary system proved to be flexible at times, and perhaps not surprisingly, as I discuss in the following chapters, dependent upon the subject's ability to approximate middle-class norms.

The following exchange recounted in Brewton Berry's *Almost White* reveals the elasticity of southern racial etiquette: "Do you call Croatans 'Mr.' and 'Mrs.'?" the researcher asks a white dental receptionist regarding now Lumbee Indians in North Carolina.

> "That all depends," she replied.
> "Depends on what?" said I.
> "Well," she said with a wink, "some Croatans have money." (1963, 82)

The wink lets us know that we are party to a conspiracy about race: it is contingent and linked to class status. In the next section, I explore briefly the labor determinates of fixing difference on the South's racial continuum before moving to another axis of social status, sexuality.

## *The Interstitial Asian*

In 1851, Mississippi writer Joseph B. Cobb offered the following assessment of the American Indian of the South:

> The Indians of our day, besides having a full share of all the lower and degrading vices of the Southern negro, such as stealing, lying, and filthy tastes, are noted for cowardice, and craft, and meanness of every description. They possess not, so far as my observation and experience go, a single admirable virtue, or magnanimous or noble quality of heart or mind. The Southern slave, much more the native, free-born African, is his superior in every sense of the word; and although slaves for life, and begetting slaves, I do not know a negro that would countenance an exchange of situations

with a Choctaw or Chickasaw Indian. As a general thing, these are hardly above the animals. (1970, 177–178)

True to the spirit of comparison, what is being weighed here is not so much character against character, but slavery as an institution; the speaker predictably justifies the practice by marking a life of servitude as superior to a life of freedom in apparent squalor. But the characterization of the Indian as the inferior of slaves is obviously as expedient as its obverse, characterizing mestizos as white. As Frederick Law Olmsted recounts in his 1860 travel narrative, *A Journey in Back Country*, the "whiteness" of Mexican bond servants was likewise invoked in the justification of slavery, specifically, in support of fugitive slave laws and their international reach. In discussing the implications of the law with a plantation owner, Olmsted points out that when Mexican "bounden servants" crossed into American territory, "the United States government never took any measures to restore them, nor did the Mexicans ask it": the slave-owner replies indignantly, "[T]hose are not niggers, are they? They are white people, just as white as the Mexicans themselves, and just as much right to be free'" (Olmstead 1970, 173). In both cases, American Indians and Mexicans become placed within an interpretative frame of approximate status to contrary conclusion but identical effect—the defense of slavery. This fluidity reveals the purposes that classification serves: the economic exploitation of not the subjects at hand, but of others. In the post-bellum South, this convenience becomes apparent in representations of "coolies" from Asia as planters and politicians alike looked to alternative pools of labor to supplant those of the freedmen. The relationship between the "Chinese Question" and the "Negro Problem" is the subject of Najia Aarim-Heriot's *Chinese Immigrants, African Americans, and Racial Anxiety in the United States, 1848–82* (2003); I want to suggest those resonances here as they emerged in the South, the other regional manifestation of what Dan Caldwell deemed the "Negroization of the Chinese stereotype" in the West and the ways in which Chinese intelligibility hinged upon their interchangeability with African Americans (1971).

On the subject of "Coolies as a Substitute for Negroes," *DeBow's Review* contributed to importation fervor in 1866 by reporting favorably on the productive use of Asian workers in the Caribbean, publishing an assessment of labor costs and exportation output in Trinidad for 1859–1861, the years "immediately anterior and posterior to emancipation." Noting the impressive increase in the production of sugar, the report illustrates, in "hard" numbers, "the advantages of the coolie system—a system which these once impoverished countries have adopted—a system that has raised them from almost entirely ruined to highly flourishing dependencies." [4] A year later, *DeBow's* continued to trumpet importation by lauding the habits of the "strange celestials" who had been brought in to work a Louisiana plantation, habits of work and self-maintenance conducive to maximizing labor extraction: they are "always quiet, working steadily the whole day long" and "without murmuring do whatever is required, working as freely in knee-deep ditch mud as in the field." [5] *DeBow's* goes further to cite a piece in a Nashville paper that rendered the comparison of Asians to African American workers in explicit terms: "Chinese coolies are more apt to learn than negroes. They are more skillful in the use of their hands and muscles. Their imitative capacity is unlimited. . . . They are more active and more industrious than the negro. Their natural intelligence is far superior to his. They are docile and obedient." [6]

As southern schemes to import Asian labor into the post-emancipation South gained currency, comparisons continued. In a memoir published the year after the Civil War, Reid Whitelaw reveals that southern planters were already speculating on how to recruit cheap labor. He records this pronouncement:

> Let the Yankees take the niggers, since they're so fond of them. Why, I was talking, down to Selma, the other day, with Jim Branson, up from Haynesville. We figured up, I don't know how many millions of coolies there are in China, that you can bring over for a song. It will take three of 'em to do the work of two niggers; but they'll live on next to nothing and clothe themselves, and you've only got to pay 'em four dollars a month. That's our game now. And if it comes to voting, I reckon we can manage that pretty well! [7]

The prospect of chastened freedmen returning South only to find themselves replaced was, as George Bentham depicts in 1880, a gleefully anticipated comeuppance: "'No, sah, the Chinee's the man for us; a free nigger is no possible 'count for nothin'. By 'n by, when the Yankee gover'ment gits 'nough of their cussed freedom, we'll have our niggers back ag'in; till then I'm goin' for the Chinee.'" [8] This southern "experiment" echoed that of British sugar planters in Trinidad who looked to labor from India to fill their shortages. The movement resulted in the importation of 144,000 Indian agricultural workers to Trinidad between 1845 and 1917. [9] In 1871, *Every Saturday* prophesied that the "prospect of John's crowding Sambo from [American] soil may be much nearer than we imagine":

It has taken but twenty years for him of the cue [sic] and almond eyes to come over and do half the labor that is done in Cuba. He has long done most of the work in the Southern colonies of the Dutch, French, and Spanish; and why he may not be destined to rejuvenate our crippled South, is more than a mere every-day philosopher is prepared to say.[10]

While the "Negroization" of Asian labor takes obvious forms, as in these examples weighing the relative capacities of field hands, it could also be more subtle. In 1872, one southern lady in Pine Bluff, Arkansas cheerfully recounted, "One of the pleasantest incidents of Christmas week was a little visit we had from two of *our* Chinamen."[11] The possessive casts the workers within the familiar discourse of colonialist paternalism; the visit is described in diminutive terms, but, by implication, so too are the people. The writer's proprietary ownership infantilizes those who, in working for her, also live under her apparent patronage and largesse.

The history of the most noteworthy southern labor importation scheme, the Chinese Labor Convention or Memphis Convention, has been ably documented in the work of Gunther Barth, Etta B. Peabody, Lucy M. Cohen, and most recently Moon-Ho Jung among others.[12] After Arkansas planters took the initiative in forming the Arkansas River Valley Immigration Company, 200 southern delegates converged in Memphis in 1869 to explore the feasibility of importing Chinese workers to help mitigate agricultural labor shortages. Addressing the convention, labor contractor Cornelius Koopmanschap assured delegates that "coolies" could be recruited from San Francisco—even more cheaply than from China—on five-year contracts for $10–$20 per month. Commercial agent Tye Kim Orr attested to efficacy of Chinese labor in the post-emancipation West Indies. The conventioneers agreed to raise a million dollars to further importation plans and formed the Mississippi Valley Immigration Company. Intended as an overt wedge against newly emancipated black labor, this recruitment was decried shortly thereafter by Frederick Douglass as inviting "a kind of Asiatic slave trade":

In the vigorous efforts now making to import Coolies from China—a kind of Asiatic slave trade—with a view to supplant the black laborer in the South, in the unwillingness to allow the negro to own land in the determination to exclude him from profitable trades and callings, there is clearly seen the purpose to crush our spirits, to cripple our enterprise and doom us to a condition of destitution and degradation below all other people in America.[13]

The adversarial relationship between Asian and black labor was played up by southern media; in 1870, the *New Orleans Times* provided a colorful depiction of black response to witnessing a boatload of Chinese workers steaming down the Mississippi and putting in to a Memphis levee. Imported from San Francisco to work the Houston and Texas Central Railroad, the Chinese were expected to work the sugar and cotton fields once the railroad job was finished.[14] Divining the thoughts of those on shore and in keeping with the momentum from the Convention, the *Times* exulted, "The Chinese are coming, huzza! huzza! . . . and Sambo does not seem to like it. He gathered his hosts upon the river bank at Memphis and expressed his dislike of the newcomers by threats and murmurs. If anything was lacking to convince us of the importance and value of this latest immigration movement[,] it is this fact."[15] "Sambo's" dislike lay in his apparent recognition that he was about to be displaced by another form of "colored" labor, one that would, the planters hoped, work more cheaply, efficiently, and tractably. The *Times* went on to anticipate that such competition would force the "Negro" to overcome his "natural indolence" as "a necessity of [his] very existence."[16] Unlike their counterparts in the Caribbean, however, southern planters failed in their importation schemes and contractor Koopmanschap declared bankruptcy in 1872 (Barth 1964, 195).

Politics, the cost of transportation, and the failure to attract labor to the United States were primary reasons for the failure of mass importation schemes, but the much-touted docility of Chinese workers imported on a small scale also proved to be unfounded. Clayton Powell, then governor of Arkansas, later declared efforts to utilize Chinese labor "a disastrous failure": "Planters soon learned that after all the negroes, as laborers in the cotton fields, were better in all respects than the men of any other race, and in a little while the Chinamen sagaciously learned the purposes for which they were introduced" (1969, 214). The hope of "John's crowding Sambo from the soil" in the experimental importation of Chinese workers to the Millaudon plantation in Louisiana, for example, was likewise recognized to be "a decided failure" by 1872. One journalist reported that not only had all but 25 of the original 140 workers deserted, but that the plantation agent would give those remaining "five dollars apiece to run away."[17] In spite of the aesthetic interest they added to the southern landscape, the "picturesque heathen" simply ran off when dissatisfied with their contracts or with the treatment of the overseer.[18] While the movement to recruit such workers relied upon the contrast between Sambo and the "strange celestial," southern disappointment with the fact that "coolies" were unwilling to take up their intended role was expressed through racial comparison as well. Thus, the hope that the Chinese were just like "the Negro" paradoxically shifted to disappointment that the Chinese were just like "the Negro":

> The Chinese in Louisiana are said to be not only lazy, but turbulent and unmanageable, while they are fond of changing about from place to place; and if they hire at a stipulated price, they will leave their employer as soon as any one offers them higher wages. At the penitentiary in Baton Rouge, one hundred and fifty-one were at one time employed, but they were soon discharged for general worthlessness. From several plantations where large gangs of them were employed, they have deserted in a body; and at the places where they have remained great dissatisfaction is usually expressed by the planters with their work and behavior. . . . [I]t is evident that hereafter there will be little demand for cheap Chinese labor in that region.[19]

The experiment to displace black workers with other "colored" labor became an anomalous if "picturesque" addition to southern history.

By the turn of the century, moreover, southern support of immigration had turned; attempts to encourage even European immigrants to the South became curtailed.[20] As in the American West, resistance to the influx of Asian immigrants and the fear of economic competition found expression in the established discourse of black racial inferiority. By 1905, Robert De Courcy Ward argued against importing Chinese and Japanese labor to the South, cautioning against the expectation that "they would be more docile and more servile than either the negro or the European."[21] Wary of the South's push to encourage "the immigration of Asiatics, of illiterates, and of aliens" (616), he warned that while such importation "might give a temporary relief where labor is now scarce, it would bring in its wake, in the future, many vast and complex problems which the South has not yet had to face. *It would soon add another race problem*" (614–615; emphasis added). A decade after the establishment of the Yamato Colony in 1904, an experimental agricultural community founded by Japanese immigrants in what is now Boca Raton and Delray Beach, public sentiment toward "alien" settlers in Florida had likewise shifted. A Jacksonville newspaper documented public opinion via a now well-worn trope, the loss of property values due to undesirable neighbors, in this case, "Japs":

> I don't want to see any great hordes ef Japs comin' into Floriday . . . they never makes good neighbors fer white payple, an' just as soon as a few ef

theim get settled in wan community, property in that section ez not worth as much as it was befoor they came, because no wan but a Jap will buy et. Tis just th' same as ef th' niggers wuz thrifty, saved their money an' bought property. Ef ye had a farm an' twas surrounded by farms of niggers, how much could ye get fer et an' wouldn't you be tryin' to sell et? [22]

Such sentiments underscored growing opposition to increased Japanese immigration, contributing to attrition and the colony's eventual decline.[23] As historian George E. Pozzetta notes, the promotion of immigration from the Pacific Rim to Florida following the Civil War was viewed as disturbing the tenuous racial balance of the state, in particular, its investment in racial polarity: "With the introduction of orientals and other 'exotic' nationalities . . . many Floridians became concerned over the possibilities of new and potentially more dangerous race problems. Would the state have to establish accommodations and laws to cover white, black, *and* yellow?" (1974, 179). By 1900, efforts to import "new race elements" in the South had reached their peak (Loewenberg 1934).

I mark these sentiments in order to suggest the ways in which racial anomaly became addressed within an established epistemological frame. The "Negroization" of Asians in the 19th and early 20th centuries likewise applied to southern American Indians, as I show in the next chapter, and surfaced within the discourse surrounding European and Arab immigration to the South.[24] At stake was not an ontological distinction between racial groups, but a grosser assessment of how best to extract surplus value and from whom. But southern culture's indirect investment in fixing the status of the "partly colored" through such comparisons was not only harnessed to ruling-class interests. Later segregation-era commentary by African Americans did not necessarily center sympathetically on their shared condition as workers, as in Douglass's rebuke regarding "Coolies" as ersatz slaves. Rather, commentary highlighted the injustice of perceived Asian mobility in the context of Jim Crow restrictions. That is, as turn-of-the-century white resistance to Asian immigration became articulated through "Negro" proximity, contrarily, African American critiques of segregation found expression in the figure of the approximately white "Oriental."

Charles W. Chesnutt's protagonist in *The Marrow of Tradition* (1901) benignly observes, "At the next station a Chinaman, of the ordinary laundry type, boarded the train, and took his seat in the white car without objection" (2003, 38). This mild comment gave way to more animated expression; African Americans conveyed outrage over what they saw as an unevenly applied color line. The appearance of Asians traveling freely in the South, albeit in the border regions of Dixie, Maryland, and Washington, DC, seemed particularly unjust. In 1926 syndicated columnist George Schuyler notes that Japanese traveling in the South could ride in Pullman cars, eat in white restaurants, and stay at first-class hotels "while the Christian Negro is huddled in a crowded jim crow half-coach and dare not ask for accommodations due a citizen and which he is willing and able to pay for." One middle-class African American woman in Baltimore writes in 1933, "Our leading white churches gladly welcome Chinese and Japanese . . . but if a *respectable* colored person should dare to enter the so-called House of God, he would not be allowed inside" (both cited in Shankman 1982; emphasis added). The injustice of being denied equal rights is made more acute in witnessing those rights bestowed upon those who do not formally "deserve" them—those who are alien to the cultural norms that define community and without a legitimate claim to the protection of the state. This racial inequality is rhetorically emphasized as an affront to class status; similarly, feminist activist Mary Church Terrell writes about living in the nation's capital in 1907, "Indians, Japanese, Chinese, Filipinos and representatives of other dark races can find hotel accommodations, as a rule, if they can pay for them. The colored man or woman is the only one thrust out of the hotels of the National Capital like a leper" (1968, 383–384). These comments emphasize race advocacy as class commentary, the belief that having capital should make for equality. The outrage over Asian mobility hinges on an implicit parallel; they are likewise one of the "dark races" and, furthermore, potentially lesser in status being neither Christians nor citizens. Nevertheless, such resentment was not simply competitive, but foregrounded the uneven application of the color line. The irony that these writers inscribe is invoked more famously and to similar effect in the dissent to *Plessy v. Ferguson* (1896) upholding "separate but equal." In his minority opinion, Justice Harlan noted that "a Chinaman can ride in the same passenger coach with white citizens of the United States, while citizens of the black race in Louisiana . . . are yet declared to be criminals, liable to imprisonment, if they ride in a public coach occupied by citizens of the white race."[25] These persuasive analogies advance arguments about the irrationality of segregation, yet they project a freedom of mobility that was by no means uniform. Members of the "dark races" are revealed to be flexible subjects available to serve shifting agendas across southern cultures.

I mark this history of the "interstitial Asian" in the South not to give more evidence of what has become axiomatic in Critical White Studies, that there are degrees of whiteness, but to restore a certain dissonance of expectation to segregation-era history. Like the photograph that begins this chapter, the evidence that there ever was (or continues to be) another referent for the pejorative term "colored" is hidden in plain sight. That no one "refers to Chinamen or Japanese or Indians as 'colored'" (Chesnutt 1999, 566) was and was not accurate. What these examples uncover is not so much a deliberate repression within southern history, but a conveniently flexible referent invoked by whites and blacks alike: the racialized subject who can *go either way*.

The ambiguity of interstitiality could also be exploited in the subversion of segregationist logic, and in the expression of interracial solidarity. Terrell recounts an instance in which a family member attempts to take six little girls to a matinee, five of whom are "fair enough to pass muster." The last child is stopped by the ticket-taker:

> "I guess you have made a mistake," he called to the host of the theatre party. "Those little girls," pointing to the fair ones, "may be admitted, but this one," pointing to the swarthy one, "can't." But the colored man was quite equal to the emergency. "What do you mean? What are you trying to insinuate about that little girl? Do you mean to say that Filipinos are excluded from the theatres of Washington?" This little ruse succeeded brilliantly, as he knew it would. "Beg your pardon," said the ticket taker, "don't know what I was thinking about." (1968, 392)

Here, the sly anecdote may itself be "passing" as fact, making light as it does of the risks of passing and the social stigma of being stopped at the door.[26] But this testimony regarding preferential treatment is the occasion to set southern inconsistency against itself. Belief in the "colored" status of other "dark races" was likewise invoked to opposite effect, in critique of American imperialism. In the *Brownies' Book* published in the 1920s by the NAACP, African American children were encouraged to identify with the Philippine independence movement in order to promote global racial solidarity:

> Betty and Philip went with Uncle Jim to the "movies" that rainy afternoon, and there they saw a picture of two young colored girls.
> "Look, Phil," whispered Betty, "there are some colored folks just like us. Who are they?" . . .
> "They're from the Philippines. . . . And they are colored—that is, their skin is not white; but they belong to a different division of people from what we do. You see, we colored Americans are mostly of the black or Negro race; whereas these girls belong to the brown, or Malay race."[27]

The impromptu geography lesson about places with "queer, pretty names" ends with the American "colored" children playing at being other "colored" children across the globe fighting for their independence against the United States, in anticipation of the panracial internationalism of W.E.B. Du Bois's *Dark Princess*.

Nevertheless, as C. Vann Woodward notes in *The Strange Career of Jim Crow*, this convergence between international and domestic politics was likewise harnessed to the defense of segregation. Southern leaders of the white supremacy movement were fully able to appreciate the parallel between imperialist rhetoric and that of American race relations. As Woodward recounts, one senator asserted that, "Not even Governor Roosevelt, will dare to wave the bloody shirt and preach a crusade against the South's treatment of the Negro. The North has a bloody shirt of its own. Many thousands of them have been made into shrouds for murdered Filipinos, done to death because they were fighting for liberty" (2002, 73).[28] The belief in racial superiority that supported colonial endeavors was easily buttressed by the discourse of racial paternalism that already existed in the South and vice versa. As white southerners took Washington's caretaking governance of the "colored races" overseas as a vindication of their attitudes toward African Americans, the treatment of people of color at home and abroad became mutually reinforcing. As Woodward argues, southern compliance with Washington's foreign policies in the Pacific emerged in part in exchange for the North's turning a blind eye to southern treatment of African Americans.

I cite these examples not only as evidence of what scholars have established as the mutually constitutive nature of racial formation and, more specifically, the political and class determinates underlying racial assignment. Rather, the proximity of the "partly colored" to either pole along a racial continuum reveals a flexible economy of cultural representation conveniently harnessed to varied political and economic interests. These anecdotes establish a cultural terrain of oscillating representation that reveal the space of intermediacy to be not a neutral zone, but one characterized by displaced hostility. In this sense, the "anomaly" of the Asian in the South gestures to the very anxieties surrounding Asian American location vis-à-vis the nation in the late 20th century and into the next: an ambivalence about the nature of Asian minority status.

Sociologist Edna Bonacich's "Towards a Theory of Middleman Minorities" (1973) underscores this ambivalence in offering an analysis of hierarchy based on triadic ethnic-racial social structure. Drawing upon the work of Hubert Blalock, she argues that "middleman minorities" assume a comprador or interstitial economic position between the elites and labor that serves as a buffer to protect elite business interests during times of crisis. Looking at the function these populations serve, she writes, "In contrast to most ethnic minorities, they occupy an intermediate rather than low-status position. . . . They play the role of middleman between producer and consumer, employer and employee, owner and renter, elite and masses" (1973, 583). The middleman minority concept initiates a relational understanding of status that is not tied to racialization per se but to modes of production enforced by colonialism. It articulates an interrelation between ethnic difference and class position in terms of social treatment but also affirms their irreducibility: that is, economic advancement does not lessen, but in fact may exacerbate cultural difference, marking racialized populations as targets of hostility for both the underclasses and the state, which benefits from their labor at the same time that it may sacrifice them in times of social upheaval.[29] Bonacich's understanding of the intersection between race and class formation both supports and extends Immanuel Wallerstein's recognition that race is "a particular form of status-group in the contemporary world" that represents a "blurred collective representation of classes" (Wallerstein and Balibar 1991, 200). Thus, class and racial intermediacy play out differently across national sites—from Idi Amin's expulsion of Indians from Uganda in 1972 to the attempts of East Indians in Trinidad to write themselves into the postcolonial national imaginary in the late 1980s (Munasinghe 2001).

Claire Jean Kim (2000) and Neil Foley (1997) have written compellingly about triadic community structures in the United States, engaging Korean Americans in New York and Mexican Americans in South Texas, respectively.[30] In particular, in her study of the 1990 Red Apple Boycott in which black nationalists initiated collective action against Korean-owned grocery stores in Brooklyn, Kim challenges a simple account of misdirected racial scapegoating. Rather, she rewrites interethnic conflict in the context of racial triangulation through the lens of self-conscious political organizing, countering media portrayals of the boycott as African American irrationality. Her analysis of racial triangulation in this contemporary context is a reminder that the structural positioning I describe here does not simply reflect being "caught in the middle" of equal and opposite forces; rather, it is a top-down imposition of status that, more often than not, adheres to the needs of the dominant at the same time that it offers a cultural and legal conundrum. In the absence of established Asian communities in the American South, the "Oriental" becomes a trope that assumes a specific burden of representation; the "Chinaman," "coolie," "Jap," or "Malay" finds convenient stability according to the interests of segregation-era culture. In this, the southern archive is, ironically, remarkably consistent.

Even the law, the seemingly final arbiter of status, reflects this convenience. For example, as a number of scholars have shown, courts in south Texas counter-intuitively classified Mexican Americans as "co-whites" in order to support the racial status quo by denying them equal rights in jury selection and education. As George Martinez notes, Anglo judges ruled that "Mexicans were co-whites when this suited the dominant group—and non-white when necessary to protect Anglo privilege and supremacy" (1997, 212). As he and others reveal, Mexican American legal classification as "white" in south Texas may have been formally recognized by the courts, but did not translate into white status within culture.[31] Thus, attempts to fix ambiguous status along a black-white continuum reveal both the subtle and less-than-subtle work of white supremacy. Racial intermediacy represents a flexibility of convenience.

In keeping with my interest in social status at the nexus of class and race relations, I turn to the simultaneously most visible and least visible example of Asians in the South, the Siamese twins, Chang and Eng Bunker. Their cultural treatment reveals not the overt processes of southern racialization that constructed the Asian as a wedge against black labor, but as his counterpart, the white planter.

## Foreign Sex

One of the first and most well-known instances of Asian presence in the antebellum and later post-bellum South is also one of the most anomalous. In 1839, the celebrated Siamese twins, Chang and Eng Bunker, elected to settle in Wilkesboro, North Carolina and take up residence as gentlemen farmers. They married the Yates sisters, Sarah and Adelaide, in a double wedding, maintained separate homes, and had 22 children between them. All things considered, Asianness seemed to be the least remarkable thing about them. Even this briefest of biographies prompts the much asked and still titillating question: How did the Siamese twins have sex?[32]

Mark Twain's 1869 "The Personal Habits of the Siamese Twins" introduces but sidesteps the question, offering only that the foursome "lived together, night and day, in an exceeding sociability which is touching and beautiful to behold, and is a scathing rebuke to our boasted civilization" (1992, 297). Recent biographers' offering, that Eng "channeled," imagining himself elsewhere while Chang coupled with his wife and vice versa, offers a biased assessment of what we imagine their sexual practices to be—biased in its failure to transcend the consciousness of the single-bodied. Would an alternative psychological state seem necessary to men who were not familiar with "normal" sexual practices enough to know how deviant their own might be? Darin Strauss's contemporary novelization of their life, *Chang and Eng*, as Rachel Adams has noted, merely disappointingly confirms our notions of bourgeois social norms and individuated subjectivity in its representation of Eng's desire for separation, normalcy, and privacy arising from his (unrequited) love for Chang's wife (Adams 2001).

The fact was that the brothers' sex lives did adhere to—if not exactly monogamous—procreative, martially sanctioned, heterosexual imperatives. Interestingly, the salacious speculation of a threesome (or more) seems to obscure another taboo transgressed, that of miscegenation. Chang and Eng, for all their monstrosity, functioned as white men in a society segregated by race: they took white wives, seemed well-respected and integrated in the community, and enjoyed the prosperity and status of independent, southern farmers. Most tellingly, they also owned slaves.

During the Civil War, they lent their sons to the Confederacy. Notwithstanding this political bias, the Siamese twins served as a literal reminder of how the national brotherhood could not be torn asunder, a metaphor that also lent itself to expressions of the folly of cross-racial brotherhood epitomized by the Union cause. In a passionate rant confined to the pages of her journal, diehard southerner Eliza Frances Andrews wrote of the white, Yankee occupying forces, "I wish every wretch of them had a strapping, loud-smelling African tied to him like a Siamese twin . . . Oh, how I hate them! I will have to say 'Damn!' yet, before I am done with them."[33] The humor in the image of conjoined twins fighting for opposing sides of the war was not lost upon Mark Twain, who fancifully reported that Chang and Eng took each other prisoner on behalf of the Confederacy and Union, respectively, but that "the proofs of capture were so evenly balanced in favor of each that a general army court had to be assembled to determine which one was properly the captor and which the captive" (1992, 297). Maxine Hong Kingston's imaginative portrayal of the brothers performing a minstrel show-type patter, Chinkus and Pinkus, puns on the metaphor of national solidarity. Upon joining the Union Army, Eng says to Chang, "I'm on your side. And a good thing too. If you were to join the Confederate Army, I don't see that we have enough room to shoot long rifles at each other" (1989, 293).

Kingston's routine simultaneously marks the brothers as both black and white men in blackface, a deliberate and ironic comment on their status as slaveholders. Her portrayal of an exchange between Chang and Eng and Millie and Christine McKoy, "the Carolina Black Joined Twins," highlights the fact that their racial, southern, and sexual status cannot, like the twins themselves, be viewed separately:

ENG: I'd like to buy you from Mr. Barnum. You be my slave. I have thirty-one slaves. You won't be lonely.

MISS MILLIE: Why, no, sir. I won't be your slave. Mr. Barnum pays me an *artiste's* salary, the same as you. I'm a free woman.

MISS CHRISTINE: You are making her an indecent proposal, sir. (1989, 291)

Here, the idea of *sexual* impropriety applies to Eng's status as a slaveowner, appropriating the idea of bodily perversion to the social perversion of owning another human being. Kingston's portrayal also mines the twins for their metaphoric portrayal of Chinese American hyphenation as yet another manifestation of conjoined oddity: "We know damned well what you came for to see," Chang charges, "the angle we're joined at, how we can have two sisters for wives and twenty-one Chinese-Carolinian children between us. . . . You want to look at the hyphen. You want to look at it bare" (1989, 293).

Chang and Eng's "hyphenation" as Chinese-Malay and American apparently was not an issue in North Carolina. Rather, it is the extent of their integration that seems almost perverse. Far from imputing an intensified racism to antebellum southern regionalism, for example, one contemporary journalist speculated that in "Wilkes County, N.C., they had a better chance than they would have had in most places, for the mountain people are given to accepting or rejecting strangers on their merits, and are not frightened by personal peculiarities."[34] (Nevertheless, upon discovering the numerous descendants of Chang and Eng, the same journalist felt impelled to assure his readership that the Bunker descendants "do not look Oriental in any slant-eyed or 'sinister' sense" (70).) The community's acceptance of the twins is historically borne out despite initial objections over their marriages: they became citizens in 1839 and were also made honorary citizens of North Carolina, apparently in spite of the inadmissibility of Asian naturalization at the time.

Their Asianness did not seem to be incredibly exploited in their public showings; rather, guests were treated to depictions of Chang and Eng in Western dress, seated in a Victorian parlor or demonstrating their agility at battledore and shuttlecock. As Cindy Wu notes, they were "racialized very differently from contemporaneous others of their racial group," Chinese laborers (2008, 34). What was remarkable about the twins, the exhibitions seemed to imply, was their normality. The place they assumed in their rural southern community suggests that the very fact of their embodied difference served to obviate their racial difference. In assessing Chang and Eng's impact on Asian representation in New York's commercial culture in the 1800s, John Tchen argues that the association between Asianness and physical difference was enforced by public showings of the twins. Noting that racial stereotyping limited the options of Asian Americans in New York, he writes that the "twins' physical abnormality heightened perceptions" of Asian racial difference and that "the racially charged commercial marketplace impacted all who sought to enter it" (1999, 153). Ironically, however, the link between bodily and ethnic difference may not have been operative in their own case. Rather, it seems as if the twins' physical abnormality rendered their racial difference *less* extraordinary. After all, what is most remarkable about the life story of Chang and Eng Bunker is its utter banality, its approximation of the lives of white, propertied, landowning southern patriarchs.

Alien to established notions of subjectivity, they nonetheless embodied less striking differences that were readily rescripted by international celebrity. The twins were thus not simply strangers, aliens, or foreigners; in the most banal sense, everybody already knew them. Nevertheless, the very heightened nature of their differences may have enabled their integration into southern culture: as "freaks," they were beyond the familiar modes of interpellation even in a region like the South where eccentricity is said to be tolerated. Even more prosaically, their racial, sexual, and physical differences may have paled against what they brought to their rural North Carolina community—their income. And while their example obviously complicates notions of social status based on a single axis—the continuums that define normativity and difference intersect at multiple points—what interests me is the way in which their right to slave ownership became overwritten by celebrity, by sexuality, by metaphor. If the example of Chang and Eng represents an anomalous account of Asians in the Reconstruction-era South, their life history suggests the very flexibility of southern culture to reconcile and incorporate difference.

This flexibility was likewise reflected in the realm of the law where the "partly colored" were only partially addressed.

## Anti-miscegenation Laws and the Approximately 'Colored'

Anti-miscegenation laws are intrinsic to understanding the sexual dimension of the color line. Such laws are rightly remembered as part and parcel of the infamy of segregation, the ways in which the law reached into the realm of the private to abrogate the civil liberties of African Americans—and secondarily, white Americans as well. To what extent did southern culture create other "colored" subjects through anti-miscegenation laws? In the West, historian Peggy Pascoe notes that such laws "were enacted first—and abandoned last—in the South, but it was in the West, not the South, that the laws became most elaborate. In the late nineteenth century, western legislators built a labyrinthine system of legal prohibitions on marriages between whites and Chinese, Japanese, Filipinos, Hawaiians, Hindus, and Native Americans, as well as on marriages between whites and blacks" (1991, 6). While southern anti-miscegenation laws do not reflect this range or degree of specificity, nevertheless, the South's commitment to segregation extended to other groups as well. Mississippi, North Carolina, Georgia, and Virginia statutes named additional subjects of prohibition in ways that testify to their proximity to "the Negro" and the lack of uniformity in the legal apparatus of Jim Crow. The law's address thus reflects the inconsistencies of cultural representation of, to echo Matthew Frye Jacobson, those both "inconclusively white" and inconclusively black (1998, 65). More importantly, if these subjects of prohibition have become erased in the history of discrimination, in what ways have they become likewise erased in the history of its redress? As anti-miscegenation laws in the Deep South reveal, the color line was not always neatly drawn even as its legacy continues to shape understanding of race in the United States and the construction of the proper subject of both moral and legal grievance.

In 1944, Gunnar Myrdal saw the "aversion to amalgamation" as the primary reason for segregation's existence, postulating that anti-miscegenation laws were the foundation upon which the entire system of legal and cultural prohibitions rested. The relative significance of each social and legal enactment of separation was "dependent upon their degree of expediency or necessity—in view of white people—as means of upholding the ban on 'intermarriage.'" Sexual intimacy, Myrdal saw, was the greatest cause for white resistance to integration: "In rank order, (1) the ban on intermarriage and other sex relations involving white women and colored men takes precedence before anything else. It is the end for which the other restrictions are arranged as means" (1962, 587–588). It goes without saying that to Myrdal, "colored" men meant African American men. The distinction between segregation in public facilities and within the realm of sexual relations is represented as a matter of the degree of white aversion; one anti-integrationist explained his opposition to educational desegregation in Little Rock, with the rallying cry, "The key that opens the door of the schoolroom . . . unlocks the door to the bedroom, too!" (cited in Dykeman and Stokely 1957, 26). As Robert Penn Warren reported in 1957, one community organizer went as far as to link amalgamation to nothing less than the decline of civilization:

> [T]here's just two races, black and white, and the rest of them is a kind of mixing. You always get a mess when the mixing starts. Take India. They are a pure white people like you and me, and they had a pretty good civilization, too. Till they got to shipping on a little Negro blood. It don't take much to do the damage. Look at 'em now. (cited in Warren 1957, 35)

Segregationists pointed to Latin American creolization to justify anti-miscegenation statutes; former Georgia governor, Herman Talmadge, wrote in 1955, "In Cuba, in Mexico and in the South American countries, segregation has never been practiced. As a result, the races have intermarried and become a mongrel race in which the strongest and best features of both races have been destroyed" (1955, 43). The white southerner's liberalism on race matters, Myrdal suspected, could be ascertained according to how much he was willing to concede to this primary taboo. As late as 1944, he noted, "Hardly anybody in the South is prepared to go the whole way and argue that even the ban on intermarriage should be lifted" (1962, 588).[35]

In the South, the "door to the bedroom" was uniformly locked in the year following the Civil War, yet southern state statutes did not dwell upon fears of racial intermixture with Asians, Americans Indians, or mestizos.[36] This may reflect what Pascoe has exposed as the fallacy of anti-miscegenation laws' gender-blind application. She speculates that in the West,

> [T]he laws were applied most stringently to groups like the Chinese, Japanese, and Filipinos, whose men were thought likely to marry white women. They were applied least stringently to groups like the Native Americans (who where inconsistently mentioned in the laws) and Hispanics (who were not mentioned at all), groups whose women were historically likely to marry white men. (1991, 7)

Thus, in the West, the protection of white women led to identifying additional subjects of prohibition.[37] In the South, a focus on the less elaborated groups of intermarriage prohibition exposes not necessarily a supposed "gender-blind" application of the law—although southern anti-miscegenation laws likewise reflected it—but the "equal application" of segregationist law. That is, defenders of anti-miscegenation laws claimed that it affected whites and blacks equally. Yet few southern states prohibited marriages between African Americans and other nonwhites, revealing the law's investment in maintaining white purity at its core.[38] For example, Alabama enacted legislation specifically targeting whites attempting to circumvent the white-black intermarriage prohibition by "passing" as Indian.[39] Because the state had not outlawed Indian-black intermarriage, it made clear that whites could not evade the law by claiming to be "partly colored" or somehow less than white. In southern state statutes, slippages between the terms "colored" and "Negro" were unintentional; the law viewed them as indistinguishable. For example, the language of Louisiana's 1958 law prohibiting marriage between Indians and blacks made this clear; marriages between "persons of the aboriginal Indian race of America and persons of the colored or black race" were forbidden.[40] In contrast, Louisiana's 1894 interracial marriage laws prohibited "marriage between white persons and persons of color"—the latter designation encompassing a potentially broader segment of the population—only to be changed to "persons of the Negro or black race" in 1908 and back again to "colored" in 1910.[41] The shift reflected a desire to broaden the definition of blood quantum as a criterion for blackness; it was not motivated by a contestation over what other races might be encompassed within the term "colored" itself.[42]

Nevertheless, four southern states had extended the white intermarriage prohibition more broadly to other people of color in ways that testify to the social status of Asians, American Indians, or Latinos as like "the Negro" in the mongrelizing threat they posed. Such variation within southern states' uniform allegiance to miscegenation taboos unveils another history: the ways in which the legal bureaucracy of segregation created other subjects of discrimination. Yet both the presence and absence of their address within anti-miscegenation laws in the South reveal ambiguities within segregation's administration similar to those reflected in cultural representation. In Mississippi and North Carolina, for example, naming additionally taboo subjects coincided with a "partly colored" population's visibility. In Mississippi, prohibitions to white intermarriage applied specifically to "Negroes" and "Mongolians" to the third generation.[43] This may not be surprising given that the Chinese population in Mississippi was determined to be "colored" by the Supreme Court in *Gong Lum v. Rice* 1927, a suit that originated in that state. However, Mississippi's anti-miscegenation statute predated that federal judgment by 35 years. The state had outlawed white-Chinese intermarriage in 1892, a time in which the Chinese population was not extensive, but, as indicated earlier, saw the South abandoning its postwar attempts to recruit "coolie" labor.[44]

In contrast, one of North Carolina's largest American Indian populations became visible to the state precisely as a result of segregation's rise. While white-Indian marriages were banned in the region as early as 1715, subsequent state laws continued to affirm such prohibition in generic terms throughout the 19th century. The community once known as a "tri-racial isolate" was recognized as the "Croatan Indians" in 1887 by the North Carolina legislature. As I discuss in the next chapter, as a consequence of this visibility, the state granted them separate Indian schools in recognition of their interstitial status; yet, ironically it simultaneously took pains to affirm their relation to African Americans by naming them within state anti-miscegenation statutes, a provision subsequently covered each time the legislature recognized the tribe's name change.[45] While the state affirmed the community's nonblack status in the realm of public education, it nonetheless refused to do so within the institution of marriage. The issue was not merely that southern American Indians were ambiguously placed along a continuum from white to black, but that they were inconsistently hailed within specific arenas of segregation's administration. Echoing Myrdal's perception of a hierarchy of racial aversion among southern whites, the state conceded in the realm of schooling with a tripartite system; in contrast, the anti-miscegenation statutes leveled against the community revealed no such concession despite the fact that, as I discuss in the next chapter, white amalgamation lay at the heart of their historical claims to Indianness.

Of the southern states, Georgia and Virginia enacted the most widely encompassing prohibitions against interracial marriage between whites and the "dark races." Georgia legislators recognized the discrepancy between the terms "Negro" and "person of color" by 1927. In taking pains to delimit linguistic ambiguity, the state legislature instituted one of the most global anti-miscegenation laws in the United States, extending Georgia's 1910 intermarriage prohibition with an "Act to define who are persons of color and who are white persons." Reflecting the codification of the "one-drop" rule, it amended its specific generational prohibition from "one-eighth Negro or African blood" to the all-encompassing, but practically more vague, "any ascertainable trace" of such blood. Its definition of "persons of color" was then extended to include "West Indians" and "Asiatic Indians."[46] The amended law specifically constructs South Asians as illicit subjects for white intermarriage, but makes no mention of other Asian groups. Ironically, however, the subsequent section of the same civil code, which specifies that individuals must identify his or her race to the State Registrar of Vital Statistics in order to comply with the marriage statute, offers a more extensive list. To assure the legality of the license, the Registrar is asked to identify individuals as "Caucasian, Negro, Mongolian, West Indian, Asiatic Indian, Malay, or any mixture thereof, or any other non-Caucasic strains" in addition to "what generation such mixture occurred." While the registration process takes what amounts to a negative definition of color—it is anyone who is "non-Caucasic"—it was unclear how the discrepancy between the registration identification process and the more specific list of taboo subjects of white intermarriage was to be managed. While racial identification within the registration process was characterized as being in service to its anti-miscegenation statute, those groups identified within the process were more expansive than those addressed within the marriage law itself. Not only was the scope of laws forbidding intermarriage uneven across southern state lines, they appear to be ambiguous within them.

Virginia's law, ultimately challenged by the Supreme Court in 1967, was similarly expansive in defining what constituted color: the absence of whiteness. In 1924, Virginia made it illegal for a white person to marry "any save a white person" under a law entitled, "Preservation of racial integrity."[47] The term "white person" applied only to those who had "no trace whatsoever of any blood other than Caucasian"; the law made an exception for those with one-sixteenth or less American Indian blood, ostensibly to honor the descendants of Pocahontas and John Rolfe. Ironically, as scholars have pointed out, after 1924 and the passage of "racial integrity" legislation, that very union would have been a felony.[48] The expansiveness of Virginia and Georgia laws reveals that "colored" was not simply synonymous with "Negro." Despite its historical construction, southern conception of the "one-drop rule"—here to be adjudicated by visual inspection—did not apply exclusively to African Americans. As the amendments passed by Virginia's legislature in 1924 and Georgia's in 1927 reveal, the color line was movable and expanding.

The upshot of my inquiry into this arena of Jim Crow culture is not merely to point out that the designations "persons of color" or "colored persons" applied to groups other than African Americans. Indeed, such a resurrection of anomaly does not fundamentally alter our understanding of, to echo James Baldwin, the spirit behind segregation, its commitment to white supremacy. The language of the Mississippi, North Carolina, Georgia, and Virginia laws provides evidence of white perception of other groups' proximity to the "Negro" and their shared status as threats to white purity even as the very absence of address in other southern state statutes testifies to Jim Crow's unevenness, an unevenness not merely confined to questions of etiquette or cultural representation. But I would also emphasize that the law's role in racial formation is particularly significant in regard to the South because of the prominence the region holds in the American national imaginary; that is, racial discrimination in the era of formal segregation has been constructed as normative to American understanding of racial injustice, encoding both racism's proper object and the subject of injury. If the abrogation of the rights of other racialized subjects is incidental to our understanding of Jim Crow, so too can the redress of those rights appear to be incidental to our understanding of civil rights.

The events leading up to the landmark civil rights case that overturned anti-miscegenation laws, *Loving v. Virginia* (1967), represent a case in point. On behalf of the plaintiffs, Mildred and Richard Loving, a black woman married to a white man, *Loving v. Virginia* ruled that such laws were violations of the equal protection and due process clauses of the Fourteenth Amendment.[49] Yet interestingly, 12 years earlier the Supreme Court had rejected hearing a challenge to Virginia's interracial marriage prohibition in *Naim v. Naim* (1955).[50] As Randall Kennedy recounts, in 1952 Ham Say Naim, a Chinese sailor, and Ruby Elaine Lamberth, a white woman, traveled from their home in Norfolk, Virginia to Elizabeth, North Carolina to wed in order to evade Virginia's restrictive law.[51] A year later, Ruby Naim filed for annulment claiming that the state's "preservation of racial integrity" act rendered their marriage null at the outset. After a trial court affirmed this annulment, Ham Say Naim appealed to the Virginia Supreme Court of Appeals arguing for the validity of the marriage by challenging the Virginia law's federal constitutionality. When the Supreme Court of Virginia affirmed the state's power to "regulate the marriage relation so that it shall not have a mongrel breed of citizens," Ham Say Naim subsequently appealed to the U.S. Supreme Court.[52]

*Naim v. Naim* remains a footnote in the history of civil rights in part because the Supreme Court declined to hear it. That decision forestalled another potential anomaly: a second landmark civil rights case heralding the end of segregation, this time undertaken on behalf of a Chinese man. There were a number of reasons why the justices declined to hear to case, none of them directly invoking the imperfect racial identity of the plaintiff. As Kennedy notes, the justices believed that it was a matter of timing; moreover, the case did not have the support of the NAACP:

[B]ecause it came on the heels of the Court's recent invalidation of de jure segregation in public schooling, the same justices worried that it might be imprudent to consider *Naim*, which might well result in the majority striking down racial segregation at the altar. One unidentified justice reportedly remarked, "One bombshell at a time is enough." That sentiment was seconded by Thurgood Marshall, the chief lawyer for the NAACP, who notably declined to support Ham Say Naim's appeal in the belief that its proximity to *Brown v. Board of Education* was a real detriment. (2003, 270)

Asserting that the record was insufficiently clear, the Court remanded the case back to the Virginia Supreme Court of Appeals, which affirmed its decision in favor of the annulment and thus the "integrity" of Virginia's Racial Integrity Act.[53] One cannot dispute that timing played a major part in the Court's refusal to hear the case; the question of the constitutionality of interracial marriage prohibition had been posed seven years earlier in California by *Perez v. Sharpe* (1948) and the Court had likewise declined to hear *Jackson v. Alabama* in 1954, cases also involving white-black intermarriage. Yet this historical footnote nevertheless raises some speculative issues given my context here. The Loving case was certainly sympathetically normative as well as aptly named: its plaintiffs were part of a nuclear family hoping only for the right to return home to Virginia with the dreaded symbols of amalgamation, the children, in tow. The case had the support of not only the NAACP and the American Civil Liberties Union, but the Japanese American Citizen's League as well. In contrast, *Naim v. Naim* dealt with complications regarding annulment, state residency, and citizenship, marking Ham Say Naim as an imperfect plaintiff in more ways than one.

The Loving case was normative in another way; it involved marriage between a white man and a black woman, a union that represented transgression albeit one that, because of its gender variation, failed to represent what Myrdal noted as "the end for which the other [segregationist] restrictions are arranged" (1962, 587). Its circumstances engaged a significant crossing of the color line, but one that was already implicitly sanctioned within southern culture if unspoken in polite company. Such is the fixity of this case in historical memory that it is startling to recall that Mildred Loving was part American Indian, Rappanhannock on her mother's side and Cherokee on her father's— and identified as such.[54] As a landmark in civil rights legislation, *Loving v. Virginia* fulfilled the function of challenging a primary taboo while simultaneously presenting the nation with appealing plaintiffs. In comparison, *Naim* involved the messier circumstances of divorce and annulment, questions of social status in regard to the law beyond a single emphasis on race, and an implicit challenge to the state's ability to protect white womanhood. Significant to my context here, however, *Naim v. Naim* reflects the ambiguity of a racial subject interpellated as "colored" under the law, yet without either the weighty historicity of offense or its moral appeal. This speculation poses a question not only about the linearity of stories about Jim Crow culture, but its dismantling. The issue is not exclusion or lack of representation, but the ways in which the narration of American racism enters popular imagination seamlessly and without complication.

Ariela Gross writes that "[L]aw has been a crucial institution in the process of creating racial meaning at every level. . . . And while many cultural institutions participate in the creation of racial meanings, legal institutions often had the final word" (2008, 12). Nevertheless, I place these legal cases alongside racial representations in popular culture not to privilege one arena as more definitive than another, but to highlight the inconsistencies in both. In later chapters, I include literature in this cultural field in order to highlight multiple terrains of (uneven) subject formation. As Mae Ngai reveals in her study of the ways in which immigration laws and public policy create racial subjects, "illegal alienage is not a natural or fixed condition but the project of positive law; it is contingent and at times unstable" (2004, 6). In reading court cases here, I am interested in their omissions as well as their constructions; as Ngai's work likewise reveals, the law's evolution exposes politically expedient elisions and conflations as well as the ways in which specific rulings emerge into public visibility.

In this case, ambiguity's erasure complicates our notion of the proper racial subject of civil rights. Legal historian Juan Perea has made a compelling argument to this end in his discussion of the absence of court cases involving Mexican Americans and school segregation in the history of civil rights. Arguing that conceptualizing a "Black/White binary paradigm of race" (1997, 1214) in the United States is both an impediment to understanding Latino/a history and gaining a broader understanding of equality, he writes, "Whites can ignore [Latino/a] claims to justice, since we are not Black and therefore are not subject to real racism. And Blacks can ignore our claims, since we are presumed to be aspiring to and acquiring Whiteness, and therefore we are not subject to real racism." (1232). In regard to race in the segregated South, such a paradigm exists for obvious reasons; nevertheless, Perea's points are particularly apt with regard to the scholarly treatment of desegregation efforts involving nonblack plaintiffs: seminal cases brought by Mexican Americans contesting racial segregation in schools remain absent in scholarly casebooks of constitutional law. *Mendez v. Westminister School District* (1946) challenged *Plessy v. Ferguson* in the realm of public schooling on behalf of Mexican Americans in California, a successful suit that prefigured the *Brown v. Board of Education* ruling by eight years.[55] Yet its omission in scholarly treatment of civil right amounts to, as he notes, "academic colonialism" (1251). This critique of the limiting effects of the black-white binary in scholarship, a critique of the ways in which "'other people of color' are deemed to exist only as unexplained analogies to Blacks" (1258), has been most powerfully leveled by Latino legal scholars such as Perea and Richard Delgado in addition to Asian American scholars.[56] As Delgado explains in the persona of his fictional alter-ego, Rodrigo: "[Antidiscrimination law] assumes you are either black or white. If you're neither, you have trouble making claims or even having them understood in racial terms at all" (1997, 1186). As Cindy I-Fen Cheng shows, civil rights cases involving residential segregation brought by Asian plaintiffs in California were also dropped from Supreme Court consideration; the neither-nor status of Asians is not cited as an overt reason for their exclusion; rather, the mitigating factors of citizenship status complicated their inclusion (2004).

The question is not one of competition between oppressed groups, but the ways in which grievance becomes narrated—or not—in the history of its redress. As legal scholars have revealed, scholarship on constitutional law rendered the "partly colored" only partially visible in the history of civil rights, and thus the history of discrimination as well. This elision has stakes for understanding racial discrimination as it overlaps other categories of normativity and difference, as well as how we come to grant, both culturally and intuitively, the subjects of racial grievance moral authority.

## *Ambiguity of Convenience*

To cast a lens on the "partly colored" does not minimize the potency of belief that the problem of the "color line" in the South was identical to the "Negro problem." My claim is not that this anomalous archive displaces the primacy of the black-white division that serves as the foundational haunting of southern regionalism. On the contrary, the black-white paradigm has structured American race relations so centrally that one can, as Houston Baker, Jr. suggests, situate the South as a microcosm of the national (2001). In our collective imagination, the era of formal segregation is straightforwardly understood to be an infamous period in American history. That past has become iconic and essential to national self-definition: it demarcates a line between what we once were and now are not.

Yet as numerous scholars have pointed out in regard to interracialism and passing, the business of white supremacy and the maintenance of black-white polarity was not always straightforward. Given the symbolic significance we assign to the segregation era and the South as a region, what interests me is what has become partially erased: segregation's *interpretive* necessity, its nuance. Mildred Loving's Indian heritage, the most famously unacknowledged Asian American slave owners, Mexican American legal challenges to segregation, the never-materializing "Asiatic slave trade," the racial identity of the faceless man at the "colored" drinking fountain—these do not fit as neatly into the version of segregation and its legacy that we have scripted. They are signs of discrimination's unevenness, its contingencies. As such, they deliver only partial knowledge. Nevertheless, they are reminders that those who claim an identity as "people of color" do so not merely in abstract coalitional affirmation with African Americans, but in the context of literal, if veiled historical referents, those communities and individuals subject to the same forms of discrimination, for the same reasons, and in the same place and time. For Asian Americans in particular, a group whose claims to racial oppression are often met with skepticism or disbelief, this is especially important.

To return to Bubley's photograph of segregated drinking fountains, how can we make visible what can no longer be conceived within reified cultural systems of representation? Between the dominant and the minor, the interstitial is a site of powerful cultural work and forced disappearance. It exposes the processes of status-making, and race's interaction with other axes that define cultural capital, among them, sexuality. Southern regionalism is essential to understanding, as I have documented here, multiple constituencies' investment in black-white relations, and their uneasy place as the subjects of racial redress. As I show in the next chapter, intermediacy may represent the space of cultural ambiguity that serves to suture those relations.

# The Interstitial Indian

## The Lumbee and Segregation's Middle Caste

We're an anthropological delight—everybody comes to study us. . . . And you can see with these curly locks and pale complexion, that something strange has been going on here.
                    —Bruce Barton, Lumbee Indian[1]

Karen Blu's 1979 study of the Lumbee Indians of North Carolina, *The Lumbee Problem: The Making of an American Indian People*, introduces a chapter on tribal activism with this sentence: "Not being content with changing their status from 'mulatto' to 'Indian' and with establishing separate schools, the Indians of Robeson County have gone on incessantly, stubbornly, and apparently tirelessly seeking to better their lot" (1979, 66). Graffitied next to this sentence in my library's copy of the book is a single word: "YUCK."

The distaste that this anonymous reviewer conveys could have been elicited by a number of things: resistance to the quintessentially American narrative of progressive self-advancement, to the academic's attribution of calculated class striving, or to the implication that being Indian is not good enough. Or the reaction could have been prompted by something more embedded, the fact that Lumbee mobility appears to have been purchased at the cost of African Americans. Blu's characterization unintentionally echoes one African American's view of the Chinese in Mississippi, the subject of the next chapter: "They play the white man's game better than white people do" (cited in Quan 1982, 54). For the Lumbee, another question arises: are they "playing the white man's game" or are they, in fact, white?

In regard to American Indians, the attribution of whiteness seems counter-intuitive. There are well-documented instances of indigenous resistance to being "whitemanized" whether through armed struggle or a refusal to vanish in response to genocidal or assimilationist policy. Forced by the rise of Jim Crow, Lumbee status shift from "mulatto" to Indian itself seems to defy expectation; in the context of the romanticized, popular conception of American Indians as a timeless people existing outside of history, were not the Indians always Indian? Moreover, when a color line is invoked in regard to American Indians, it usually refers to the division between Indian and whites. As novelist Louise Erdrich writes about her fictional Chippewa family, by "giving" the government one of her sons and withholding the other, the Kashpaw matriarch, "gained a son on either side of the line. Nector came home from boarding school knowing white reading and writing, while Eli knew the woods" (1984, 17). The line is not one defined by color, blood, or descent but cultural practices, epistemologies, and ways of being.

As with other tribes remaining in the South after removal, the Lumbee in North Carolina presented Jim Crow with a dilemma. What accommodation would be made for these formerly designated "free persons of color"? The answer is deceptively straightforward, though not without controversy: when faced with intermediary status between black and white, the Lumbee became Indian.

This simple declaration of Indian identity has been defended and questioned. Malinda Maynor's short 1996 film, *Real Indian*, on Lumbee failure to be perceived as authentic articulates the tribe's contemporary situation thusly: "Other Indians even argue that Lumbees can't be real Indians because we're not traditional enough: no reservation, no ancient language, and too much bad blood." In other words, not only do the Lumbee lack the traditionally authenticating markers of tribal culture, but consistent with the residual laws of hypodescent, they compromised their claim to Indianness by intermixing with blacks, hence, "bad blood." Commissioned to research Lumbee tribal origins in the 1970s, American Indian anthropologist Robert Thomas found that the community's authenticity was challenged for a number of reasons:

> A great many whites really do not "buy" the identification of the Lumbees in Robeson County as Indians of any tribe. Further, some people in other Indian groups feel the same way as do whites about the Lumbees. Many Lumbees have obvious black blood. Lumbees do not have a distinct language and a distinct tribal religion. Different individual Lumbees present themselves as members of different tribes. (1980, 63)

The tribe has undergone numerous official name changes (both with and in spite of community input) in the 20th century prior to voting to rename themselves the "Lumbee Indians of North Carolina" in 1951, a geographic designation derived from the Lumber River. The tribe was first recognized as the "Croatan Indians" in 1885, a misnaming with considerable influence, but was renamed the "Indians of Robeson County" in 1911, and then the "Cherokees of Robeson County" in 1913. Later proposals to change the tribe's name to "Cheraw Indians" and to "Siouan Indians of Lumber River" failed to reach state and federal legislatures.[2] Thus, the "something strange . . . going on" in Robeson County is not necessarily racial amalgamation as much as the contentious and long-standing effort to establish identity through government petition, the effort to establish Lumbee origins as Hatteras, Cherokee, Tuscarora, Saponi, Cheraw—or as "tri-racial isolates."[3] And, given the issue of amalgamation, some question whether they are, in fact, Indian.

The tribe is recognized by the state of North Carolina, but is refused—for reasons subject to multiple and contentious interpretation—full federal recognition and benefits. To claim that the Lumbee *became* Indian in response to the rise of segregation is, of course, disingenuous. It appears to question the traditions and values that define a people and ignore the affirmative identifications that inform collectivity irrespective of social status. To invoke N. Scott Momaday, the Lumbee have possessed an unequivocal "shared idea of themselves" as Indian for over three hundred years—the emergence of segregation as a cultural system in the late 19th century did not change that. Racial status was neither the starting nor ending point for defining this North Carolina community. Nor is American Indian identity simply established through the movement between blackness and whiteness, the top-down imposition of external categories of peoplehood that adjudicate status. "The not-White and not-Black expression of Lumbee identity," notes Blu, "embody only two facets of their multifaceted sense of collective selfhood" (1979, 234).

That collective sense of selfhood was, from the community's perspective, unwavering and unambiguous. Nevertheless, the rise of segregation at the end of the 19th century and into the 20th forced the community into an interstitial position that had to be mediated within public documents that disclose impassioned attempts at resolution. As the cultural representation of the community both during the Jim Crow era and beyond it reveals, Lumbee positioning between black and white began to structure what would be marked as a symbolic third caste. This positioning was by no means unique to this southern community, especially for native populations in the South resisting removal. The Choctaw who remained in Mississippi after the tribe's forced relocation to Indian Territory in 1831, for example, petitioned the federal government for relief in 1913, citing, for one, their educational disadvantages off-reservation.[4] The majority of Choctaw in the South, wrote the Mississippi, Alabama, and Louisiana Choctaw Council, "cannot, with hardly an exception, read or write, and . . . the majority of them are unable to speak or understand the English language, living in communities where the Choctaw language is universally used . . . [F]or this reason their children are unable to attend the state schools and are reared in the same unfortunate circumstance as their parents."[5] Unlike the Choctaw, the tribe that would become known as the Lumbee could not argue for separate schools, either on the basis of cultural difference or physical isolation in a county that was almost evenly divided between whites, blacks, and Indians. The absence of forced migration marks the history of these North Carolina Indians as distinct from the "trail of tears" narrative that structures that of other tribes, situating that history as already anomalous. Yet that absence set the stage for cultural interpretation of the community according to the mores of Jim Crow and the racial continuum it inscribed. This interpretative process is reflected in government documents representing tribal advocacy by members of the community and outsiders; the narrative that emerges perhaps predictably centers on the discourse of genealogy and bloodline. Yet what makes this southern archive surrounding the community noteworthy is the degree to which the representation of blood quantum level focused not on "Indian" blood, but on that of whites and blacks and, more specifically, their latency.

In this chapter, I explore segregation-era culture's carving out of a space deemed "Indian" within the interstices of the meanings ascribed to the signs "colored" and white. The enormous historical, governmental, and popular cultural archive centering on the question, "Are they or aren't they white or black?"reveals the ways in which Indian advocates and community members came to uphold the tenets of white supremacy and the class structure it supports in the making of this middle caste. Their history reveals how, contradictorily, the evidence of modern subjectivity legitimated the Lumbee's status as a tribal people.

The history of the Lumbee reflects the fraught narrative of native authenticity that surrounds tribal history in the United States. Due to their southern placement and the absence of removal, the contestation over Lumbee tribal origins had a specific resonance, reaching back well before the rise of segregation and popularized in the theory of the Lost Colony. Recounted in the language of legend, it is said that when European settlers arrived in North Carolina in the 1730s, they found "located on the waters of the Lumbee, as the Lumber River was then called, a tribe of Indians, speaking English, tilling the soil, owning slaves and practicing many of the arts of civilized life" (McMillan 1907, 25). From 1783 to 1835, these Indians had the right to vote, joined the military, and had their own schools and churches. As "free persons of color" they were denied franchise in 1835 by constitutional convention, and although the ban was removed in 1868, they were nonetheless barred from white schools. In spite of efforts to compel them to attend "Negro" schools, they refused; thus, as state legislator Hamilton McMillan notes in 1888, "Hundreds have grown up to manhood and womanhood in perfect ignorance of books. This they preferred to association with the colored race" (1907, 37).

In 1885, McMillan proposed that the North Carolina state legislature establish funding for separate Indian schools and recognize them as the "Croatan" Indians.[6] In linking these two actions, their recognition as an Indian tribe became inseparable from the recognition that they were, neither in blood nor in status, "colored." The evidence was based on the "common sense" visual inspection of race, the belief that "blood tells." What it tells, however, is not a narrative of Indianness as much as the negation of blackness, a story reflecting those European immigrant disavowals that, as numerous scholars have shown, was key to the construction of European American whiteness. Nevertheless, state recognition of their Indian specificity comes to reveal what white blood signifies as well; the theory that the Croatan Indians were descended from the English survivors of Sir Walter Raleigh's Lost Colony of 1587 was instrumental to the formation of their separate Indian status. Here, the oppositional discourses of black and white blood become contradictorily united. While black disavowal was key to establishing Indian specificity, so too was the acknowledgment of not just white blood, but foundational whiteness: McMillan's advocacy on behalf of those he called the Croatan Indians was inextricable from his belief that in this tribe, one could settle a historical mystery. His booklet, *Sir Walter Raleigh's Lost Colony* (1888), musters evidence to prove that the colonists amalgamated with Indians friendly to the English and eventually removed with them from Roanoke Island to what is now Robeson County, North Carolina.

I want to trace this narrative of racial interstitiality, the space between black abjection and white normativity, in key documents published during the Jim Crow era that propagated this theory of white amalgamation in the service of tribal advocacy. These include not only McMillan's 1888 work, but historian Stephen B. Weeks's *The Lost Colony of Roanoke: Its Fate and Survival* (1891); Indian agent O. M. McPherson's *Indians of North Carolina: Report on Condition and Tribal Rights of the Indians of Robeson and Adjoining Counties of North Carolina* (1915); and George Butler's "The Croatan Indians of Sampson County, North Carolina. Their Origin and Racial Status. A Plea for Separate Schools" (1916). These documents reveal that government intervention on behalf of the tribe was partially based on belief in the Indians' distinguished white ancestry, which rendered them suitable candidates for racial uplift. This segregation-era attempt to fix the caste status of this southern community set in motion a field of representation that extended beyond the de jure end of segregation. The Lumbee's 1958 portrayal in *Life* magazine highlighting the community's routing of a Klan rally enforces the narrative of self-sufficiency and ethnic pride originating within turn-of-the-century texts. As revealed in Adolph L. Dial and David K. Eliades's 1975 community history, *The Only Land I Know: A History of the Lumbee Indians*, this narrative took on a more anxious cast as federal desegregation orders were seen to compromise hard-won Indian schools.

The Lumbee's efforts to establish who they were to whites and seemingly against African Americans reveals one historically situated response to the implicit demands of capitalism: the state intervenes to produce subjects capable of being managed distinct from and in concert with their own conceptions of peoplehood. As the belief in the Lumbee's foundational English bloodline became harnessed to a narrative of emergent bourgeois conformity, their segregation-era history bares the meaning behind whiteness and the class-based tenets underlying racial hierarchy. My intent in this chapter is not to affirm or contest any one account of the Lumbee's tribal origins, but to trace the ways in which racial belief became essential to leveraging a position of approximate likeness, the interspace between black and white.

## Black

In 1914, Indian agent O. M. McPherson was on the verge of submitting a report on the "Croatan" Indians of North Carolina at the behest of the U.S. Senate, then charged with adjudicating federal tribal status. After assuring community members that they need not show up in Washington in a body to support the presumed advocacy, McPherson received this missive from a Robeson County resident and community member:

Dear Sir:

Please grant me this privilege of writing you. I am well and trust you are enjoying life with the greatest of pleasure. I do this to hear from you. Can you tell me anything that is good about our affairs? Would you like to have my picture with my hunting suit?

And if so, I will mail you one.

> *Yours truly,*
> A. *Chavis* (cited in McPherson 1915, 250)

The quaint and proactive offer was declined on the basis that the agent "could not use one picture to advantage in [his] report," although he welcomed the picture for his personal collection. While charming, the gift of one's photo in a hunting suit is not wholly innocent: it betrays a self-consciousness as to how visual documentation affects one's status as Indian, especially in regard to government visibility. Native authenticity was and continues to be somewhat predictably associated with signs of proximity to the natural world. The incident is merely one example of the many ways in which visual inspection was central to the Lumbee's attempts to advocate for tribal recognition on both the state and federal levels.

Visual epistemology has been a stock feature of determining racial status in popular culture, legal discourse, and in "scientific" assessment as well. Working for the Smithsonian in the 1930s, anthropologist John Swanton records, "My first encounter with a Robeson County Indian was in the office of Mr. Mooney a few years before his death. He called me in on this occasion, pointed to a tall swarthy individual standing near and asked me if I did not clearly recognize the Indian features" (1933, 1). Such an inspection held material stakes: the government dispatched physical anthropologist Carl Selezer to the area to examine 209 volunteers from the community "to determine Indianness on the basis of anatomical and physiological features" and thereby their eligibility for benefits under the Indian Reorganization Act of 1934 (cited in Dial and Eliades 1975, 19). As a result, a mere 22 individuals were determined to be half-blood or more, the minimum requirement of eligibility for Indians not members of previously recognized tribes. Yet the southern placement of this North Carolina tribe dictated that the visual evidence of Indian blood rely less on establishing blood quantum level as much as another type of visible proof: that of nonblackness. As legal historians Ariela Gross and Ian Haney Lopez point out, legal determinations of racial identity were always partly dependent on the appearance of the plaintiff or accused.[7] Gross writes, "Litigants seeking to prove a person's whiteness almost always sought to exhibit him or her to the jury. And witnesses' descriptions of appearance—skin color, hair, eyes, and features—were ubiquitous in racial identity trials, even if the person being described was a long-dead ancestor" (2008, 41). Particularly in southern cases that dealt with challenges to slave status and later, one's status as "colored"—most famously in *Plessy v. Ferguson*—reading the signs of race on the body were structured by a black/white dichotomy. How, then, did the discourse of black disavowal imposed by Jim Crow culture come to legitimate the interstitial caste position called "Indian"?

George Edwin Butler's 1916 petition for the restoration of separate schools for the Indians, "The Croatan Indians of Sampson County, North Carolina. Their Origin and Racial Status. A Plea for Separate Schools," reveals the ways in which Indian authenticity in the South became adjudicated through visual distinction. His petition self-consciously submits photographic evidence of the community's Indianness in addition to the recitation of the genealogies of selected extended families. The occasion for Butler's plea for the reinstatement of state funding originated with a crisis over the blurring between Indian and black after the children of an Indian and a "mulatto woman" attempted to enroll in an Indian school. While the teacher and trustees refused their admission on the grounds that "these children contained negro blood to the prohibitive degree" (Butler 1916, 31) (in this case, to the fourth generation), nevertheless, as Butler notes, "the fact that they were excluded created confusion and friction in this Indian school, annoyance to the County Board of Education, and was the chief cause which led to its repeal by the legislature of 1913" (32). It is this repeal that Butler's document hopes to redress. In mustering evidence toward this end, he presents a number of arguments—their status as taxpayers, the treatment of Indians in neighboring counties, the lack of additional cost to the state—but his chief argument concerns their racial status. In the course of asserting that they are, as one subtitle proclaims, "Easily Recognized as Indians," the document provides visual evidence not so much of Indianness as proof of their distinction from "negroes."

As the document reveals, visual inspection was an instrument of black disavowal, half the battle toward status elevation. "We have procured from the homes of these Indian families a few photographs, showing the type of these Croatan Indians today living in Sampson Country," Butler writes. "It will be readily seen that they are neither white people, negroes or mulattoes. They all have straight black hair, the Indian nose and lips, their skin a light brown hue, mostly high cheek bones, erect in their carriage, steel gray eyes and an intelligent countenance. Where the white blood predominates many of them have beards" (1916, 46). What follows is a series of portraits with a narrative overview of the genealogy of specific families, for example, that of Enoch and Sarah Manuel and William and Nancy Ann Bledsole.

As authenticating documents, photographs such as these rely on the associative link between blood and the body: because the physiological signs of race are taken to be definitive, the absence of other markers of Indian authenticity in the photographs—the attire, context, and cultural objects intrinsic to the tradition of late 19th-century Native American portraiture—goes with-

Portrait of Enoch Manuel and Sarah E. Manuel in George Edwin Butler's *The Croatan Indians of Sampson County, North Carolina: Their Origin and Racial Status, A Plea for Separate Schools* (Durham, NC: Seeman Printery, 1916). Used with permission of Documenting the American South, The University of North Carolina, Chapel Hill Libraries.

Portrait of William J. Bledsole and Nancy Ann Bledsole in George Edwin Butler's *The Croatan Indians of Sampson County, North Carolina: Their Origin and Racial Status, A Plea for Separate Schools* (Durham, NC: Seeman Printery, 1916). Used with permission of Documenting the American South, University of North Carolina, Chapel Hill Libraries.

out comment. Instead, Indianness is distilled into a set of physical features—or more appropriately, the *traces* of those features. A narrative pedagogy of racial visualization is necessary to supplement the photographs; the viewer must be told how to read them. The signs of race that Butler instructs the viewer to look for—straight black hair, light brown skin, high cheek bones, erect posture, gray eyes, and "intelligent countenance"—are not, in fact, readily apparent without prior coaxing—nor are they unambiguously Indian.

The photographs in Butler's petition for separate Indian schools would at first seem to bear no relationship to Native American *carte-de-visites*, hobbyist portraits, advertising images, or before-and-after shots of Indian children enrolled in BIA boarding schools that were popular in that era.[8] These are not public and exoticized images of American "aborigines" intended to inspire curiosity, nostalgia, desire, or repulsion. Nor do they represent the silent testimony of an illiterate people, the objectification of natives subject to a colonizing gaze. The accompanying narrative co-authored by two Indians from Sampson County, Enoch Emanuel and C. D. Brewington, "Brief Sketch of a Few Prominent Indian Families of Sampson Country," represents self-produced testimony geared toward community advocacy. The photographs are nonetheless a form of anthropological evidence and submitted as authenticating supplements. What they intend to authenticate stems from the pressures of 1916 Jim Crow culture.

In their genealogies of Indian families included in Butler's document, Emanuel and Brewington take a somewhat different approach from Butler's emphasis on the visual inscription of race; commentary on the physical features of those pictured is subordinated to a narrative of bloodline based on descent. Such minute genealogies attest to the families' admixture with "pure whites" while assuring against their mulatto status. Disavowing hints of the "tarbrush," they accept the segregationist logic of hypodescent even as they contest their treatment under Jim Crow. For example, Emanuel and Brewington's sketch of county resident William Simmons informs us that

William's mother was Winnie Medline, who married Jim Simmons in Fayetteville, and she made an affidavit in 1902, in order that her son William could vote under the grandfather clause, that her mother was a white woman and that her father was an Indian. She further states in her affidavit that there was not a drop of negro blood in her veins or those of her children. Her son, William Simmons, had dark brown eyes, straight hair and high cheek bones and light brown skin. He claimed that his grandfather and grandmother, on his father's side, were Indians and came from

Roanoke River, and never affiliated with the negroes. William Simmons has eighteen grandchildren whose parents have not intermarried with the negro race, and these children are without school advantages except by private subscriptions. (Butler 1916, 62)

While this discussion of physical features testifies that Indianness should be evident in the body, its focus lies in establishing untainted lineal descent. It relies not on establishing an affirmative sense of Indianness as much as the negation of blackness: it is a statement against affiliation, against intimacy, against amalgamation. It represents race by (non)association and assures the white reader of shared values—the claim of superiority over the reviled caste. While group cohesion is always predicated on some type of disavowal, the rise of segregation forces that process to be both self-consciously practiced and juridically overt. In this sense, the apparently neutral assertion of identity, "we are who we are," lends itself to status elevation. This Jim Crow history of an anomalous southern tribe lends ironic support to Toni Morrison's claim about racial hierarchy as intrinsic to immigrant belonging. "[T]he move into mainstream America always means buying into the notion of American blacks as the real aliens," she writes. "Whatever the ethnicity or nationality of the immigrant, his nemesis is understood to be African American" (1994, 98). The forced assertion of identity around the color line reveals the mutually constitutive nature of racial assignment, whether immigrant or, in this case, indigenous. Unlike European immigrants, however, this distinction was not linked to assimilation coded as the progressive movement into abstract universality coded as white, but leveraged on behalf of, ironically, the support of social separation, the desire to be free from state interference.

The testimony of black exclusion in the genealogies of these "prominent Indian families" supplements what Butler readily acknowledges as his selectivity in choosing which members of the community to profile. Introducing the photos he notes, "There are a few of these people that have intermarried with mulattoes, but all those of negro blood have been excluded from this sketch and no demands or claims are made in their behalf, as under the law they are properly classed with the negroes" (1916, 46). In its contestation of Jim Crow one sees the acceptance of segregationist logic: it is not a challenge to racial hierarchy per se, but one's place in it. Carving out a previously unimagined space within the black/white caste system entails the forced disappearance of those who cannot be interpellated within its boundaries, those figures of Indian-black amalgamation. Like the mixed-race children whose presence initiated the closure of all Indian schools in Sampson County, the families "excluded from this sketch" on the basis of "negro blood" are lost to history as Indian.

Needless to say, the discourse of white blood figures differently in these segregation-era petitions given the absence of any one-drop rule in regard to whiteness. But even accepting the belief that white admixture does not make one white, one would assume that white ancestry would not be advantageously foregrounded in petitions claiming Indian specificity and upholding the separation between races. Such depiction leads to unspoken ironies within these documents that lobby to establish Indian status or trace specific tribal origins. Under the heading "Easily Recognized as Indians," Butler testifies:

> The above list of Indians will be readily recognized from their general appearance. . . . They do not resemble the negroes or mulattoes, in that their hair is perfectly straight. They have high cheek bones, they do not have flat noses, or thick lips. Many of them have grey eyes, and often have rose tints on their cheeks. They are usually tall and erect, they are cleanly in their habits and mode of living. They are usually land owners, and more thrifty and industrious. They live and congregate in certain localities, and are clannish, and in numerous ways show Indian traits. (1916, 33–34)

In the effort to demonstrate the physical and cultural characteristics that deny blackness, the language here introduces a seed of doubt about the Indians of Robeson County, one that would only emerge as an issue years later. That is, in its attempt to militate against blackness, Butler's language shows his subjects to be indistinguishable from whites. The very assertion that they reveal "Indian traits" as a testament to Indian ancestry begins to betray their collective petition: if they live in white-approved ways and possess "white" features, what remains of their Indianness?

This, moreover, is the ultimate irony of the photographs themselves. While they intend to testify against traces of the "tarbrush," they nonetheless fail to establish a positive "Indianness" perhaps by virtue of the fact that the very historical context would render such empirical content unnecessary— if, as I have noted, there is no intermediacy within the metaphor of the color line. While one could say that features of the men depicted are obscured by heavy beards, it is the very presence of those beards that begins to question their Indian status. Unlike signs of blackness, this indication of whiteness— facial hair—does not need to be explained away, at least in 1916. Reflected here and in other segregation-era documents, white blood and "civilized" cultural practices become counter-intuitively linked both to the establishment of Indian status and to theories of tribal specificity. The claim that the Indians of Robeson County were descended from the English survivors of Raleigh's Lost Colony of 1587 was intrinsically tied to the initial allowance for separate Indian schools under segregation. Belief in this narrative of foundational white amalgamation—and in the latency of white blood—rendered them suitable candidates for racial uplift. Nevertheless, while this narrative of white descent became crucial to establishing their racial distinction at the beginning of the 20th century, it serves to complicate that distinction at the century's end in unexpected ways. This interplay between black disavowal and white proximity characterizes the narrative by which the Lumbee Indians carved out an interstitial place within Jim Crow's racial binary.

## White

Legislator Hamilton McMillan's intervention on behalf of the Indians of Robeson County in 1885 seems to have stemmed partly from his belief in their august ancestry. His 1888 booklet, *Sir Walter Raleigh's Lost Colony: Historical Sketch of the Attempts Made by Sir Walter Raleigh to Establish a Colony in Virginia, with Traditions of an Indian Tribe in North Carolina, Indicating the Fate of the Colony of Englishmen Left on Roanoke Island in 1587*, introduces the theory that the English colonists survived by seeking refuge with friendly Indians and removing with them to the interior. The story of the Lost Colony has entered into national consciousness not as one potential birthplace of America, but as an unsolved mystery. Replayed in many historical documents—not to mention tourist sites—the history of the colony is this: under the auspices of Sir Walter Raleigh's charter to explore territory in the New World under Elizabeth I, Governor John White left a colony of 117 men and women "planters" on Roanoke Island in 1587. Among the colonists were his daughter, Eleanor Dare, and his granddaughter, Virginia Dare, whose distinction lies in her recognition as the "first Christian child born in Virginia." Delayed by three years due to England's war with Spain, White returned to the colony in 1590 to find it deserted. The only clues as to the whereabouts of the colonists were the "fair Roman letters: C. R. O." carved into a tree on the beach and the word "CROATOAN" carved onto a tree near the abandoned dwellings. Confronted with the dismantled fort, White was nonetheless optimistic that the colonists had departed with Indians friendly to the English to "Croatan," an island to the south of Cape Hatteras and the seat of this tribe and their leader, Manteo. His journal reads, "I greatly joyed that I had safely found a certain token of their being at Croatan, which is the place where Manteo was born, and the savages of the island our friends" (cited in McMillan 1907, 10). Other signs added to his optimism: heavy iron items had been buried, indicating an intent to return, and the message carved into the tree was not accompanied by a cross, a previously agreed upon symbol of distress. Nevertheless, the colonists were never seen again—or rather, as McMillan's version of the story goes, they were never seen by white men again. Weather inhibited White's landing at "Croatan" and subsequent efforts to ascertain the whereabouts of the colonists in succeeding years, including inquiries undertaken by the colonists at Jamestown 20 years later, were unsuccessful. The fate of the original colonists is therefore uncertain, but their likenesses resurface every summer on Roanoke Island where one can "relive the exciting story of The Lost Colony" in an outdoor theater—$30 for the Queen's pass and $15.50 for youth.

While there are various interpretations of what happened at Roanoke, all of which theorize the cause of the colonists' demise—they were slaughtered by hostile Indians, perished on the sea in an attempt to return to England, or died of starvation—McMillan's alternative explanation postulating amalgamation with friendly Indians found the remnants of the colony alive and well and living on the banks of the Lumber River 300 years later. Thanks to McMillan's research and legislative initiative, the Indians of Robeson County thus became (mis)named the "Croatan Indians" by the state of North Carolina, granting them formal government recognition. The evidence that McMillan compiled has since been advanced, embellished, or countered in numerous documents, some which seek to establish the tribe's genealogy, and others to petition the government as to their racial status under segregation-era pressures. These include, among others, Stephen B. Weeks's *The Lost Colony of Roanoke: Its Fate and Survival* (1891); O. M. McPherson's *Indians of North Carolina* (1915); the aforementioned 1916 document by George Butler advocating the reestablishment of separate Indian schools; Angus W. McLean's "Historical Sketch of the Indians of Robeson County" (n.d.); and John Swanton's "Probable Identity of the 'Croatan' Indians" (1933). Moreover, McMillan's research remains significant in contemporary explorations of Lumbee origin.[9] Those who advance the link between the Lost Colony and the modern-day Lumbee do so not only to explain a historical unknown, to allow the colonists' history, as historian Stephen B. Weeks announces, "to emerge again from the darkness and dust of oblivion" "after a lapse of three hundred years" (1891, 127), but to put that history into the service of the tribe.

In the context of this chapter, my concern is not to validate or contest McMillan's theory but to explore the ways in which belief in the tribe's legendary white ancestry produced Indian collectivity in the eyes of the state. I focus not so much on how that belief impacts Lumbee's "shared idea of themselves"—although this is part of their oral tradition—but on how it inspired outsiders to advocate on their behalf during an era of forced racial separation. In this sense, the "legend" of the Lost Colony was itself a production of segregation-era southern culture. If the disavowal of African American intermixture was intrinsic to the then "Croatan" petition for separate Indian schools, in what ways did the discourse of white intermixture support such advocacy for a "third" space in Jim Crow culture?

I want to sidetrack the temptation of historical explication, the reason why the story of the Lost Colony continues to beguile. What is intriguing is the way in which that legend unveils the meaning behind whiteness—or rather, its residues. In effect, McMillan's belief that the Lost Colony survived in the form of a mixed-blood people in North Carolina provoked him to intervene on their behalf. His historical research was taken up by others who began to link the tribe's latent white blood to their cultural worthiness and to highlight those community practices that would, ironically, prove Indian distinction from African Americans after the turn of the century. McMillan's evidence is intriguing in and of itself.[10] Yet, writing 100 years later under commission to report on the probable tribal origins of the Lumbee, anthropologist Robert Thomas found that while McMillan was an "honest scholar and fairly thorough," his evidence of the colonists' survival "stretches my credulity beyond its limits" (1980, 5). Nevertheless, McMillan's arguments were persuasive, especially to the North Carolina legislature, which passed his proposals to fund their separate schools and have the state recognize them as "Croatan" Indians, a geographic naming reflected in the colonists' apparent indication of their destination. The link between ancestry and advocacy is made overt in McMillan's pamphlet: "The action of the North Carolina Legislature in establishing separate schools for this people and recognizing them as descendants of the friendly Croatans known to the English colonists, was one great step toward their moral and intellectual elevation" (1907, 38).

While benevolent in intent, the theory of Lost Colony descent mutated into a subtle testament to white supremacy during the rise of Jim Crow as the discourse of white blood supported testimony of group exceptionalism. Status elevation is a means of recognizing and producing a specific kind of subject, one who demonstrates a progressive movement toward some measure of bourgeois normativity through self-betterment. Positing white origins singled out candidates for racial uplift and became a justification for offering "Indians" educational opportunity, the symbolic vehicle of democratic possibility and precondition of "moral and intellectual" improvement. This action on behalf of the newly designated Croatan Indians not only rewards them for their friendly services, albeit 200 years later, but uplifts national history from a narrative of failure to one of enduring survival. It is an account of founder perseverance engaging enough to overcome distaste for miscegenation and the potential rape of white women that lie at its core—a story allegorically imagined but with requisite condemnation in *The Tempest*. To draw an analogy, McMillan's theory might ask us to believe that Caliban has indeed "peopled . . . /This isle with Calibans" but also to "think but nobly" of Miranda, simultaneously would-be conqueror and conquered, her survival contingent upon the loss of her English virtue. Nevertheless, the legend survives despite the transgression of these taboos. As I note in the previous chapter, if the state of Virginia could make an exception in its anti-miscegenation laws for the descendants of John Rolfe and Pocahontas, then this becomes less difficult to believe.

Of course, there are other explanations for McMillan's intervention more efficacious than historical revisionism. In speculating on his motivation for sponsoring the legislation, Karen Blu suggests that McMillan was attempting to court the Indian vote in order to ensure conservative Democratic control in a state whose stronghold was being threatened by Reconstruction Republicans.[11] Nevertheless, McMillan's text suggests another motivation; for one, his very minute exploration of historical documents regarding the Lost Colony indicates a history *aficionado* inspired by the will to know. More importantly, McMillan's advocacy on behalf of the tribe extended beyond his term in the legislature; in effect, both his booklet and subsequent correspondence reveal a benevolently paternal attitude toward the tribe reflective of the discourse of native sympathy in the West popularized by Helen Hunt Jackson's *Ramona*.[12] "To the charitable, who are interested in the moral uplifting of humanity," his treatise concludes, "we heartily commend the Croatans" (1907, 46). The saviors of our white forefathers, these Indians were worthy candidates for state intervention. It is thus that, irrespective of grosser political motivation regarding the fortunes of the Democratic Party, McMillan is inscribed as "one of the best white friends the Indians of Robeson County ever had" (cited in Dial and Eliades 1975, 8).

A narrative of progressive development and self-betterment became intrinsically linked to the question of racial status not only in McMillan's mind, but in that of the historians and Indian agents who began to embellish his work. Not incoincidentally, following the rise of Jim Crow, the community's purported "hatred" of black association became more pronounced in the rhetoric of its white advocates. In response to Indian Agent O. M. McPherson's request for information about the Croatan Indians in 1914, McMillan responded, "Since their recognition as a separate race they have made wonderful progress. Their hatred of the Negro is stronger than that entertained by Caucasians" (cited in McPherson 1915, 243). The unwitting placement of these two statements side by side in his personal correspondence reveals how closely advancement and African American repudiation were connected. Marking the community's concerted distaste for "Negro" association is represented as another sign in their favor, an indication of class drive. In 1891, historian Stephen Weeks embellishes McMillan's 1880 evaluation that the Indians "preferred ignorance" to integrated schooling: "[T]hey were obliged to patronize the negro schools. This they refused to do as a rule, preferring that their children should grow up in ignorance, for *they hold the negro in utmost contempt, and no greater insult can be given a Croatan than to call him 'a nigger'"* (1891, 131; emphasis mine). George Butler's 1916 petition extends this discourse by establishing "ignorance" as preferable to an "association with a race *which they hold in utter contempt"* (1916; emphasis mine). What is striking is not only the need for this continued iteration, but its progressive emphasis over time. This narrative of interstitiality, then, perhaps predictably follows the rise of white supremacy.

In contrast to Butler's petition, which presents straightforward "proof" of nonblackness in order to reestablish separate school funding, the evidence of specifically derived white ancestry of 300 years' standing becomes subject to tautological use: while McMillan recommended the Croatans as candidates for racial uplift based on their presumed ancestry, a few years later, Stephen Weeks represented their civilized cultural practices as proof of their white ancestry. That is, while one harnessed the theory of descent to a benevolent charitable mission, the other takes the evidence of their "civilized" lifestyle as an indication of descent. Weeks's 1891 extension of McMillan's theory, *The Lost Colony of Roanoke: Its Fate and Survival,* differs from the other documents discussed here in that it does not intend to lobby the government on behalf of the tribe. Nevertheless, its positive assessment of Croatan character represents a subtle sign of white supremacist belief in its emphasis on the latency of white blood surviving the passage of centuries. Weeks's ethnography of Croatan "character and disposition" is offered as proof of McMillan's theory of the colonists' survival, notwithstanding the obvious points that cultural practices are not irrefutable signs of blood and that white-Indian amalgamation could have taken place merely a generation earlier rather than in 1587.[13] Nevertheless, Weeks offers the following evidence:

> [The Croatan Indians] are found of all colors from black to white, and in some cases cannot be distinguished from white people. They have the prominent cheek-bones, the steel-gray eyes, the straight black hair of the Indian. Those showing the Indian features most prominently have no beards; those in whom the white element predominates have beards. Their women are frequently beautiful; their movements are graceful, their dresses becoming, their figures superb. (1891, 131–132)

Beauty, it seems, is proof of white amalgamation as is, the passage goes on to enumerate, the professional achievement of individual Indians.

Interestingly, as a footnote to the "superb" figures of these Indians, Weeks introduces the infamous Indian folk hero/outlaw, Henry Berry Lowrie (also Lowery) who successfully eluded the authority of the North Carolina Home Guard during the Confederacy.[14] Anecdotal evidence identifies him as a physical specimen embodying perfect human form and, not incidentally, western features: "The face was pure Greek in profile; the eyes *steel blue*, the figure of perfect mould and the man as easily graceful in his attitude as any gentleman in a drawing-room" (1891, 143). This portrayal of the renegade Indian is not at odds with Weeks's purpose, which is not only to show the latency of white genes, but the result of racial hybridity: the tribe bears, in his words, "traces both of savage and civilized ancestry" in its "habits, disposition, and mental characteristics" (1891, 143). Even now the subject of local legend for resisting the unjust treatment of Indian people, Henry Berry Lowrie provides Weeks the perfect case in point for demonstrating the amalgamation of supposedly contradictory tendencies. A bandit capable of suffering privation and exertion that "would have killed a white man or negro," he nonetheless also surfaces in Weeks's text as "a perfect Apollo" with a strict code of ethics. This, we are informed, includes the most definitive sign of chivalry: his refusal to insult white women (1891, 140). The depiction operates within the veiled discourse of blood that provides the evidentiary supplement to the historian's case: what could the amalgamation of white and Indian produce but this embodiment of pure opposition—the ultimate savage forced to live outside the law who nonetheless behaves as honorably and with the discrimination and grace of any "gentleman in a drawing-room"?[15]

The duality, though relegated to a footnote, emphasizes the historian's overt intent: English ancestry surfaces within an innate nobility that battles savage recidivism. Dilating on the contradictory nature of the tribe, his text moves from character traits to cultural practices:

> These Indians are hospitable to strangers and are ever ready to do a favor for the white people. They show a fondness for gay colors, march in Indian file, live retired from highways, never forget a kindness, an injury, nor a debt. They are the best of friends and the most dangerous of enemies. They are reticent until their confidence is gained, and when aroused are perfect devils, exhibiting all the hatred, malice, cunning, and endurance of their Indian ancestors. At the same time they are remarkably cleanly in their habits, a characteristic not found in the pure-blooded Indian. Physicians who practise among them say that they never hesitate to sleep or eat in the house of a Croatan. (1891, 139–140)

In contrast to Butler's petition, Weeks's goal is not to prove that the Croatan Indians are deserving of schools (at this point, they already have them), but to muster sociological evidence of descent. This surfaces, for one, in their admirably sanitary housekeeping, which sets them at odds with their "innate" tendencies. These tendencies, one cannot help but notice, reflect belief in a premodern code of honor often attributed to "developing" peoples. What I would emphasize here is, again, not an assessment of the truth value of any of these representations of the community's origins, but, in keeping with my later emphasis on Asian Americans, the very ways in which the community became subjected to a specific frame of representation imposed by segregation-era culture. In this case, "Indian" was a site of forced intelligibility, one subject to reincorporation in ways that conformed to regional norms. That this process of white/black approximation began to suture other *American* values becomes clear as racial depiction is linked to economic self-sufficiency. Racial intermediacy, then, becomes the occasion to affirm normative class values.

In this sense, the racialization of the Lumbee in cultural representation reflects what Gross has noted as the performance of whiteness within litigation over racial status particularly in cases involving inheritance and property rights following the rise of Jim Crow. That is, plaintiffs argued that they "performed" civic virtues—citizenship, character, and honor for men and sexual virtue for women—as a means of convincing juries of their white status. As she shows, these cases arising from the "one-drop" rule did not make crossing the color line impossible: "Indeed, in racial identity litigation, juries often seemed to reward people who 'passed' successfully into whiteness for doing such a good job at performing as whites" (2008, 298). In the case of the Lumbee, caste elevation represented a recognition of not only lifestyle, but class and kinship conformity.

Weeks's text demonstrates this type of ethnographic testimony later reproduced in Butler's petition and implicitly underlying McMillan's advocacy on their behalf: it offers evidence of their ambition and, contrary to notions of tribal communalism, their adherence to kinship structures that facilitate the accumulation of capital. "Likeness" is thus not merely racially coded, but reflects national values. Liberally borrowing from McMillan's booklet, Weeks informs us, "They are almost universally land-owners, no two families occupying the same house, but each having its own establishment. They hold about sixty thousand acres in Robeson county. They are industrious and frugal, and anxious to improve their condition" (1891, 131). These normative cultural practices and values—individual property ownership, nuclear family arrangement, work ethic geared to futurity and advancement—are all offered here not to recommend the tribe per se, but to support the speculation that these structures must stem from the residual traces of superior ancestry. The information testifies to the ways in which they have forgone any tribal organization and have assimilated the values and household structures that work in concert with the dominant culture. Weeks's document, then, is in keeping with the covert agenda of the Dawes Act, which, in the effort to enforce individual property ownership among Indians, ended up divesting tribes of communally held reservation land. Weeks's document perhaps unintentionally holds up this southern community as a model for Indian assimilation in the West.[16] The irony is, of course, that with varying degrees of directness, this information about their normativity also advocates for their Indian specificity. These anti-communal social structures translate into less subjective information of the type necessary to render groups visible to government agencies: well-defined heads of households, income levels, number of taxpayers, dollar value of property, etc. When, 20 years later, McMillan attests to the fruit of his 1885 proposal to establish their separate Indian schools— "Since this action on the part of the State they have become better citizens"— his criteria for such an assessment goes unmarked (1907). Nevertheless, the information gathered in 1914 by McPherson in order to fulfill his charge to investigate "the condition and tribal rights of the Indians of Robeson and adjoining counties of North Carolina" indicates the community's viability in contributing productively to the state economy. Good citizenry, then, implies neither advanced literacy nor loyalty to any political party, but an ability to add to state coffers. Status elevation is its reward. What these segregation-era texts reveal is not so much that "Indian" was anomalous to the black/white dichotomy enforced within southern culture, but that such anomaly could be resolved in the eyes of the state via the normative discourses of class.

The belief that a consistent propensity toward self-help might translate into continued state aid (and thereby separate caste status) is overtly acknowledged by 1916. Butler's petition to reestablish funding for Indian schools in Sampson County after the "confusion and friction" caused by "mulatto" Indian children attempting to gain admission concludes:

> It is marvellous [sic] that they have been able to maintain their racial status so well under the adverse social and political status which has been forced upon them by the white people. It shows that they have an ambition to improve their condition and to build themselves upward, morally, socially, and educationally, rather than to be pulled down to a level with the inferior race, with whom they would be socially classed. It is nothing but common justice to these people that the white race, which has done so much and is now endeavoring to do still more, for the education and material progress and welfare of all the people of the State, of every race, that the efforts of these Indians to build up and maintain their superior social and intellectual status from the negro race, should be encouraged in every proper way. (1916, 34–35)

Like other documents advocating for the "Croatan" Indians during this time, Butler's petition validates the underlying premises of white supremacy by recognizing those whose cultural practices render them fit subjects. Self-consciously addressing an audience liberal enough to accept responsibility for the injustice of a social status erroneously "forced upon them by the white people," it nevertheless appeals to conservative and presumably shared values of property ownership, civic duty, and spiritual improvement. The basis of its argument for status shift, their distinction from the "negro race," lies in their work ethic and consistently demonstrated desire for group advancement. The document unintentionally highlights one of the ironies of Jim Crow: racial status is something to be earned, caste placement of the presumed biologically distinct group is yet based on meritocracy. In suggesting that what distinguishes these Indians from African Americans is the performance of good citizenship thereby insisting on gradations of color, the document might appear to offer a theoretical challenge to segregation, its classification by biological descent and narrow, bipolar distinction. Nevertheless, it operates well within the logic of white supremacy and racial hierarchy even while laying bare the terms upon which recognition is based. Status recognition and potential funding by agents of the white supremacist state are means of validating those subjects fit for (contingent) incorporation based on conformity of values. In these documents surrounding the interstitial status of the tribe that would later be recognized as the Lumbee, one can witness the ways in which ambiguity found resolution within the processes of governmentality, shifting relations to capital, and a black/white axis. As in the following chapter, in which the designation of "near-whiteness" comes to characterize a formerly "colored" community's class advancement, here "Indian" emerges as a caste position to be recognized insofar as it can be integrated within the ideal category, citizen. That is, if intermediacy found grudging stasis, it was not wholly because a "third" category could emerge distinct from the racial associations that segregation inscribed, but because intermediacy could be reconciled by other axes that likewise defined social status and communal belonging.

## Indian

The characterization of this now unequivocally Indian community as worthy citizens enacting national values continued into the post-1954 era. The narrative of representation that emerged within (and due to the needs of) a previous period in history now also served the purpose of the times, in the 1950s, the promotion of American democracy during the rise of the Cold War. Evaluating the tribe's candidacy for uplift was now more nationally invested: the Indians of Robeson County provided evidence of equal opportunity for communities of color. This is amply reflected in two *Life* magazine photo layouts that take as their context the community's attempt to combat white supremacy. Just as Henry Berry Lowrie's legendary resistance became part of the tribe's oral tradition, so did their routing of a Ku Klux Klan rally intended to intimidate them in 1958. *Life*'s coverage of the event, "Bad Medicine for the Klan: North Carolina Indians break up Ku Kluxers' anti-Indian Meeting," granted the tribe national recognition in its depiction of, in cinematic fashion, a heavily armed scuffle between Klansmen and North Carolina Indians.[17] The attending text reads: "The Indians and whites, as well as a large Negro population, live apart and have their own schools. In its continuing efforts to keep Robeson County's three-way segregation rigid, the Klan had recently burned crosses to warn an Indian family that moved into a white neighborhood and an Indian woman who had dated a white man" (26). Community response was overwhelming: over 350 Indians, "most of them from the fiercely prideful Lumbee tribe," appeared at the site of the rally, successfully shutting it down without resorting to violence. The brief text is accompanied by a full-page photograph of two Indians who, having "captured" the KKK flag, are now wrapped in it, winking for the camera.

The caption calls attention to one subject's V.F.W. cap and identifies him as a flight engineer in World War II who "took part in first U.S. raid on Berlin." Such information marks the Indian within the purview of national community at the same time it provides ironic contrast: just as this Indian fought against fascism in Europe, he fights against fascism at home. Of course, there is no mention of whether he did so from within the confines of a segregated unit. Once again, race is at the center of narrating the tribe in ways consistent with the representation generated during the Jim Crow era; this time, however, the values they model are those that define national community through the repudiation of racist hierarchy.

After their initial coverage of this successful defeat of Klan attempts to dictate appropriate behavior to the tribe, *Life* reporters returned to Robeson County two months later to report on the Indians' return to normalcy—in more ways than one. "Indians Back at Peace and the Klan at Bay" informs us that the interlopers have since retreated, and takes the opportunity to assure us that the Indian lifestyle is very much like our own: "For years their people, like those shown on these pages, had quietly and profitably tended tobacco, corn and cotton, sent children to the good—if separate—schools and on to college. They had won tolerance and respect from the vast majority of their white neighbors."[18] There is, of course, an unspoken story underlying the caveat, "good—if separate—schools," one that I have highlighted. But in concert with their representation around the turn of the century, this 1958 portrayal of the tribe shows them prospering even as the racial deck is stacked against them. In adhering to the law, "those shown on these pages" represent a community modeled on peaceable and progressive development—somehow a natural inclination if allowed to proceed "quietly," that is, without outside interference. In concert with the belief that education levels the barriers to mobility, *Life* focuses on schooling: the caption to a photograph of second graders testifies to the fact that the "all-Indian" (read: segregated) schools are "well-equipped." Other depictions of "normal" life in the community highlight educational achievement: "COLLEGE SENIOR Mergie Chavis, 20, weaves a rug for her course in home economics at Pembroke State," and "FARMER Burleigh Lowry, 68, has sent four of his 11 children through college and has two more there now" (36A). As supplements to those dealing with the trial of the one Klansman arrested after the aborted rally, these pho-

The Lumbee as depicted in *Life* magazine, 1958.

tographs testify to the emergent class status of tribal members and represent a selective and leading portrait of the community, one invested in educational advancement, but whose "fierce" pride obviates an integrationist stance. Klan attempts to teach them their place through racial intimidation are thereby implicitly evaluated as unjust not only because the Klan itself acts undemocratically and thereby aberrantly, but because the tribe is simply not deserving of mistreatment—their values are also our own. The portrayal lends itself to an overlapping yet dual reading: does *Life* object to the Klan rally because it represents values antithetical to democracy or because, industrious and independent, these people do not need to be told how to act? Popular culture images show the community as having prospered because it played by the rules, both those of segregation and, later, of a nation that came to define itself in opposition to segregationist values.[19] The interstitial Indian was made to serve a *new* function during the rise of the Cold War and to that newness, anomaly could also be reconciled. As in the previous chapter, the "partly colored" provide a conveniently flexible referent.

The link between educational opportunity and segregation lends irony to post-1954 portrayals of scholastic pride in texts that also serve as vehicles of tribal advocacy. In the 1975 study, *The Only Land I Know: A History of the Lumbee Indians*, tribal members Adolph Dial and David Eliades devote a chapter to education whose title, "Out of Darkness," unintentionally resonates with the segregation-era legacy it chronicles. If schooling served to enlighten members of the tribe, it lightened them as well. The separately funded school system was official acknowledgment that they were not black; as Dial and Eliades write, "Their goals in education were to become a basis for pride and dignity, *as well as providing recognition of the people as an identifiable race* with deep roots as original owners of the land, as well as part of the beginnings of the nation" (1975, 90; emphasis mine). In this history, establishing Indian schools takes on a romantic cast in which the tribe is seen as taking an individualist stance against government intrusion. This reflects George Butler's 1916 characterization of "Croatan" educational history as a heroic defiance of the state's attempts to place them, erroneously, within its caste system. "[R]ather than *surrender* their racial status," Butler writes, "they will continue to support the public schools by taxation and support their own schools by private subscription" (1916, 45; emphasis mine). Their resistance is portrayed as both a matter of principle and autonomy from prejudiced authority— the selfsame values that Henry Berry Lowrie's legend signifies in collective memory. As anthropologist Robert Thomas notes in 1980, "it is the Lumbee conception that they have gone through a great deal of persecution because they were Indians and a great deal of persecution as well, because they would not become black and continued to declare themselves to be Indians" (1980, 60). The perceived ability to hold fast to a self-determined conception of who they are invests the tribe with very American traits: iconoclasm coupled with a morally informed position against unjust persecution. Ironically, this also represents resistance to the federal government's assimilationist agenda toward American Indians in the 1970s. In essence, segregation-era history allows any vestige of tribalism to be rewritten in terms of the rugged individual, one hallmark of the Americanizing process. In this sense, as well as in the simultaneous claim of indigenous and founder descent, the figure of the Lumbee Indian makes for a potentially satisfying national symbol. This is not lost upon North Carolina, which sent two former Miss Lumbees to the Miss America pageant to represent the state in recent years. The narratives of self-sufficiency and pride that attend the Lumbee transcend periodization, the division between segregation-era representation and that in the post-1954 moment.

Post-segregation era portrayals of this interstitial community highlight the processes of communal reconciliation to the class-based values that underwrite national norms, processes that mark continuity between the end of the 19th century and the latter part of the 20th. In this sense, assimilation was conveyed not through racially saturated terms—like whites or unlike blacks—but within the unifying discourse of nationalism, including pride in autonomy. Given the community's history, in which "Indian" emerged to allow for Jim Crow's continuance, it is only somewhat ironic that the tribe was then made to stand in for the national as a community defiant of white supremacy. As one historian declared in 1985, the Lumbee "emerged as a powerful force for racial equality in North Carolina."[20]

## Red, White—and Blue?

Looking at the racially interstitial, those whose claim to specificity did not formally signify in the Jim Crow South, unveils the cultural accommodations that could assure the continuation of white supremacy. But more significantly, advocacy both on behalf of and by members of the community produced a durable narrative that simultaneously inscribed "Indian" both as "not-black" and as residually white in specific ways. In effect, it produced a narrative that could render the community comprehensible in the eyes of the state, and left an important but complicating paper trail for Lumbee attempts to seek full federal recognition as a tribe. In compelling Indian visibility, its segregation-era history bears ongoing significance for contemporary debates about tribal self-definition and federal recognition. Just as Jim Crow enforced caste status based on the one-drop rule, its overdetermined discourse of blood is also reflected in contemporary determinations of who counts as Indian: blood quantum level has long been employed by the state as a determiner of Indian authenticity. Those narratives about blood initiated by the rise of segregation become echoed in contemporary arguments about descent, genealogy, and the political status of the tribe. The cultural work that went into establishing a "third space" between black and white thus resonates with contemporary attempts to assign political meaning to race.

The question points to the possibility that the very narratives of uplift that succeeded in distinguishing the Lumbee from African Americans might serve to distinguish them from other American Indians as well. To what extent does the history of advocacy occasioned by the rise of segregation now contribute to doubts about their authenticity as a tribe? The questions are intriguing, not necessarily for what they yield in a positivist sense, but for the ways in which contemporary attempts to respond to them rely on the idea that "blood tells" no less than they did at the beginning of the 20th century. While in a previous era the struggle was to be recognized as Indian against the taint of "Negro" association, the contemporary Lumbee struggle for recognition may now be waged against whiteness. Blood quantum level, an individual's degree of Indian blood, has long been a government criterion for determining Indianness; the Certificate of Degree of Indian Blood is required by the Bureau of the Interior to determine eligibility for federal social services and benefits. Blood quantum level emerges as an issue in the tribe's quest for full federal recognition, albeit in a minor way. In the course of reporting on intertribal resistance to the Lumbee petition, David E. Wilkins reveals that Chief Phillip Martin of the Mississippi Choctaws "submitted a report written by a tribal employee with dubious academic credentials" suggesting that the Lumbee were merely "a 'tri-racial isolate,' with the emphasis being on their alleged African ancestry" (1998, 170). Lumbee supporters roundly challenged this as "a racist view, long discarded," asserting that "no present Indian tribe would or could claim that some non-Indian ancestry disqualifies a group, since essentially all modern tribes have some, often much White ancestry."[21] In spite of the status that blood quantum level holds as a determiner of Indianness, however, it is not a major issue stalling the tribe's petitions for full federal recognition, a process that Wilkins has dubbed, the "Trail of Many Years," a pun on the history of native removal, the "Trail of Tears" that is absent in Lumbee history (1998).

While it is not within the scope of this chapter to address the vexed terrain of blood in regard to Indian status, suffice it to say, blood quantum level as both a federally imposed criterion of Indianness and one adopted by numerous tribes is subject to controversy. Blood quantum requirements are seen to hold the line against the "wannabe tribe": the number of self-reported Indians rose by 75 percent between 1970 and 1980 (Gould 1992, 85). Nevertheless, those requirements fail to speak to the complexity of intertribal intermixing and may be the instrument of statistical extermination through attrition. "Set the blood-quantum at one-quarter, hold to it as a rigid definition of Indians, let intermarriage proceed," observes historian Patricia Nelson Limerick, "and eventually Indians will be defined out of existence. When that happens, the federal government will finally be freed from its persistent 'Indian problem.'"[22]

Limerick's reference to intermarriage raises the spectre of tribal whitening, unlike the legend of foundational whiteness that served to authenticate native claims. The Cherokee, like the Lumbee, do not require a specific blood quantum level for membership. Thus, as Circe Strum writes, "The Cherokee's more open policy regarding blood has helped create the largest tribe in the United States, which continues to grow at a rapid pace, with over 1,500 applications for tribal citizenship arriving every month. Blood connections have been stretched to the point of 'Whitening the tribe' to a controversial level" (2002, 234). Blood quantum levels within the Cherokee Nation can thus range from full blood to as low as 1/2048. The fact that Lumbee tribal enrollment is also based on lineal descent helps to explain why, at 43,000 members, the Lumbee tribe is the largest east of the Mississippi River.[23] And size matters. Some federally recognized tribes oppose the Lumbee petition out of concern that their own benefits would be reduced.[24] The absence of such criteria for tribal enrollment makes possible the "something strange" of this chapter's epigraph; it would seem that the most famous Lumbee Indian claimed by some members of the tribe is blue-eyed, blonde television icon, Heather Locklear.[25] Yet the tribe's political significance in the state is unmistakable: in 2003, one of the first bills put before Congress by then freshman senator Elizabeth Dole (R–NC) requested full tribal recognition for the Lumbee, perhaps reflecting the same impulses that motivated McMillan's pamphlet in 1888.[26]

McMillan's hypothesis on ancestral migration from "Roanoke" authenticated these mixed-race people as Indian in the minds of some white southerners by suggesting tribal specificity necessary to establishing them as distinct from African Americans. The narrative of Lost Colony descent, then, not only gave the Indians of Robeson County foundational white blood but specific tribal ancestors. In 1888, McMillan was not really concerned with establishing the ancestry of the Indians of Robeson County, but he nonetheless set the stage for the widespread belief that they were of "Croatan," or more accurately, Hatteras descent.[27] While this resulted in the material benefit of school funding in the early part of the century, it perhaps did less of a service as time went on and came back to haunt late 20th-century efforts to lobby for full federal recognition.

In spite of the 1913 name change to "Cherokee Indians of Robeson County," the Senate found no evidence of "any lands or monies due them" as a result of its 1914 investigation based on agent O. M. McPherson's 1915 report, *Indians of North Carolina: Report on Condition and Tribal Rights of the Indians of Robeson and Adjoining Counties of North Carolina*. While McPherson's conclusions as to their origins have been deemed "cautiously non-committal" (Swanton 1933, 1), on the contrary, it appears that McPherson was convinced of their "Croatan" origin. However sympathetically his report recommends them, his finding nonetheless potentially absolved his bosses at the Department of the Interior from delivering "any monies due" the tribe, which may have been the case had they been found to be Cherokee (or, for that matter, any other tribe) who had a previously established relationship with the federal government. Ironically, the enduring national legend became an excuse for federal disavowal.

Thus, within or against their "shared idea of themselves" as Indian, anxiety over their precise tribal affiliation enacted on the state and federal levels for over a century has engendered debate that spills over into contemporary tribal and pan-tribal politics. As Wilkins reveals, the Lumbee tribe has factionalized into seven political entities, each independently seeking federal recognition.[28] Such divisions have produced a terrain so vexed that in 1980, Thomas elected to withhold his research on Lumbee tribal origins from publication. "I didn't want to add anymore 'fuel to the fire'" he writes, "by publishing a premature article which did not have the 'iron-clad' evidence needed to make a definitive scientific and historical argument" (1980, 1). His scholarly forbearance reveals the elevated stakes behind contemporary assignations of tribal origins, stakes with consequences as material as those revealed in the processes of defining "Indian" status a century earlier.

This chapter provides one case study of a southern community representing between the legal identities in force from the Reconstruction era to 1954, and retaining significance well afterward. And despite the ironies, contradictions, or necessarily elisions surrounding the interplay between blackness and whiteness that I have highlighted here, the Lumbee's is largely taken to be a story of successful indigenous defiance. In carving the space for interstitial Indian, the community and its advocates mounted a sustained resistance to the artificial social engineering imposed by the state and antithetical to its own self-conception. Here, the top-down imposition of racial assignment failed. On the surface, in refusing Jim Crow culture, the Indians of Robeson County worked proactively to protect their communal identity, a process that reveals that self-determined, affective ties are not the only foundations to community, but are enmeshed with the interests of academia, popular culture, representional politics, and the legal system.

In marking the era's significance for this tribe's history, I do not want to imply that the Lumbee only began to think of themselves as Indian as a result of segregation, or that they (or their advocates) fraudulently claimed Indianness to avoid being classified as black. In posing the questions, "how long have the Lumbees conceived of themselves as Indians? Is this something which came up after the Civil War during the time of segregation?" Thomas steadfastly argues against such expediency in 1980 (1980, 56). In the process of defending their Indian authenticity, he criticizes the ideologically invested motivations of those who, in positing the Lumbee as a tri-racial, refugee community, read collectivity only through the lens of social status. Such an orientation, he argues, merely reflects "the general worldview of the American middle class; a view that does not see people or communities but only individuals of differing races and ranks": "[T]hese scholars see the caste system in the South as the origin of such a community as the Lumbees. . . . I think these scholars are showing a very pronounced middle class American bias. Middle class Americans will opt for rank over and above relatives or community or anything" (1980, 18–19).[29] In electing to read collectivity as self-determined rather than externally imposed, Thomas affirms the nonhierarchical, horizontal forms of affiliation represented by community, clan, and tradition. These emphases loom large in Lumbee collectivity in the absence of those cultural markers such as political organization, language, communally held lands, and religion that traditionally define tribal identity. "There are no expectations of rain-making, bead-using, basket-weaving and canoe toting, or questions of which reservation chief or language," writes Vernon Ray Thompson, corroborating another researcher's assessment of tribal cohesion in 1973. "To be Lumbee is to be Indian" (1973). This is why the idea of bloodline or genealogy emerges as an expression of authenticity in Lumbee self-conception. For example, Maynor's *Real Indian* raises the question of Lumbee racial status by enumerating what, in comparison to popular conception of American Indians, her people lack: the visible signs of "Indianness" in addition to traditionally conceived indices of culture. The film validates those internally defined ties of genealogical continuity, connection to the land, and community solidarity. In doing so, Maynor affirms a notion of Indianness located in interdependency that does not register on the radar of government bureaucracy. She recounts her father's advice in a voiceover: "Malinda, you can go into any of these houses and tell them you're Waltz Maynor's daughter and Wayne Maynor's granddaughter and they will take you in, take care of you, because your family is their family." "That's my tradition," she concludes, "and that's what's real."

"What's real" is also based on interiority—something even less visible than those traces of blood purported to be obvious under Jim Crow, but no less important a source of horizontal comradeship. These internally derived notions of peoplehood cannot be disputed or quantified. "Everything I view, I view from a Lumbee's eyes," says David Wilkins, "because that's the essence of who I am."[30] In defiance of cultural expectations of "rain-making" or "basket-weaving," being Lumbee is said to be "not merely a physical foundation, but a state of mind" (Dial and Eliades 1975, 23). This "state of mind" produces noteworthy social cohesion, as witnessed by the small number of family names that have persisted over centuries: Chavis, Maynor, Oxendine, Lowry, Revels, Brewington, Braveboy, Locklear. If there is a conception of "Indianness" among the tribe that predates the segregation-era narratives that I highlight here, narratives that made the classification viable in the eyes of the state, then it resides in these expressions of communal affiliation and belonging. These extended family networks signal a political structure formed around blood ties, a structure that nonetheless fails to signify "in the mechanistic and process-oriented criteria devised by the BIA" in the late 20th century (Wilkins 1998, 162). Nor did they signify to agents of a southern segregation-era bureaucracy who enforced the black/white dichotomy in the realm of public schooling; internal definitions of collectivity were shown to be inadequate to reconciling the community to the cultural norms of Jim Crow. Yet, even as they lobby the federal government on behalf of their contested tribal origins, the Lumbee maintain the unduped status of natives who do not need state agencies to tell them who their relatives are.

Thus, foregrounding status in the (self) making of the Lumbee Indians does not situate the Jim Crow era as the origin of tribal unity, but it does reveal that the self-evident expression "we are who we are" is never neutral or organic. What one might see as a "middle class American concern" that stresses "rank over relatives" in the Jim Crow history of the Lumbee is ironically exactly that, a narrative at its core about the class-invested cultural practices that are seen to give meaning to presumed biological descent. Situated between black and white, the tribe's example complicates any academic theory of American Indian subjectivity produced out of the dialectical interplay between civilized and savage or predicated upon a history of removal. The state accommodated this "third" race by creating a middle caste position that did not challenge the logic of juridically enforced racial hierarchy. But as the documents working to establish that position attest, it does bare the terms on which that hierarchy was based. If biological distinction ascertained through negative visual inspection—the absence of black features—was a criterion of Indianness, it had to be supplemented by beliefs surrounding whiteness and the class-inflected structures and values that attend them. Those beliefs corroborate a narrative that, however unintentionally, accounts for the mysterious origin of modern subjectivity in an indigenous people, an account that ironically then circles back to legitimate Indianness. The space of intermediacy reveals the interplay of multiple forms of status—race, class, nation—that define both integration and segregation in excess of the symbolic meaning we ascribe to those terms.

Whether or not "incessant," "stubborn," or "tireless," the history of Lumbee political advocacy reveals that in response to the pressures of Jim Crow, the Lumbee did not become white, but Indian. The process reveals more about the state's investment in race-making than it does American Indian authenticity or inauthenticity; its involvement in this one historical example seems minute in comparison to Jack D. Forbes's claim that indigenous North American populations did not vanish as a result of genocide, they merely became Hispanic (1990). If populations of color exist only insofar as they become visible to the state, the Lumbee example shows those processes of recognition to be predicated on writing collectivity through the lens of normative social structures.

Lumbee history succeeds in questioning—and continues to question—the meanings behind the hard-earned designation, "Indian." In 1975, Dial and Eliades wrote that the Lumbee "are determined to achieve political, social, and economic equality with the whites, while at the same time preserving their distinctiveness as a people" (1975, 23). It is a tall order: no less than forcing race and ethnicity to signify *against* the implication of inferiority. Belief in Lost Colony descent initiated this process by imbuing the tribe with qualities ascribed to America's would-be forebears, effectively overwriting their anomaly: pride, independence, desire for opportunity and self-betterment, the will to prosper in the wilderness. Segregation-era advocates perhaps looked at a New World community peopled by Calibans in order to persuade others of that community's singular triumph—that they take after their mother.

The story, however, generates its own absences: the mixed-race children whose presence forced the closure of Indian schools, those families deemed not Indian enough to appear in the photographs of Butler's petition. They indicate, perhaps, that Raleigh's was not the only colony lost to history.

CHINA, MISS. From left, Sammy Chow, Alice Chow, Sandra Chow, Audric Chow, Bradley Chow, L. K. Pang, Lisa Chow, Sally Chow, Jennifer Chow and Gilroy Chow on the family's farm near Clarksdale, Miss.

"East Meets West at a Delta Table," *New York Times,* 2003.

# White Is and White Ain't

*Failed Approximation and Eruptions of Funk*
*in Representations of the Chinese in the South*

Some are born white, others achieve whiteness, still others have
whiteness thrust upon them.
—Eric Liu, *The Accidental Asian*

The Lumbee's struggle for state and federal recognition was partly
based on the segregation-era representation of the community's upstanding
qualities. The southern context exaggerated the connection between visibility and communal incorporation to produce an enduring narrative that continues to frame this ethnic community. They were "like" whites, which is to
say, like those who shared American values of hard work and thrift. These
efforts to reconcile anomaly to the national are likewise evident in the representation of Asian Americans in the South. Case in point: the Chinese in
the Mississippi Delta. "[I]n the Delta, home of the blues and Muddy Waters,
cooks are sizzling catfish and collards and crayfish every day and night. But
you don't expect to find those home chefs stir-frying them or steaming them
in a giant backyard wok." So begins a feature in the *New York Times* about the
Chow family of Clarksdale, Mississippi, titled, "East Meets South at a Delta
Table: Chinese-Americans bring the tastes of their ancestors down home"
(Nathan 2003, D1).

The hook for the reader's attention is based on simple juxtaposition: Crayfish? Woks? The unexpected hybridity produces what can be seen as quintessentially American—immigrant ingenuity and adaptability—or so we are
led to believe as the Chows descend upon Washington to demonstrate the
aforementioned stir-fry on the National Mall.

In their anomaly, the Chows are made to represent American normativity,
albeit through a circuitous route. They are only representable insofar as their
eccentricity is both asserted as a point of interest (Chinese who say "y'all")

and reinscribed within dominant values and expectations (Ms. Chow is a finalist in the contest to find a new image for Betty Crocker). This progression is subtly reenacted within the feature as well; it introduces the Chow's backstory, how they ended up in Mississippi as it is enmeshed in Reconstruction-era politics and racialized labor competition, only to end with the image of three generations linking hands around the table to say grace. The radical implications of the aberrant presence of Chinese in a region dominated by black-white relations and the sedimented class hierarchies of the plantation system become resolved by the Chow's use as model citizens; they exemplify adaptation, proliferation, and belief in divine providence. A tall order for a piece about cooking, indeed.

Such a portrayal reproduces a dominant narrative governing American racial representation since the Civil Rights Movement: a progressive chronology of racial uplift that buttresses a liberal vision of ethnic incorporation. The use of Asians as evidence of this movement has become ubiquitous in popular culture, hence, the simultaneously laudatory and derogatory designation of Asian Americans as "honorary whites" and model minorities. Inspiring distaste from both the white majority and other people of color against whom it is directed, the charge nevertheless becomes an instrument of Asian racial subordination. Thus, the comment, "the Chinese in Mississippi play the white man's game better than white folks do" resonates well beyond southern regionalism, prefiguring a dominant representation of Asians in the United States (cited in Quan 1982, 54). Nevertheless, for this southern community during the era of formal segregation, the ability to "play the white man's game" took on *literal* stakes.

James Loewen's influential 1972 study, *The Mississippi Chinese: Between Black and White*, argues that when faced with a binary racial system that had no accommodation for a third race, the Chinese engineered a shift in status from "colored" to white in the course of one generation. The Chinese in Mississippi, Loewen claims, "worked systematically . . . in order to rise from Negro to white status" (1988, 72) in the period following World War II, and once crossing over, left "the black world behind without a second glance" (194). While the Supreme Court Ruling *Gong Lum v. Rice* had formally established the "colored" status of the Chinese in Mississippi in 1927, by the time that sociologist Loewen arrived to do fieldwork in 1967, the Chinese were apparently card-carrying white people—or at least they were according to the "W" on their driver's licenses. His study attempts to show what transpired between the years 1941 and 1966, the twilight of formal segregation. What he postulates is an Asian community's shift from a reviled caste to what one could call a less reviled caste, but what he chooses to call, perhaps for lack of a better word, "white." Loewen attempts to account for the shift not simply by positing acculturation to white norms and values as intrinsic to the processes of Americanization. Rather, as in the case of the Lumbee of the previous chapter, he depicts a community who, not content with their social address as "colored," began to engineer a "transition from near-black to near-white" (1988, 135) as a response to segregation's racial dichotomy. This narrative—with differing prophecies and conclusions—is repeated in a number of studies of this community, an archive that provides empirical evidence as to the ways in which cultural ambivalence became resolved; Christine Choy, Worth Long, and Allan Siegel's 1984 documentary film, *Mississippi Triangle*, is the most well known of these.[1] As a southern ethnic community garnering academic interest, they are rivaled only by the Lumbee.

Loewen's thesis about caste rise and the framework it engendered suggest why Asian Americans have become such a fruitful site for uncovering national ambivalences about race, class, and equal opportunity. In looking at the representation of Chinese in the South, my intent is not to replicate Loewen's work by focusing on the historical process of how caste shift occurred—which, as in the last chapter, has do with a certain kind of modeling back of cultural norms including, ironically, the tacit agreement to respect the color line. Rather, I'm interested in what lies in excess of this population's purported success, and where that narrative of progressive advancement becomes interrupted. What does it mean to claim "near-whiteness" for a population formerly known as "colored"? What becomes erased in that story and to what extent do those occlusions disrupt the naturalized teleology of racial advancement that governs American rhetoric on race?

A number of academic studies with intentionally provocative titles have highlighted the mutually constitutive nature of racial formation and the emerging and precarious racial status of European immigrants: to wit, *How Jews Became White, How the Irish Became White, Are Italians White?*[2] These titles reflect what has become known as Critical White Studies, which includes foundational works such as Alexander Saxton's *The Rise and Fall of the White Republic* (1990); David Roediger's *The Wages of Whiteness* (1991); Ruth Frankenberg's *White Women, Race Matters* (1993); Ian Haney Lopez's *White by Law* (1996); George Lipsitz's *The Possessive Investment in Whiteness* (1998); and Matthew Frye Jacobson's *Whiteness of a Different Color* (1998). Robyn Wiegman locates three strains of thought within "Whiteness Studies": "[T]he race traitor school (which advocates the abolition of whiteness through white disaffiliation from race privilege), the 'white trash' school (which analyzes the racialization of the permanent poor in order to demonstrate the otherness of whiteness within), and the class solidarity school (which rethinks the history of working-class struggle as the preamble to forging new cross-racial alliances)" (1999, 121–122). One tenet of the latter is that white privilege is the compensation for the labor subordination of the European immigrant working class; all expose "whiteness" as a historical formation dependent upon other projections of difference. Despite the lack of similarly provocative title, *The Mississippi Chinese: Between Black and White* is an unacknowledged precursor to Critical White Studies; in positing Asians under segregation as ersatz white people, in 1972, it recognized whiteness as a detachable, transferable social status. Thus, while cited in a number of general Asian American histories, Loewen's book is not ultimately about Chinese Americans; it is self-consciously not intended to be merely an ethnography or community study. Rather, it purports to analyze "how status hierarchies are maintained and perpetuated using the segregated South as a site which exaggerates, in particular, racial status." As a national, not merely regional process, racial hierarchy under the American version of apartheid merely reveals its heightened stakes and formal privileges, "whiteness" as it potentially designates mobility, equality, civic participation, or identifications with power. In short, any narrative about the place of Asians under segregation is one in which assimilation is racially measured within a black-white axis through degrees of distance or proximity. The status shift enabled by the Chinese in Mississippi is not significant in and of itself, the narrative suggests, but insofar as that shift sheds light on the division between African Americans and whites. In response to the question, "Where did the Asian sit on the Jim Crow bus?" the study answers emphatically: first, near the back, and later, near the front.

In its provocative conclusions, Loewen's study helped to inaugurate what is now taken to be axiomatic in critical and comparatist race studies; a social formation distinct from any naturalized concept of biology or descent, race emerges out of intersectionality, contestation, and historical context. But the claim here of Chinese "arrival" differs from these studies focusing on the whiteness of whites. It engages a period and region subject to the formal pressures of segregation; racial status had to translate into legal subjectivity. The presumption is not only that racial identifications (and disavowals) are intrinsic to consolidating group status, but that those identifications had to be acknowledged by the state, whether tacitly or overtly. Loewen's influential thesis on Asian near-whiteness served as a script for subsequent representations of the community as well as serving as evidence for theorizing other "middleman minorities" whose economic niche depended upon the gap between elite and masses (Bonacich 1973). Yet there is an obvious dissonance to that claim: the community neither asserted "whiteness" as an identity nor would they have been successful had they tried. Is the story of their "successful" integration the equivalent of having, in Liu's terms, "whiteness thrust upon them"?

The incommensurability—people of color posited as near white—is, of course, a claim that was (presciently) not about identity but social formation and intended to contribute to a radical understanding of racial hierarchy. Nevertheless, that narrative coincides with a national discourse on race existing prior to but emerging in full force out of the rubble of a segregated past: a belief in a progressive chronology of self-betterment and racial uplift. The post–Civil Rights moment has enforced this narrative so optimistically as to render the period of segregation itself a historical aberration in the script of inevitable pluralist unity. Whose interests do such narratives serve? In 1972, it could not be foreseen that postulating Asian "whiteness" would emerge as a dominant instrument of Asian American racial subordination a scant generation later. The representation of this seemingly anomalous community of Chinese in Mississippi thus exaggerates what has emerged as a liberal view of minority integration and prefigures mainstream discourses surrounding Asian Americans in particular. But these consequences were largely unseen; it is thus that the claim to "near-whiteness" warrants critical scrutiny. What goes missing in the attempt to narrate caste rise?

Interestingly, the same anxieties of representation evident in early attempts to fix the status of this interstitial community reemerge in subsequent depictions of their upward trajectory. I want to focus on these anxieties, particularly as they appear in *Mississippi Triangle,* the documentary that attempts to visualize Loewen's findings. My focus is thus not on the processes of status-making as in the last chapter, but on the jarring moments and incommensurabilities that attend the claim of progressive racial uplift here and in legal, academic, visual, and popular cultural depictions of Asians in the Deep South. In surprising ways, the class and caste position of the Asian in the South is at times mediated through representations of gender and sexuality, underscoring the interaction between axes of difference. Loewen has suggested that Chinese transition to "near whiteness" in Mississippi was enabled, among other things, by their willing disassociation from African Americans, particularly in regard to interracial unions—ironically, this applied to whites as well: "The final step [of status elevation] was for the Chinese to convince Caucasians that they too believed in racial integrity and had no intention of mixing with anyone. . . . [T]he Chinese simultaneously denied that they married Negroes and explicitly vowed that they would never marry whites in the future" (1988, 79). The paradox of caste elevation was that it seemed predicated on respecting Jim Crow's primary distinction, on upholding the color line in both directions and repressing a history of intimacy with African Americans.

Yet, as this chapter highlights, figures of Chinese-black amalgamation are never wholly buried, even at moments that intend to testify to the community's "successful" transition. What is repressed in the discourse of status shift necessarily comes back to the surface as, to use Toni Morrison's description of working-class disturbances to the lives of class-conscious African Americans, eruptions of "Funk." That is, what disturbs the emergent black bourgeoisie is the resurfacing of the residues of an ignominious past strategically left behind.[3] Such eruptions reveal and unsettle the terms of racial hierarchy both within and beyond the historical context of the South's second peculiar institution. What I am proposing, then, is a method of reading anomalously within the anomaly—to resurrect what threatens the logical coherence of specific narratives about race, democracy, and segregation as they emerge within a field of representation surrounding one seemingly aberrant interstitial community, the Chinese in the South.

Within every narration of status transformation, there lies both an ambivalence and incompletion that can unveil the stakes underlying its emergence. What I want to focus on here, then, are the moments of failed approximation in Asian racial representation in order to uncover what white is . . . or, more significantly, what it ain't.

## Race-Class Incommensurability

The legal status of the Chinese as "colored" was formalized in the 1927 Supreme Court ruling *Gong Lum v. Rice*, which assigned members of the "Mongolian race" to "colored" schools. In 1924, Gong Lum brought suit against school trustees in Mississippi district court charging that his daughter Martha had been unfairly prevented from attending Rosedale Consolidated High School, where the student body was exclusively white. Upon the court's decision in her favor, school officials appealed to the state, which reversed the decision. In upholding the Mississippi Supreme Court's decision against the plaintiff as the case went before the Supreme Court, Chief Justice Taft asserted that as a "member of the Mongolian or yellow race," the plaintiff was "not entitled to attend the schools provided by law in the State of Mississippi for children of the white or Caucasian race." "The question here," Taft wrote, is whether a Chinese citizen of the United States is denied equal protection of the laws when he is classed among the colored races and furnished facilities for education equal to that offered to all, whether white, brown, yellow or black. Were this a new question, it would call for very full argument and consideration, but we think that it is the same question which has been many times decided.[4]

The decision both fixed the intermediate racial status of the Chinese in the South and affirmed the constitutionality of *Plessy v. Ferguson*. This use of the Asian American in the affirmation of "separate but equal" doctrine is indeed ironic, as the dissenting opinion to Plessy invoked Chinese privileges under segregation.

That seeming privilege notwithstanding, sociologist Robert O'Brien prophesized in 1941,

> as the number of Chinese in the Delta increases it will become more difficult to maintain an intermediate position between the Negro on one hand and the whites on the other. . . . [A] study of the relationship of the Chinese, whites, and Negroes in [the Mississippi delta] seems to point inescapably toward an inferior position of the Chinese in the southern communities. (1941, 386)

While recognizing the pressures of intermediacy that occasioned such prophesy, 20 years later, however, others were coming to the opposite conclusion. Despite *Gong Lum* and an earlier association with African American labor, third-generation Chinese Americans were, as George Rummel III concludes from fieldwork done in 1964, "trying to live down their previous image" and formed an "almost exclusive social and economic identification with the dominant white community rather than with the lower-class Negro community" (1966, 49). As if to confirm that Asian identification with the dominant culture in the South is articulated via white approximation, filmmaker Rene Tajima Peña interviews a pair of aging Filipina sisters in New Orleans while on the road to find "Asian America" for the documentary, *My America (. . . or honk if you love Buddha)* (1997). In the course of recounting their pasts as belles of the French Quarter, the sisters cheerfully assert their white status as it is confirmed on their birth certificates and by their schooling, romantic partners, and the cemeteries that house their ancestors: "Filipinos were not considered a race other than white. Because Spain owned the Philippines. So they were just considered white."[5] These representations attest to the ways in which racial ambiguity became adjudicated, disciplined, or rationalized in disparate cultural forums; what remains constant from the 1920s through the 1990s are the narratives in which this community was placed: either racial backsliding or promotion.

The sisters' testimony on how colonial subjugation might confer elevated racial status is likewise reflected in Christine Choy's assessment of the Chinese American community in the South. After her work on *Mississippi Triangle*, the filmmaker concluded, "these Chinese who are in between the blacks and whites have inherited, as neocolonizers within the system, the values of the capitalist system. They have become racists: they think they are socially white. They have become the dividers" (cited in Dittus 1985, 39). There is a baldness about this pronouncement that one does not see, for example, in discussions of other interstitial populations such as Korean Americans in south central Los Angeles; its openly condemnatory tone is one that Loewen's study scrupulously avoids. Nevertheless, while Choy's statement does not entirely do justice to the nuanced point of view of her own film or the academic study it takes as a script, the statement represents a bottom line to Loewen's findings on Chinese caste shift in the South: economic stability as a necessary but not sufficient precondition of status elevation.

The economic function that racial interstitiality plays is addressed in Hubert Blalock's statement, "the stranger may actually perform better than the in-group member in market situations requiring objectivity and impersonal dealings" (1967, 81). That is, as Loewen suggests, the outsider status of the Chinese was instrumental to their establishing a market niche between black and white; they were not (initially) influenced by social taboos around business practices enforced by Jim Crow etiquette. Having not yet inherited the prejudices or value system of the host country, they did not assign symbolic significance to service-oriented labor addressed to the African American community. Which is to say, money knows no color other than green.[6]

In marking the apparent caste transcendence of the Chinese as it is linked to the accumulation of capital, his analysis nonetheless self-consciously refuses an economically determinist understanding of racial formation. In situating the agential nature of the community's status rise, he points to its cultural intervention: "I would rank economic success the most important basic cause of the upward racial mobility of the Chinese," he writes. "But wealth in itself was not the means of solution. Their situation was transformed only as a result of the process of image change, parallel institutions, and behind-the-scene negotiation" (1988, 98). Loewen details six concessions that the Chinese made in response to white pressure to distinguish themselves from blacks and set the groundwork for their apparent shift from black to white:

- They accepted unequal social treatment in order to secure economic advancement.
- They assured whites that they had no intention of intermixing with either group and took steps to ostracize black-Chinese.
- They acculturated their children into white norms.
- They self-segregated, setting up cultural institutions patterned on white models—dances, churches, birthday parties, etc.
- They agreed to move into residential neighborhoods rather than continue residence behind grocery stores in black neighborhoods.
- They cultivated white benefactors who could institutionally intercede on their behalf.

What is noteworthy about this list of social concessions that preceded Chinese status shift is, first, the embedded assumption that the state's interpellation of the Chinese was relatively inconsequential to the upward rise it documents. Thus, neither *Gong Lum v. Rice* (1927), nor *Brown v. Board of Education* (1954) figures as consequential to Loewen's argument on racial status shift. Race is seen as adjudicated not by invisible agents of the state but in the context of small southern towns, by a white oligarchy. The study's situating state power as concentrated in the hands of influential white men explains its emphasis on individual agency in the processes of racialization: white pressure to conform to segregation's racial etiquette and Chinese response to this pressure are not positioned as indirect or internalized, but conscious and overt. In this study, power is personal; favors are granted and privileges are extended by a white elite rather than through the diffuse processes of hegemony, and its members become lobbyists on behalf of the increased integration of the Delta Chinese. Thus, while acknowledging the economic base and its cultural taboos that created a small business niche to be exploited by the Chinese, status shift is viewed to be a result of their own social engineering. Situating any subaltern group thusly produces inherent ambivalence: to what extent are they to be seen as oppressive agents or merely responding to the power of a white oligarchy?

What is also interesting about these concessions is the degree to which they upheld segregation. What made the white southerner "accept" the Chinese, Loewen notes, was their ability to convince of a likeness of values. The actions enumerate forms of mimicry that made no demands on white people—most of the conditions precluded social intimacy with them. Moreover, they assured whites that they had no intention of intermixing with blacks and took steps to ostracize black Chinese unions. What these concessions imply, however, is the paradox of presumably unsustainable interstitiality, how upholding the color line in both directions translates into status elevation. This contradiction at the heart of narrating racial status shift is worth looking at insofar as it confounds a neat progressive linearity consistent with the discourse of American immigrant uplift. Rather, the discourse on the emergent class status of people of color is fraught with elision and contradiction, particularly as it engages Jim Crow etiquette. The very precariousness of asserting middle-class status for nonwhites erupts at the moment of its attempted enunciation. In what follows, I want to situate such moments that, taken together, form a counter-narrative that unsettles the discourse of Asian communal self-transformation supporting post–Civil Rights narratives of unimpeded racial progress.

Loewen's study implies that, as a group, the Chinese capitulated to cultural practices that acceded to their lower racial status as a strategy to increased economic status. He writes:

> In addition to sexual equality with whites, another potential demand the Chinese gave up was equality in etiquette. Even today most Chinese adults interact with Caucasians from a position of deference. This is another of the "nonessential" slights the Chinese have been willing to accept in order to secure their more essential goals—economic security and an education for their children. (Loewen 1988, 80)

Such an analysis produces a paradox: how could the acceptance of racial subordination—the concession of "equality in etiquette"—eventually translate, as the study suggests, into increased social status? His research uncovers "deep resentment among the Chinese toward the ways whites speak to them" (156), but he sees its repression to be a consequence of a conscious strategy for long-term status advancement: "The Chinese have not pressed whites on the matter but have played along in order to seem polite and unthreatening, while focusing on more tangible goods." What this conveys without marking it as such is the fine art of Uncle Tomming; that is, one mimes the expectation of servility in order to placate or curry favor with those in power. Duplicity here is not positioned as a key to survival; rather, capitulation to racial etiquette—addressing a white man as *Mister*, for example—is considered a calculated bid by the oppressed rather than as coercion backed by threat of reprisal. They are willing participants in maintaining the public appearance of their inferiority in order to advance as petit-bourgeois; according to this logic, one foregoes social equality on the way to increased class status, which in turn is presumed to translate into social equality. Or does it?

Herein lies the inexactness of race and class commensurability: one accepts racial subordination as a condition of class rise, which, according to the study, subsequently enables a rise in racial classification. The contradiction hinges on an orderly chronology; the Chinese are initially capable of such action because, as outsiders to the social system of the South, they have not yet been habituated into the colonial mentality necessary to its maintenance. Uncle Tomming does not decrease self-esteem, which is seen as being supported from outside the system. This is similar to his argument explaining the rise of the small grocery as an ethnic labor niche; service to a black clientele was not initially viewed by the Chinese as a servile profession. As I discuss in the next chapter, the logic depends upon temporality: at what point does the performance of racial servility become indistinguishable from the actual effects of social conditioning? (And, conversely, at what point does the outsider internalize his/her superiority to the lowest caste?) In this case, the argument hinges on the idea that the practice of inferiority did not translate into an abject identity either for this generation or the next, and that social relations were always capable of being abstracted from selfhood. The tautology—class status is only achievable through acceptance of diminished cultural status—results from the desire to detach race from class only to reattach it at a later point.

The emergent class status of people of color no doubt generated southern discomfort in a white population confronted with the specter of the Asian professional above and beyond those revealed by etiquette and modes of address. One catches a glimpse into how the incommensurability between race and class status was reconciled—or rather, failed to be reconciled—within the incidental depiction of "four Chinamen" in Jonathan Daniels' 1938 memoir/travelogue, *A Southerner Discovers the South*. Sexuality as a vehicle for reading race relations is the topic of chapters 5 and 6; similarly, the invocation of sexual deviance here queers the testimony about the Chinese and functions as one moment that cannot be reconciled to the narrative of Chinese American arrival. In describing a casual exchange on a ferry crossing the Mississippi River, Daniels writes,

A fat and effeminate man got out of the sedan in which he rode with four Chinamen.

I looked at him with careful distaste but I asked, "Tell me, what do the Chinese do for a living in Mississippi? Do they farm?"

He looked back at his companions. "Oh, no, they're business men. And that one yonder is a preacher, a Presbyterian preacher. Oh, they're fine gentlemen." His eyes filled with a pleasant dream. "You ought to see a Chinese boy I know. He's just fifteen. I tease him. And he just smiles so sweet, so sweet!"

He mimicked a monstrous coyness. And he pursed, in imitation of the China boy's smiling, a mouth like the sessile, fleshy suckers on the tentacles of an octopus.

"I'm sure of it," I said, "Excuse me." (1938, 194)

Here, the status of these Chinese Americans as "fine gentlemen" is not only overtly confirmed, but validated circumstantially: they travel in the company of a white man. But their professional status is marked as grotesque and unnatural as it becomes grafted onto the queerness of the messenger. Both the aping of femininity by the white man and the aping of gentility by his Chinese companions inspire the curiosity and distaste of the white, middle-class speaker. His response indicates how the "fat and effeminate" man's status as white—and indeed, given his bestial description, as a man—is demoted by his presumed homosexuality. His pedophilic desire—he is not quite right—renders him the fit companion of the not quite white. The class status of those formerly known as "colored" becomes queered and thereby challenged: through associative intimacy it is not true gentility, only a "monstrous imitation." In this, the bourgeois status of the Chinese is only an approximation revealing how social status is multiply mediated. Color triangulated by queerness emerges as a class sign. Anxiety about the middle-class person of color becomes grafted onto other signs of difference; aberrant sexuality is another form of "Funk." The "careful distaste" that their professional status inspires and here expressed by contiguity must be distinguished from the violent repercussions suffered by middle-class African Americans.

While representations of the Chinese in Mississippi might successfully abstract the meaning of white status in anticipation of contemporary academic discourse on race, as in this case, they also nonetheless reveal their own discursive slippages that indicate what must be repressed in order to render persuasive the testimony of racial status transcendence. The more obvious inference of status through association is, of course, to be drawn from Chinese intimacy with African Americans. It is this, in the words of Gross, "race by association" (1998) that had to be dislodged in order for "near-white" status to be achieved. While I do not doubt that those acts of repudiation existed in multiple forms, what I would like to question here is how successful they were. That is, it would seem that the repression of cross-racial intimacy within the discourse of Asian American subjects and those who represent them is itself only approximate.

## Eruptions of Funk

> [W]hen you look at the Chinese stores down by the river, you get a totally different picture. They're right down in nigger town, and what goes on there, God only knows. When those yellow people first came here, nobody really know what to think, but some of them have proved themselves, and we've accepted them, but those that stayed down with the niggers, well *we just let them go.*
> (white informant in Mississippi, cited in Rummel 1966; emphasis mine)

Those interstitial subjects who fail to perform the dual gesture of white identification and black disavowal according to the script of racial uplift are written off or "just let go." Evidence of those incorporated into African American communities often only surfaces within the anomalous trace. In the "colony" of Black Chinese in Calvert, Texas, for example, the only vestiges of Asian ancestry lie in the surnames of extended black families—Moy, Yepp, and Chopp—or in its traces, such as the black patriarch who insists on eating with chopsticks.[7] Unlike the case of the Lumbee, wherein the repression of black amalgamation informed a strategy to put forward an unambiguous government petition in 1916, the Chinese attempt to "let go" signs of that intimacy is represented as a willing response to white pressure. Loewen writes, "The final step [to white status] was for the Chinese to convince Caucasians that they too believed in racial integrity and had no intention of mixing with anyone. . . . [T]he Chinese simultaneously denied that they married Negroes and explicitly vowed that they would never marry whites in the future" (1988, 79). Through their "outspoken emphasis on endogamy" (117), Loewen argues, the Chinese assured the elite that they had no interest in fraternization, no desire to break the taboo of familiarity with whites. In other words, they appeared to have no plans to seek a horizontal comradeship that would be interpreted as a sign that they thought themselves to be equal. The assurance against intimacy—they had "no intention of mixing with anyone"—produces this conundrum: the Chinese became white by agreeing not to come near whites.

Or for that matter, blacks. Both the study and the film, *Mississippi Triangle*, reveal that one strategy in the community's bid for whiteness was the repression of signs of black-Chinese intimacy. In discussing the pariah status of those who crossed over, Loewen suggests, as subsequent studies on the mutually constitutive nature of racial construction would, that integration is won partly through repudiating African Americans. The hypothesis depends on the repression of its obverse, that the Chinese also became black. The source of disavowal is seen as the Chinese community itself; the social ostracism of black-Chinese is seen as deliberately enacted by the community as a means of disassociating from the most reviled caste. The study represents this as a form of barter and social insurance, thus privileging the exchange nature of the social contract rather than highlighting coercion or threat. Narratives about violence are markedly absent in representations of this community; in the case of the Mississippi Chinese, white power was expressed not in its most bald form—the threat of vigilante violence—but in overt and implied *requests* to modify cultural behavior.

Nevertheless, hints of such reprisals are not wholly repressed; for example, a moment of dissonant speculation emerges precisely at the point in which *Mississippi Triangle* attempts to establish the willingness of the Chinese community to repudiate those who consorted with African Americans. By the early 20th century, Chinese Exclusion laws and their precursor, the 1875 Page Act, had severely restricted the immigration of Chinese women to the United States, truncating the growth of Chinese communities across the country. At the same time, Mississippi's anti-miscegenation laws expressly forbade intermarriages between a "white person and negro or Mongolian."[8] In looking at interracial marriage between Chinese and blacks, then, documentary filmmakers Choy, Long, and Siegel recognized that they had a visceral template for depicting Chinese caste movement: the transition from black to white intermarriage. Yet, the following testimony of Chinese-black ostracism can be read in a dual register:

INTERVIEWER: When the Chinese married some black people, what happened?

RAY JOE: Well, they, the Chinese people, scared to be with them no more. Not acquaint with them no more.

Joe's testimony supports the study's thesis that black-Chinese families were consciously shunned to curry favor with the white community. Nevertheless, while the informant's testimony validates that forcing pariah status on interracial unions had taken place, the very language that he chooses questions Chinese motivations for what can also be read as self-motivated social engineering—is it pride or fear? "Scared to be with them no more" marks the community's intent ambiguously, leaving unnamed the source of anxiety: is it the censure of other Chinese they fear or the censure of whites themselves? The latter hints at the violence that underlies upholding Jim Crow, even as the study and film emphasize the subaltern's willing capitulation to a social contract that situates disapproval of interracial mixing as essential to group advancement. Even as the informant gives evidence of this dynamic, his rhetoric introduces uncertainty at the moment of utterance.

The centrality of black-Chinese individuals in the film is perhaps due to the fact that biracial Ludwig Goon served as the cinematographer, and it was through his acquaintance that Choy, Long, and Siegel were first alerted to the aberration of an Asian community in the Deep South. To underscore the racial chronology of the study—from black to white—the film gives symbolic centrality to another such figure, Arlee Hen, an elderly Afro-Chinese woman. The film grants her prominence not only in its frequent return to her voiceover, but in her use as a framing device. Beyond her value as an informant imbued with privileged access to the history of Chinese origins in the Delta, the filmmakers clearly found in her a symbol of black-Chinese amalgamation, the embodiment of the original taboo. This proof of intimacy between two "colored" races had to be repressed in order to facilitate Chinese status shift, a point that Loewen's book takes pains to document. But to what extent does her representation exceed its intended use?

Both Loewen and the filmmakers acknowledge Hen's exile from the Chinese American community in the Delta. As Loewen notes in a caption to her photo included in the 1988 edition of his book, "[Arlee Hen] was living in Greenville when I did my fieldwork, but because her mother was black, the Chinese community never mentioned her, and I learned of her lonely existence only when Third World Newsreel filmed her just before her death in 1982" (n. p.). As Christine Choy notes, Hen's "discovery" was policed by the community to the extent that the crew had to concoct an elaborate ruse to gain access to her without the community finding out:

[The Chinese American community] refused to take us to the black-Chinese areas. No one wanted us to talk to the elderly black-Chinese woman who became a major character in the film. So we made an announcement in Greenville that we were leaving town. Word traveled quickly from Jackson, Mississippi to Memphis, Tennessee. All the gossips spread the word.

We went down to Jackson, spent the night, and then sneaked back into Greenville. We parked the car in an alley behind the woman's house, and stayed in her home for two days of filming. The Chinese community didn't know we had any relationship with this woman. When they saw the final film they were very upset. (cited in Dittus 1985, 40)

In documenting Hen's communal repudiation, the story lends credibility to Loewen's assertion that the majority of Chinese in the Delta were white-identified and actively disavowed the existence of interracial marriage between blacks and Chinese as part of their bid for acceptance among the white elite. In a subtle parallel, with its hints of skullduggery and doubling back in the dead of night, the story resembles those of Civil Rights activists trying to do their work under threat of violence by white supremacists, only in this case, it is Chinese Americans whose disapproval—and implied power—provokes such machinations. What the story also conveys is Hen's significance to the filmmakers who went to such lengths to secure her interview.

The film's staging of Hen's pariah status as proof of the community's racism is undermined by an alternative assessment of her acceptance. In *Chinese American Portraits: Personal Histories 1828–1988*, Ruthanne Lum McCunn reports that Hen worked in the most prominent Chinese grocery store in Greenville, Mississippi.[9] While focusing on Hen's triple ostracism, Lum McCunn nonetheless notes that "Arlee and her sister . . . were both accepted by the local Chinese community and never left Greenville" (1988, 82). The disjunction bespeaks a potential rupture in the narration of Chinese caste elevation. The disavowal of African American intimacy (Hen's "lonely existence") may be a matter of public self-representation to the outsider, whether filmmaker, independent scholar, or, like Loewen, Harvard graduate student.

Nevertheless, the film chooses to use Arlee Hen as a reminder of the ignominious class and color roots of the community. A symbol of black-Chinese amalgamation, Hen exists as an eruption of "Funk" that disturbs the dearly won "near-white status" of the Chinese community. Throughout the film, she testifies to discrimination against blacks and Chinese perpetuated by whites even though, ironically, one of the film's few "integrated" scenes occurs at Hen's birthday celebration in which, bedridden and frail, she receives both black and white well-wishers. In effect, the party is filmed as if it were a funeral; Hen's supine body lies in state to receive those who pay their last respects. It is as if the tri-racial society can be sanguine precisely because what she represents is likely to die soon; all can afford to be gracious at the demise of those lingering signs of a past intimacy.

The film pointedly addresses southern Asian racism via Hen's actual death in ways that bolster Loewen's thesis on Chinese American crossover—at the same time, I would argue, that Hen's use in the film can be said to question it. At the end of the film, we see a coffin being lowered into the ground. Hen's voice rises over the image of a field in spring, her words depicted in subtitles for emphasis: "I couldn't be buried in a Chinese cemetery . . . I'm mixed with Negro, you know . . . and I couldn't be buried in a Chinese cemetery." Choosing to end with this reference to segregated burial, the film achieves multiple purposes: it signals the "end" of the community as a natural conclusion to the testimony of Chinese Americans who express the financial insupportability of the small grocery businesses and prophesize the next generation's out-migration. More importantly, what is being buried is evidence of amalgamation now lost to near-whiteness. Choosing to close on these words, the filmmakers succeed in conveying that Hen's ostracism represents a collective repudiation of the community's previous racial status—that past is being buried with her.

Nevertheless, this figure of miscegenation does not remain underground: Hen's voice, and with it the community's "colored" past, pops out of the grave to haunt what the film has previously inscribed, albeit ambivalently, as Chinese American crossover to white norms and values. In refusing to "just let go" a figure like Hen, the filmmakers ensure that black-Chinese intimacy, the origin of community, is not erased. The film pointedly refuses to mark Hen as an abject figure and sees to it that, even in death, she has the last word. Nevertheless, the only overt testimony of Chinese racism that she makes in the film is given prominence. Thus, the film has it both ways: it documents the crossover at the same time it tethers that crossover to the community's deliberate repression of the Chinese who, in excess of Loewen's thesis, became black. In allowing for eruptions of "Funk" in biracial Arlee Hen, the film succeeds in marking white status as contingent—it does not dispute the fact that white-identification has occurred, but it does mark that status as tenuous. In addition, the penultimate sequence witnesses three separate racial spheres in the Delta: a white country club and bar, black workers in a fish-processing plant, and a Chinese American wedding. This visualization of the on-going processes of segregation is certainly ironic in the context of the film's chronological progression depicting Chinese crossover. In effect, it wants to show the Chinese as de facto white people without ever showing them *with* white people. Apart from one interracial romance and a few white pastors, no Caucasians are ever seen socializing with Chinese in the film. This absence produces a rupture similar to that in Loewen's study:

the "middlemen" have taken on the prejudices of the elite without achieving social integration.

Community reaction to the film reveals a similar slippage indicative of approximate status, the anxieties of the "partly colored": when the film premiered in town, Chinese Americans were not happy with it. Rather than being angry about their portrayal as racists mouthing the pieties of a white elite, they were upset that they were not portrayed as white enough. That is, in the peculiar tangle of class-as-race logic, they were not represented as being more prosperous or successful. As Adria Bernardi reports, "Most said they didn't think it portrayed the progress of the Chinese-Americans. Some objected because they thought it left the impression that Chinese are linked more closely with the black community than the white. Certainly the scenes in small country stores and interviews with people of Chinese and African-American ancestry did not sit well with the Chinese audience, most of whom were successful merchants" (22).[10] This response conveys an inherent duality: on one level, in expressing anxiety about black association as class demotion, the reaction lends credibility to sociological claims of their white, middle-class identification. At the same time, it reveals the degree to which they feel the incompletion of status elevation; the fact that it needs to be publicly validated testifies to its fragility. This vulnerability is likewise uncovered in Robert Seto Quan's fieldwork done over a decade later. "In nearly every conversation, the Delta Chinese of the first two generations spoke of the respect shown them by the whites," he writes. "Such emphasis may mean that some Chinese have doubts as to how the whites feel about them" (1982, 86). The fact that white association needs to be publicized and affirmed bespeaks both its desirability and an awareness of its instability. The need for reassurance unveils the tenuousness of an incomplete status shift.

These discursive ruptures emerge out of an inherent contradiction: the move to document the transference of white status to an "outsider" population proceeds against the commonsense awareness that people of color can never "be" white. As I discuss later, this presented the filmmakers with a visual conundrum: how to depict the community's "whiteness" when confronted with Chinese faces, especially if its achievement means embodying what is normative and hence, invisible. The disjunction reveals itself in the rhetoric of both researcher and informant. As one college-age, southern Chinese American remarks in an interview with Quan in the late 1970s, "The whites will accept you at every level, but not socially" (1982, 124). "Near whiteness" is revealed to be an inadequately blunt instrument to define the nuances of social status. Loewen marks the incommensurability between racial classification and equal treatment: "Although they still do not enjoy full equality, the Chinese are definitely accorded white status, affirmed for example by the "W" in the appropriate blank on their driver's licenses" (1988, 96). His statement questions the determinants of white classification above and beyond the study's self-conscious examination of its artificiality. In other words, what is the value of "white status" if it does not ensure full equality? What does it mean to be accepted "at every level" *except* socially? That is, "whiteness" (or proximity to it) is not an independent indicator of social status and does not guarantee entry among social elites. Each citizen's constitutional guarantee of equal rights, his presumed abstract universality under the law, does not obviate the material enactments of racial hierarchy attending the citizen's embodiment. Such dissonance in this case points to the disjunction between the state's (or, rather, the oligarchy's) interpellation of the Chinese as "white" as bestowed by a single capital letter on state identification and the social practice of whiteness. Again, a black-white continuum becomes an inadequate framework for measuring cultural assimilation. Thus, even as Chinese American informants attest to the privilege of inhabiting an invisible norm— their ability to avoid being targeted as the objects of racial violence, ridicule, ostracism, or discourtesy, for instance—their testimony reveals ambivalence.

As I discuss in the next chapter, scholars themselves are not immune from rationalizing their own treatment within an unjust system. In documenting his fieldwork among multiple communities in the American South, Korean American sociologist Choong Soon Kim poses the question, "Had a proverbial 'southern hospitality' been extended to Asians?" (1998, 138). His answer simultaneously acknowledges racism as it is expressed via social etiquette at the same time that he negates the possibility that he himself has been a target of it: "The early Chinese in the Mississippi Delta might have a different answer, but most Asians, including myself, who came to the South recently, would have a positive answer to the question" (1998, 138). While one can grant the autonomy of the individual's mediation of his own experience, Kim's affirmation of the courtesies whites show him provokes the same uneasy questioning that underlies those expressed by the Chinese in the Delta. Kim observes:

Despite my observations of racial discrimination exhibited toward others, I wish to emphasize that I have never been subjected to it during my ten years of living in the South. It is true, though, that southerners are more openly ambivalent about foreigners. . . . Sometimes, whites have refused to shake my hand or to have close contact. . . . However, these incidents should not be interpreted in terms of racial discrimination. Such curiosities in relation to foreigners are rather natural. (1977, 122)

Kim's analysis of his own racial status in the South points to the inherent unreliability of the ethnographer as ethnographic subject; there is simply no alternative interpretation that can logically supplant the one he chooses to deny—he is snubbed because he himself is seen to be "partly colored," a point I take up in the next chapter. What his testimony reveals is that one cannot enter an embedded system of social relations without developing mechanisms to avoid internalizing one's inferior status. Segregation produces psychic violence in the form of denial and rationalization. Both are readily apparent within the discourse of the willfully unknowing subaltern subject.

In highlighting what lies in excess of the subject's apprehension of the social meaning of his own experience, I do not mean to substitute one narrative for another, in this case, one in which the evidence of racial oppression counters the assertion of its attenuation. Rather, I would claim that the pressures of representing incompletion produce a counter-narrative existing in dialectical tension with the narrative at hand, something that also characterizes attempts at situating Asian Americans as a vehicle for affirming racial progress in the post–Civil Rights moment. This duality can be witnessed elsewhere within the sketchy and ambiguous archive of Asians in the South. As part of the Federal Writers' Project of the Works Progress Administration from 1936 to 1940, over 1,200 interviews were conducted to document folklore and life in the South over a range of occupations and ethnicities. Within the archive, there are two interviews with Chinese laundry owners, one in Georgia and the other in South Carolina.[11] These transcripts depict dramatically different accounts of Asian American integration, delivering evidence of both social separation and inclusion. In the first, an unnamed WPA worker interviews the prosperous and charismatic businessman Gerald Chan Sieg, also know as Chung Tai-pan, in 1939 Savannah. The transcript reveals a politically savvy and self-consciously aware individual who enjoys the spotlight cast by his questioner. During the course of his interview, he holds forth on his views on interracial intermixing, revealing that his wife is half Chinese, half "Spanish American," and that two sons and a daughter have out-married. When his daughter "ran off" to marry a white man, he reports, "I bow my head." But he dilates more expansively, "Young people got to fall in love. He teacher's son, must have plenty courage to marry Chinese girl. Then I think maybe good thing to mixee up all races, makee better world" (17). In its historical context, these are notably progressive statements even as one reveals a telling shift in perspective, from the Chinese man's consideration of his own views of intermarriage to that of his recently acquired white son-in-law. The interviewer's stereotypical attempts at dialect notwithstanding, what emerges is a portrait of a benevolent, self-satisfied patriarch, one whose Chinese American family is so acculturated to life in the South that, as he jovially claims, "If I ever getee Chinese son-in-law I drop dead" (18).

In marked contrast, the 1938 WPA interview with Joe Shing of Spartanburg, South Carolina paints a self-consciously ambivalent picture, a life of social isolation marked by suspicion and bordering on despair. Interviewer Ruth D. Henderson displays a remarkable flair for narrative here, a flair that one anonymous commenter (her supervisors at the WPA?) attempts to rein in. The Chinese laundryman, she writes, "smiles incessantly, but the somber glow of his small, dark, penetrating eyes leaves one with the feeling that he is, in reality, melancholy" (3). On the original typed manuscript someone has penciled in, "How do you know?" leaving the trace of an ethnographic dispute. Henderson's well-embellished portrait was apparently necessary: her subject, Joe Shing, can't or won't speak; he refuses to indulge what appear to her to be innocuous questions about his life history. That is, he satisfies her queries on the sociology of laundries (he has run it for 50 years, employing two "Negro women"), but declines over the space of 14 pages to divulge anything personal. He refuses to name the town in China from which he immigrated ("velly muchee bad luck") or the names of any living or deceased relatives. He willingly demonstrates how his family name is written in Chinese, but immediately crumples the paper up, denying her a quaint souvenir of her visit. This attempt at an objective account of southern life at the margins becomes an exercise in futility, interesting for its omissions. In the absence of definitive ethnographic information, Henderson has seemingly no recourse other than to substitute her own narration for that of her reluctant informant. It is not clear whether or not she understands Joe Shing's polite resistance as evidence of his fear of deportation, his awareness that the authorities might trace the pathways of his presumably ambiguously legal immigration. Henderson betrays no self-consciousness about her role as an agent of the state; nevertheless, she sympathetically ascertains that the upshot of her subject's protective secrecy is not entirely self-imposed segregation. She does not probe about his relationship with his African American workers, but queries his state of mind regarding his distance from (white) public culture given the seeming absence of wife and family. The laundryman responds agreeably but noncommittally, "Sure [I] get lonesome sometimes." Undermining the requisite distance between ethnographer and informant, at the interview's end, Henderson invites him to come for an outing "as a friend," an invitation that he declines.

Taken together, these two WPA interviews provide an inconsistent picture of Asians in the South—the expansive, integrated participant in southern life on one hand, and the solitary marginal man on the other. This ethnographic record testifies to the color line's ambiguity but also provokes other questions about how to account for the startlingly distinct portraits of two Chinese laundry operators in southern culture of the 1930s. Can the difference be attributed to regionalism, the difference between Georgia and South Carolina? The pressures of legal status surrounding Chinese immigration and prohibitions to Chinese women's immigration? Or is it simply—and what filters through these two interviews most forcefully—the difference in individual disposition that succeeds in projecting such opposite futures for these subjects? In any case, within these portraits, the "facts" of living Jim Crow for the "partly colored" do not emerge with evidential clarity; what one takes from this Depression-era archive is the quiet toll of the color line and the fragile and inadequate gesture of one white woman who attempts to reach across it.

In other cases, the duality of representation that creates dissonance is overtly acknowledged; contradicting points of view are portrayed side-by-side in competition and irresolution. Historian Judy Yung's representation of the Asian American experience in the South engages this strategy. In *Chinese Women of America: A Pictorial History*, the contradiction produced by the simple question, How were Asians treated in the Deep South? must be resolved by the reader/viewer who is confronted with two versions of the Asian southern debutante: a cheerleader and a churchgoer.

While the parallel images might speak to the assimilationist success of the Chinese, the captions deliberately introduce dissonance between the image and the text. While one caption attests to the fact that the girl from Arkansas "experienced no prejudice," the other caption cites its subject from Mississippi as saying, "We were made fun of all the time . . . [and had to] deal with those who could not totally understand us as Chinese" (1986, 92). Such a division generates no comment in this pictorial history; rather, it merely asks the reader/viewer to process the contradiction as a result of individual experience—or, perhaps, the difference between Mississippi and Arkansas.[12] Yung's representation introduces an inherent duality in the ways one can read history by presenting the reader/viewer with the incommensurability between two women's experiences as well as between the verbal testimony and the

4 Louise Gee, one of eight children, grew up behind the family grocery store in Dumas, Arkansas. With so few Chinese in Dumas, she experienced no prejudice. On the contrary, she was selected cheerleader three times by her classmates. On special occasions like the prom, she was allowed by her parents to date white boys, since there were so few Chinese boys around, but she always knew she was expected to marry a Chinese.
*Louise Gee Collection*

5 A unique racial hierarchy in the South gave the Chinese intermediate status between whites and blacks. Chinese Americans began attending white schools and churches in the mid–1950s, but interracial socializing was kept to a minimum. Nancy Bing Chew (right), shown accepting a sceptre for achievement at the Lalu Baptist Church, found it difficult being a Chinese American in Mississippi: "We were made fun of all the time. . . . We had to meet certain expectations that our parents wanted of us and at the same time, deal with those who could not totally understand us as Chinese" (Chew 1982).
*Nancy Bing Chew Collection*

92

From Judy Yung's *Chinese Women of America: A Pictorial History* (Seattle: University of Washington Press, 1986). Reprinted with permission of the author.

image. Both photographs ask the viewer to infer a relationship between each girl's class position and femininity and her level of integration. While both are depicted in poses of heightened civic presence—the school and church as twin stages for the production of public femininity—according to no apparent logic, feminine sexuality deflects race-baiting for one but not the other. Yung's choice to represent the community in a disjunctive parallel partially undermines situating the photographs as evidence of Chinese American class attainment in the South via the communal rituals of womanhood. As in the WPA interviews with Chinese laundrymen in the South, while the cheerleader confirms a salutary racial invisibility as a testament to achieving white normativity, the other provides evidence of the obverse. Rather than attempt to reconcile the two experiences, Yung places them in dialectical tension. The photograph captures the latter subject side-by-side with her white female peers as if to imply that she is their equal, but her accompanying testimony betrays what the photograph makes obvious: she is different. This tyranny of the visual would present a certain conundrum for any film taking Loewen's thesis on Chinese caste shift as its script. *Mississippi Triangle*'s resolution to this mirrors the historical shift from white supremacy to liberal anti-racism: while the camera is not color-blind, the same cannot be said of discourse.

## *A Whiter Shade of Pale: Color-blind Discourse after Segregation*

I want to turn to another form of dissonance that arises in Asian American representation, one that also engages the disjunction between visual and rhetorical representations of race. While I have previously discussed the paradoxes exposed in the chronology of ever-approximate whiteness of Chinese Americans' asymptotic relationship to an idealized norm, I want to look at how that status might be enacted in the post–Civil Rights moment. In visualizing Loewen's thesis, the dilemma of *Mississippi Triangle*—how to portray the white status of nonwhites—was very specifically surmounted: it depicted them as subjects who had access to a privileged mode of discourse, that of color blindness. What shifted in the interim between the 1960s and the 1980s was the way in which white supremacy could be upheld within the discourse of deracinated liberalism. In the minority opinion to *Plessy v. Ferguson*, Justice Harlan's assertion of the color-blind nature of the Constitution foreshadowed the ways in which white privilege might come to be expressed after *Brown v. Board of Education*.

Catching two generations not only between black and white but between a pre- and post-Civil Rights moment, *Mississippi Triangle* witnesses an uneven historical transition in the way that race is invoked in public discourse. The only social engineering overtly articulated in the film is the continued shunning of black-Chinese families, which, as I have discussed, is realized in the figure of Arlee Hen. Instead, the film implies that what leveled the playing field for the Chinese in Mississippi was the Civil Rights Movement. White identification, therefore, is conveyed as a mindset—through the portrayal of

Asian Americans *speaking as* white people. As Robyn Wiegman has noted, "The hegemonic formation of white identity today must be understood as taking shape in the rhetorical, if not always political, register of disaffiliation from white supremacist practices and discourses" (1999, 118). The hollowness of that disaffiliation is held up to critique in the film's depiction of a southern private school in which a disembodied voiceover pronounces, "We say that anyone—any race, creed, color—can come to our school" at the same time the camera pans over only white faces in its classrooms. The film thus shows how post–segregation era liberalism comes to support white interests. In this case, however, the southern Chinese become the unwitting vehicles of that expression.

In order to convey "near-whiteness," the film chooses to show community members accessing the discourse of equal opportunity in ways that support the racial status quo. This is evident in an exchange between a second-generation Chinese American girl, Linda Wing, and her African American, would-be suitor. The film marks her working-class status as she emerges from a trailer home in an alley next to her father's grocery store. After depicting a homey scene in which the father and daughter are seen socializing with the unnamed black man, the camera cuts to a shot of his hands on her car as if to imply not only familiarity but possession. He leans into the car window as she sits in the driver's seat:

MAN: Your people don't want you to be seen with me?
LINDA WING: Why you think that?
MAN: The way you act. Your attitude.
LINDA WING: You see, my people, you know, they think that blacks shouldn't belong with Chinese people. They want me to marry someone . . . so that we'll have our own color . . . Shouldn't mix the blood up. I don't have anything against you. I don't have anything against any color. I was raised around black people. I'm not going to turn against black people because the white people told me not to. I have my own life to live.[13]

Wing's repudiation of any version of racial supremacy, white or Asian, takes the form of denying its effect on her own thinking: "I don't have anything against *any* color" (emphasis added). While her reply acknowledges systemic cultural pressure to adhere to racial hierarchy and separation, she implies that intimacy is a matter of volition, of choice seemingly irrespective of status. At the moment she asserts her autonomy from culture, her statement invokes another influence: white people. Segregation's enforcement, which the African American ascribes to "her people," is tellingly redirected by the end of her reply. The slippage in attributing the interracial marriage prohibition from the Chinese to whites can be read as a subtle defense of the Chinese at the same time it acknowledges a vertical line of power situating white people as the final arbiters of the color line. As if to heighten the contradiction of the exchange, the literal meaning of her statement is garbled at a crucial point: one presumes she meant to say, "I'm not going to turn against black people because the white people told me to."

Following Wiegman's recognition, white privilege in the post-segregation era appears as the very disavowal of bias. For the person of color mimicking this disavowal, professing free will is also contrarily a hedge against rejection by whites.[14] The film shows Wing explaining, "I have a lot of white friends too, but I don't see them. I don't hang around no crowd. They be in their own crowd." Asserting systemic autonomy acts as a balm to soothe her exclusion from the upper caste at the same time that her use of ebonics marks her social distance. Here, however, the retreat into individualism against the prevailing racial hegemony nonetheless marks near-white privilege in the same way that the private school's mantra of equal opportunity—"any race, creed, color—can come to our school"—upholds racial separation. Linda asserts that she is an equal opportunity dater as a means of rejecting her black suitor. The rhetoric of free choice becomes the acceptable means of disaffiliation from African Americans in the post-segregationist era, a means of ostensibly claiming a position of unmarked universality that is, in effect, unavailable to her. There is a duality about the film's portrayal: it simultaneously marks white desire at the same time that it registers the Asian subject's distance from that invisible norm. The space of the interstitial is marked by multiple partial truths.

If deracinated rhetoric marks privilege, it would seem that in *Mississippi Triangle*'s portrayal of Chinese "whiteness," such privilege is inexpertly practiced, perhaps as a sign of the community's still precarious place in southern culture. In another scene, an interviewer has apparently asked Chinese American Audrey Sidney about her views on Chinese-black unions. Stumbling over a definition of interracial marriage after a series of fits and starts heightened by the editor's cuts, she begins to rephrase a response: "I don't think that they will marry black, my children. Personally, I think Chinese people tend to . . ." With an embarrassed smile, she finally stops to explain, "You put me on the spot." Her flustered response, its gaps and self-conscious elisions, bespeaks the liberal's awareness that one cannot gracefully convey one's disassociation from African Americans without being overtly racist. To invoke Minnie Bruce Pratt's words, the "horrid, cheerful accents of a white lady" (1984, 12) mark this Chinese American's "whiteness" perhaps more definitively than what must no doubt be the "W" on her driver's license. Yet a glib answer revealing her stand on interracial marriage is not readily forthcoming, perhaps due to her own emergent status and the fact that the rhetoric of deracinated liberalism has not become entrenched. She is "acting" white, but with rough edges showing; her rhetoric around the minefield of black-Chinese intimacy is fitful and halting precisely because it has not become second nature. What is caught on camera is a not-quite status, a failed approximation.

The film's contribution to Critical White Studies is dual: it portrays the rhetoric of a "postsegregationist antiracist whiteness" (1999, 124) that takes the form of asserting autonomy from systemic influences or a disassociation from the past. This stance is put in greater relief in its articulation in the mouths of a racialized population, Asian Americans speaking in the heavily coded language of what has emerged as a means of supporting the status quo under the guise of liberalism: disavowing prejudice. Asserting "choice" in one's associations, then, supports the old framework of intensely realized class and racial segregations. At the same time, the film introduces an ambiguity that questions who really speaks from the space of disembodiment. As a generation on the cusp of two historical periods, the end of segregation and the beginning of the Civil Rights Movement, the community's inability to perform convincingly deracinated universality both supports and undermines the "near-whiteness" that they had presumably achieved. The decade between *The Mississippi Chinese: Between Black and White* and *Mississippi Triangle* marks the emerging shift from white supremacy to anti-racist liberalism and with it a shift in the ways that whiteness itself is rhetorically invoked in the maintenance of racial hierarchy.

To question the narrative of progressive modernity as it is affixed to this "rising" interstitial population, not the oscillation between poles along a racial continuum, but a developmental movement, is to question a broader narrative based on a pre- and post-1954 periodization, a before and after national snapshot that sees segregation as the dividing line between racial ignorance and enlightenment. Because one difference between the study and the film is its historical address, the filmmakers attribute Chinese status elevation not, like Loewen, to behind-the-scenes concessions to white oligarchy, but to the Civil Rights Movement. For example, one Chinese American public official—his position itself a testimony to change—claims, "The Civil Rights Movement helped the Chinese to attain certain status among the white world, more or less, whereas we didn't have anything to gain in the black world because they didn't have nothing for us to step in to." Nevertheless, the film perhaps unintentionally presents a more complicated and inherently ambiguous picture of post–Civil Rights race relations in the Delta in ways that question a progressive chronology that conflates the end of state-enforced segregation with the end of racism.

Yet that historical cusp occludes a more fragile boundary between past and present, a fragility that is disturbed by eruptions of "Funk." After establishing that the demise of Jim Crow created opportunity via education, the film cuts to a high school pep rally as the site of integration, as a symbol of the fruit of civil rights activism. As if to support Loewen's comment in a new afterword to his study that the 1980 Greenville High School yearbook is an "integrationists' dream" (1988, 191), the camera pans the bleachers of a Delta high school to give evidence of black and white fellowship in this "new" era of race relations. The cheerleading squad, the marching band, the pep rally performers, and the general assembly all display blacks and whites (and a few strategically placed Chinese Americans) mutually involved in constructing school spirit. The sequence carries the weight of the film's suggestion that public education was the white supremacists' last line of defense. Yet this sequence, designed to convey at least the surface level success of desegregation, ends up witnessing something beyond the filmmakers' overt intent. Serendipitously, the crew witnesses a student pantomime that is itself highly suggestive when read in the context of Chinese crossover to white status.

After establishing shots of interracial unity, the film briefly depicts a performance being enacted at the rally: a mock funeral complete with coffin, distraught mourners dressed in black, and a minister of ceremonies. After calling for silence, the student playing the preacher ponderously intones over intermittent cheering, "We have gathered here, my children, on this very sorrowful occasion to pay our last respects to our dearly, *dearly* departed School Spirit of 1982." His discourse is rudely interrupted by the presumed corpse who leaps from the coffin, to the horror of the mourners and delight of those in the bleachers. The "Spirit," a girl made up in ghostly white, scampers around the floor of the basketball court only to be chased down by the funeral-goers who, to the glee of the crowd, catch her, hoist her aloft, and triumphantly bear her back toward the coffin. The scene reverses melancholic mourning: the lost love object's restoration erupts, in Anne Cheng's terms, as pathological euphoria.[15] The scene confronts the viewer with a positive image of desegregation: boys and girls of all races together enacting the (very vocal) rituals of community. It intends to confirm the Civil Rights Movement's reach into the institutional state apparatus of the public school system. But the sequence carries meaning beyond that intended by the students (school spirit is not dead) and by the film (segregation is dead).

What to make of this sequence in a film about the Chinese American caste elevation, a sequence in which few Chinese Americans appear? Fittingly—or perhaps ironically—school spirit in the pageant is performed by an African American girl in what looks like "whiteface." Intended merely to give her an other-worldly appearance as a ghost, her get-up nevertheless carries other resonance in a film about race relations, the attempts of a formerly "colored" community to shift its status, and the historically saturated context of black-face minstrelsy in the South. However subtly, this staging of whiteface suggests that while such pressure was thought to be dead in this new era, instead it rises up to disturb the recently achieved interracial harmony. This ghost of the past cannot be fully contained and thus must be subject to capture: ironically, the film portrays African American students giving chase. Just as the white paint cannot disguise the performer's blackness, white face is itself an inadequate costume, an offense to the interracial assembly. Beyond this, there is inherent ambiguity in the film's witnessing of this meaning-saturated pageant: the sequence cuts off at the moment that the African American girl in whiteface is borne away amid the crowd's increasing hysteria. Is the Spirit of 1982 going to be restored to her grave to make way for the Spirit of 1983, for example, or does she symbolize a unity triumphantly resurrected and now on display for former naysayers? In either case, whiteface figures ambiguously. As the crowd roars its approval, the students lay hands upon her either to restore her to her rightful death or fete her as the embodiment of their solidarity, a solidarity then contingent on impersonation. The sequence at the high school ends moments later with a similar image: two male students, one black, the other white, are lifted above a crowd—presumably the football team—as a token of honor, their heroism on the field celebrated as a point of school pride and unity. The girl is made to fulfill a similar symbolic function, but—as with all women made to serve as symbolic boundary markers of community—she figures more ambivalently: is she a symbol of communal loathing (bury her) or the corporeal icon of their collectivity (parade her)?

Inadvertently highlighting the assimilative pressure to mimic whiteness as a condition of people of color's civic presence, the film's portrayal of this visual pantomime questions the premises of Asian caste elevation by opening up the space of farce. The newly acquired racial status of the Chinese in the Delta can likewise be read as merely "acting" white, a tomfoolery that deserves, like the School Spirit of 1982, to be buried as a retrograde artifact of the past. If touted as a sign of unity between black and white, the performance reveals the uneven, incomplete transference of status, one that is so blotchy that the darker shades cannot help but show through. Designed to incite unity in a high school gymnasium, the students' staging of this mock funeral is certainly beside the point of the film's own self-conscious staging of race, but like the ghost itself, it pops out perhaps inopportunely to disrupt any uncomplicated or unironic portrayal of a post–Civil Rights landscape. The pep rally asks the viewer to consider what lies in excess of the communal celebration of post-1954 integration not only for Asian Americans but for African Americans as well.

## Reading Anomaly within Anomaly

The claim that the Chinese in the South left "the black world behind without a second glance" (Loewen 1988, 194) places in hyper-relief Morrison's assertion that the Africanist presence underwrites immigrant assimilation. "Only when the lesson of racial estrangement [from African Americans] is learned" she writes, "is assimilation complete" (1994, 98). If indeed "yellow is a shade of black, and black, a shade of yellow," as Gary Okihiro has suggested in emphasizing the shared subordination of Asian Americans and African Americans, it must be acknowledged, then, that yellow is also a shade of white (1994, 34). In situating Asian American racial formation within a comparative context, this is a significant reminder. Yet the regional assertion of Asian "success" in stretching the color line curiously prefigures what would only later emerge as the dominant national discourse on Asian Americans: their portrayal as white-identified, model minorities. This chapter has been a caution against using this community as a symbol of immigrant triumph, something that Loewen recognizes in his 1988 afterword to the second edition of *The Mississippi Chinese* and is reflected in the careful politics of *Mississippi Triangle*.[16] Both resolutely refuse to take either a celebratory or condemning tone toward caste shift, placing ironic quotation marks around the "success" of their subjects.

The post-1954 period witnessed the mass exodus of second-generation Chinese from the Delta at the same moment in which it was claimed that they had achieved what the previous generation had worked assiduously to engineer. The reasons for the out-migration of this now emergent middle class—those presumably near or at the top of the status hierarchy—are attributable to the loss of economic opportunity, to competition that threatened small merchant businesses. Yet, as Loewen notes in highlighting the white-but-precarious status of the Chinese in the Delta, "the most important single reason for leaving is the continued discrimination the race still faces in Mississippi" (1988, 181). This acknowledgment of ongoing racism against Asian Americans not only indicates the incomplete transformation of status, but the fact that, under segregation, "full equality" and white status are two different things. This social vulnerability serves to reveal the privileges of "whiteness" that this population does not share: political influence and civic participation—neither of which were enjoyed by working-class whites. That is, place-marking along a black-white continuum is an inadequate means of measuring degrees of assimilation or equality and will yield only a partial narrative.

This acknowledgment may be one reason that, in the midst of documenting caste rise, the pressures of intermediacy intrude upon the documentation itself—this is true even within both Loewen's text and its visual counterpart, *Mississippi Triangle*, which attempt to maintain a scrupulously careful ideological balance. Charting dissonance within the field of representation surrounding the Mississippi Chinese in multiple disciplines reveals a counter-narrative, however muted or repressed, that disrupts the narrative of racial uplift wittingly or unwittingly ascribed to this interstitial population. In this sense, the community resists its use as historical evidence of racial self-help or as an affirmation of the trickle-down effects of the Civil Rights Movement. Both these optimistic stories render the period of segregation itself as nostalgic, as a historical aberration rather than something convergent with national interests and imparting a lasting and continuing legacy of racial hierarchy; they produce representations that are themselves funky, that cannot quite stand up to scrutiny. The fissures and gaps within representations of segregation-era history question the stability of any narration of caste transcendence and draw attention to its function in the post–Civil Rights era.

The Asian's uneasy relationship to power in this historical context is likewise reflected in the uneasy discourses that intend to convey it. For the "partly colored," white identification is revealed to be a failed approximation. The space between black and white measures the distance between the social enactment of an identity and its idealization, highlighting the structures that consolidate social power in its multiple manifestations. Yet this ambivalence surfaces not only as an anxiety about status, but as an anxiety within discourse itself. As in the next chapter, the residues of a repressed or unacknowledged history—of intimacy, of discrimination, of collusion, of self-degradation—emerge within a field of representation surrounding the historical context of intermediacy. What surfaces only as a discursive haunting nevertheless interrupts the drive to create linear chronologies out of the untenability of middleman status. Racial interstitiality, then, may be conceived as a site where identifications with power go unrecognized or remain unfinished. Within every narration of status transformation, there lies both an ambivalence and incompletion that can unveil the stakes underlying its emergence. If there is a messiness to living in the interstices, it is revealed in the very discourses that seek to represent it.

# Anxieties of the 'Partly Colored'

While it is impossible to defend racial segregation in a democracy, it may still be observed without any implication of such
defense that human beings seem to prefer a definite and understandable social role to one that is ambiguous, even though that
role be one in justice unacceptable.

—Foreword to Charles S. Johnson's
*Patterns of Negro Segregation*

Objectivity does not simply involve passivity and detachment;
it is a particular structure composed of distance and nearness,
indifference and involvement.

—Georg Simmel

German sociologist Georg Simmel has noted that one characteris-
tic of "the stranger" is a seeming lack of commitment to the social norms
of the new group, a perhaps felicitous objectivity or dispassion (1950). For
his student of the influential Chicago School, Robert E. Park, migration
makes possible a new interpretive lens, the viewpoint of the "marginal man"
whose distance from his home culture emancipates his vision, allowing him
to "interrupt the routine of existing habit and break the cake of custom"
(Park 1928, 885). For "strangers" setting up shop in host countries, remaining
aloof from local culture is conducive to business. Edna Bonacich asserts that
comprador ethnics or "middleman minorities" do not allow the status hierarchies of their host cultures to interfere with the impartiality of capitalism
(1973). While the distance of the outsider is the occasion for suspicion—witness reaction to Hannah Arendt's admission in "Reflections on Little Rock"
that as a European, she has "difficulty in understanding, let alone sharing,
the common prejudices of Americans in this area" (1959, 46)—the outsider
is often regarded an ideal observer.[1] This view complements a belief in the
ethnographer's distance as a requisite for the absence of predetermined bias.
As Ralph Ellison notes regarding Gunnar Myrdal's 1944 analysis of Ameri-

can race relations, *An American Dilemma: The Negro Problem and Modern Democracy*, "The reviewers have made much of Dr. Myrdal's being a foreigner, imported to do the study as one who had no emotional stake in the American Dilemma" (1964, 313).

For Asians in the South, this presumption of objectivity takes a racial cast. Reviewing V. S. Naipaul's 1989 travel narrative, *A Turn in the South*, C. Vann Woodward comments approvingly, "Whether in colonial, antebellum or postemancipation times, most visitors arrived with preconceptions about race relations. Unlike his precursors, V. S. Naipaul comes with an ethnic neutrality bred of his ancestors from India" (1989). Of course, no one with a knowledge of South Asian history would claim that Indian ancestry breeds ethnic neutrality; what Woodward grafts on to Naipaul is not only a belief in the foreigner's detachment, but an American belief in the Asian's neutrality in what is seen to be a primary struggle between blacks and whites.[2] As if to echo this, the Japanese American protagonist of Cynthia Kadohata's novel, *kira-kira*, set in Georgia in the 1960s confirms, "White people were not really mean to me, but they were rarely nice, either" (2004, 153).

This projected neutrality offers a ready trope in African American literature: in channeling a persona seemingly apart from the system of American race relations, African Americans have repeatedly invoked the image of the turbaned outsider whose costume displaces skin color as a central marker of difference. The turban has been represented as a talisman against blackness: "It was a standard joke among us [at Harvard]," notes an African American scholar in the 1950s, "that all you had to do to get away from unpleasantness was to put on a turban and pass as an Indian" (cited in Isaacs 1962, 358). Foreigners are often perceived to have diplomatic immunity from American preconceptions about race. As one man confronting changing race relations in south Florida suggested, "It's not color—it's background. That was true even 10 or 12 years ago, in the South—a dark-skinned person from another country, speaking with an accent or wearing a turban, got better treatment than American citizens of the same color" (cited in Egerton 1969, 22). Or, as the narrator of Chester Himes's *If He Hollers Let Him Go* assures his girlfriend who is nervous about entering a restaurant patronized by whites, "I'll tell them I'm an East Indian if you think that'll help. Next time I'll wear a turban" (1973, 60).[3] The turban becomes the alternative fetish of difference that compensates for color; the anecdotes betray the view that the Indian stranger's distance results in heightened status.

This assumption regarding the Asian's partial privilege under Jim Crow is reflected with ironic twist in Asian American writing about the South. Putative objectivity toward relations between black and white offers Asian American writers a specific means of self-location: that of impartial cultural critic whose intervention assumes the veneer of credibility. That said, this positionality may also signal a convenient retreat, an illusory denial of investment. While the previous three chapters have engaged the ways in which interstitial communities became represented in academic, governmental, legal, and popular cultural discourses over time, I want to turn to the individual's self-representation in memoir. Racial intermediacy became worked out in the public sphere in ways that established enduring but ambiguous narratives about the racial uplift of two communities; what does personal narrative reveal about the "partly colored" subject?

Counter to its circulation as Orientalist trope in Asian American Studies, "foreignness" offers a paradoxically liberating positionality for Asian American writers engaging the region—it represents a presumed "outside" to the social mores both publicly displayed under Jim Crow and highlighted in the southern canon. In this sense, interstitiality becomes the occasion for an affected posture toward southern-as-American race relations: that of innocence. This posture is strategically assumed in the two memoirs that I foreground here, Choong Soon Kim's 1977 *An Asian Anthropologist in the South: Field Experiences with Blacks, Indians, and Whites*, depicting the ways in which Kim's racial location impacts his data collection, and Ved Mehta's *Sound-Shadows of the New World* (1985), which, along with his autobiography, *Face to Face* (1957), tells the story of his tenure as a student at the Arkansas School for the Blind in the 1950s. Both Mehta and Kim assume an objective distance from black-white relations as a conduit to offering somewhat mild-mannered liberal critiques of race in the United States.

Kim's *An Asian Anthropologist in the South* takes as its central conceit the idea that being a Korean "foreigner" in the South enhances his observation of three racially defined communities: "[M]y neutral position facilitated my objective observation of each group. Each group was willing to present its side to me, because these people knew I did not represent any side" (Kim 1977, 117). Within the status hierarchies of the South, "Asianness," he implies, can appear to be neutral, unaligned, a DMZ of American race relations, enhancing his professional role as participant-observer. This concept of a racial neutral zone takes another cast in Ved Mehta's creative nonfiction set in Little Rock. Mehta mines the literal and metaphoric potential of his disability from the perspective of his own "precarious" position as an Indian foreign student. "If you rub your nose in the nigger business too much, you'll become one yourself," a white student warns, "and remember, whatever else you Indians are, you aren't white" (Mehta 1957, 243). Affecting a tone of innocence intended to destablize racial logic, Ved offers a faux naïf meditation on the visual epistemology of difference from the perspective of the blind, literalizing the idea of a color-blind world in the tumultuous year of Little Rock's forced integration. "White, black," he muses, "It registered nothing":

> "White is clean; black, dirty," I said to myself, but "clean" and "dirty" meant nothing, not, at least, in that way. . . . If I could only remember the colors. I'd always heard that the blind lived in a world of darkness, but that couldn't be, because I didn't know what darkness was, except maybe the smell and the quiet of the night. Two birds fluttered over my head. I wondered how dark I was, how much I looked like a Negro, and what my kinship was with him. (1957, 244)

The moment's lyrical tone resonates with theoretical significance. Ved's wistful desire to access color in order to understand the meanings ascribed to it succeeds in denaturalizing race for his sighted readership: why would color have intrinsic meaning? Would seeing those differences render them any more explicable? Occupying two sites of cultural outsidedness, not white and not sighted, grants him the moral authority to expose the irrationality of the color line from a position of destabilizing innocence. In the context of 1957 Little Rock, this is not an insignificant card to play.

Yet this confrontation with race relations is ancillary to Mehta's primary narrative charge. He comes not to advocate for racial integration, but for the integration of blind among the sighted; the regional context of his story at first appears to be incidental to his cultural intervention. In contrast, Kim takes on southern race relations in a self-conscious way: his work is only partially invested in detailing the results of data collection among black and white workers and the demographics of the Choctaw community; he wants to explore the ways in which his own racial position impacts his fieldwork and cultural reception. Nevertheless, what these two southern memoirs have in common is not their overt commentary on race, the force with which they critique Jim Crow or its continuing legacy. Rather, their southern context brings to light one dynamic of racial interstitiality that I have been arguing underlies Asian racialization in the United States, that of black disavowal— in this case, in regard to the self.

Kim's and Mehta's southern memoirs have heretofore flown under the radar of both Asian American and southern writing; what makes their regional engagement significant is the way in which cultural intermediacy comes to highlight a broader set of relations. As the texts inscribe narrators well-defended against the presumption of being interpellated as "colored," they can be read as primers on how individuals deal with a loss of status—or, more existentially, the loss of self. That is, to be "partly colored" necessitates a partial consciousness, particularly in terms of how the subject mediates dehumanizing treatment. Studies of race often proceed with the expectation that the subaltern will convey his experience with a certain kind of clarity, whether with an activist's righteousness or, as I have noted earlier, with Fanon's philosophical poignancy. But what I am interested in here are the traces of the individual's awareness of his racial place that refuse the overt recognition of Fanon's "Look, a Negro!" What intrigues me are not only those situations in which status is inconsistent or in flux, but the ways in which it assumes a dual register and becomes unevenly enacted.

Both Kim's and Mehta's narratives reflect the anxieties of the "partly colored"; they betray subtle instances of African American disavowal that contrast their understated racial liberalism, their overt if muted opposition to segregation in its formal and de facto forms. This nuanced repudiation does not always address black subjects, but surfaces in the Asian individual's resistance to interpreting his place in southern culture if it threatens the inviolability of his subjectivity. Intermediacy produces what can be seen as a poetics of disconnection in regard to a self-implicating blackness—how one reads over the signs of differential treatment as a hedge against the implication of one's inferiority, a hedge against the full consciousness of "how much I looked like a Negro, and . . . my kinship with him." But that poetics also suggests a corresponding analogue: whiteness is exposed as the unmarked ideal that the subject only uneasily attempts to inhabit; Asian American southern literature jars into visibility the abstract, universalist notion of transcendent subjectivity characterized by the term "white." These regional narratives inscribe not straightforward attempts to establish "Asianness" as distinct from American investment in the terms "black" and "white," but the point where white supremacy becomes normative, the point where it becomes, in effect, national.[4] Thus, it is not simply that the Asian American subject is constructed within the South's racial continuum, but that the irresolution of his southern location nudges our investment in an unmarked norm into grudging visibility. Both the privileges and degradations that attend interstitiality are to be found in what goes unsaid, what is to be read between the lines. What the southern context of Asian anomaly enables, then, is an understanding of racial latency.

As Simmel has theorized about the place of the "stranger" in the opening epigraph, if objectivity involves an equal measure of indifference and involvement, the nature of that involvement is not at first clear. How does a social location that is at once above and below nuance the individual's understanding of "his place" within a culture governed by multiple forms of separation, division, and hierarchy? Kim's text reveals an investment in seeking a space seemingly *outside* those relations, the position of the "foreigner." While he views role-playing as a pragmatic professional strategy that solicits the goodwill of his informants, I want to highlight its other use to him: the role of the foreigner is only desirable because of what it is not—that of a minority. It becomes a point of identification because it appears to render him immune to the social structures that define individual status in the United States. Foreignness is a defense against becoming familiarized, becoming knowable within the historically sedimented hierarchies of the still segregated South. Yet Kim's performative gesture ironically mirrors that exacted from African Americans. Similarly, racial segregation casts a long shadow upon Mehta's text: it impacts his treatment in a white school, it hovers on the borders of his commentary on integration among the sighted, and it obliquely structures his depiction of (interracial) dating. The racial resonance of his memoir surfaces as a veiled counter-narrative within discussions of caste in India and of disability.

The presumed neutrality of Asians in the South authorizes both writers' overt commentary on American race relations. It is a position that grants the illusion of immunity and distance, but it is one that cannot be maintained over time. My focus is less upon the empirical ways in which ambiguous cultural placement is sociologically documented by the individual as the inverse, the ways in which it is both unconsciously—and at times resolutely—banished or occluded. In other words, uneven status produces uneven or anxious narratives that oscillate between the conscious recognition of racial injustice and a resistance to seeing its self-implicating, conditioning effects. It invites a method of reading race akin to what Eve Kosofsky Sedgwick has called "paranoid" interpretation, a hermeneutics of suspicion regarding the repression of same sex desire that she reconceptualizes as a critical method intended to expose homophobia and heterosexism (1997). To invoke Naipaul, what the Asian American "turn in the South" offers is not simply a pluralist addendum to an archive that supplements our understanding of either Asian American or southern diversity, but an alternative interpretive focus that brings to light the other effect of white supremacy: the degree to which its values are internalized by those subjects who do not at first appear either to bear the weight of its leveling apparatus or to share unequivocally its privileges. Looking at Asian American memoirs of southern segregation, I want to explore the poetics of the *unevenly* oppressed.

## Asian Neutrality?

Predating postmodern anthropology's exploration of academic self-location, Choong Soon Kim's 1977 *An Asian Anthropologist in the South: Field Experiences with Blacks, Indians, and Whites* presents its findings about American race relations in the context of a personal narrative, one that is both self-consciously and unwittingly an ethnography of the ethnographer. Well in advance of James Clifford's *Writing Culture: The Poetics and Politics of Ethnography* (1986), which explores anthropological "fictions" in the creation of narratives about the native Other, or Ruth Behar's *The Vulnerable Observer: Anthropology that Breaks Your Heart* (1996), which makes the case for personal narrative in ethnographic practice, Kim inscribes himself as a character in the drama of his own research. Transplanted from South Korea in order to attend graduate school in Georgia and later, to become a professor of anthropology at the University of Tennessee, Kim highlights his field experiences among racially segregated crews of pulpwood workers in Georgia, as well as with the Choctaw Indians. The conceit of his "experiment" lies in determining how his identity is to be read by his southern American informants. Self-consciously playing with the hierarchy between investigator and native, Kim embarks upon a study of the Choctaw living in Tennessee, and later on the reservation in Mississippi. He is "anxious to see the responses of the Indians toward an Asian anthropologist" (70). In noting the antagonistic relationship that Vine Deloria has articulated between Indians and white academics, he comments, "I was interested to know whether I would be treated differently in comparison to white anthropologists, since the Indian and I shared morphological similarities. Certainly, I did not fit the stereotype portrayed by Deloria. I am not a tall, gaunt white, but a short, squat yellow" (70). And, as he finds, being short, squat, and yellow *does* make a difference in the racially divided South—it determines how he solicits cooperation, who gives him access, and, eventually, how his self-conception is challenged. But for a narrative that engages not his research findings per se, but the ways in which his Asianness has impacted his work in the field, it is curiously opaque; the statements he makes about southern racism (or lack thereof) are in constant tension with his anecdotal evidence—and, I would claim, what is omitted.

Asian neutrality at first appears to authorize his judicious weighing of the South's racial legacy: both blacks and whites, he concludes, seem culpable in perpetuating the legacy of Jim Crow into the 1970s. In the context of these two communities, Kim emphasizes his distance from his informants, a distance that is represented as a professional bonus lending him the air of objectivity, an enhancement of his role as participant-observer. In being chosen to work on a project comparing black and white workers, his white senior colleague reveals that he "thought of [Kim's] position as neutral in the racial perspectives," enabling him to "alternate easily in observing blacks and whites in the South" (21). Once in the field, this presumption appears to be borne out: an African American informant and work crew supervisor, a Mr. Swain, extends to Kim a rare dinner invitation to his home, a dwelling whose exterior is deceptively and deliberately dilapidated. Swain's willingness to allow Kim a glimpse into the well-kept interior of his newly remodeled home is revealed to be a function of Kim's apparent neutrality, the fact that he does not seem to signify within the South's established racial codes. Whites, Swain believes, would not approve of his middle-class pretensions, while fellow African Americans would "line up the next day askin'" for loans (58). Accounting for the rarity of his invitation, Swain informs the anthropologist:

If you were a white, I don't think you'd come in my house for a meal. And if you were a black, frankly I'd be more cautious about invitin' you to my place. You're a foreigner. I figure you don' care for local gossip or anythin' like that. And I don' have to worry about yo' to puttin' on airs about us. (Kim 1977, 59–60)

His informant's testimony establishes their shared intermediacy; Swain's class position elevates him above his peers while Kim's position forestalls racial hubris. This encounter pleases the author despite its implications about how his own status is read; his text maintains a mildly liberal view, which aligns him with a national readership but potentially distances him from a southern one. Swain's commentary seems to confirm Kim's claim that his outsider status facilitates his data collection: "Each group was willing to present its side to me, because these people knew I did not represent any side" (117).

In effect, this interspace is continually constructed as an opportunity for alliance along the lines of Bill Hosokawa's depiction of Japanese Americans interned in Arkansas:

In 1942 the evacuees who were sent to Arkansas had been astonished to find they were regarded as white by the whites and colored by the blacks. The whites insisted the Japanese Americans sit in the front of the bus, drink from the white man's fountain and use the white man's rest rooms even though suspecting their loyalty to the nation. And the blacks embarrassed many a *Nisei* when they urged: "Us colored folks has got to stick together." If there was no middle ground in the South's polarized society of black and white, in the rest of the country after the war, a *Nisei* could live as a yellow-skinned American without upsetting too many people, and he also discovered it was not particularly difficult to be accepted into the white man's world. (Hosokawa 1969, 473)

Hosokawa's sentiments reflect the hope that having "no place" may translate into mobility between both groups, something also operative in Kim's narrative. "Foreignness" thus appears to have a positive professional resonance: in echo of Simmel and Park, the stranger is free from local biases and his transience renders him inconsequential to established social structures; he has no people and no history and is, in the words of Park, free to "interrupt the routine of existing habit and break the cake of custom" (Park 1928, 885). The efficacy of this encounter prompts Kim to capitalize on the posture of innocent foreigner as a strategic means of soliciting cooperation among all three communities—black, white, and American Indian—throughout his fieldwork in the South. His implicit sense that each will respond favorably to this cultivated persona derives not only from the performance of innocence, but to its actuality: they simply appear to him as three distinct communities existing side by side in the American South. That is, he does not see how each is implicated in each's racialization, much less his own.

Yet the Asian "foreigner" is not a positionality that lies outside the embedded status hierarchies of American race relations; Kim's continued role playing reveals not only the nuances of the color line for Asian Americans, but the subject's unspoken struggle to maintain his humanity.

## The Performative Impulse

In order to facilitate his fieldwork, Kim stumbles upon the most enduring of all Oriental stereotypes: that of the bumbling but ingratiating alien. As critic Tina Chen has argued, being Asian American in some sense requires one to "impersonate" the public identity assigned to him, that of the perpetual alien (2005). Yet this self-conscious impersonation takes on specific resonance in the context of the South's racial polarity. Encountering hostility from a white sheriff in Georgia who demands to know how a person from an "underdeveloped country" could conduct an investigation of "the most advanced society," Kim concludes that he should thereafter "play the part of the Asian stereotype: be humble, polite, appreciative": "I told him that, being a foreigner, I could not adequately express my way of thinking in English. Furthermore, I told him I did not know southern customs since I was in the process of learning American ways" (52). This tact proves to grease the wheels of his study among white southerners by indulging their belief in their superiority and, in turn, allowing them to perform paternalism and "southern hospitality." In performing the stereotype, Kim allows himself to be read as someone whose helplessness is contingent upon his failure to apprehend cultural codes, the position of the social innocent and teachable child. Such a persona may easily function as a catalyst for exposing the prejudices of those around him—witness Sacha Baron Cohen's fictional persona, Borat, in the 2006 movie of the same name, whose politically incorrect innocence is put to comically exaggerated use in the American South. Like Baron Cohen's alter-ego, Kim views his actions as a professional strategy, as acting.

Kim acknowledges the racial resonance of his strategy in reflecting, "I learned from this relationship why some blacks would 'Uncle Tom' the whites" (52).[5] Yet he later expresses befuddlement over a similar posture among African Americans who, he observes, are irrationally agreeable to their white bosses even when confronted with tasks that they know cannot be completed. The self-conscious connection—and one of the few in which he draws a parallel between his own behavior and that of African Americans—recalls an instance in Richard Wright's *Black Boy* in which he is belatedly schooled in how to act like a "Negro" in the South. A friend informs Richard, "[Y]ou may think I'm an Uncle Tom, but I'm not. I hate these white people, hate 'em with all my heart. But I can't show it; if I did, they'd kill me" (Wright 1993, 219). For African Americans, such duplicity is not based merely on efficacy, but on survival. Like Wright, Kim understands that feigning ignorance and docility is a strategic posture, one that he can, for its lack of habituation, abstract from his own identity. Unlike Wright, he does not recognize it as a form of psychic violence that is coerced from him as a condition of white tolerance.

The transference of such behavior between racial groups is nonetheless highlighted in the work of a researcher studying the racial attitudes of white southerners who staffed the internment camps in Arkansas. In noting how their paternalist attitudes "toward Negroes have carried over to . . . the Mongoloid race," the author writes regarding Japanese Americans:

There are two noticeable results of this paternalism: a breakdown of individual initiative and the development of lackadaisical work habits on the part of evacuees; and the use of subtle and indirect methods of getting concessions from the administration. . . . The animosity of the evacuees is usually concealed beneath a polite, sometimes servile demeanor, but is definitely there. (McVoy, 1944, 189–190)[6]

In essence, the researcher marks a dialectical correspondence between racialized behaviors; white expectation, he claims, is self-fulfilling. Japanese American behavior is portrayed as a façade disguising the "true" feelings of those under the authority of white overseers, a subterfuge enacted as a survivalist accommodation to living Jim Crow, here in the context of the hyper-surveillance of a concentration camp. In contrast, neither Kim's own performance of servility nor that which he witnesses among African Americans during his fieldwork appears to him as behavior exacted by the legacy of Jim Crow. Rather, he blames the victim for the continuation of racial hierarchy, noting that in exhibiting such behavior, working-class blacks themselves encourage "the build-up of white supremacy in the South" and that the races are "mutually responsible" for it (131, 48). More to my point here, Kim's recognition that he is playing to expectation does not translate into an awareness that he himself may be understood to be "partly colored" and that the evidence lies in the very necessity of his resorting to deception as a means of ingratiating himself to southern whites. Rather, the posture of helplessness is—initially at least—constituted as a part that may be played to his advantage among all three racialized communities. In this sense, the impersonation assumes an equal valence: it is not a role played "for" those in authority and is therefore not perceived to be a tax levied on him by white supremacy.

Yet impersonation enables only a contingent mobility tolerated as long as the color line remains unchallenged. As Kim himself reveals in his portrayal of an Asian American who has taken the side of power, there is a toll extracted in the exchange—the capitulation to irrationality. One of the few instances in which he documents overtly racist behavior in the South comes in his depiction of a Korean American man who had been adopted by a white family. After the fellow Asian chastises Kim's black associate for coming into his segregated neighborhood, Kim comments, "Wilson's attitude was ludicrous in my view, for he also appeared to be a colored person if yellow is a color. Orientals would be treated just like a white so long as they stayed away from blacks" (121). That "yellow is a color" seems oddly estranged from the context of its utterance; yellow is not merely a color, but "colored." Kim's liberal commentary assumes a perhaps strategic but nonetheless obstinate innocence.

The tax, then, for the Asian man's attempt to inhabit the unmarked norm of whiteness lies not merely in mimicry and disconnection, but in the tacit understanding that he will not test the boundaries of the color line, making it manifest where it may be ambiguous. This is the case in Kim's refusal to enter a segregated theater, particularly after he finds that, although his presence in public facilities in the South undergoes discomfiting scrutiny, it has not heretofore been challenged. In recounting an opportunity to test his interstitial placement while working on the Mississippi Choctaw reservation, the text reveals that maintaining the illusion of neutrality within that environment confounds narrative logic. While supervising white students doing data collection in 1974, Kim is informed of their outrage regarding a movie theater's segregationist practices:

> The blacks and the Choctaws were charged less than the whites but had to sit in the balcony. Once, several of my [white] students went to the theater and asked to be seated in the balcony. They were not being activists; they had simply thought it would be economical. When they were not allowed to do so, they left. One angered student asked me to see how I would be treated racially at the theater. It would have been an interesting experiment, but it would have brought about their embarrassment as well. Such embarrassment might have had unpredictable effects. I thought I should avoid such temptation and continue to enjoy my unique status. (109)

In recounting the incident, Kim's refusal hinges upon a professional rationale: he does not want to be humiliated in front of his students and suffer a loss of authority. Nevertheless, his recharacterization of his students' presumably militant challenge as "tempting" experiment is telling: in casting what he might discover as empirical "evidence," he can professionally distance what he might take away from the action, namely, the full weight of how he himself is viewed in southern culture. It is this road not taken that allows him to affirm about his experience in the South, "I was surprised to find no form of segregation against a nonwhite Asian" (47).

What Kim does not do and does not say, then, forms an uneasy backdrop to his investigation into race and American culture; his repeated attempts to maintain a sense of professional abstraction above the culture he describes come to challenge his narrative reliability. Defying his belief in Asian racial neutrality, a Japanese American couple advises him, "Don't try to be equal with these people. Don't compete with 'em. If you do, then they'll pick on you and step on you" (54). Upon finding that he has children in the United States, they urge repatriation to South Korea: "You better go back to your homeland as soon as you finish your study no matter what your status will be after you get back home. I don't want to see any second or third generation Orientals go through what I have gone through." Once familiarized and read into the established hierarchies of color, the couple suggests, the Asian American's place in the system becomes known, and, in turn, he is made to know his place. After establishing his informants' belief that Japanese American internment was motivated by racism, Kim blandly comments, "That concluded an unusually active day of my living in Pinetown." Whether indicative of the dispassion that the anthropologist affects or ethnic animosity over Japanese imperialism in Korea, his lack of commentary here is noteworthy. Asian American testimony contests his own professed fluidity, his belief that as an Asian "foreigner," he is partially exempt from the prejudices held by natives in the field and of the host country in which he initially thinks of himself as a sojourner. Here, he offers neither support nor refutation.

Yet Asianness cannot continue to signify in a vacuum; Kim later reconciles this slippage between participant and observer by drawing a distinction between the "foreigner" and the "minority": "As long as a foreigner is obviously a foreigner, they see him as a foreigner. But if a foreigner has succeeded in America and appears to be American, then they treat him as a member of a minority group" (76). That is to say, they treat him as one who does not warrant the pretense of "southern hospitality." There is a strange contradiction within the commentary itself: success is simultaneously equated with acculturation over time, yet successful integration carries with it the implication that one has been stigmatized. Familiarity breeds contempt. Regarding fieldwork in Mississippi, Kim notes that he could not expect individualized treatment as a distant visitor because "the whites of the region were familiar with Orientals, mainly Chinese" (96), who, he knows from James Loewen's work, were formerly known as "colored." The role of foreigner is revealed not to have positive content—it is not ethnically specific, it is merely that which has not already been abjected. The thin line between the minority and the foreigner is an epistemological one: the outsider who is known versus the outsider who is not. Thus, the disconnection that Kim effects is not from African Americans per se, but from Asian Americans who, he recognizes, have already become "partly colored" minorities in the eyes of southern whites. The source of narrative anxiety stems from whether or not to open the possibility that this national enculturation applies to the self, and whether or not it can be defended against.

This is perhaps why there is a notable omission in his statement, "I have never deluded myself that I belonged to the native groups of southerners— the whites, blacks, or Indians. In order to conform to the expectations of natives in the field, *I had to* behave as a foreigner so that I could get maximum assistance from them for successful fieldwork" (126; emphasis mine). Asian Americans are also "native southerners," but does he likewise belong among them? By the end of *An Asian Anthropologist in the South*, the question is whether or not Kim's role-playing can ever translate into an affirmative identity. He concludes, "As to reduce unnecessary competition with anybody in my school and community, I have again remained a humble foreigner in this setting as well. Even in the classroom with my students, I feel I am an outsider. . . . Having two American-born sons and ten years of residence in the American South was not enough to break down the barrier between 'our' and 'your.' At the same time, I know I can no longer fit into my native Korean society. Thus I remain a marginal man who belongs nowhere" (126).

Kim's phrasing echoes Park's assertion in his 1928, "Human Migration and the Marginal Man," that in the migrant one can find "a new type of personality, namely, a cultural hybrid, a man living and sharing intimately in the cultural life of two distinct peoples; never quite willing to break, even if he were permitted to do so, with his past and his traditions, and not quite accepted, because of racial prejudice, in the new society in which he now sought to find a place" (Park 1928, 892). Yet the "marginal man" was potentially an ideal type for social science researchers; it was an identity that Asian American intellectuals associated with the Chicago School of the 1920s and 1930s readily embraced. Historian Henry Yu writes, "As part of the Chicago sociologists' map of the Oriental Problem in America, the marginal man theory provided a shortcut for Oriental sociologists in their own intellectual journeys of self-understanding" (2001, 110). The end of Kim's narrative indicates why such intellectuals sought a theory in which professional detachment could redeem personal estrangement, highlighting the dual register of Park's own theory, which articulates a view similar to Du Bois's concept of "double consciousness." To some extent, Kim recognizes that performative duplicity is not a result of his own volition, but is coerced by the very social norms that he purports to study ("I had to behave as a foreigner"). In the context of the segregated South, the very necessity of dissimulation before whites locates him as like African Americans who, as in Paul Laurence Dunbar's poem, "wear the mask that grins and lies." Even while testifying to the fact that he was "treated very well" by southerners, he does recognize this as an acceptance contingent upon his ability to maintain an agreeable façade. Insights such as these skirt the full recognition that his professional strategy owes its effectiveness to a deeply embedded racial caste system. This keen and impartial observer will tell you what he sees about American class and race politics using himself as a barometer—without the recognition that he himself has internalized it. "Foreignness" is a pragmatic, short-term, self-conscious act readily distinguishable from subjectivity. It appears to have no real content—it is not the performance of Koreanness, for example, and appears to be deracinated in refusing an identification with either pole in the racial spectrum of the South. It is a self-proclaimed "neutral position" that facilitates the "objective observation of each group" (117) in which he appears to have no personal stake.

Nevertheless, its use as a strategic persona opens up an alternative reading to what I have presented here: to what extent are Kim's narrative disjunctions and omissions "coerced" by his expectation of a southern readership? That is, does his commentary become skewed by his effort to make his race liberal-ism palatable to a southern audience? What he details as being performed for his informants, the humble Oriental stereotype, may likewise be performed by a writer hoping to be accepted by his readers. Yet it would seem that, like Zora Neale Hurston collecting folklore in the South, Kim, too, places much faith in "the spy-glass of Anthropology" as means of framing his subject and distancing himself from it; in this case, however, it is not clear whether or not the "spy-glass" produces a specific distortion, the illusion of objectivity (Hurston 1978, 3).

The figure of the foreigner or alien is one that is irreducibly tied to Asian racialization in the United States. I want to nuance that construction by exploring how it is—however falsely—construed as a position of relative power. That is, "the foreigner" is a point of identification that resists one of lesser status, the "minority" who is understood to be something less than white. Kim's work contributes to our understanding of how Asian social status becomes adjudicated within the space between black and white—or more precisely, within the crucible between "not black" and "not white." It is simultaneously a signifier of objective distance and nonbelonging. That space also both consciously and unconsciously suggests, in Clifford's words, "the partiality of cultural and historical truths" within ethnographic knowledge production: "Ethnographic writings can properly be called fictions in the sense of 'something made or fashioned' . . . But it is important to preserve the meaning not merely of making, but also of making up, of inventing things not actually real" (Clifford 1986, 6). In this case, it is not only the native Other that is the invention, but the Other within the self. The subject inscribed in Kim's narrative suggests the "partiality of cultural and historical truths" in more ways than one; it represents a partial understanding of the Asian's place within segregation's lingering racial continuum and a veiled meditation on the individual's investment in rationalizing the loss of social equality within American democracy. *An Asian Anthropologist in the South* reveals a clear understanding of why Kim's African American informant maintains his home's run-down façade to disguise a comfortable and comforting interior. This duplicity represents a concession to the race/class norms of where he lives, but its consequence is isolation. Kim's performative impulse represents another division between surface and interior with similar costs. An accommodation to living in a racially stratified society, ironically, acting Oriental does not reflect the actions of an outsider or impartial social scientist, but those of a minority.

## The Psychology of the Unevenly Oppressed: Ved Mehta's Little Rock Integration

> [F]rom the very beginning I had taken care to seem like every-
> one else at the school, and kept my different, Indian background
> a dark secret.
>
> —Ved Mehta

Hurston's spy-glass metaphor takes vision as a requisite to cultural framing, yet prolific author Ved Mehta, blind as a result of childhood meningitis, nonetheless provides a penetrating if incomplete account of southern culture of the 1950s in his 1957 autobiography, *Face to Face* and his 1985 memoir, *Sound-Shadows of the New World*. Both depict the South Asian adolescent's time at the Arkansas School for the Blind from 1949 to 1952, yet neither portrayal is primarily a commentary on race relations in the United States. Rather, Mehta's goal is to allow the "sighted" a glimpse into the consciousness of the blind. What is intriguing about Mehta's American memoirs is their contribution to Disability Studies and their portrayal, however muted, of what has become an overdetermined site in the history of American race relations—Little Rock of the 1950s. He reveals that he is a figure of local curiosity, not only among the sighted as he tests his mobility on the streets of Little Rock, but among his blind peers at the "white's only" school that he has the privilege to attend. An impassioned journal entry records one racial affront perpetrated by a white, partially sighted classmate, the meaning of which he understands despite strategic protestations about color's inaccessibility:

> Evelyn said that she didn't want to hear what a "darky" had to say. I don't generally lose my temper—Daddyjee gave me strict training in controlling it—but today I did. I have been called a Negro before and been mistaken for a Negro once, and it didn't bother me, but I was enraged because Evelyn dismissed my opinion on the grounds that my skin is darker than hers. . . . More than ever I am determined to write a book one day and discuss this attitude that many Southern people seem to have. (1985, 387)

Ved's outrage bespeaks the reformer's zeal to combat regressive and ignorant attitudes on behalf of society as a whole. Yet Mehta's exposé of the American South never materializes despite his subsequently impressive literary output (*Sound-Shadows* is the fifth of eleven books so far making up his "Continents of Exile" series) and recognition as a cultural critic in the United States (he won a MacArthur Fellows "genius" grant in 1982). Moreover, his righteous response seems to be reserved for his being mistaken for a "darky"—elsewhere he has informed a peer who questions his white status that his people are "fair-skinned Aryans" from northern India, "not dark-skinned, like the Dravidians" in the south, a distinction that he has been taught and repeats but for which he has no reference. That regional difference, historian Sucheta Mazumdar notes, has been traditionally invoked by diasporic South Asians as a hedge against their status as "black" (1989). Indeed, Mehta's character-ization reflects the infamy of *United States v. Thind* (1923) in which Bhagat Thind contested his exclusion from naturalized citizenship on the basis that he was, as a South Asian, of "Aryan" stock and hence, white.[7]

Elsewhere, however, Mehta capitalizes on his disability as that which pro-vides a destabilizing perspective on the visual signifiers of race: "Maybe see-ing was an illusion," he recounts wistfully, "but I wanted to have that illusion, if only for a moment, to find out where and how I fitted into the social cross-word puzzle" (1957, 244). Figuring out his place in the American "puzzle" means accessing the meanings assigned to lines drawn around color, ability, nationality, and sexuality. His meditation on where he stands "in the shad-ings from white to black" offers a twist to the visual epistemology of race, yet what is notable about the 1985 narrative set in Arkansas of the early 1950s is that race relations are, in fact, infrequently mentioned. Nevertheless, I would suggest that Mehta's narrative on blindness resonates with a post–Civil Rights awareness of southern race relations and the significance of Little Rock in national memory. Mehta's subject, disability and consciousness, unwittingly calls forth the abstractions that we associate with the history of race relations: segregation and integration, two separate spheres, normativity and inferiority. In this case, seeking an understanding of the Asian's place along a racial continuum reveals the ways in which multiple forms of social difference and privilege become mediated and enmeshed, marking not merely one interspace, but other axes that mark privilege and difference, including gendered concepts of beauty and individual worth.

## Race and Disability: An Analogy of Beasts

Race becomes visible in Mehta's memoir within an analogy to disability. His advocacy derives from his firm conviction that disability need not be a handicap even as he engages a beastial analogy to depict the relationship between two worlds, the sighted and the blind:

> Mr. Chiles, almost totally blind himself, introducing one of the social-adjustment classes, had remarked, "To be blind is an uphill struggle. You've got to sell yourself to every seeing man. You've got to show him that you can do things that he thinks you can't possibly do."
>
> It was true enough if you were a donkey in a world of horses, you had to justify your worth and existence to the horses. You had, somehow, to prove to them that you could carry as much weight as they could, and if you couldn't move as fast, you at least were willing to work harder and put in longer hours.
>
> "Anything you do wrong in the world of the seeing . . . people around you will chalk it up to your blindness. They'll call you poor wretches, feel sorry for you, and they will commit the worst sin of all by excusing it because you're blind." (1957, 248)

Mehta's characterization inadvertently resonates with ideas of species differentiation and evolutionary hierarchy, metaphors harnassed to the segregationist's justification of racial separation. His response is telling: Ved accepts his teacher's philosophy and makes an effort in the sighted world both for his own self-advancement and family pride, and as a form of advocacy on behalf of the disabled collective. While donkeys may feel more comfortable among their own—forestalling a consciousness of their shared limitation as donkeys—as a precondition for social change, it behooves them, he suggests, to integrate into a world dominated by horses.

Mehta's 1985 elaboration of his analogy introduces the idea that *voluntary* segregation provides the oppressed a false sense of security. He is only mildly sympathetic to the separatist sentiments expressed by his blind peers: "We don't give a damn about being blind, but to be blind among people who have eyes, that's what's hell" (164). This "voluntary" separatist expression was certainly an outgrowth of dominant belief regarding the disabled at the end of the 19th century. As Douglas Bayton has noted, immigration officials believed that individuals with mental or physical "defects" warranted institutionalization, another form of segregation.[8] Raised "mostly among the sighted," which is to say, integrated, Ved nonetheless commiserates,

> Out in the world, there was no getting away from the feeling that we were indeed donkeys—beasts of burden, scorned and under valued, ever condemned to compete with natural prancers and jumpers. No matter how we might excel in our own terms, next to horses we would always appear to be jackasses. In some ways we were worse off than jackasses, because at least they had no consciousness, no idea that they were deficient in gait or in mane. Would that we had their innocence! For the first time, I had an inkling of why many of my fellow-students talked as if they would like to go straight from the school to a sheltered workshop, and pass the rest of their days among their own kind. (164–165)

The difference between the two groups is actual, the analogy implies, a biological distinction then exaggerated by the social attitudes ascribed to it. Again, this distinction invokes race not in an overt parallel, but insofar as his characterization of the blind and sighted takes on the very resonances we ascribe to race—a species difference that carries implications of inferiority and superiority, natural ability and natural limitation. The awareness of the distance between what one is and what one could be is represented as an additional burden of consciousness akin to that expressed in Richard Wright's depiction of living Jim Crow. The passage's rhetorical yearning for an Edenic innocence devoid of man's awareness of his oppressed condition is strategically faux naïf: the ambition to want more than one's place in the world underlies Mehta's portrayal of subaltern subjectivity in the autobiography as a whole. The prejudices against his "kind" are intended to be offset, no doubt, by this display of the lyricism. Unlike his peers who would like to remain among their own, he retains a greater belief in his potential than is socially acknowledged.

That is, Ved is not willing to accept his partial "donkeyness." While understanding the desire to retain one's sense of self through the comfort of voluntary segregation, he is nonetheless determined to combat prejudice by winning the grudging acceptance of the dominant. His narrative, then, centers around his attempts to negotiate the sighted world of Little Rock, Arkansas on his own. Here, the racial dimension of his experience as an Asian in the South becomes trumped by his *other* difference: riding the streetcars or shopping in town are exercises in refusing solicitous intervention, not being refused service; joining the Little Rock chapter of the (white) Boy's Club is about proving oneself equal in bouts of (Braille) chess where, again, the markers of black and white are not seen but nonetheless felt. While his species analogy exposing (confirming?) the hierarchy between the sighted and the blind is not intended as a commentary on race relations, it is the very historical location of his efforts at integration that push it to the surface.

In terms of disability, Ved becomes a model minority. He takes an individualist solution to social prejudice; accepting the terms of the dominant culture, he models himself on its ideals—in short, trying harder to approximate being a horse among horses. His means of ameliorating social attitudes engendered by preconceptions about biological difference covertly resonate with accommodationist theories of racial uplift. The parallel between Asianness and disability is acknowledged only in passing and to the same effect. In keeping with his theme on the responsibility of the blind to challenge the ignorance of the sighted via an ethos of self-help, in *Sound-Shadows*, Mehta embellishes the philosophy that has become his own: "Most sighted people shy away from handicapped people," Ved is informed by the same teacher. "They're frightened off by anyone who's not like them, so you have to make an extra effort to make them feel that it's worth their while to get to know you. You have to convince them that you're not very different from them, that you're a likable fellow, and that they'd enjoy being around you" (136). This fear of difference, Ved acknowledges, may extend to his own place among white folk within a segregated institution. He takes pains to conceal his ethnicity, race and skin color there remaining only imagined: "[F]rom the very beginning I had taken care to seem like everyone else at the school, and kept my different, Indian background a dark secret, instinctively realizing that it would get in the way of my acceptance and add to the feeling of separateness that I carried like a burden" (137). What Mehta represents as being learned during his tenure at the Arkansas School for the Blind is something that he already instinctively knows: if difference is an excuse for ostracism, one must compensate for it by approximating the norm. This is the only moment in his southern memoir in which he acknowledges that as a South Asian, he is becoming habituated to the cultural norms of place, that he is at risk of assuming the consciousness of a *racial* "donkey": "[M]y wish to win acceptance at the school was so strong that to me, often, everything in my background seemed inferior, everything in the backgrounds of the other students superior" (137). Again, what is most striking about this reflection is its rarity; it is the only moment in a 400 page account of Arkansas of the 1950s that he confesses an anxiety regarding cultural difference, and then, his reaction to race hierarchy is identical to the philosophy he advocates in regard to the hegemony of the sighted. To some extent, the elision of race in the narrative is both a form of privilege (he can approximate "whiteness" as unmarked ethnicity well enough among the blind and makes no mention of accent discrimination), and indicative of the opposite: "Indianness" is hidden from the reader in the same way that it is hidden from his (blind) peers. It represents a dark secret.

Nevertheless, the very nuances of Asian racial place in the segregated South are what I want to restore to visibility above and against the racialized subject's consciousness of that place. As in Kim's (mis)interpretation of the white man's refusal to shake his hand discussed in chapter 3, Asian American intermediacy signals a duality of interpretation, particularly as subjects read over signs of their different treatment. A case in point: the degree to which Ved is subject to segregation within the white school that he attends. In spite of the fact that he has deliberately downplayed his ethnicity, he is moved out of the boy's dormitory and into a converted broom closet. The move is represented as an administrative concession to Ved, an unusual privilege granted to him alone in order to accommodate his need for privacy ("You want a place where you can shut the door and be by yourself, keep on with your typing and reading, listen to Indian music and think of home. Am I right?" (285)). Whether this separation can be understood as anything other than voluntary and self-initiated is not mentioned: is he singled out for "special" treatment because he has made a case for his exceptionalism, or does the closeting represent a concession to time and place, one whose motive remains veiled? It is the very ambiguity of Asian location that allows for both readings: the move *within* the white school *away* from white boys may be read in the spirit of "separate but equal"—a privilege, even—or as another tier of segregation, an accommodation for a third caste. The former interpretation does not cross the threshold of the text's narrative consciousness for good reason; being treated "like white" is unremarkable and therefore goes unremarked. Nevertheless, neither does the latter; being treated "like black" necessitates a disconnect, one that reveals subjects who are well defended against the signs that they are constructed as "poor wretches." This racial aside exists only in the traces of narrative disclosure, what is visible only by reading between the lines and outside the closet.

## Caste's Dual Register

The interface between Asian Americans and southern regionalism is intriguing for this simultaneity of interpretation. Mehta's narrative is one example: a counter-text exists in tension with the surface of his narration. As in the last passage, what is not said exerts pressure on his account of events; this is also the case in Mehta's (non)narration of caste in India, which never disturbs his understanding of caste in the United States. Interestingly, Mehta's thesis on the responsibility of the individual to diffuse his difference and integrate into society appears only in the context of American culture and most forcefully in regard to the blind among the sighted. Despite Mehta's mild condemnation of the color line and the attitudes it breeds, its obvious parallel to caste distinction in Indian culture is represented marginally, but significantly. In the context of the heightening Cold War, parallels between caste in India and what Ellison referred to as American "soiled democratic linen" were necessarily repressed given that they compromised American claims to moral leadership on a global stage (Ellison 1964, 313). The irony was not lost upon Eleanor Roosevelt, who cited Britain's emancipation of India after World War II as an ethical model for the United States and its segregationist practices. A 1956 cartoon in the *New Yorker* rendered the comparison ironic: a man reading the *Bombay Times* in front of an Orientalist backdrop comments to another, "More controversy in Alabama! You'd think those people were being asked to send their children to school with Untouchables!"

One country's caste taboos are not another's, yet the cartoon holds the willful distinction up to ridicule. On one level, one could say that Mehta's text succeeds in eroding the caste system that places restrictions upon the disabled in the United States. Moreover, one could say that the road not taken here—an overt parallel between caste in India and in the United States—is an indication of Mehta's near white status. In effect, he reveals that he can inhabit the invisible norm in a crucial arena: interracial dating. Thus, to this mix of intersections that determine the "puzzle" of social status, I would add another: the privileges of masculinity. Mehta's brief defense of the Indian caste system is depicted through letters from his father, who is cited with

Ed Fisher © 1956 The New Yorker Magazine Inc.

"*More controversy in Alabama! You'd think those people were being asked to send their children to school with Untouchables!*"

"More controversy in Alabama!" New Yorker, 1956.

particular reverence. "Daddyji" sends his son abroad partly in the hope that he will marry an American and avoid inevitable caste demotion at home. Disability is mediated by sexuality and class; one can exploit differences between national contexts and their systems of value because foreigners do not adhere to the cultural conventions that matter to "us"—that is, intimacy only among members of one's own caste. Of course, this assumption relies upon an erasure: Ved has been sent to a place invested in its own caste system, one that applies to him in uneven ways.

My focus on sexuality here suggests a parallel to Mehta's earlier speculation on the arbitrariness of race's visual inscription, an inquiry into beauty
as a form of social ranking for *women*. Is his perspective one that disrupts
the dominant culture's emphasis on feminine aesthetics or depends upon it?
His father tells Ved, "Oh, you could get married here [in India], all right,
but not in our caste group and education group, and therefore not well, not
happily. . . . Because of your blindness, no parents in our education group
would give their girl to you" (24). His father's logic rests on his assessment
of the social demotion that blindness represents in India, one that renders
Ved outside its endogamous system of marital exchange.[9] Daddyji's desire
to see Ved make a match in the West proceeds without the thought that his
son's nonwhite status might function as a leveling factor, or perhaps Mehta
does not himself choose to represent this concern. Rather, his father's commentary introduces yet another category of community, that of religion, and
an evaluation of how it mediates social rank and the fear of difference. Western Christian girls, his father believes, are inclined to be more sympathetic
toward disability than Hindus ("That's why even Indian Christian girls make
so much better nurses" (25)). That race constitutes a form of caste in the
United States is not mentioned, even as his son apparently has been denied
admission to all schools for the blind in the West excluding one. More telling
is his father's unspoken expectation that his son marry a sighted woman; that
expectation is so normative that, like whiteness, it remains invisible.

Ved's racial and cultural difference seems not to have been insurmount-
able within his co-ed boarding school, at least within the text's representation of dating among the blind. What is interesting about the discourse of
sexuality is that, as in his speculation on the meaning behind color, blindness
complicates the traditional markers of beauty that are, especially for women,
forms of cultural capital. Unable to access the visual signs of attractiveness
that the sighted place into definite hierarchy, he and the other boys nevertheless "know" which girls are most desirable, an evaluation of personality, voice,
and, he acknowledges matter-of-factly, whether or not they are partially
sighted. In a noteworthy confession, his wish for sight in another instance
is based on a desire to judge the worth of his date beyond the segregated
community of the blind: "Would I be better off with a more desirable date
than Barbara? Then it occurred to me that everyone now and again thought
the grass was greener on the other side, but that our grass was without color.
At that moment, more than ever, I wanted to see grass—also to see Barbara's
face" (325). The confession is self-conscious, a contrast in tone to the rhetorically poignant desire for vision in *Face to Face* that will presumably allow

Ved Mehta in Little
Rock, 1950.

him to understand where he fits "in the shadings from white to black." In
that case, he recognizes that sight would merely grant the illusion of knowledge, reveal the arbitrary markers that determine social relations. What is
portrayed as an evocative yearning to understand his own racial place is represented here as a sheepish concession to masculine vanity, one that demonstrates a straightforward belief that one *can* determine where a woman
stands, to borrow from his own characterization of skin color's continuum,
within the shadings of feminine beauty from pretty to ugly. Neither portrayal
of Ved's longing for vision is self-pitying; interestingly, both instances fall
within the context of the desire to understand what seems to be of great significance to the sighted and thus to him as well: feminine beauty and color
as signs of social rank. Yet while his wish to comprehend Asian racial placement is conveyed with requisite neutrality perhaps because of his positive

reception in Arkansas—it is neither self-aggrandizing nor self-abasing—he is nonetheless self-conscious about his hope to raise his own cultural capital through that of his partner, readily bypassing any commentary that indicates that dating a white woman is already one indication of that capital. Perhaps a function of heterosexual male privilege, he offers no musings on his own attractiveness to the sighted—or lack thereof. He does, however, indulge the sighted by including a photograph of himself in the book, ironically, shirtless. Thus, he displays to the sighted reader what is partially hidden from his peers, the ambiguity of physical beauty, the ambiguity of brownness.

In a homosocial world, what matters is the esteem of other men; wanting to know a woman's social rank through her appearance betrays the vulnerability of the blind even among the blind: they are conditioned by sexual norms that they can access only figuratively. In actuality, this is the only access for the sighted as well.

Mehta's intimate account of disability conveys the ways in which multiple axes of difference and social status overlap like "a social crossword puzzle": ability/disability, white/black, American/Indian, attractive/unattractive, sighted/unsighted. His work represents advocacy for the blind and casts an unsettling perspective on the visual epistemology of difference. Of course, at one level this denormalizing perspective cannot be sustained; the conventions of the dominant culture(s) intervene in subaltern consciousness. To claim to be racially "color-blind" in a literal sense is perhaps as disingenuous as it is in the world of the sighted. Mehta's 1985 southern memoir is marked by the absence of African Americans; it would seem that in all his encounters there is no one he can (or will) identify by race other than himself. It is as if the necessity of depicting characters as "sighted," "blind," or "partially sighted" obviated any additional identifying markers other than those of gender. Mehta's work will not be remembered for its depiction of southern race relations, nor is he likely to be embraced as a "southern" writer. In this sense, my focus has been admittedly artificial—one initiated by his rare asides, but more significantly by what I see as a series of discursive convergences surrounding the depiction of multiple cultural differences as they intersect and come to structure one another. *Sound-Shadows* can be read as a pro-integrationist text at least in regard to the blind. To draw a simple racial analogy in this regard, even one derived from the very overdetermined historical context of the narrative, would underplay the inconsistencies within its treatment of multiple axes of difference. He expresses outrage for the plight of the "Negro," but fears being mistaken for one. He questions the arbitrary visual distinction between white and black, but accepts visual distinctions among women as indicators of their worth. He exposes the systemic prejudices of the sighted, but counters them with an individualist philosophy. In this, he cannot imagine what lies outside the scope of his vision—disabled rights or the broader movement that served as its symbolic origin, civil rights.

The end of *Sound-Shadows* finds Ved graduating and leaving the South for the West. His tone is not one of bitterness in spite of his feeling that he has been overly sheltered in ways that work against his goal of becoming "a well-adjusted member of the seeing society outside" (428). As he leaves Little Rock, a school administrator asks him, "Son, what's the most precious thing that you're taking from us?" and he replies without hesitation, "Mobility" (430). As Mehta was no doubt aware, by 1985, mobility in Little Rock had come to signify something else. Ironically, another school for the blind figures tangentially into that other history of integration, mobility, and border crossing between separate spheres. In defiance of court orders, Governor Orval Faubus called out the Arkansas National Guard in September 1957 to prevent the integration of Little Rock Central High School. While the other members of the "Little Rock Nine," the African American students attempting to enroll, decided to meet off campus and enter the school in a body surrounded by white and black ministers, Elizabeth Eckford failed to receive the message: her home lacked a telephone. Eckford's lone attempt to integrate public education entered collective visual memory in the form of photographs taken by Will Counts who was covering the standoff for the *Arkansas Democrat*. His images capture her stoicism in the face of adversity, her ramrod straight posture and carefully cultivated indifference as a white woman curses her back.

According to Eckford's account of that day, she is turned away from the door of the school three times by armed Guardsmen as anti-integrationist protesters surround her. Holding her emotions in check, she makes it to a bus stop bench as the mob circles, taunting her with epithets about lynching. Ultimately, she escapes through the intervention of a sympathetic white woman who steers her to a city bus. According to Eckford's story, the bus delivers her to "the School for the Blind" where her mother works in the laundry room.[10]

It is not, however, the school that Mehta attended, but the Negro School for the Deaf and Blind in the same city. Contrary to his literalizing a color-blind world, the site cannot be a place where black and white no longer signify, but the very indication that no such place exists. This is the telling irony of Mehta's story of separation, integration, and mobility in Little Rock of the 1950s: 400 pages and not a black person in sight.

## Racial Disconnection, Racial Paranoia

In seeking to recover the historicity lurking within Asian American narratives (not) about race, my reading of the places where the illusion of objectivity breaks down in Mehta's and Kim's autobiographical writing may appear to be overly subtle. I am arguing, in part, that the work of white supremacy is not always dramatic and clear cut but nuanced; in the subject's struggle against making conscious his social demotion, the anxieties of intermediacy come to the surface as avoidance or elision. Jamaica Kincaid's assertion, "Everyone in every place needs a boundary; in America the boundary is the phrase 'I am not black,'" takes on another resonance (1997, 73). Internalizing the phrase is not necessarily proof of cultural assimilation; rather, it can also be read as resisting American norms particularly as they apply to racial self-consciousness. As in chapters 2 and 3, the cultural work of such disavowal may be abundantly obvious—for example, denying that black intermarriage within American Indian or Chinese American communities has taken place. Here, memoir likewise indicates the ways in which "not-blackness" takes shape. That boundary becomes a structuring narrative absence akin to Toni Morrison's concept of the Africanist presence that underwrites canonical American literature: "Even when American texts are not 'about' Africanist presences, or characters or narrative or idiom," she writes, "the shadow hovers in implication, in sign, in line of demarcation" (1992, 45). Kincaid's boundary is not merely the African American subject, but a metaphoric repression of, in Morrison's words, "reined-in, bound, suppressed, and repressed darkness" (1992). Tracing "the shadow" represents a significant critical methodology appropriate to "minor" canons as well, here, Asian American memoir. Like Morrison, I have great faith in what lies beyond the frame of either historical or self-imagining.

What I inscribe here is more broadly a method of reading that reflects the Freudian dialectic between exposure and concealment echoing Paul Ricoeur's "hermeneutics of suspicion." The contradictions within rhetorical expression become signs of the repressions necessary to maintain the illusion of wholeness against the pressures of cultural ambiguity. In other words, the unevenly oppressed produce uneven testimonies. For example, Nobuo Honda's account of the time he spent in Georgia while stationed at Fort Benning in 1951 not only provides evidence of Asian status under Jim Crow, but works to establish Asian and African American coalitional sympathy by paralleling the plantation legacies of the South and Hawaii. Honda's racial advocacy, the assertion of solidarity among people of color, likewise produces its own ambiguities. The website, "The History of Jim Crow" recounts the Japanese American serviceman's experiences on a bus in Atlanta where he has taken a seat in the back row only to be motioned forward by the driver. Honda recalls:

> When I reached him, he pointed to a seat up toward the front and said, "Soldier, you sit here." Being new to the United States, I did not want to argue with the bus driver so even though I didn't know the reason, I acquiesced to his order. After a few minutes sitting up front, I began to realize what was happening—that I was in the American South where they have different rules and regulations where Blacks all sit in the back of the bus. Not wanting to cause any disturbances, I just obeyed the customs and rules of the American South. When I got off the bus in Fort Benning, I had to choose between the black and white bathrooms. Not being black or white, I nevertheless made the conscious choice to go to the white bathroom. After having been scolded by the bus driver, I didn't want to get into any more trouble. (www.jimcrowhistory.org)

In many ways, Honda's account reflects the textual anxieties that erupt in narratives of interstitiality, anxieties that have been the focus of this and the preceding chapter. On the surface, it testifies to Asian "near whiteness" if read simply as ethnographic evidence. Of course, it may certainly be that the primary sign being read here is not Asianness but the uniform. As if to echo this resonance, Honda's rhetoric reflects an almost military hierarchy that oddly refuses to recognize his place on the bus as a sign of favor, marking it instead as submission. Changing seats is represented as the acquiescence to a command that he "just obeyed" as a newcomer to the United States (n.b.: Hawaiian statehood came in 1959), a country that he has nonetheless (and with all the ironies attending Japanese American treatment on the mainland during World War II) sworn to serve. Honda's "choice" is a calculated concession ("I didn't want to get into any more trouble;" "I just obeyed"). Moreover, such testimony is itself not uniform: as K. Scott Wong reveals in his study of Asian Americans in World War II, other veterans reveal, for example, that a Hawaiian regiment sent to Camp McCall, North Carolina years earlier "would not accept 'their Place' in the South," would flirt with white women, and therefore "had a lot of trouble" (2005, 151). Like the dual testimony that historian Judy Yung portrays regarding the public rituals of assimilative femininity in the previous chapter, this account of favored status simultaneously calls to mind its inverse, Honda's experience as a subject of racial prejudice.

"That was my first introduction to Jim Crow in the South, but not to discrimination," Honda continues. He goes on to parallel his awareness of African American treatment under segregation to his experiences growing up in Hawaii on a Dole plantation, a "highly discriminatory society" with residential segregation by ethnic and racial groups. The parallel explains, indirectly, why he represents his favored status in the South as submission to white authority: it is simply an extension of the life he has been leading in a company town where power likewise accrues to race. The website upon which his testimony appears is intended as a resource for teachers developing units on southern segregation; it includes the helpful but weighty question: "How was the type of discrimination Mr. Honda experienced as a boy on Lanai the same or different than southern Jim Crow discrimination?" In citing parallel forms of racial inequity and discrimination against "non-whites," those "settlers" imported from Asia to work the plantations, Honda omits a crucial reference that would mirror the triadic social hierarchy of his example in the South: an indigenous underclass. The displaced native Hawaiians here are subsumed within the distinction between whites and "non-whites" or rendered otherwise invisible. His interstitial placement on the islands remains veiled in his attempt to establish coalitional sympathy with African Americans. Yet his decision not to mark an existing hierarchy among "non-whites" occludes his slightly privileged status as ethnically Japanese on Lanai. That history exists merely as a trace that haunts his depiction of discrimination, an uneasiness likewise reflected in his previous account of seemingly coerced white identification in his encounter with Jim Crow conventions. In effect, his coalitional gesture, he is "like blacks," is predicated on an absence, what is not said about who occupies the symbolic position of racial abjection in the caste system on the plantation in Hawaii or just beyond its boundaries. The poetics of affirmation take the same shape as the poetics of disconnection.

In readings such as these, I highlight the complexity of what it means to be caught in the middle, a complexity that reveals itself within the spaces of rhetorical disjunction. Race flares up against overt intent: other motives surrounding Ved's move out of the dorms into a broom closet, what goes unsaid within Kim's depictions of southern hospitality. In emphasizing the pressure that elision places on interstitial narratives, I am aware that my project here might be characterized as critical paranoia. That is, why read racism where it is not manifest? Why read what is not really there?

In two cases in which I previewed sections of this work, this seemed to be the question. My interest in the "partly colored" derives from personal curiosity, what my Chinese American parents did not say about growing up in Jim Crow culture. I speculate on the very dynamics that I engage here, how people create stories that allow them to detach from potentially leveling experiences, in an essay entitled, "Meditations of the 'Partly Colored'" (2007). In exploring my parents' responses to their experiences— my mother's self-directed preference *not* to socialize with white people, my father's being cheated out of being named valedictorian—I suspected that there was another story to be told, one about the ways in which we rationalize the limitations that culture places on us. In discovering that a retired academic who, like my parents, had grown up Chinese in the South was circulating the piece electronically, I invited him, a social scientist, to share his response with me. His commentary was polite, but corrective. "You can never know what your parents felt about being Chinese in Arkansas," he wrote. "Indeed, you imply that even they didn't know . . . or that their views were inaccurate because they did not match what you thought they would be." His comments are a salutary reminder that one cannot simply write over the stories told by others, to submit them to another kind of erasure. The will to recast these narratives into a post–Civil Rights perspective is no less a product of history. It would be a violation, an affront—paranoid, even—to point a finger as if to say, "You experienced racism and didn't know it!" On the other hand, there is this disciplinary divide: where the social scientist looks for accuracy in ethnography, I look for multiple and conflicting truths.

In another instance, my attempt to bring narrative anxiety to light was likewise received with uneasiness. In a subtle response to my reading of *An Asian Anthropologist in the South*, after our panel at a professional conference, a Korean American anthropologist mentioned in a brief but pointed aside: "I know Professor Kim. He has done *very* well. He's *very* well respected." It was a rebuke: she let me know that Choong Soon Kim holds real status in the real world. On a more figurative level, I could not help but hear behind her words, "Professor Kim is definitely not 'colored'—*and neither am I*." My reading had been received as an attempt to level Kim's professional standing and perhaps his ethnic identity as well, while on the contrary, I was attempting to establish the significance of his work, albeit not in the way he intended. Ironically, I read this aside along the same lines that I approach Kim's text itself, the ways in which we work to defend against the implication that we are, even by proximity, somehow made to be lesser. Here, as in the text, the individual resists a potential loss of cultural capital via an association with one who has been (unfairly?) disrespected, whether professionally, racially, ethnically, or generationally.

The anthropologist's brief comment may also have been a reaction to my attempt to turn the ethnographic gaze back on the ethnographer, a disciplinary breach—of etiquette, of critical method. The exchange brings to mind the more emotional story that anthropologist Ruth Behar recounts concerning her response to two literary critics at a meeting of the American Ethnological Society (Behar 1996). Behar tells the story about taking two English professors to task for their insensitive reading of anthropologist Renato Rosaldo's essay, "Grief and a Headhunter's Rage." Famously depicting the death of Rosaldo's wife, anthropologist Michelle Zimbalist Rosaldo, during fieldwork in the Philippines, the essay is written in the first person; at the meeting, the critics apparently offer an interpretation of Rosaldo's mourning his wife as a conduit to putting himself in the place of his indigenous subjects, allowing him to feel as they feel.[11] In response, Behar finds that the agency that these white male critics grant Michelle Rosaldo is patronizing; moreover, they are "disrespectful and insensitive in the way they speak about her as merely a body" (171). Their reading is an affront, she argues, akin to talking about someone when he is not in the room—an affront somewhat literalized in her speculation that the author in question, Renato Rosaldo, is himself just outside the conference room door. It is their very objectivity that is insensitive, unfeeling.

In both cases, mine and the white, male English professors', the inability to bridge disciplines—the difference between "real" and textual bodies—was coded as disrespect. For the literary critic, "Kim" and "Michelle" cease to be parents, spouses, or anthropologists and become rhetorically constructed personas, a shift that defines one risk in writing personally.[12] Yet in her affirmation of that intermediate space between the professional and personal, one bumpily traversed, Behar asserts, "anthropology that doesn't break your heart just isn't worth doing anymore" (177). What strikes me is not her call for disciplinary change, an affirmation of risk-taking and a place for emotion, but the value we assign to detachment. Kim's work reflects Behar's call in structure but not in content: the anthropologist has put himself within the frame of analysis while studiously avoiding a pedagogy of affect. Nevertheless, what I have tried to show is that there is also pathos in disconnection, in the *retreat* to objectivity. In other words, detachment can also break your heart.

Reading racial latency may represent a paranoid critical method, yet paranoia may not merely represent a delusional will to see what is not really there, but a particularly appropriate means of "outing" the uneven or seemingly secondary and underacknowledged effects of southern racism. I use that term deliberately because, as Eve Kosofsky Sedgwick has theorized, "paranoia" has become a means of describing the dominant hermeneutic practice within queer literary reading. Critics, she argues, have wrested paranoia away from Freud and his concept of pathologically repressed homosexual desire in order to define a critical practice that places faith, for one, in exposure. Following the work of Guy Hocquenghem, Sedgwick establishes a methodology of suspicion intrinsic to the critical enterprise of queer theory:

> If paranoia reflects the repression of same-sex desire, Hocquenghem reasoned, then paranoia is a uniquely privileged site for illuminating not homosexuality itself, as in the Freudian tradition, but rather precisely the mechanisms of homophobic and heterosexist enforcement against it. What is illuminated by an understanding of paranoia is not how homosexuality works, but how homophobia and heterosexism work. (Sedgwick 1997, 6)

My conceptual parallel to race then presumes the latency of southern racism and its repression within the residually "colored." The discursive interruption becomes its symptom, one resurrected within the (multiply suspicious) critical enterprise. Mine is, as Sedgwick outlines for "paranoia," a practice that places "extraordinary stress on the efficacy of knowledge per se—knowledge in the form of exposure" (17).

Nevetheless, Brian Carr questions "paranoid interpretation" as a critical strategy, noting that "When a queer hermeneutic is nearly indistinguishable in structure from the cultural logic of homosexuality, the queer project finds itself complicit with the homophobic imperative to read for homosexuality. Homophobia and the critical reading of homosexuality often share an interpretive impulse to identify homosexuality's flare up, the betraying gesture, outbreak, or textual symptom" (2004, 288). His methodological caution clarifies the interpretive practice at the center of this chapter, which reads the "flare up, the betraying gesture, outbreak, or textual symptom" of racism within texts that (partially) refuse to name it as such or become visible only through analogy. Carr's wariness also seems appropriate given the two self-reflective examples I discuss here. Yet there seems to be a fundamental difference between interpretative projects that aim to resurrect the traces of either racial or homosexual latency in order to pathologize its "closeted" object versus those that attempt to identify and understand the effect and scope of such repression, the historical and material consequences that drive it to the surface only within the discursive trace. I mark my critical enterprise as "paranoia" disingenuously; convincing of the idea that Asian Americans in the South repress unequal racial treatment might be as simple as drawing yet another analogy: would one presume to say that seeing racism's latency in southern African American literature likewise represents a critical projection? Rather, one might be delusional for refusing to see it.[13]

As in the previous chapter, in highlighting the anxieties of the "partly colored," I want to register culture's incomplete work and incompletion as a function of interstitiality itself. My reading of Mehta's and Kim's accounts of the South, like those of my parents, does not intend to make an ethical judgment about the accuracy of one's self-knowledge, but hopes to illuminate what is part and parcel of living in a hostile environment. Freud's theory of "reaction formation," defense mechanisms that prevent the ego from making conscious sources of anxiety or threat, has become synonymous in pop psychology with denial or self-deceit. But denial is not merely a form of self-protection, but a social balm, a coping mechanism that is inherent to forging community. In *Almost White*, Brewton Berry's African American informant notes regarding mixed-race American Indians confronted with segregated railways, "I feel sorry for those people. They don't know where they belong. . . [T]hose Red Legs, they don't know when they supposed to get on, and they don' know where to sit. That's how they are all the time, and I feels sorry for 'em" (cited in Berry 1963, 70). Yet his pity may be misplaced; in effect, there is no doubt that they reconciled ambiguous belonging in ways that allowed them to lead their lives as best they could. They most probably did not "feel sorry" for themselves despite the sentiment expressed in the preface to Charles S. Johnson's *Patterns of Negro Segregation*, "[I]t may still be observed without any implication of such defense [of segregation] that human beings *seem to prefer a definite and understandable social role to one that is ambiguous*, even though that role be one in justice unacceptable" (cited in Johnson 1943, xi; emphasis added). As the southern memoirs here reveal, the subject has the wherewithal to render potentially dehumanizing treatment consistent with his self-knowledge—even as a counter-narrative to that understanding may surface. My point is that in reading interstitially, interpretation can, like the subject, go either way—and both have their uses.

In the American South, the figure of the Asian outsider may not immediately signify within the norms of place. The presence or absence of historical referent marks the difference between, for example, the "foreign student" and the despised "Paki." This is something that Avtar Brah learns upon her permanent move to Britain after being rendered stateless as a result of Idi Amin's explusion of South Asians from Uganda. "I was no longer a 'foreign' student, a visitor on a temporary sojourn [in Britain]," she writes. "Rather,

I was now constituted within the discourse of 'Paki' as a racialised insider/outsider, a post-colonial subject constructed and marked by everyday practices at the heart of the metropolis" (1996, 9). With settlement comes the loss of a neutral point of identification: she is no longer seen as transient, alone, and therefore inconsequential to her host culture, but inextricably part of a community vilified over time through the work of colonialism. One could say that Brah's survival and ability to flourish depend upon this recognition of how she is seen. On the other hand—in the spirit of what I have focused on here—one could also say the opposite.

In the context of the United States, there's a cost to racial consciousness, whether black or white. When writer Minnie Bruce Pratt becomes aware of the ways in which her "home" in southern white womanhood has been underwritten by injustice, she recounts that the breakthrough "did not feel like liberation, but like destruction" (1984, 36). And Ralph Ellison writes, "It is only when the individual, whether white or black, *rejects* the pattern [of segregationist southern culture] that he awakens to the nightmare of his life" (1964, 92). The "nightmare" here is not simply being at odds with home or place, but being asked to question the very foundations of the self, the certainty of one's own humanity and its autonomy. It is easy to see why this consciousness might be resisted: the stakes are too high. Still, the dynamics I have traced here are not so much akin to what Ellison has written regarding Richard Wright, that the challenge for Wright was not simply to reject the white South, but to "reject that part of the South which lay within" (92). Instead, what I've witnessed here are the points prior to that, the resistances to internalizing that "part of the South" that would coerce the subject into seeing himself as even partly "colored." What these Asian American authors reveal is not necessarily empirical experience of what I have been calling racial interstitiality, but the ways in which it is resisted. In this sense, Asian American literature reflects the central struggle of southern letters, the struggle between blacks and whites—even where none appear.

# Productive Estrangement

*Racial-Sexual Continuums in Asian
American as Southern Literature*

You are a stranger here. I can tell by the way you do.

Sexuality is an overdetermined category in southern discourse. As
Patti Duncan bluntly puts it, the perception is that "southerners have this
really perverse, fucked up sexuality" (2001, 38). Donna Jo Smith asserts that
the "terms *southern* and *queer* both come laden with a host of stereotypes"
so much so that "the term *southern queer* is redundant." She asks, "Since the
South is already an aberration, what is a southern queer but deviance multi-
plied? In other words, did Truman Capote really need to tell the world that
he was a pervert? After all, he was from south Alabama" (1997, 370). Such
an insight complicates Duncan's own claims to sexual difference as an Asian
lesbian living in the South. She notes regarding Asian and Pacific Islander
lesbians in Atlanta,

> [C]laiming that we're sexually different in the South . . . raises all kinds
> of issues for me, here we are being told that the South already has this
> really deviant sexuality, and then here we are as queer women and as Asian
> Americans and Pacific Islanders being told that our sexuality must be per-
> verse or different, that we're hypersexual . . . somehow sexually wrong.
> (2001, 38)

Embracing "deviance" does not authenticate her regional identity despite
C. Vann Woodward's reference to the South as "the perverse section" of the
nation (1951, xi); instead, Duncan's sense of herself as Asian and lesbian is
continually measured against her claim to belonging. For her and the other
members of her Asian lesbian support group, such a claim is symbolically
contested by the intensity of scrutiny from both whites and blacks on the

most basic of levels: "It's like, Is it a boy or a girl? Is it black or white?"( 2001, 37). The obsessive attention causes them to question, "Is it because we're dykes?" [or is it that] "we're just foreign" (37)?

The speculation, dykes or foreigners, offers a symmetry of exclusions: both transgenderism and Asianness are categories of difference that confuse understanding of normative oppositions—boy/girl, black/white—that locate her in southern culture. Her outsidedness is rendered somewhat ironic by the symbolic role that immigrants play in the New South; they testify to its cosmopolitanism, its connection to the global. As Bharati Mukherjee ventriloquizes a white, southern yuppie, "Dear old redneck Atlanta is a thing of the past, no need to feel foreign here. Just wheel your shopping cart through aisles of *bok choy* and twenty kinds of Jamaican spices at the Farmers' Market, and you'll see that the US of A is still a pioneer country" (1988, 79). The portrayal invigorates aberrant southern regionalism with national resonance: the new migrants render its purported parochialism into a vision consistent with America itself, dislodging its antiquated reputation. But the cheerful disclaimer that all Americans were once foreigners belies the specificity of Duncan's meaning. A seeming outsider to the South's sexual and racial mores, she is a figure of forced intelligibility. Representing as neither a boy nor girl, she becomes a site of cultural anxiety in more than one arena; she becomes an occasion of interpretive necessity.

But in what sense can this uneasiness signal a site of productive reinvisioning? In the context of segregation, one's outsidedness might be gauged by a failure to apprehend local racial etiquette—a perhaps felicitous failure. In the 1940s, sociologist Charles Johnson recounts an anecdote about an African American traveler from the North who takes his place in line with white patrons at a post office in Mississippi. "This was so unusual that it attracted the attention of both Negroes and whites," Johnson writes. "The surprised white people made no comment, but one of the Negroes who [was] patiently waiting until the white people were through remarked to the visitor, 'You are a stranger here. I can tell by the way you do'" (1943, 38). The actions of the unschooled visitor mirror the cultural norms of place in discomfiting ways. The outsider not yet assimilated into established modes of behavior and expectation unsettles the surface of convention, or, to echo Park in the previous chapter, breaks the "cake of custom" (1928, 885). In Johnson's anecdote, the stranger literally cuts the line, assuming an unsanctioned place within the established hierarchy.

Defined as that which is "introduced from outside into a place where it does not belong," the foreigner is a figure of only partial comprehensibility, one that must be self-consciously interpreted into the context of the local. He is nonetheless essential to collective definition. As I have noted elsewhere, accusations of betrayal work to secure group cohesion and define the borders of communal belonging (2001). Thus, as Julia Kristeva notes, "the foreigner lives within us: he is the hidden face of our identity" (1991, 1). This dynamic underlies Constantin Cavafy's "Waiting for the Barbarians," in which a community's fearful anticipation of "the barbarians" is replaced with the opposite anxiety:

> [N]ight has fallen and the barbarians have not come.
> And some who have just returned from the border say
> there are no barbarians any longer.
> And now, what's going to happen to us without barbarians?
> They were, those people, a kind of solution. (1995)

The invention of "the barbarian" does not require reciprocal awareness either of the appellation or the implication of inferiority that accompanies it. Edward Said writes, "It is enough for 'us' to set up these boundaries in our own minds; 'they' become 'they' accordingly, and both their territory and their mentality are designated as different from 'ours'" (1978, 54). These abstract processes of assigning communal, often national differences are not simply reversible between the First and Third Worlds: witness the codification of cultural differences into racial distinctions as a justification for colonization. Thus, although the inhabitants of the remote Swiss village where James Baldwin takes up residence have never seen a black man, the history of European colonialism nonetheless informs their collective relation to him, a lone "African."[1] Baldwin is not merely an object of wonder, but also something less. "People are trapped in history and history is trapped in them," he writes in "Stranger in the Village" (1955, 163); that is, they are already enmeshed in what Immanuel Wallerstein recognizes as the "international status group" of race and its "basic division between Whites and non-Whites" (1991 199).

In the context of American history, the use of the racialized stranger for national self-definition belies the image of the United States as a crucible of immigrant acceptance. For Asians in particular, belief in the unassimilability of the "Oriental" was foundational to the 1790 Naturalization Law restricting naturalized citizenship to whites and, in the 19th century, the escalation of racial exclusion laws first levied against the Chinese and later extending to other Asian nationalities. As Lisa Lowe notes, "[T]he figuration of the Asian immigrant as a transgressive and corrupting 'foreignness' . . . continues to make 'Asians' an object of the law, in the political sphere, as well as national culture" (1996, 19). The Asian "stranger" produces anxiety over the coherence of the national body, an anxiety that serves a collective function, securing cohesion out of the spectre of Asian difference.

In contrast, as I discuss in the previous chapter, Asian/American writers Ved Mehta and Choong Soon Kim attempt to exploit the cultural innocence of the stranger by positioning their status as foreigners as the occasion for postures of strategic dispassion toward southern conventions. Yet their uneven attempts at self-location reveal an inability to remain aloof from American race relations despite their presumed distance. Their uneasiness about their proximity to African Americans contrasts their liberalism, their overt sentiments opposing segregation in its formal or de facto forms. But in what ways can detachment represent a strategic response to embedded southern race relations? Here, I want to take narratives of Asian "foreignness" to southern culture in another direction, shifting to Asian American texts produced from a post–Civil Rights perspective and deliberately playing off southern histories of social division and their continuing legacies. These texts mark the revisionist potential of racial intermediacy, situating it as a fluid template against which white southern collectivity is performed. This chapter (and the next) deviate from previous chapters that focus on interstitiality as a social location subject to cultural pressures of incorporation and repudiation; rather, Asian American literature about the South deliberately engages the oscillation between positionalities within the South's historical racial dyad in order to expose the stakes that underlie lines of affiliation and division, lines that go beyond those defined by color.

The pathology of difference is not merely racial but, as readers of southern literature well know, sexual. I have heretofore explored the notion of a racial continuum legislated by the poles black and white in order to reveal the cultural anxieties surrounding the "partly colored." Social status is decided in part via proximity to an idealized, invisible norm, or, conversely, a stigmatized racial community. But race is only one arena of cultural location; my focus on the South's racial continuum finds an analogue in feminist theorist Gayle Rubin's 1984 "Thinking Sex: Notes for a Radical Theory of the Politics of Sexuality," which unveils a covert continuum of sexual practices from invisibly normative, and thus socially sanctioned, to deviant.[2] Rubin focuses on the prosecution of subjects whose erotic behaviors have marked them as targets of social and community discipline during periods of sexual panic. "Sexuality in Western societies," she notes, "has been structured within an extremely punitive social framework, and has been subjected to very real formal and informal controls" (1993, 10). In the course of highlighting examples of the ways in which individuals and groups are stigmatized across historical periods and geographies—from reforms over prostitution in the Victorian era to homosexuality during the McCarthy era—Rubin argues that sex acts are placed within a "hierarchical system of sexual value" wherein heterosexual, marital, monogamous, reproductive sex represents the standard against which other sexual practices are negatively evaluated.[3] Thus, in her view, a radical theory of sex "must identify, describe, explain, and denounce erotic injustice and sexual oppression" while developing a "critical language that can convey the barbarity of sexual persecution" (9). In effect, "Thinking Sex" offers a framework for understanding the ways in which social status becomes assigned according to values placed on a continuum of erotic practices—from natural to illicit, from "vanilla" to perverse, from healthy to immoral.

Rubin depicts the sequence of ever-increasing sexual pathology in two graphics, one portraying concentric circles and another, brick walls. In the first, a small circle represents the "charmed inner circle" of socially approved sex: at home, same generation, married, heterosexual, not for money, etc., while the larger, surrounding circle represents its "outer boundaries"—those acts deemed "bad, abnormal, unnatural, damned." In the second graphic, three walls demarcate the borders between acceptable and unacceptable sexual practices: between "healthy" sex, acts subject to suspicion and social condemnation—areas of "contest"—and, finally, the most despised "sexual castes," which include "transsexuals, transvestites, fetishists, sadomasochists, sex workers such as prostitutes and porn models, and the lowliest of all, those whose eroticism transgresses generational boundaries" (12). The "walls" separating poles on a continuum of sexual practices from normative to "queer" represent moral lines that distinguish between erotic behaviors; as Rubin notes, "Arguments are then conducted over 'where to draw the line,' and to determine what other activities, if any may be permitted to cross over into acceptability"—or conversely, those that transcend disapprobation to be characterized as criminal, as cause for prosecution (14).

While Rubin's work elicits controversy, what interests me here is her identification of a sexual continuum from normative to reviled that provides a conceptual analogy to the racial continuum that has been my subject, segregation's legislated distinction between "colored" and white. But my interest lies not in exploring sexual interstitiality, the middle space or erotic buffer zone of "partly" perverse sexual practices. Rather, Rubin's metaphor of crossing the conceptual barrier or wall that creates the sexually abject subject—the pedophile, the queer, the ruined woman—parallels the processes by which culture assigns communal belonging. While I have explored this conceptual polarity as the uneasy oscillation between white normativity and black abjection that the "partly colored" negotiate, Rubin's work names another axis by which individuals must likewise approximate an idealized norm or become subject to the disciplining and punitive community or state sanctions that legislate individual behavior. In highlighting the ways in which proximity to presumed sexual aberration levels status, Rubin's work identifies a sexual line akin to the color line, one that likewise does not become manifest until it is transgressed.[4]

The relevance of Rubin's continuum is clear in the context of the "perverse section" of the nation, where rape and miscegenation represent foundational repressions, but perhaps assumes a less obvious connection to the context of racial interstitiality that has been my subject. While I have explored the ways in which intimacy with African Americans became central to the racial status of interstitial subjects—or, as in the previous chapter, the repression of what the subject sees as "colored" within himself—Rubin's work suggests an alternative deciding point. That is, proximity to sexually "deviant" subjects may tip the balance toward the racial degradation of the uneasily placed Asian in the South. How is racial outsidedness reinforced via intimacy with those who have transgressed the boundary between "acceptable" and "unacceptable" erotic practices? To what extent does "foreignness" apply not only to racialized subjects but to sexual acts? In prompting these questions, Asian American literature gestures outward from the material circumstances of segregation that inform the first part of this book toward both the conceptual and contemporary resonances of social division writ large.

Asian American literature is "foreign" to the southern literature for perhaps obvious reasons; authors such as H. T. Tsiang, V. S. Naipaul, Cynthia Kadohata, Lan Cao, Elena Tajima Creef, Patsy Rekdal, Abraham Verghese, Ved Mehta, Patti Duncan, Ha Jin, Susan Choi, Choong Soon Kim, and M. Evelina Galang, who set Asian American prose narratives in the South or inscribe southern Asian American characters, are not widely recognized to be "southern" writers.[5] Nor do they necessarily inherit, as Alice Walker notes regarding southern African American writers, a sense of community or social consciousness that identifies "with remarkably silent accuracy, the people who make up the larger world that surrounds and suppresses [their] own" (1983, 19). Recognition of southern Asian American literature lags behind southern Asian American film: *Mississippi Triangle, Mississippi Masala, Miss India Georgia, Daughter from Danang, The Delta,* and, as I discuss in the next chapter, *Mai's America* assume a more visible profile than their literary counterparts. The lack of awareness may hinge on the belief that Asians in the South move through southern culture without, in Baldwin's words, the "rather desperate advantages of bitterly accumulated perception," without an awareness of the full weight of segregation's prohibitions (1955, 145). Yet that perspective is neither innocent of racism, nor wholly defined by it. This incompletion makes possible, I would claim, an expanded notion of caste. In denormalizing the entrenched social etiquette of race, the outsider might also force scrutiny of embedded sexual conventions and taboos that expand and extend those surrounding anti-miscegenationist fears. This chapter explores another resonance of interstitiality as Asian American writers envision forms of collectivity and intimacy that challenge traditional conceptions of southern belonging and integration in the post-segregation era.

Both Susan Choi's 1998 novel, *The Foreign Student*, and Abraham Verghese's 1994 memoir, *My Own Country: A Doctor's Story of a Town and Its People in the Age of AIDS*, follow Asian protagonists through a Tennessee landscape in order to make visible sexually defined forms of segregation. Choi's novel depicts the delicate relationship between Chang, a foreign student from Korea who arrives in University of the South in the 1950s, and Katherine, a white woman whose sexual reputation has been compromised. In the gradual unfolding of their traumatic pasts—his stemming from the Korean War, and hers from a cross-generational relationship—the text unveils the ways in which seemingly arbitrary lines of affiliation are both policed and transgressed. Abraham Verghese's *My Own Country*, a memoir of his practice in infectious diseases in the early 1980s, represents an early form of AIDS advocacy, but the narrative is as much about the doctor's tenuous attempts at integration, at finding a home, as about his southern and largely white, gay male patients. A "Foreign Medical Graduate," Dr. Verghese passes as an upstanding citizen-worker in his small southern town until he becomes pathologized through an association with his patients, effectively "outing" his racial difference. Both Choi and Verghese draw upon colonial and postcolonial histories of exile order to produce commentaries on domestic race relations, segregation's ongoing legacy, and the unfulfilled promises of democratic enfranchisement in the United States.

In keeping with previous chapters, these works suggest that the "partly colored" subject's movement into white universality is asymptotic and ultimately denied. Highlighting the multiple axes of social status and dual caste systems, they suggest that what refuses this movement is proximity to projected sexual perversity. Both Choi and Verghese uncover an alternative political valence to racial interstitiality: Asian "foreignness" becomes the conduit to exposing the division not between white and black but between other lines that define superiority and inferiority, normativity and deviance. In twinning Rubin's grid of sexual practices alongside what I have been positing as an American racial continuum exaggerated in southern culture, I want to explore the ways in which belonging and exclusion are defined by the lines drawn between monogamy and promiscuity, heterosexuality and homosexuality, wellness and contagion.

## *The Racial DMZ: Susan Choi's* The Foreign Student

> [T]he so-called non-West's turn toward the West is a command.
> That turn was not in order to fulfill some longing to consolidate
> a pure space for ourselves, that turn was a command.
> —Gayatri Chakravorty Spivak

Linking the fall of Jim Crow culture and international politics, historian Mary Dudziak has shown that American concerns about its image as a democratic world power were instrumental in dismantling segregation as a formal system and hastening civil rights legislation.[6] Highlighting the interaction between domestic race politics and foreign policy in the postwar period, she notes that the demonstrations against integration in 1957 Little Rock "threatened to undermine the narrative of race and democracy carefully told in U.S. propaganda" (2000, 16). Race prejudice was, in the words of Ralph Ellison, part of America's "soiled democratic linen" compromising its reputation abroad as the Cold War began to escalate (1964, 313). Susan Choi's 1998 novel, *The Foreign Student*, likewise implicates the southern segregation in global politics in its portrayal of the Korean War and Sewanee, Tennessee during the 1950s through the eyes of an immigrant protagonist, once called Chang and newly dubbed "Chuck." While the novel draws a parallel between international human rights in postcolonial Asia and domestic civil rights in the United States, her novel's post–segregation era perspective is less a literal commentary on rights than a philosophical inquiry into the ways in which imaginary lines of division and affiliation are drawn. At first glance, however, it is simply a love story.

Faulkner scholar Diane Roberts suggests that in *The Foreign Student's* comparison between two "souths," Choi is "helping reinvent the Southern novel for the new millennium." The Asian American author, she writes, "explores race and class but bypasses the expected avenues of Jim Crow, shack dwellers and white columns in favor of looking at the South through the eyes of a man who has no purchase on its magisterial systems of prejudice . . . [Chuck's] civil war, his ruined lands are behind him in Korea" (1998,12L). Yet in depicting Chuck Ahn's movement through a 1955 southern landscape, Choi does not exactly bypass stock features of southern literature, the "shacks" and "white columns" that signify the expanse between black and white, nor does she ignore the other hallmark of southern literature, its veer toward the gothic. As a refugee of indeterminate status and a stranger to southern customs and norms, her Asian American protagonist is the vehicle of the novel's embedded commentary on the artificiality of the color line and the sexual taboos that surround it, but more expansively, its inquiry into the making of social divisions. *The Foreign Student* is not merely a meditation on reading difference between black and white, but turns back, in Spivak's words, the "command" function of the West by engaging Korean history in its exploration of civil freedoms.

The novel's engagement with the Korean War mines the symbolic resonance of the three-mile border that came to divide north from south. The demilitarized zone or DMZ represents a buffer space; it is the place of intermediacy that stands for a putative neutrality, the space of nonalignment. The DMZ manifested both symbolically and physically at the 38th parallel at the end of the war; in 1945, the temporary line was intended to demarcate areas of American and Russian authority in administering the Japanese surrender from the peninsula. The expedient division assumed greater stakes in the ensuing civil war between two newly established states, the Republic of Korea under President Syngman Rhee and the Korean People's Republic under Premier Kim Il Sung, both nations buttressed by competing superpowers.[7] For Choi, this history becomes an abstract meditation on the formation of lines of division and affiliation: "The thirty-eighth parallel ceased to be a set of points sharing an angular distance from the equator, and manifested itself as a thing. . . . When each nation set about establishing a Korean government under its own auspices, on its own terms, and in its own zone, the thirty-eighth parallel ceased to be a line and became a border, and soon was not only a border, but one made of mirrors" (Choi 1998, 64). Affecting a tone of objectivity, Choi blunts a critique of American stewardship. Her careful approach might be attributed not so much to politics as to distance: she has acknowledged that she had little awareness of Korea or the Korean War, growing up watching the television show, *M\*A\*S\*H*.[8] Her character's clumsy attempt to sketch this civil war for his American audiences in the South highlights this haziness. In a telling parallel between the two sites of the novel, Choi writes that Chuck "would groundlessly compare the parallel to the Mason-Dixon line, and see every head nod excitedly" (51). But the association between two nations here is not entirely groundless; the interspersed narratives, one in 1950 South Korea told in flashback and the other set in the novel's present time, the United States in 1955, are bound by their historical proximity and more significantly, by their abstract resonance. The 38th parallel is represented as an arbitrarily enforced line, one that is simultaneously irrational and worth dying for. In the context of American history, the once purely geographically descriptive Mason-Dixon line became invested with similarly heightened stakes. The two civil war histories allow Choi to hold up to scrutiny the processes underlying national and regional boundary-making and the ways in which these "imaginary" lines that specify allegiance and belonging become punitively enforced. The novel mines other metaphors to suggest this resonance as well.

In highlighting Chang's role in South Korea as a translator for an American news service agency, for example, Choi foregrounds her protagonist as himself a figure who requires interpretation: "Chang had done enough translation already to know that there weren't ever even exchanges. You wanted one thing to equal another, to slide neatly into its place, but somehow this very desire made the project impossible. In the end there was always a third thing, that hadn't existed before" (67). In suggesting the symbolic implications of translation, the passage reflects what Lowe sees as the intrinsic infidelity of translation, its lack of faithfulness to an original (1994). Translation thus signifies betrayal, but also becomes a metaphor for the impossibility of fixing meaning, an impossibility that extends to the sociopolitical world, especially one already in flux. Derided for his disingenuous belief that he does not have to take sides in the war, Chang leaves others to translate or (mis)interpret where he stands; he himself is a figure of inexact correspondence. The novel's second portrayal of graphic bodily violation, Chang's torture by agents of the South Korean government, is based on a misalignment of his identity—he is taken to be a traitor and a spy for North Korea even as he has been previously accused of collaborating with the Americans. Chang has no place in either emerging nation because he claims no allegiance and cannot fit into the dyad required by war: "He was the third thing . . . Translation's unnatural by-product" (84).

The contentious realm of postwar politics finds its correspondence in the social divisions of the segregated South where Chang, incongruously rechristened, "Chuck," also lacks a straightforward place. The novel's discourse on the arbitrariness of the 38th parallel, the line that divides the peninsula into north and south as a result of civil war, finds its analog in the United States as Chuck occupies a racial DMZ between the lines that define other forms of political community. The novel's engagement with international history exists not merely as a backdrop to characterization—even as it echoes a stock feature of migrant narrative, that a traumatic past travels across geographic expanses to elucidate a present conflict in the diaspora. Nor is the reader meant to see, as one reviewer optimistically put it, that "the Souths of Korea and Tennessee—are not that different after all."⁹ Rather, the two locations suggest a conceptual parallel; both are invested in the imaginary lines that define, in a visceral way, inclusion and exclusion. Reversing the usual hierarchy of the West as a primary lens through which to read the developing world, Choi situates Asia as a vehicle for a commentary on domestic race relations, here, from the perspective of the interstitial Asian, the foreign student.

"Translation" applies to the slippage of social meanings assigned to people; once in the South, Chang/Chuck's status as an unnatural "third thing" describes his racial standing, which rests in inexact measure somewhere within Jim Crow's embedded continuum. The former translator must be translated into the etiquette of place; in Tennessee, he is repeatedly situated as an object of both impassive and malicious surveillance. The signs of Chuck's privilege, his near-white status, remain unmarked in the novel: he "integrates" the University of the South as an outsider who yet lives as an equal among the region's native sons; his presence in "whites-only" establishments is observed but not prohibited. Roberts implies Chuck's symbolic standing by placing Choi's depiction of his prewar past in the context of the antebellum South; in Korea, Roberts notes, Chang is gentry, a man of the manor with servants and a landed country house. Her parallel locates the Asian American character within a specific southern literary tradition—the white one. Moreover, *The Foreign Student* makes clear Chuck's distinction from African Americans through the rituals of southern etiquette. A lone resident in student housing during holiday break, Chuck encounters social awkwardness in the kitchen where the "colored" help have their dinner. The absence of white people produces a temporary social vacuum: "'We're glad you're here, Mister Chuck,' Louis said. 'Let me make you a plate.' They had cooked themselves a pan of baked chicken and mashed a pot of potatoes. He found a plate and tried to serve himself, as the others were doing, and Louis physically obstructed him. 'Let me make you a plate,' he said firmly" (166). In portraying the ways in which intermediacy is subject to fixity, Choi makes clear that *Mister* Chuck does not occupy the same place as African

Americans while simultaneously implying that her character's fragile place in society is contingent upon submission to southern conventions practiced by both the elite and subaltern. Yet submission to white authority, even when seemingly benevolent, is, of course, not without cost.

Chuck's foreignness to place becomes a conduit for highlighting the processes of communal self-definition and validation; the stranger, writes Georg Simmel, is "an element of the group itself." This use of the stranger is particularly enforced by Choi's engagement with regionalism: how one reacts to an outsider, Chuck quickly perceives, is a sign of breeding, the hallmark of what creates a certain class of white southerner:

> He felt safe on the mountain because it was a point of pride for the people there that he would prefer Sewanee to his home. They thought of him as a romantic castaway, whose presence among them confirmed everything that was best about themselves. In this way they were like Crane's father, who had viewed his hospitality toward the stranger as the prerogative of a prosperous man. Chuck understood this line of thinking very well, and he understood what was required of him. (145)

What is required of him is a form of what Tina Chen identifies as Asian American "double agency," the imposture of a dominant cultural projection (Chen 2005). The stranger becomes the canvas that provides the template against which communal norms are written, here, with particularly regional resonance: "Manners," V. S. Naipaul recognizes, are "part of the South's idea of itself" (1989, 98).[10] Choi depicts Chuck's acquiescence as both a response to undisclosed post-traumatic stress—a protective guardedness against revealing the self—and as behavior subtly exacted by white supremacy. Chuck accedes to Orientalist expectation in ways that enforce the clear demarcation between the First and Third Worlds. Thus, hints of Korean cosmopolitanism provoke vague disappointment or incredulity in Americans hoping for self-affirming primitivism: "Chuck told Mrs. Crane about his father's library. Something in her excessively attentive listening posture made him feel that she didn't believe him" (59). In Choi's subtle encoding of the Asian's place in the South, the success of Chuck's educational lectures on his homeland hinge upon slides such as, "Village Farmers Squatting Down to Smoke."

In depicting the ways in which Chuck's interactions with whites are bounded by racialized projection, *The Foreign Student* highlights what writers Frank Chin and Jeffrey Paul Chan call "racist love," the idea that others cultivate their superiority through condescension, in this case, the projection of Oriental docility (Chin and Chan 1972). "Racist love," then, might aptly describe southern paternalism toward people of color, a paternalism reflected in, for example, southern sociologist John Shelton Reed's reading of Choong Soon Kim's *An Asian Anthropologist in the South*: "The story of how different Southerners reacted to an unusual stimulus—that is, to Professor Kim—is often fascinating, informative, and (he will know I do not intend the word to be patronizing) charming" (2003, 103). Colonialist paternalism is easily recognizable within the southern legacy of race relations, the mythology of faded gentry notwithstanding. In the case of the "Oriental," difference can be "charming" insofar as it does not disturb; as Chin and Chan bluntly state, "we" are not black. Inclusion, then, is predicated on submission to condescension cloaked in terms of praise ("He knew that for Crane he was an easy and dependable possession, as if at any time Crane might announce to someone, "My man Chuck" (41)) or exaggerated hospitality ("What have you brought us? . . . You are an emissary from a distant land. I hope we can make you feel welcome" (59)). The novel exposes white aristocratic pretension as an extension of the benevolent impulses of colonial education. Thus, Chuck's relationship with a supposed mentor later turned rival, Professor Charles Addison, is "patronizing" both in the literal and figurative senses. Of their casual tutorials purported to help Chuck with English fluency, Choi writes, "mostly their conversations went like this: 'Thistle.' 'Thistle.' 'Thistle!'" (16). Despite his obvious privileges, Chuck is made the object of paternalist interest, a hallmark of Asian racialization within and beyond American borders. Like Korea itself, he both is and is not the real colonial object; he is and is not "colored." Far from revealing that Chang/Chuck represents, in Roberts's words, "a man who has no purchase on [the South's] magisterial systems of prejudice," the novel explores the nuances of Asian placement in the South, which are perhaps less iconographic than those overt acts of violence recorded by African American writers, but are no less informed by the "magisterial" forms of white racism characterized by *noblesse oblige* and Christian-tinged charity. In this sense, Choi's work is a self-conscious rendering of the nuanced behaviors that serve to create the "partly colored" above and beyond those state processes I discuss in chapters 1 and 2.

Choi situates her Asian American protagonist as an object of forced intelligibility, highlighting the processes of scrutiny and judgment that are, in part, how identities become fixed. In keeping with the tradition of southern literature, Choi's interest also lies in sexual behavior; her depiction of her characters' violation of the miscegenation taboo is both subtle and cataclysmic. As I discussed in chapter 1, unlike the Virginia, Georgia, and Mississippi state statutes that expressly prohibited marriage between whites and "Mongolians" prior to 1967, Tennessee did not forbid unions between Asians and whites. In the novel, resistance to Asian-white interracial dating is portrayed through heightened surveillance. The implied coupling between Chuck and Katherine Monroe in Tennessee of the 1950s becomes the occasion not for outrage, but for a muted, yet palpable scrutiny underwritten by the tension of uncertain expectation. The novel thus adds another valence to southern depictions of transgressions of segregation etiquette; when Katherine, a white woman, is on her first social outing with Chuck, the stares they receive push her into the conceptual place of the foreign student, the place of the alien, the stranger:

> They might have been watching a ship come in, Katherine thought. For a moment she could feel it. The arrival in a strange land, and stepping onto the gangplank as the whole harbor paused in its work and turned a single gaze toward you. She stood there with him in a half circle of constant, unshy observation. (Choi 1998, 37)

Their gaze forces Katherine to assume the Asian man's social location as object, while simultaneously suggesting the possibility of a new beginning in the shared position of migrant. Elsewhere, Choi describes reaction to the couple as an "unremitting scrutiny, disguised as politeness" (54) or as the "tension of careful indifference . . . and steady observation" (146). The continuous, electrified air that attends their public presence together—a couple? not a couple?—succeeds in conveying not simply the ripple of interest that surrounds something new to see in the landscape, but a feeling of slight and impending menace. As David Mura reveals about Japanese Americans interned in Arkansas in the 1940s, "There was an unspoken message all about them in the camps, especially in the South: Things are bad now, but they could be worse. We aren't lynching your kind. Yet" (Mura 1995, 236). This tone is enforced by the threat of casual violence that underlies the novel's single reference to lynching; Chuck's white roommate, Crane, lazily speculates about the Klan in his hometown, Atlanta: "They don't hang Orientals . . . There aren't any down there to hang. I don't think they'd know one if they saw him. I wonder if they would hang him. They might mistake him for a nigger and hang him or have the sense to see he's not a nigger and not hang him just because of that" (56–57). In contrast, "going North" for Chuck is marked as a free zone insofar as it promises (racial) anonymity: in Chicago, "no one's gaze seemed to rest on him. He was surrounded and invisible"

(240). The gray zone of Jim Crow culture that the Asian inhabits is simultaneously marked as similar to and distinct from that experienced by African Americans; the novel intimates that the "privilege" of suspended or withheld evaluation is temporary and contingent on unspoken rules—rules that, having not been broken, have yet to become manifest.

Reflecting Patti Duncan's self-consciousness about how the southern gaze interprets and defines, Chuck's comment about being observed unwittingly suggests the active processes of subject construction in its attempt at idiomatic English: "They don't know what to make me," he observes (37). The missing preposition highlights the sense of racial speculation that would write the foreign student into the social hierarchy of place. Because the white locals don't know what (or how) to *make* him, there is no communally agreed upon response to his social outing with a white woman: because he is not black, it avoids overt hostility and confrontation, but because he is not white, their surveillance is uncensored and undisguised. Chuck's response to being the object of a judgment temporarily withheld recalls James Baldwin's sense of being at a disadvantage among the French; Baldwin's expatriate uneasiness is tinged with hopefulness as he notes, "I did not know what they saw when they looked at me" (Baldwin 1955, 145).

What tips the balance of Chuck's fragile social location is, of course, the growing seriousness of his relationship with Katherine. In crossing the color line's sexual taboo, the outward signs indicating that he knows "his place" are shattered by this presumptive claim of equality; an Asian man, he is seen as trying to "become white" by possessing the body of a white woman. Chuck's lack of fluency with both language and culture again affords Choi the opportunity to mine the symbolic resonance of translation and approximate linguistic fluency: Chuck "did not know precisely what boundary he had overstepped, only that there had been one, and that he'd forgotten himself. He tested a phrase he had learned. *'I carry away. I am carried away'*" (156). "I carry away" implies that he has stolen something from another, in this case, Katherine from Charles Addison, her white lover. "I am carried away" constructs him as the incidental object of someone else's volition; placed together, the two phrases imply a reciprocity of action, a mutual theft. The love story is marked as exactly that, but its consequence is unevenly borne; as the novel reveals in a brief aside, the Asian man perhaps predictably suffers a demotion from his racially nebulous, "third thing" status. After being accused of stealing money—of carrying away what does not belong to him—he is stripped of his scholarship and, as a condition of his readmittance to the University of the South, is consigned to the kitchen with African American service workers until his debt can be paid.

This fixing of intermediacy is perhaps foreshadowed by the novel's repeated echoes of canonical African American literature despite—or in addition to—its heralded critical parallel to the tradition of Faulkner. Chuck's movements recall that of African American characters: his trip to Chicago reflects the "Great Migration" of blacks out of the South; the period Chang spends in hiding during the war ("He lived in that hole for three months, from the twenty-ninth of June to *liberation*" (emphasis mine, 102)), evokes Harriet Jacobs's confinement while eluding slave catchers; the irrationality of Chuck's white boss at a book bindery is reminiscent of both Ellison's *Invisible Man* and Wright's account of looking for work in *Black Boy* ("'Boy, do you steal?' Only an idiot would have answered: 'Yes, ma'am. I steal'" (Wright 1993, 172)).[11] As in both southern canons, Choi's novel reveals that transgressing the border makes it real; her Korean character is no longer the "foreign" outsider, but something less. Ultimately, however, it is not the transgression of segregation's interracial sex taboo that links *The Foreign Student* to the tradition of southern gothic. Rather, it is the novel's careful portrayal of pedophilia.

In previous chapters I focused on the ways in which the social space of racial intermediacy hinges upon an interpreted proximity to both literal and figurative conceptions of blackness. *The Foreign Student* suggests that such intermediacy may also be decided via proximity to sexual perversity. I marked the portrayal of Chang's torture—a violation of international human rights—as the novel's *second* rendering of graphic bodily violation. The first is Katherine's rape. Yet "rape" may not register as an accurate descriptor of the novel's representation of cross-generational sex: Choi depicts sex between Charles Addison and 14-year-old Katherine ("Kitty"), between man and child, in the aestheticized language of literary—not sensationalist—fiction and the muted cadences of flashback. Because their relationship is portrayed as consensual and Choi imbues her underage protagonist with desire, the scene stands in marked contrast to the no less crafted, but decidedly more horrific portrayal of child rape in, for example, Dorothy Allison's *Bastard Out of Carolina*.[12] There is nothing about Choi's tone or perspective that bespeaks pedophilia, a practice that Rubin identifies as the "lowliest of all" in the "hierarchical valuation of sex acts" (1993, 11). Moreover, the reader takes the cue of the community in evaluating the "affair," which is not made known until after Katherine achieves the age of consent and then provokes censure of *her*: she is, in Choi's deliberately archaic term, "ruined." Southern tolerance of eccentricity seems only to extend to white men; thus, Addison is not a former pedophile, but a charming rake. Yet Katherine is his "whore" and "[e]verybody knows that" (221).

I invoke Rubin's sexual continuum in the context of the novel not to subject Choi's portrayal of cross-generational eroticism to social discipline, although I would point out that she highlights a gendered and racial double standard regarding sexual transgression. (From the communal viewpoint portrayed in the novel, for example, the derogation "sick business" is reserved for the interracial relationship (221)). Rather, Rubin's work suggests that interstitial social status applies not only to what I have established in this book as segregation's racial continuum, but to a sexual one as well. As a figure who has also crossed the line that defines sexual normativity, Katherine inhabits an uneasy middle space within a sequence of sexual practices that names subjects from normative to deviant. In delaying marriage, Katherine not only refuses what Carole Pateman calls the "sexual contract" for women, but her extramarital affair places her outside the boundaries that define her racial, regional, and gendered subjectivity—white, southern womanhood (Pateman 1988). As in Minnie Bruce Pratt's recognition of the fragility of that idealization, Katherine has stepped outside "that protected circle . . . marked off for [her] by the men of [her] kind"—either virginity, or in Rubin's terms, the "charmed inner circle" characterized by monogamous, heterosexual, marital, procreative sex (Pratt 1984, 27). In flouting norms, she is not merely one of many aging women—spinsters and widows—who have a useful but sexless place in the small town. Like the stranger, she is essential to communal self-definition, the Hester Prynne of Sewanee. More-over, what pushes Katherine over, in Rubin's graphic, the wall separating the middle caste of still-tolerated but suspect behaviors, is her association with perversity at the abjected end of the sexual spectrum. As the object of pedophilic passion, she prematurely and presumptively crosses the line between girl and woman. As a child with (slightly masochistic) desire, she is socially unintelligible, likewise a "third thing," woman/not-woman. As Choi makes clear, the consequence of being approximately perverse is unspoken social demotion. Which is to say, Katherine herself is already "partly colored" at the moment she takes an Asian lover.

This associative twinning highlights similarly disciplining systems—sexual morality and white supremacy—but more specifically, the uneasy middle space between the normative (hence, invisible and naturalized) and the deviant. Both Katherine and Chuck occupy interstitial places within mirrored racial and sexual caste systems, finding overlap and thus camaraderie within and in spite of these pathologizing continuums. The consequence of intermediacy—a crossing of the "walls" that separate acceptability from suspicion, and then suspicion from condemnation—is outsider status, a place they assume not as violently repudiated criminals, but as mildly censured social pariahs. I would claim that it is the shared and lonely space of cultural intermediacy that underwrites their connection.[13] Choi enforces this sense of shared location in multiple venues; for example, Katherine's gift to Chuck early in their acquaintance is Robert Penn Warren's *Band of Angels*, a southern novel not incoincidentally also about interracial desire, mistaken identity, and limited freedom where, in the words of William Bedford Clark, "true love vies with a certain sadomasochistic titillation" (Clark 2006, 177). Moreover, not only are Choi's protagonists both revealed to have survived traumatic pasts involving bodily violation, but they are pushed beyond the confines of polite society by the accusation of theft. For Chuck, the charge breaks the tension of his temporarily ambiguous social status, marking him thereafter as symbolically black. Katherine is stigmatized at summer camp after being accused of stealing (or she is accused of stealing because she is stigmatized), a reaction to an intuitive understanding of her difference from other 15-year-old girls. Ironically, Charles Addison accuses her of "robbing the cradle" in her relationship with his student; as implied by Chuck's inexpert English, she is the agent who carries him away. As a metaphor of usurpation, the accusation of theft is intended to be socially leveling. Of course, as in torture, the point of such a charge is not to seek information, justice, or confession; a venue of discipline and power, it secures group cohesion by locating subjects within a sequence of behaviors from socially sanctioned to indefensibly criminal. Choi's interstitial characters unveil the processes by which a presumed deviation from "universal" norms becomes associated with pathology. In sharing the consequences of a refusal to submit to social convention, both Katherine and Chuck seek a DMZ beyond the hierarchies of race and sex; their house, as Katherine muses, lies "in the middle of the ocean" (292)—not within a specific region or nation but in a mythic space beyond territorialism.

The novel's contribution lies not in expanding notions of southern literature through immigrant addition, or expanding Asian American literature's regional reach, but in understanding how borders, categories, and groupings come into being—punitively so—and how they can be remade or redefined. Choi highlights multiple contexts of connection and division, both those historically contextualized and those suggestively metaphorical; the arbitrary yet weighty lines that divide nations, races, and ideas of proper womanhood, for example, find parallel in other systems of relationally defined association. Language provides one such analogy; as previously noted, Chang is a translator, a pointedly poor one ("Grab your mechanical-gun-that-shoots fast and get into the car-with-no-top!" (Choi 1998, 67)), highlighting the nature of linguistic infidelity and imperfect correspondence, a point that symbolically gestures to Chang's political allegiance and Chuck's racial location as well as to Choi's use of names: Chang is not exactly Chuck, nor is Chuck, Charles. Calculus is asked to bear similar allegorical resonance. Choi's protagonist (like her father, Chang Choi, a professor at Indiana University, South Bend) aspires to be a mathematician, in effect, to enter a world characterized by a closed system made up of an infinite, imaginary continuum of numbers where, unlike the slippage of words to things or people to identities, units bear exact if hidden relationships to one another. An innocent reference to calculus assumes heightened significance in a work about the uneasy, often asymptotic nature of social belonging. Following his self-imposed sequestering during winter break, Katherine impinges upon Chuck's solitude by appearing one day and inquiring about his course of study. He replies:

> "I determine groups. What law describes them. Which belongs with each other."
> "Does everything belong in a group?"
> "Yes. I think so."
> "What will happen when you put everything in its group?"
> "Then we see the structure. How it works."
> "Of the world?"
> "Of the universe." (169–170)

Professor Chang Choi's article, "On Subgroups of M24. II: The Maximal Subgroups of M24," does indeed enumerate the structure of groupings, albeit with no reference to a world outside mathematics where correspondences can be reassuringly sought and known.[14] His daughter, in contrast, takes this seemingly arcane investigation to be a metaphor of philosophical import: her vocation intervenes in the cultural logic of subgroupings, the laws that govern them, and the social and political structures that connect and divide. Chang's/Chuck's attempt to understand mathematical relationships mirrors the ambiguities of his belonging in a newly divided Korea and the American South. Giving weight to the dynamics of understanding "which belongs with each other," the novel closes on yet another scene of mistaken identity: after Chang is released from prison, his mother turns him away from the door, initially taking him for a beggar. "In his mother's failure to recognize him," Choi writes, "his duty to his family was done," setting him "free" (325). This symbolic disavowal releases Chang from the one collective that still holds claim to him, leaving him open to seek another. Thus, loyalty to family, to the state, or to the Asian ethnic community in the United States becomes supplanted by the novel's romantic resolution, its suggestion that the central characters belong, in the end, together. Nevertheless, it does not merely evoke the "universal" theme of outsiders finding affinity in estrangement. Engaging multiple sites wherein everything is put "in its group," whether through conscription, torture, community surveillance, or love, the novel becomes a meditation on how collective affiliations and loyalties—including those enforced by southern culture—can be both forsworn and remade.

*The Foreign Student* can be read on many levels—as a love story, as an imaginative, pseudo-ethnographic account of an Asian's uneasy place between black and white.[15] The novel that grew out of an anecdote about a woman who had been nice to Choi's father at Sewanee recalls the most popular treatment of an interracial love story involving an Asian American in the South, Mira Nair's 1991 film, *Mississippi Masala*. In exploring resistance to the contemporary relationship between a South Asian woman and an African American man, the film draws upon flashbacks to an alternative site of state-imposed segregation, Uganda during Idi Amin's expulsion of the Indian population. *Mississippi Masala*'s temporal movement between continents is meant to parallel the irrationality of clannishness and racial separation in each. As in the film, the novel's use of postcolonial flashback does not merely explain the Asian protagonist's past trauma, but puts diasporic history in the service of a critique of American fears of difference and the restrictions this places on individual freedom. Engaging both postcolonial Korea and the segregation-era United States, Choi's novel represents a critique of "colonial" practices within the First World, turning back the "command" of the West by invoking Asian history as a means of commenting on domestic American politics. It does not merely parallel oppressions or depict the immigrant resilience revealed in one Indian motel owner's response to the signs put up by his white, southern competitors: "American-Owned." "It doesn't get us down," the businessman insists. "If we survived Idi Amin, a couple of redneck motel owners aren't going to bother us much."[16] Rather, the novel's politics encompass segregation-era prejudices surrounding race and those involving sexuality; *The Foreign Student* invites comparison to, in Roberts's words, "the old-time religion of William Faulkner, Ralph Ellison and Eudora Welty" in terms of its craft and southern context, but perhaps also in its exploration of the line between convention and perversity.[17] Thus, the racialization of a Korean man in Jim Crow culture engages both a racial continuum and other processes of assigning social status as well, both gendered and sexual.

The stranger's difference is never absolute, but represents a convenient template upon which community norms are written. As a figure both within and outside the local, the foreigner occupies the space of temporary immunity; the occasion for interpretation, he can likewise provoke a productive estrangement from those norms. "Foreignness," the novel proposes, is something that a southern white woman and Asian man share; in doing so, it creates an alternative community through the intimacy of two. However romanticized, this recasting of a basis for alliance and belonging asks us to reconsider the criteria for patriotism and the irrationality of racial divisions, and to explore the potentially punitive boundaries we place around affiliation, loyalty, and identity. We may not be entirely free from the social significance of "subgroups," but like Choi's characters, we may be partly free to remake them.

As in the next section, Asian difference in the South and the experience of postcolonial exile are strategically situated as a means of refiguring collectivities. Placing Gayle Rubin's poles that define sexual practices alongside the one I have highlighted in this book reveals the multiple ways in which "subgroups" come into being through proximity to normativity or deviance, a process that is both disciplining and defining of community.

## Racial Latency in Dr. Verghese's My Own Country

Abraham Verghese's *My Own Country: A Doctor's Story of a Town and Its People in the Age of AIDS* (1994) is likewise an Asian American's search for place in the South even as the book is noteworthy primarily for its contribution to early awareness of Acquired Immunodeficiency Syndrome (AIDS). Dr. Verghese's memoir calls upon the history of Asian postcolonial exile to comment on southern segregation, not in its racial connotation, but on behalf of individuals infected with the Human Immunodeficiency Virus (HIV) and their caregivers. An immigrant of South Asian ancestry, Abraham Verghese is an infectious disease specialist who comes to treat then-called "AIDS patients" in rural Tennessee in the mid-1980s. In recounting the time he spent in practice at the Johnson City Medical Center (aka the Miracle Center), he produces diverse character portraits of HIV-infected patients in order to give a face to the disease in the period before increased public knowledge about HIV transmission. AIDS was first diagnosed in 1981; by 1991, the Centers for Disease Control had diagnosed 196,000 cases of HIV infection (Diehl Elias 1994, 16). A National Book Critics Circle Award finalist, the book contributed to public enlightenment about the virus that enabled the shift between speaking about "risk behaviors" and "risk groups," and of managing an "HIV-positive" diagnosis and "having AIDS."[18] Deliberately countering ignorance and paranoia surrounding fears of a pandemic, *My Own Country* vividly depicts not only AIDS's toll on the body, but its social toll, the stigma created by infection as it affected the gay community in the rural South in particular. In providing compassionate sketches of diverse subjects outside the urban epicenters of the disease, the book represents an early form of sentimental advocacy akin to the AIDS Quilt; it personalizes pain and loss, extending awareness and grief into the public sphere. What unifies the narrative is not merely the shared plot trajectory detailing the progressive deterioration of each subject profiled, but the doctor's modeling a perspective for his mainstream reader, one of empathetic identification with the text's largely white, gay, working-class, rural, southern male characters.

Verghese's story of AIDS in the South represents, as one reader on amazon.com calls it, "a compelling portrait of parallel developments of the man and the epidemic." This consistently personal perspective, Verghese's constant insertion of his persona into the frame of his narrative, is nonetheless deemed by another anonymous Amazon reviewer to be a "disappointing exercise in egocentrism": "So often in the book, he relates some terrible anecdote and then goes on to say how it reminds him of his own situation—which, of course, is utterly absurd. The value of the book lies in the stories of the AIDS patients, and I'm left wishing that Verghese had made this book more of a 'patients's story' than a 'doctor's story.'"[19] Nevertheless, it is clear that the point of view of the slightly homophobic, but liberal, heterosexual, educated, healthy, monogamous, feeling man of science is essential to the book's effectiveness as AIDS advocacy. It creates the space for the reader's own progressively sympathetic consciousness. But to that list of descriptives, I would add a crucial one: race. Or in this case, its latency within a narrative that takes both homophobia and pathophobia as overriding interests. The title, *My Own Country*, invokes the Asian doctor's search for belonging as part of the Indian diaspora, a search that allows him to find a contingent "home" in the American South—not through an embrace of region, but through meaningful connections with other "migrants," in this case, gay men who have returned home to Tennessee. Inscribing an expanded sense of community along alternative axes—not black or white—like Choi's, the text exposes other continuums that define exclusion and belonging. As the doctor's own difference becomes "outed" via proximity to a projected medical and sexual deviance, *My Own Country: A Doctor's Story of a Town and Its People in the Age of AIDS* twins the seemingly distinct stories of the doctor and his patients in ways that effectively expand notions of segregation and integration in the rural South.

At first glance, Verghese's narrative trajectory seems to reverse a standard feature of Asian American literature: it begins with a counter-intuitive statement of regional belonging only to depict over the course of 400 pages the ways in which that sense of community becomes eroded. The story is not one of increasing acculturation, but of heightened distance and progressive alienation that is assuaged only by a less anticipated sort of communalism at the narrative's end. Taken from a Malcolm Cowley poem, the title, *My Own Country*, intends to invoke the diasporic condition, the Indian exile's search for place presaged by his parents' immigration to Africa a generation before.[20] The label, "expat," Verghese notes, evokes in him "a sense of tremendous desolation" born of childhood experiences growing up in Ethiopia, where he was taunted with the epithet, "ferengi," ironically, the Hindi word for "foreigner" (Verghese 1994, 233). If transnational rootlessness drives the doctor's personal story and delivers its narrative tension, the reader does not wait long for resolution. In defiance of southern stereotyping, at the outset of his new life in Johnson City, Abraham finds acceptance seemingly easy and he is readily embraced as "Doc," a fellow "good ole boy." Verghese writes, "Stateless and roaming for so long, I wanted to put down roots. Johnson City was going to be my town. I felt at peace in this corner of east Tennessee. Finally, this was my own country" (45–46). Thus begins a testimony about fluid movement among multiple communities in the South—the "parochial" world of fellow diasporic Indians, the medical establishment, and the secular white community of east Tennessee. Yet the early resolution of the exile's search for home is short-lived; the "doctor's story" that I would emphasize here is not one of medical discovery or a successful "humanizing" of affliction via testimonies of individual suffering or resilience. Rather, the narrative movement depicts a gradual attenuation of regional (and national) inclusion as the doctor's lifelong quest becomes mapped alongside the ambivalent homecomings of his HIV-infected patients. *My Own Country's* movement, like that of early AIDS literature, is one of rising melancholy and inevitable loss, the end result of which is not only the deaths of most of its characters but the doctor's increasing isolation and subsequent "exile" from home as his relationships with his patients and their caregivers begin to disturb the normative categories that he inhabits as heterosexual, middle class, and "safe."

Abraham's identification with his patients is expressed through Verghese's rhetorical association between homosexuality and foreignness. Because he earned a medical degree outside the United States, the identity, "Foreign

Medical Graduate," or FMG, is a source of potential stigma in his new post. In a piece for the *New Yorker*, Verghese delivers an ironic portrayal of being in the all-powerful position of granting visas to fellow Indian FMGs hoping immigrate to the United States. Taking advantage of post-1965 changes in American immigration law that replaced racial quotas with occupational specialties, these graduates, disproportionally Asian for historical reasons, must pass selective interviews, but are nonetheless, in Verghese's view, treated as secondary citizens within the hierarchy of American medicine.[21] Verghese places his own sentiments into the mouth of a colleague who opines, "Look here. We foreign medical graduates are an embarrassment to this society, a problem. . . . Alas, we problems wouldn't exist if the United States economy didn't depend on us. . . . We are like transplanted organs— lifesaving, and desperately needed, but rejected because we are foreign tissue" (Verghese 1997, 79). Here, the medical analogy is placed in the service of distinct populations: the skilled but nevertheless exploited (partly) racialized labor. Verghese's self-consciousness about being an FMG in *My Own Country* represents a similar invocation and displacement of race: echoing the characterization of Asian labor initiated in the 19th century, the "foreign" body introduced to the national host is ultimately in but not of it. Nevertheless, the slippage allows Verghese specific flexibility: "foreignness" can be overcome or at least disguised via a mimicry of the host—an ironic echo of the way in which HIV replicates itself on the cellular level. Initially figuring Asian American social placement as "foreignness" allows Verghese to insert himself within the frame of his narrative about his patients in specific ways.

Reflecting Choong Soon Kim of the previous chapter, outsider status here is likewise constructed as lending a professional advantage. In this case, presumed objectivity establishes one avenue of sympathetic identification with the gay men who come to Abraham seeking treatment:

> Bobby and Ed left my office with fistfuls of multicolored, multiflavored condoms [and] plenty of literature on safe sex . . . I wondered after they left whether there was an element of relief on their part to discover that the doctor they had come to see was a foreigner, an outsider. Their sexual proclivities would have made them like Martians in their community. To come to a doctor's office . . . and tell their sexual secrets to a Caucasian face that could just as well have belonged to a preacher, a judge, or some other archetypal authority figure in their town, might have been difficult. I may have been flattering myself with these thoughts, but I had the sense that a patient was opening up to me for this very reason, *because* of my foreignness. (Verghese 1994, 116)

The doctor speculates that his undefined status in the town's social hierarchy grants him a measure of patient trust—in contrast to another Asian doctor's testimony regarding white patients from rural southwest: "We get patients from West Texas, and they don't see many Asians or minorities in general. You can kind of see that they're uncomfortable" (cited in Dhingra 2003, 126). But this apparent openness can be read as social condescension: despite his authority as a physician, their indifference reflects the idea that as a stranger to their community, his moral judgment doesn't really matter. Nevertheless, rewriting this hypothetical lack of deference as "flattery" enables him to establish a bond with those who, as the narrative succeeds in establishing, come to represent a stigmatized community. Resonating empathy, Verghese's characterization of Bobby and Ed as "like Martians" becomes a metaphor describing his own other-worldly status as "alien." Later, his self-descriptor, "man from the moon" unwittingly exaggerates the xenophobe's view of the Asian diaspora in the United States. Even so, in the context of this narrative about the rural South, it is infection, not race or citizenship, that establishes a metaphoric overlap between doctor and patient, writer and subject: with the importation of the disease into Johnson City, the "hometown boy was now regarded as an alien" (Verghese 1994, 11).

Verghese's analogy between doctor and patient is more explicit as he weighs dual forms of acculturation to dominant culture(s) defined by unmarked sexual and ethnic norms. In philosophizing about gay men, he notes:

> Society considered them alien and much of their life was spent faking conformity. New immigrants expend a great deal of effort trying to fit in: learning the language, losing the accent, picking up the rituals of Monday Night Football and Happy Hour. Gay men, in order to avoid conflict, had also become experts at blending in, camouflaging themselves, but at great cost to their spirit. My adaptation had been voluntary. I lacked a country I could speak of as home. My survival had depended on a chameleon-like adaptability, taking on the rituals of the place I found myself to be in: Africa, India, Boston, Johnson City. I was always reinventing myself. (58)

Here, the new immigrant's tests of adaptation are strategically marked by masculine heterosexuality as occasions for male bonding—watching sports, drinking, hitting on women. The comparative gesture gently erodes the distance between dissimilar social positions. But Verghese's distinction between mimicry that is coerced and adaptation that is chosen reveals an elision:

being an immigrant is positioned here as a matter of ethnicity, not of race. At the outset of the narrative, this elision allows him to depict communal belonging as a voluntary shedding of cultural difference, the cost of which does not at first appear to be high. It is only when, as described 300 pages later, due to his contact with AIDS patients, Abraham faces increasing ostracism from the medical community of other doctors, hospital administrators, nurses, and pharmacists, and then the town as a whole ("I could not handle [another] crack about 'homos'" (309)) that Verghese comes to mark his social location in Johnson City as a racial one:

> Sometimes it was possible to have the illusion that I was so much a part of the town, so well integrated, that I even looked like the townsfolk. . . . I had fought the clannishness of the Indian community, felt embarrassed by their refusal to integrate. Did they understand something I did not? . . . Was there some place in this country where I could walk around anonymously, where I could blend in completely with a community, be undistinguished by appearance, accent or speech? (308–309)

Segregation takes on a familiar cast: not self-imposed ethnic "clannishness," but forced racial distance based on skin color, which cannot be erased despite one's willingness to, as Abraham does, put on cowboy boots and master the rituals of line dancing. Nevertheless, the narrative defamiliarizes the pathway to this critical consciousness, routing it through an affinity with another "minority," one pathologized by the medical community and occupying a reviled place on Rubin's continuum of sexual practices.

As the doctor's growing identification with those infected with HIV and their families begins to expose his own difference in the South—not merely cultural (I am not American) but racial (I am brown-skinned)—Abraham's estrangement from community is described, like that of his gay patients, in sexual terms. Thus, when his vocation draws his time and attention away from home, his wife Rajani flatfootedly accuses him of homosexual attraction, a challenge he readily dismisses: "I felt she had entirely missed the point. I couldn't believe my wife was capable of reducing my complicated feelings to something just sexual" (142). Clearly, however, she perceives that her husband's libidinal energy is focused on his work in ways that erode his marriage, a circumstance that later finds redirection in the more prosaic form of a sexually aggressive single woman. Mira Nair's film version of the memoir, *My Own Country* (1998), heightens the connection between sexual infidelity and the doctor's passion for medicine by placing the temptation of sex and the temptation of AIDS research into close proximity.[22] That is, the scene depicting Abraham's flirtation with a provocative blond while Rajani is out of town directly precedes the moment in which he elects, instead, to return home and produce a map of AIDS's entry into the rural South. The film visualizes this medical breakthrough as a frenzy of triumphant typing and discarded paper that is only interrupted by the return of his (still) disapproving wife. As in the text, AIDS work here has become the unmentionable mistress who queers Abraham's home life (288). Of course, it is not simply that the physician betrays Rajani by having an "affair" with medicine, but that she has likewise betrayed him by reacting to the disease with ignorance: for example, in asking him to wash his hands before touching their son, she becomes one of "them," on the outside of the emerging community created by compassion toward HIV-positive individuals. AIDS work thus becomes cast as a sexual drive within the context of heterosexual cliché—illicit, inexcusable, outside the home.

This metaphoric depiction of Abraham's relationship to his object of study, his passion as it were, lies in distinct overlap and juxtaposition to a previous metaphor that depicts his work as homosocial yet similarly disruptive of his home life: "AIDS was like another wild friend, a friend from a different social stratum, a friend I indulged but no longer brought to the house or even discussed with [my wife]" (171). Verghese introduces a rhetorical slippage between the dual objects of his emotional attachment, medicine and his largely male, gay patients, in ways that further a sense of shared intimacy with the latter. The threat to monogamy simultaneously takes the form of a desirable white woman and an uncouth, alpha male, both disruptive of heterosexual nuclear domesticity, both potential homewreckers.

Other parallels between the heterosexual, Indian doctor and his patients are less overt but succeed in conveying the bond of sympathy that carries the emotional authority of the narrative, its successful rendering of affect that marks the book's effectiveness as AIDS advocacy. For example, a subtle association between doctor and patient, between race and gender, occurs via flashback to Boston in 1983 in one of the text's earliest depictions of Abraham's encounter with an HIV-infected patient: "When I approached, a pair of close-set eyes looked at me with suspicion from behind a *purda* of sorts: he had coiled the bed sheet around his head and across his face" (28). The description lends a disorienting foreignness to this figure of social and medical curiosity, his "first gay patient." It is an Orientalizing and feminizing portrayal that conveys the same distance that attends the doctor's other noteworthy diagnosis of this patient—he has accessory nipples. Nevertheless, given Verghese's subsequent emphasis on his own status as a foreign medical graduate, the early portrait hints at a mirroring that becomes more overt as the narrative proceeds; the doctor, along with his patients, will enter a social *purda* of sorts. Patient joking during a rectal exam represents another inadvertent association: "When I asked Otis about whether he often had anal receptive intercourse, Fred *piped up from behind me*: 'Uh, not often enough!' . . . While I was doing Otis's rectal exam, Otis looked over to Fred and said, 'I wonder if he'll still respect me in the morning?'" (124; emphasis mine). As the doctor enacts anal penetration, he is nonetheless simultaneously positioned as anally receptive; just as the banter intends, the portrayal equalizes their relationship.

Moreover, as the narrative gradually unravels Abraham's sense of inclusion in Johnson City as he becomes more deeply enmeshed within a climate of suspicion surrounding fears of a pandemic, Verghese's descriptions of medical mastery become increasingly described as a loss of sexual vitality. Abraham's strongest identification is formed with a heterosexual, married, monogamous, white male patient, Will Johnson, who has inadvertently become infected through a blood infusion during surgery. The doctor confesses his own bias in admitting that his feelings of connection may lie in Johnson's innocence in contracting the disease, an innocence that is reflected in Abraham's own position as a medical bystander unfairly accused by a hospital administrator as responsible for, not the spread of AIDS per se, but for an increase in the number of patients who appear at their rural hospital seeking treatment. This association is furthered by his word choice: he notes that Johnson "had come to understand my sense of impotence" as medical practitioner directly following the moment in which Johnson confesses his literal impotence as a consequence of contracting the disease. That is, the language used in regard to the patients circles back to implicate the doctor.

*My Own Country*'s significance to critical regionalism and southern literature lies in Verghese's blurring the criteria for segregation and inclusion, highlighting parallel "caste" systems, and refiguring lines of affiliation away from identity categories that have traditionally configured southern community. The progressive loss of the "Doc's" sense of belonging in Johnson City is presented as a matter of taking on the "foreignness" of those he treats: "The exile I felt had less to do with being an AIDS doc than with the fact that most of my patients were homosexuals." This stigma by association produces a slippage between subject and object, a blurring that creates the "about-me" quality of the text that signifies "egocentrism" to the aforementioned amazon.com reader. Thus: "I had become the target of [the nurse's] venom—the discussion had not really been about Scotty. It had been about me" (161); and "I was . . . tainted socially by the association with my patients, even if most days I told myself I cared nothing about what others thought" (365). Certainly, this substitution worries the line between identification and cooptation, but it nonetheless succeeds in marking the text's significance as both Asian American and southern literature by drawing a subtle interconnection: the rising pathophobia of the community begins to express itself as xenophobia in ways that expose the latency of southern racism that Asian Americans experience. At first, he enjoys a seeming immunity from the embedded hierarchies of the region until he makes conscious, in tones of baffled paranoia, his social demotion due to proximity to abjection, to the sexual and medical "deviancy" of his patients. "Asianness" here signifies through social contiguity but not within the axis of white normativity and black abjection that I have previously foregrounded as central to southern regionalism. Moreover, like Choi's novel, it is not only the domestic context of American racialization that the text engages, but the global context of the postcolonial Asian diaspora. The shared association between the doctor and those under his care is conveyed through self-implicating sexual metaphors and through those of migration.

The medical breakthrough depicted in Nair's film, the scene situating research as a substitute for adultery, is Verghese's "mapping" the movement of HIV-infected patients from urban centers to the rural South. This contribution to sexual geography is less dramatically depicted in his co-authored article published in the *Journal of Infectious Diseases*, "*Urbs in Rure*: Human Immunodeficiency Virus Infection in Rural Tennessee" (1989), which provides an overview of AIDS treatment outside the "urban epicenters" of the disease and sounds the warning bell of its impending migration. Ironically, the article testifies not only to a counter-intuitive story of family and community support in the small-town South, but one somewhat counter to the dominant plot movement of *My Own Country*. He and his co-authors conclude, "[T]his phenomenon of migration underscores the importance of the family support system. . . . We believe that family involvement and the presence of an intact and complete family unit is an integral part of optimal care of patients with HIV infection" (Verghese, Berk, and Sarubbi 1989, 1054). In depicting an "exodus" from urban centers, the article maps a reverse movement from what Kath Weston, in keeping with the work of Allan Berubé, has characterized as the "Great Migration" of gays and lesbians to cities as part of their search for community from the 1940s through the 1980s. *My*

*Own Country* is largely accepting of this "standardized tale of gay migration" (Weston 1995, 284) in positioning its characters' previous moves out of the South as part exile and part quest for acceptance in the idealized meccas of sexually liberated urban spaces. The gay migration stories depicted in Verghese's work reflect the idea that, in Donna Jo Smith's words, "queers in the South not only would want to leave home but literally would be required to leave home, as a matter of survival" (1997, 381). Thus, at first glance the text appears to confirm what scholars of gay and lesbian regionalism have criticized as the myth of gay metronormativity, stories that, as William J. Spurlin notes, rely "heavily on a romanticized prototype of the queer child who saves money and gets on a train bound for New York or some other coastal city in search of a new life more compatible with his or her emerging sexual identity . . . [where he or she can] escape oppressive familial and social relations back home" (2000, 182).

In representing the early exodus of white native sons of the South as a symptom of their being misfits "bereft of community" (Weston 1995, 280), Verghese confirms a conventional expectation. Nevertheless, the concept of gay exile is essential to the book's advocacy; just as his medical research attests, these narratives of return simultaneously inscribe a landscape of continuing prejudice and of familial embrace both in its traditional and broadened senses. In effect, it portrays not gay diaspora, but rural homecoming. As Irit Rogoff reveals regarding Verghese's contribution to conceptual mapping, "Certainly, the ongoing fascination with Verghese's book is its active construction of a subject for itself which will not allow it to settle into the category of medicine, or rural geography or migration culture or alternative sexualities, but uses each to interrogate and actually *hear* the other through their contiguous spatialization" (2000, 83). To that contiguous spatialization I would add race, present here in crucial, yet veiled ways. As in Choi's novel, Verghese overlaps dual continuums that define social status.

That is, Verghese does not merely map a sexual geography, but plays with ideas about coalition and shared experience by linking gay migration to the more conventional sense of diaspora threaded within his own story of Asian transnational labor. One such instance occurs in an indirect aside about the proliferation of migrating birds who have become nuisances at the Veteran's Administration (VA) hospital where he sees patients. An innocent stroll with his son resonates with the politics of race and contagion as he speculates about the doves who thrive on the hospital grounds despite increasingly aggressive measures to drive them off:

Where would the doves go? Would they fly west to Murfreesboro where another quaint old VA of similar construction awaited them? Or would they go down to the Bay Pines VA in Florida, mimicking the migratory pattern of our domiciliary residents? Had an eccentric old domiciliary veteran *brought them here to begin with, only to have their population explode* much in the manner of the aggressive starling had first arrived in America? (Verghese 1994, 178; emphasis mine)

His musing draws a direct analogy between the doves and veteran "snow birds," but it is also inadvertently reminiscent of the proliferation of AIDS carriers migrating from who knows where to roost, unwanted and in ever-increasing numbers, in the placid, bucolic locale of east Tennessee. The subtle association is reinforced by the tone of melancholy that attends the scene; emanating from under the eaves of the hospital, the cooing of these doves, he reflects, "made it seem as if the building was grieving aloud." Within this suggestive portrayal, the doctor is himself the "eccentric" conduit to contagion, like the veteran, unwittingly inviting a proliferation that he cannot control. Yet the racial resonance attending the scene derives from a muted sense of historicity implicating the doctor's own ec-centricity to place: it was precisely the fear of population explosion that spurred U.S. immigration restrictions identifying Asians as subjects of exclusion until the shift to occupational preferences—of which medicine is a notable one—enabled a post-1965 increase in migration from Asia. Moreover, the representation of Asian immigrants as sources of contagion was central to their early racialization.[23] The doctor himself plays the part of self-conscious newcomer to his VA patients, many of whom, he has previously recounted, have been exposed to foreigners only through their military service in Asia. As a self-identified FMG, the doctor is likewise the contaminant introduced into a host, one that multiplies, like the doves, largely unwelcome.

Pico Iyer's review of the book inadvertently reinforces this association between the doctor and the infection he treats; Iyer writes that as an immigrant from Africa, Verghese "arrived in the U.S. at almost exactly the same time as the foreign disease" (Iyer 1994, 70). Abraham's tentative speculation about where the birds will migrate once driven out of Johnson City can be read as both an allusion to his patients and an echo of the narrative's essential conflict: "Was there ever going to be a place in this world for me to call my own?" (Verghese 1994, 308). The passage draws an intuitive connection between the migratory patterns of gay men and Asian Americans by invoking multiple contexts of diaspora and, in this biological metaphor, the association between immigrant populations and viral replication.

Medical language becomes an apt way to define the text's veiled but ever-present association between race and sexuality; in the manner of the disease itself, racism in Johnson City, once latent, becomes manifest as hostility toward his patients and their caregivers progresses. It is this very dormancy—marked in Choi's novel as a palpable surveillance surrounding Chuck—that distinguishes Asian American depictions of racism in the South, distinct from, perhaps, the "magisterial systems of prejudice" portrayed in both white and black southern canons. Thus, although Abraham brushes off Rajani's warning about circumspect behavior early in the narrative ("we are a very visible Indian community" (60)), his increasing dislocation from the (white) community he once embraced becomes expressed as racial paranoia, as self-consciousness about skin color and "alien" status, culminating in his decision to leave the South.[24] The doctor's desire for anonymity ("Was there some place in this country . . . where I could blend in[?]" (308–309)) ironically mirrors the situation of some of his patients whose acceptance hinges upon a dual form of closeting. The end of the narrative brings home this blurring between the writer and his subjects; after recounting the deaths of almost all of the individuals profiled in his book, Verghese's final gesture is to usurp their place. His departure from Johnson City is an extended goodbye depicted in the language of elegy: "To my tennis buddy, Earl, I leave my Datsun Z" (426). For both the Indian doctor and his patients, home in the South reflects, in Bhabha's words, "a place of estrangement that becomes the necessary space of engagement; it may represent a desire for accommodation marked by an attitude of deep ambivalence toward one's location. Home may be a mode of living made into a metaphor of survival" (Bhabha 1997, 11).

For the individuals depicted in the work, survival exists only metaphorically, their life stories channeled by Dr. Verghese and left behind, to paraphrase Edmund White on AIDS literature, like stones left behind by those entering a dark forest. While his ventriloquism might be read as an affront, as secondhand suffering, his testimony nonetheless bears powerful witness to, in White's words, the "hard work, of dying or getting someone else ready to die." Post-book, the doctor's own search for home has a felicitous ending: he gets a divorce, establishes a literary career after a stint at the Iowa Writers' Workshop, and takes a post in El Paso, Texas where, in his brownness, he is taken to be like everyone else—which is to say, Latino. ("For the first time in America, I felt as if I had disappeared. I no longer stood out" (Verghese 1997, 87).) At home on the border, where foreignness is reinscribed as normative, he sutures his belonging by marrying a Chicana. Thus, the national anxieties surrounding "alien" status expressed in *My Own Country* find resolution within romantic conventions reflective of *The Foreign Student*. As Verghese writes in a love poem, "it comes to me, my love, that from now on/my own country is simply/wherever you are" (Verghese 1996, 252). The attachments and intimacies portrayed in the memoir take a more traditional form located in shared phenotype and heterosexual monogamy. The afterstory finds Verghese embracing his interstitial "brownness," fittingly, on the border of the nation.[25]

As if to mirror its thematizing of dislocation, the book *My Own Country* has been hard to categorize; Rogoff's attempt to locate it under the sections reserved for "Biography," "Medicine," "Non-fiction" and a host of others in Barnes and Noble is unsuccessful until she unearths it under the rubric, "Health and Fitness" (Rogoff 2000). Rajini Srikanth tried to nominate the work for an Association of Asian American Studies Book Award soon after its publication, but it was deemed "not to illuminate sufficiently the Asian American experience because it was primarily about Southern white patients" (Srikanth 2004, 447). Acknowledging that by 2004, notions of Asian American literature had expanded, she nonetheless cautions that the work "will not readily spring to mind as an example of an ethnic text so long as we continue to view expressions of ethnicity in narrow terms" (447). Such a broadening would not only address the story of diasporic rootlessness invoked in the title, or even what she highlights as the paradox of insider/outsider status that the text inscribes, but expanded notions of intimacy and coalition that are likewise the purview of the discipline. That is, while I have argued that Verghese's exposing the dormancy of racism is essential to his AIDS advocacy, *My Own Country: A Doctor's Story* is not a book about racial segregation in the South. But it reveals how Asian difference becomes mediated within the confines of a community organized around race, as well as on multiple axes of difference including sexual normativity and wellness. Racial estrangement becomes a venue through which the doctor conveys kinship with those for whom he becomes a spokesperson. Such challenges to coalitions based on naturalized conceptions of shared identity effectively produce, to invoke Susan Stanford Friedman's terms, new "scripts of relational positionality" and possibility (Friedman 1998, 66). It is not the medical, the South Asian, or the white establishment of Johnson City, Tennessee to which he lays claim, but to a constituency segregated by fear of contagion. As such, the text can be read as a commentary on a form of apartheid, on the unwill-ingness of an American community to incorporate another minority, those infected by HIV and their caregivers. Integration in this part of the South becomes recast as the embrace of community, however it is defined.

## The Promise of the Interstitial

In 1994, when Ram Uppuluri was seeking to represent Tennessee's third dis-trict in Congress, he would open his campaign speeches by asserting, "My father comes from the south of India, my mother comes from the south of Japan, so we're a family of Southerners" (59).[26] A mixed-race Asian literally lobbying to become a representative southerner, Uppuluri was grasping at conceptual straws in order to seek a point of commonality. Like Duncan's awareness of being made an object of scrutiny and interpretation, the anec-dote betrays the limits to which Asian Americans in the South can become "just folks," to become, as one Delta resident informs V. S. Naipaul, "people who weren't transient, who'd lived here for some time . . . [and you] knew their families" (Naipaul 1989, 182). These regional struggles reflect the larger resonances of Asian racialization in the United States, the construction of the Asian as unassimilable alien. In turn, Asian American writers find in south-ern parochialism a representative if misguided sign of First World smugness: as Choong Soon Kim notes regarding fieldwork in a working-class African American southern community, "As Americans, they were aware that they were donors of [American] foreign aid [to South Korea] and, despite their poverty, assumed they were nevertheless among the wealthiest people in the world. Some showed me their telephone and television, assuming that I might never have seen those cultural items" (Kim 1977, 122). Likewise, in Bharati Mukherjee's novel, *Jasmine*, a white veteran in Florida establishes his superiority to the Indian protagonist: "I been to Asia and it's the armpit of the universe. . . . Don't tell me you ever *seen* a television set" (Mukher-jee 1988, 112). Such portrayals question First World/Third World distinction through the enabling if stereotypical depiction of the South as a rural back-water; these ironic exchanges disturb a presumed hierarchy among nations, effectively troubling the unexamined claims to modernity of these "represen-tative" Americans.

The addition of Asian American literature to the southern canon may well represent, in historian Victor Jew's words, the worlding of critical regional-ism insofar as it engages postcolonial histories of migration in a critique of American domestic politics.[27] "Migrancy" here does not merely add another thematic to southern literary concerns, but offers a potentially reorienting perspective on the very dynamics at the heart of the southern canon: racism, or in this case, its latency. In the works I have engaged here, the forms of white supremacy lack the immediacy of Baldwin's recognition that he is "among a people whose culture controls me, has even, in a sense, created me" (Baldwin 1955, 164). Nevertheless, southern Asian American literature here does not inscribe figures who serve merely to highlight the more complex humanity of white people, or to showcase the deeper suffering of African Americans. In keeping with previous chapters, these post–segregation era texts establish the interstitial as a site of cultural discipline, but in distinction to previous sites of my inquiry, they also give it a new direction and an alternative political valence.

The "partly colored" status of both Choi's and Verghese's Asian American protagonists is exposed via their proximity to other pathologized subjects who are judged in part by their erotic nonconformity. In placing Rubin's grid of sexual practices alongside the one central to this book, I want to highlight not merely contiguous but also overlapping and intersecting continuums that settle the place of those who generate cultural uneasiness, revealing, not surprisingly, that white southerners can also become "partly colored" if only figuratively. Against and within segregation and its legacy, then, is a sexual caste system, one that represents, for Rubin, "the last socially respectable form of prejudice" (1993, 12). These dual continuums reveal the multiple axes through which social status is constructed; in the next chapter, I consider the gender continuum from male to female in order to explore its consequences for those who represent as culturally interstitial.

Ram Uppuluri's rhetorical attempt to ingratiate his foreign origins to fellow southerners may be only a little more obvious than my own conceptual bridges. I am aware that Korea's civil war bears little relation to the American Civil War, and that the isolation of HIV-positive individuals is not identical to racial segregation. For that matter, the weight of southern history does not fall upon the backs of Asian Americans, "ruined" white women, or gay men. Nevertheless, the shift of subject offers a potentially expansive perspective on entrenched cultural norms in the spirit of anthropologist Renato Rosaldo's conception of "microethnography," a retelling of custom from the viewpoint of an outsider whose "objectifications [make] certain patterns of behavior stand out in stark relief—the better to change them" (1989, 48). As in Simmel's concept of the stranger, the outsider, is "near and far *at the same time*" (Simmel 1950, 407); he is the site of difference that questions cultural norms, in this case, American norms of racial separation that find their primary target in African Americans. Asian American texts offer a productive estrangement from historically sedimented divisions as writers think beyond entrenched forms of social organization—of collectives, of loyalties, of groups—in order to reinvent lines of connection and intimacy. Such a perspective allows artists to reconceive alliances beyond those based simply on naturalized identities; for Asian Americans without ethnic community, whether in the South or beyond it, this is an important point. As the literature reveals, Asian Americans find a contingent belonging not through the embrace of region per se, but through forging other meaningful connections, offering a reconsideration of what it means to be "at home" in the South.

The addition of Asian American writers to the southern canon cannot perform the work of idealistic pluralism by demonstrating an alternative cosmopolitanism that is expected to wipe clean the slate of a hoary past, whether one violently repudiated or mired in nostalgia. Nor can it simply graft the terms of African American oppression onto a new group or, for that matter, graft the conceptual terms central to Asian American Studies—citizenship, diaspora, migrancy, acculturation, transnationalism—onto southern regionalism. Asian American southern literature yields something more complex about the interstices of collective affiliation: that crossing the color line can mean something other than imagining oneself to be white; that claiming outsidedness can signal something other than unrepentant unassimilability. In providing a lens for re-framing a "known" history that allows us to reconceive established forms of affiliation and interconnection, Asian American literature might function within the context of critical regionalism as a reorienting space akin to Bhabha's conception of the interstitial. Critical discourse, he notes, "opens up a space of translation: a place of hybridity, figuratively speaking, where the construction of a political object that is new, *neither the one nor the other*, properly alienates our political expectations, and changes, as it must, the very forms of our recognition" (1994, 25). Asian "foreignness," then, might be reconceived as a useful alienation from entrenched southern race relations, an estrangement that provides the space for questioning norms of etiquette, habit, or intimacy—and, in the process, those of regional exceptionalism.

Throughout this book, my thesis has been that the anomaly is a productive site for revealing the investments of culture. Inscribing the ways in which "partly colored" status becomes manifest, these authors open up a "third space" of social relations that can and cannot be coded as racial. Here, integration is cast not as acceptance by white southerners or access to civil rights, but as, in a sense, kinship with those who likewise possess a queered relationship to southern culture. Asian racial difference thus becomes a catalyst for reimagining the often arbitrary boundaries of belonging both within and beyond the black-white dichotomy and a catalyst for understanding how status becomes assigned according to distinctions not only between white and black, but between illness and wellness, loyalty and disloyalty, sexual normativity and erotic deviance, "foreigner" and "good ole boy." In this sense, the racial in-between pushes us to think beyond the lines drawn by color and segregation's legacy to the partial commonalities that bind us.

# Transracial/Transgender

*Analogies of Difference in* Mai's America

I think there is a continuum of Male . . . to . . . Female; like
shades of gray from black to white.
—D. Cameron, "Caught Between: An Essay on Intersexuality"

As members of society, most of us see only what we expect to
see, and what we expect to see is what we are conditioned to see
when we have learned the definitions and classifications of our
culture.
—Victor Turner, *The Forest of Symbols*

While "colored" and "white" signs separating public facilities in the
Jim Crow South have become infamously iconic reminders of past injustice,
signs enforcing another social division remain. In the post–Civil Rights era,
the battle over segregation continues to be waged in what is a historically
laden site: the public restroom. As legal historian Mary Anne Case notes,
"Very few spaces in our society remain divided by sex . . . There's marriage
and there's toilets, and very little else."[1] The division created by "Ladies" and
"Gentlemen" signs over restroom doors does not immediately conjure up
an analogy to race so ingrained is the belief in the natural division between
men and women. Yet, among transgendered and disabled rights activists, the
bathroom, in Case's words, that "prosaic fixture of past battles against racial
segregation," is the site of continued contestation involving public accommodation and individual rights.[2]

Transgender activist Leslie Feinberg hearkens back to the Civil Rights
Movement in calling for the dissolution of gender as a legal category:

I am told I must check off M or F because it is a legal necessity. But when
I was a child, I was required to check off race on all legal records. It took

mighty militant battles against institutionalized racist discrimination to remove that mandatory question from documents. . . . Why is the categorization of sex a legal question at all? (1998, 62)

Making a similar connection between racial and transgender advocacy, law professor Patricia Williams recounts an anecdote in which a transgender student who is denied access to both the men's and women's restrooms at a California law school comes to her, hoping for a sympathetic ear. He confides to Williams his intention to seek a sex-change operation in the belief that Williams "might be more understanding" (1991, 122) because she is black.[3] Williams makes the connection that "S.'s experience was sort of a Jim Crow mentality applied to gender" (124). In effect, the student's access to public facilities was compromised by restrictive social organization:

> After the sex-change operation, S. began to use the ladies' room. There was an enormous outcry from women students of all political persuasions, who "felt raped," in addition to the more academic assertions of some who "feared rape." In a complicated storm of homophobia, the men of the student body let it be known that they too "feared rape" and vowed to chase her out of any and all men's rooms. (1991, 123)

The analogy between race and gender segregation in public facilities strikes Williams not only in a literal sense but also in terms of an abstract connection: both blackness and transsexualism as spaces inhabited by social "nobodies" (124). Williams's initial defensiveness, her feeling "put off by the implication that my distinctive somebody-ness was being ignored" (124), is offset by the recognition that she and the student share a nonidentical yet similar positionality, one characterized by having "no place else to go" (124). Transgender individuals confront the same question that I have framed here as a historical and conceptual one for the "partly colored" races: which facility?

Feinberg's and Williams's parallel between race and transgenderism provokes logical questions: What are the limits or rewards of drawing analogies between race and gender in the context of past and present forms of segregation, of drawing analogies of difference? How might the gender dissonance attributed to transgendered figures contribute to developing a lens for reading racial history? More specifically, what can be gained by drawing an analogy between individuals who are conceptually interstitial to poles that once defined or continue to define legal identity?

Feminists have often invoked racial analogies to highlight gender and sexual oppression—from Yoko Ono's "Woman is the nigger of the world," to Monique Wittig's assertion that the lesbian is an escapee from her class "in the same way as the American runaway slaves were" (1992, 108), to Gayle Rubin's assertion, "This system of sex law [that criminalizes sexual behavior] is similar to legalized racism" (1993, 21).[4] Most recently, such analogies have been called into service to highlight the injustice of attempts to prohibit same-sex marriage. Drawing a parallel to anti-miscegenation laws, Massachusetts Chief Justice Margaret H. Marshall argued in 2003 that neither interracial unions nor same-sex marriage diminish "the validity or dignity of opposite-sex marriage."[5] Such assertions recognize the rhetorically persuasive potential of comparison in advocacy at the same time that they link oppressions by acknowledging the contribution of both the Civil Rights and Women's movements to the discourse of rights.[6] Yet analogies between sexism or heterosexism and racism also run the risk of being one-sided (more often invoked by white women than men and women of color) as well as disrespectful of historical differences. As Jesse Jackson reminded the public during the height of debates over same-sex marriage, "Gays were never called three-fifths human in the Constitution."[7] As the 2008 Democratic primary contest between Hillary Rodham Clinton and Barack Obama revealed, race and gender are more readily portrayed as points of competition—as cards to be played—rather than a basis for shared vision.[8] Hence, Williams reacts warily to her transsexual student's expectation that in his black female professor he would find a kindred soul. But Williams's anecdote suggests a more abstract way of looking at the race-gender analogy beyond the discourse of rights that have come to frame race in the public sphere.

In taking literal and figurative conceptions of segregation as my context, I want to explore what it means to have "no place else to go" as a result of the dictates of social organization, to engage a spatially inflected way of looking at the construction of difference by focusing, again, not on the primary categories of division—male/female, white/black—but what lies between them. The historical context that figures as my conceptual problematic is reflected in the contemporary requirement to self-designate as male or female. To repeat a question that I pose in this book's introduction now applied to the current moment, what does it mean to represent *between* legal and cultural identities sanctioned by American culture, or between the poles of identification and legal subjectivity that enforce social hierarchy?

This chapter extends my project by seeking a conceptual parallel to transgenderism in "transracialism." The term "transracial" has been invoked in other contexts, most notably in reference to transracial adoption wherein predominately Caucasian parents adopt a child of color.[9] "Transracial" in this sense is intended to convey reaching across cultures, spanning a divide. The-ater critic Josephine Lee has also used the term in regard to "transracial" stage performance in which multiple characters of different races are played by the same actor (1997). It has also been invoked to describe interracial individu-als of black and white parentage, productively highlighting racial intermix-ture as a site reflective of similar ambivalences within segregation-era culture that have been my focus.[10] Nevertheless, in highlighting Asian American sta-tus between black and white, I want to invoke "trans" status apart from the question of racial epistemology as it engages genealogy, bloodline, and racial authenticity. While narratives about interracial passing likewise establish the instability of the black/white binary, my investment here lies in shifting away from visual ways of knowing toward both the social practices that cre-ate racialized bodies, and the more abstract resonances of being symbolically interstitial. As in the analogy between race passing and closeted sexuality, I am interested in questions of epistemology but, in contrast, I want to look at overt moments of category ambiguity that force interpretation and resolu-tion. Moreover, I seek in Asian "transracialism" a new language that derives from the historical context of this book without the derogatory baggage of my title.

The interruption of entrenched southern race relations forms the center of Marlo Poras's 2002 film, *Mai's America*. The documentary promises an "outsider's glimpse inside America" from the point of view of Mai Nguyen, an exchange student from Hanoi in the 1990s.[11] Following Mai's placement with white and black host families in Meridian, Mississippi, the film provides a portrait of American-as-southern culture by narrating the experiences of a stranger in a strange land: a Vietnamese girl is plunked down in unknown territory. The viewer follows her quest for a First World education as she trav-els to exotic and uncharted landscapes: the high school graduation, the prom, the black Baptist church, the "redneck" family reunion. Her fluid movement among multiple subcultures—black, white, gay, working class, Vietnamese expatriate, and collegiate—delivers a diverse portrait of the United States, but one punctuated by racial, class, and sexual division. The documentary narrates a specific story: America's defeat of an intrepid spirit and the illusion of the American dream.

*Mai's America* is thus intended to be a national meditation, but one that is, I would suggest, dependent on Mai's ambiguous place within the subcul-tures established by semi-rural poverty and the residues of Jim Crow. Even as Mai fails to find a sense of community within the racial communities split by the legacy of segregation, she develops a sympathetic attachment to one who likewise inhabits "no place" in rural Mississippi: a white, male drag queen. The Vietnamese foreign student finds community in the United States through her friendship with Chris aka Christy, a southern, Pentecostal cross-dresser. In the gender-ambiguous figure of Christy, *Mai's America* finds an analogue to its protagonist, one who becomes an interstitial figure in more than one sense. Through this "trans" twinning, the film models the ways in which gender dissonance challenges not merely our investment in the division between black and white, but in category distinction writ large.

In seeking a parallel between two arenas of "trans" or interstitial status, I want to stress not the progressive or temporal movement of liminality per se but a spatial notion of racial or gender formation that highlights incompletion. That is, both represent the never-finalized oscillation between, as my first epigraph suggests, poles of a socially enforced continuum. As transgender theory reveals, the interstitial subject is a site of cultural anxiety and of potential disruption, a site where status hierarchies are made visible and potentially reconciled to cultural norms. Anthropologist Victor Turner's commentary on social expectation in my second epigraph resonates with both race and gender: to what extent do the prevailing "definitions and classifications of our culture" (1967, 95) constrict our vision and do violence to those who inhabit the space between them? In highlighting two distinct but intersecting continuums, I draw an analogy between forms of cultural difference in order to consider the interventionist possibility of comparison while exploring its theoretical complexity.

My interest in twinning the terms "transgender" and "transracial," two historically distinct discourses, lies in understanding the abstract nature of interstitiality, the political valance of those who represent between the dominant racial and gender symbolics characterized (today) by the signs over segregated bathroom doors or (then) by segregated drinking fountains. Thus, I begin by invoking Jacques Lacan's iconic image of the gender-divided restroom doors marked "Ladies and Gentlemen" appearing in "Agency of the Letter in the Unconscious" (1966) as a gateway for thinking not only about the gender dichotomy challenged by transgender theorists, but the structuralist underpinnings of racial discourse in the United States. That is, how does the iconic division between "Ladies" and "Gentlemen" resonate with segregation's legacy? Subsequently, in exploring the ways in which the gender dissonance provides a lens for reading race, I turn to *Mai's America*, which suggests that shifting one's perspective to the transspace between normative social categories challenges forms of social organization that exceed those passed down by history. Crucial to the film's portrayal of its Asian protagonist's transracial status among southern subcultures is her gender ambiguity: she is a girl who transforms herself into a boy for a man who is dressed like a woman. For a lone and sojourning Asian foreigner in a landscape saturated with the history of black/white relations, "integration" takes on another cast.

Transgenderism does not merely ask us to expand categories of gender identity; it offers a perspective that questions loyalty to an entrenched dyad and suggests alternative ways of reading difference not only as mutually constituted and intersecting categories, but as continuums linked through conceptual parallelism. While feminists have often called upon racial analogies to support women's liberation, I want to reverse that gesture in order to consider how gender theory might enhance our understanding of race relations and, in doing so, highlight the importance of gender to comparative racial analysis. In drawing from transgender theory a parallel concept of "transracialism" enabled by shifting the racial gaze to that of Asian Americans, I want to explore both the fruitfulness and the limits of analogy.

## Race and Gender Interstitiality

In highlighting how a focus on interstitiality might challenge normative concepts of difference and the hierarchies they support, I turn to an alternative iconography of segregation: gender-divided restroom doors.

The illustration is well known in literary theory; it accompanies Jacques Lacan's discussion of the illusory transparency between signifier and signified in "The Agency of the Letter in the Unconscious." His point is conveyed within an amusing anecdote centering on innocent misrecognition:

> A train arrives at a station. A little boy and a little girl, brother and sister, are seated in a compartment face to face next to the window through which the buildings along the station platform can be seen passing as the train pulls to a stop. "Look," says the brother, "we're at Ladies!"; "Idiot!" replies his sister, "Can't you see we're at Gentlemen." (1977, 152)

Here, Lacan briefly references the politics of gender division in a way that enforces their dialectical dependency, but nevertheless also ironically supports the notion of "separate but equal." "Ladies and Gentlemen," he comments, "will be henceforth two countries towards which each of their souls will strive on divergent wings, and between which a truce will be the more impossible *since*

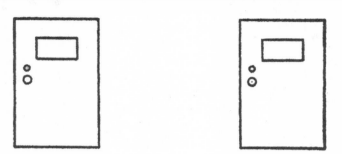

LADIES          GENTLEMEN

"Ladies" and "Gentlemen" reprinted from *Ècrits: A Selection by Jacques Lacan*, translated by Alan Sheridan. Copyright ©1966 by Editions du Seuil. English translation copyright © 1977 by Tavistock Publications. Used by permission of W.W. Norton & Company Inc.

*they are actually the same country* and neither can compromise on its own superiority without detracting from the glory of the other" (1977, 152; emphasis mine). In *The Daughter's Seduction: Feminism and Psychoanalysis* (1982), Jane Gallop engages this image in order to establish the significance of Lacanian psychoanalysis for Anglo-American feminist thought. Lacan, she argues, asks us to "consider as illusory the entire structure which makes the realm of Gentlemen and Ladies appear as defined and absolute as they do in the one-to-one correlation" (1982, 12). Moreover, Gallop draws an analogy between being inside the train and "inside" language in order to question the feminist subject's place within patriarchy. Highlighting the subject's constitution within and by language in a critique of naïve feminist goals centering on the overthrow of patriarchy, she notes, "In ethical discourse, spoken from our place as subjects attempting to signify ourselves in the signifying chain, we are all sitting on one side of the compartment or the other: we are all subject to the blindness imposed by our seats in the compartment; there is no other way of being on the train (chain)" (12). Gallop's recuperation of Lacan for an activist agenda represents a powerful caution; there is no being "outside" phallogocentrism. Yet the compartment is not only divided into sides that influence perspective, but into halves, namely, a front and back. In the context of the image, I would also suggest that Lacan draws our attention back to the social not only in terms of mutually constitutive gender division, but in terms of the artificiality of racial division. Read within the context of American southern history at the time of Lacan's writing in 1966, race resonates within his reference to "two countries" that "are actually the same country."

I invoke Lacan's structuralist iconography here not to gesture to the importance of Lacanian readings of race, but to highlight the other symbolic division that this iconography implies, one that likewise defines social status: the division between white and "colored." Both Elizabeth Abel in "Bathroom Doors and Drinking Fountains: Jim Crow's Racial Symbolic" (1999) and Maia Boswell in "'Ladies,' 'Gentlemen,' and 'Colored': 'The Agency of (Lacan's Black) Letter' in the Outhouse" (1999) have foregrounded Lacan's indirect invocation of American racial segregation via the image of separate restroom doors. In drawing out the image's racial resonance, Boswell calls our attention to both Lacan's reference to (racially unmarked) slavery and his anecdote regarding the wedding preparations of a "negress" in the passages that precede the image. Abel goes further to suggest French cultural awareness of racial segregation in the United States in 1966. His reference to "urinary segregation" she writes, "undermines, rather than reinforces, the primacy of the sexual division. . . . The racial reference signals a return of the Lacanian repressed, not a putatively natural body behind the bathroom door, but the mutual constitution of diverse symbolic systems that disrupt as well as mimic one another" (1999, 439). One can say that this indirect invocation of race denaturalizes gender segregation by pointing to its social constructedness even as Lacan bypasses discussion of the arbitrariness of gender distinction in favor of emphasizing the cultural imposition of privacy ironically ascribed to "Western Man" (Lacan 1977, 151). I say "ironically" because his unspoken analogue is not "Western Woman," but "Primitive Man." This implied racial division predicated on nature/culture distinction and signaled by the presence of doors to veil the bodily needs of the "civilized" informs Boswell's Lacanian reading of race in regard to Toni Morrison's novel, *Sula*.

Boswell's analogy between racial segregation and Lacan's gendered signs focuses on the materiality of the printed letter, its blackness on the page, as an excess to signification. Race represents an excess to the gender binary, "Ladies and Gentlemen," she argues, a relation made visible in a scene in which an African American woman, Helene, travels to the Jim Crow South by train. The character suffers the indignity of being ejected from the "whites only" coach and having to urinate outside, in nature. In the novel, Helene questions a darker-skinned black woman as to the location of the restroom. The woman gestures out the window and replies, simply, "Yonder." Morrison depicts the scene thusly:

While Helene looked about the tiny stationhouse for a door that said COL-ORED WOMEN, the other woman stalked off to a field of high grass on the far side of the track. . . . She looked around for the other woman and, seeing just the top of her head rag in the grass, slowly realized where "yonder" was. All of them, the fat woman and her four children, three boys and a girl, Helene and her daughter, squatted there in the four o'clock Meridian sun. (1982, 24)

As Morrison's work makes clear, the nicety of privacy granted by the gender-divided restroom—and intrinsic to the notion of womanhood itself—is a "whites only" privilege, highlighting the erasure of gender within race: "All of them, the fat woman and her four children, *three boys and a girl* . . . squatted there" (emphasis mine). For African American women, the non-existent racial sign ("yonder") trumps gender distinction, an erasure that is potentially constitutive of the "civilized." Boswell puts pressure on the word "yonder" in order to indicate that facilities for the "colored" exist somewhere beyond the realm of the social:

This gesture of pointing out the window, to a space occupied not by "Ladies" and "Gentlemen," nor even by "Colored Ladies" and "Colored Gentlemen," but rather to the supposed space of "Nature" is what interests me here. . . .What I want to open up is the way in which the racial other can appear set outside of the signifying chain. Designated to a space "yonder," among the grass, the leaves, and the animals, Helene and Nel are not defined as either "Ladies" or "Gentlemen," "white" or "colored," but as figures of elsewhere. They are placed outside "place," without privacy, perhaps in a space of the nonhuman. (1999, 123)

The theoretical parallel, then, is the association of blackness with excess, what exists as "waste" within signification, a gesture outside (the "outhouse") beyond culture's defining terms and meanings. "Lacan's choice of bathrooms segregated by gender," she argues, "reminds us that bathrooms segregated by race are prominent figures in various textual and experiential histories; and such segregation practices have situated some people in a realm of non-signification and nonsignificance" (1999, 119). Boswell's emphasis on blackness as excess uncannily dovetails with what Harun Karim Thomas points out regarding the historical asymmetry of drinking fountains labeled "white" and "colored" in the Jim Crow South. He notes, "The whites-only fountain [often] seems to be constructed in a way that appears to provide the water for the 'colored' drinking fountain via its *excess or run-off* (emphasis mine).[12] That blackness can only signify as an excess, as the discarded waste of an unspoken norm, is highlighted in both an abstract and literal sense. Nevertheless, the distinction between the doors veils the fact that the feminine is itself "no place" within the Symbolic; Woman represents a Lacanian "yonder." This abstract resonance is belied by the iconography of "Ladies/Gentlemen," which implies "separate but equal" and might be more accurately suggested by alternative signs above the restroom doors: "Men/Not-Men."

I want to take Abel's and Boswell's acute discussions of race and gender division in a somewhat different direction, one suggested by what I have focused on here as the interstitial place of Asian Americans and others in the segregated South. If, in the context of gender division, race functions as a "return of the Lacanian repressed" as in Abel, or a means of conveying an "elsewhere" as in Boswell, a secondary level of repression, a secondary "elsewhere" might be recalled by posing the question, "Which race?" That is, in the context of Abel's and Boswell's excellent analyses, African Americans logically serve the symbolic function of abjection as historic targets of segregationist philosophy. But what meaning might be generated by shifting the perspective away from the primary division between black and white? Just as transgenderism asks us to conceive of differently interpellated subjects, how might a parallel term in "transracialism" illuminate that division? To get at this question, I parallel Lacan's image to another iconic representation of social differentiation. Abel's investigation into the dual symbolics of the bathroom door might be cast in its overdetermined American form, perhaps not in terms of the "elsewhere," nonspace of segregated restroom facilities, but of the segregated drinking fountain.

Taken side by side, the dual images highlight a structural parallelism and represent twin forms of segregation: one repudiated in 1954 by *Brown v. Board of Education* and the other, ongoing. In thinking about how the question of the segregated drinking fountains might be different from the question of segregated bathroom doors, I would emphasize that the fountains suggest not so much a question of having "no place else to go," of being relegated to a putative "outside" of culture or signification, but of being resolutely yet ambiguously interpellated within them.

My theoretical parallel is challenged by historical specificity: not often was there such mirror-image equivalence in segregated drinking fountains. That is, as Thomas points out regarding material history, my graphic supports the illusion of "separate but equal" in ways that belie social hierarchy. This is the case in the parallel images of the restroom doors, "Ladies" and "Gentlemen,"

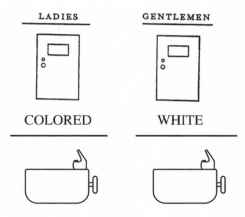

LADIES      GENTLEMEN

COLORED      WHITE

"Ladies" and "Gentlemen" from Jacques Lacan's
*Ècrits* with segregated fountains.

in which the duality veils the hierarchy between men and women. (As my students are fond of pointing out, women's restrooms are *superior* to men's— by which they mean that the level of cleanliness is superior. This is more often than not offered as subtle evidence that gender difference is really "separate but equal," a commentary that supports the (minority) opinion that gender oppression, like racial segregation, is something relegated to the past.)

Yet the shift to the imagery of the drinking fountain does not allow us to invoke race on the basis of the nature/culture, primitive/civilized divide and therefore as something beyond the gendered signs—as in Boswell's reading, where blackness is spatially "yonder" and conceptually parallel to the "outhouse" of language. In effect, the place of the Asian in the seg-regated South is marked by the ambiguity of simultaneity—as both "like blacks" and "like whites"—putting pressure on that distinction in obvious ways. Here, the interstitial denaturalizes the meanings we ascribe to both black and white by exposing race as a continuum of cultural values. "Black" is not a site beyond signification, the place of the nonhuman, but one of hyper-signification, the place where the individual submits to interpreta-tion and surveillance. As theorists of race passing likewise reveal, racial ambiguity can represent a site for exposing the stakes underlying the terms of social division.

This is, not incoincidentally, a claim similar to some offered by transgen-der theorists regarding gender. Susan Stryker writes:

"Transgender phenomena" emerge from and bear witness to the epistemological rift between gender signifiers and their signifieds. In doing so, they
disrupt and denaturalize Western modernity's "normal" reality, specifically
the fiction of a unitary psychosocial gender that is rooted biologically in
corporeal substance. As such, these phenomena become sources of cultural anxiety and semiotic elaboration. (1998, 147)

The "cultural anxiety and semiotic elaboration" of the transspace might find
material resonance in the "choice" of one door or fountain or the other, a
choice that constitutes a public performance of the subject's identification
with and culture's designation of that subject as definitively sexed or definitively raced. In the case of the fountains, how those identifications are made
or refused both by subjects and by culture has been my subject. For the "partly
colored," racial meaning is created through the interplay between two signs,
"colored" and "white," and ultimately can only rest uneasily in ever-increasing or ever-decreasing proximity to either. How the individual chooses either
door or fountain is a matter of both identification and coercion. The parallel
to gender pushes into greater abstraction what my previous chapters have
engaged in historical context. Judith Butler's emphasis on gender play in the
context of drag performance articulates this double valence. She notes:

Identifying with a gender under contemporary regimes of power involves
identifying with a set of norms that are and are not realizable, and whose
power and status precede the identifications by which they are insistently
approximated. This "being a man" and this "being a woman" are internally
unstable affairs. They are always beset by ambivalence precisely because
there is a cost in every identification, the loss of some other set of identifications, the forcible approximation of a norm one never chooses. (1993, 126)

Butler's awareness of gender as an unrealized and unstable norm that can only
be approximated highlights gendering as a cultural process that is essentially
asymptotic; it is a coercive process that can never find stasis. Locating gender
as the "forcible approximation" of normative conceptions of male and female
offers a ready analogy to race. In this case, racial identity must emerge out
of a prescribed identification with the "internally unstable" categories, black
and white, forcing the inverse process of identification into relief: the process of disavowal. My twinning of the graphics and invoking the admittedly
contested phase, "gender segregation," suggests that oscillation: to represent
as "trans" or between categories is to be subject to the sometimes obvious,

sometimes nuanced pressures of conformity. The forms of "forcible approximation" are rendered visible by the transgendered in ways that suggest an alternative term for describing the "partly colored": the transracial.

Thus, the historical process that James Loewen traces regarding the caste elevation of the Chinese in Mississippi discussed in chapter 3 is more abstractly articulated in what is perhaps an anomalous choice of sources, Sandy Stone's discussion of transsexualism in "The 'Empire' Strikes Back: A Posttranssexual Manifesto." In critiquing the ways in which individuals undergoing the first sex-change operations were pressured into making definitive gender choices, she writes, "The highest purpose of the transsexual is to erase him/herself, to fade into the 'normal' population as soon as possible" (1991, 295). That is, the cultural imperative faced by the transsexual is to represent as either male or female as a condition of communal incorporation, to make oneself legible according to social norms. Loewen's work reveals a racial parallel to this cultural imperative: Chinese intermediacy was subject to the pressures of the state, and the very certainty of what "being Chinese" signified became a question, particularly for the second-generation Chinese Mississipian. As in the case of transsexual individuals, those transracial populations can be seen as sites where culture's investments in category distinction become visible. Anne Fausto-Sterling sees in the hermaphrodite the potential for the disruption of biological sex distinction: "Society mandates the control of intersexual bodies because they blur and bridge the great divide; they challenge traditional beliefs about sexual difference. Hermaphrodites have unruly bodies. They do not fall into a binary classification; only a surgical shoehorn can put them there."[13] Her example bridges the illusory divide between activist calls for transgender rights and deconstructionist transgender theory: the "surgical shoehorn" of genital reassignment surgery is itself "unnatural." What I have been discussing in this book is the cultural analogue to that surgical "shoehorn," the processes that reconcile the "inter" to prevailing classifications dictated by the rise of Jim Crow. The representations of caste flexibility in the cases of the Lumbee of North Carolina and the Chinese in the Mississippi Delta reveal the ways in which distinctions between "colored" and "white" were sutured in the face of anomaly. These representations of communities over time reveal both the benefits and costs that attend the subject's inscription into sanctioned state-defined identities, particularly as they engage notions of class uplift and productivity that are intrinsic to American national self-conception. What Butler has identified as gender "approximation" thus finds its historical analogue in Loewen's work on race, the putative caste elevation of Chinese in Mississippi. In portraying the community's progressive encroachment upon idealized whiteness, his work unveils the multiple pressures of social conformity.

What Loewen posits as a resolution to intermediacy, the Chinese transition to "near-white status" (1988, 176), can be seen as a concession to racial apartheid: its "success," though incomplete, validates the unnamed universal of white normativity. Butler cautions against a similar dynamic in the movement for state recognition of gay and lesbian marriage. Such a desire, she notes, is driven by the illusory hope "to become universal, to become interchangeable in one's universality, to vacate the lonely particularity of the non-ratified relations, and, perhaps above all, to gain place and sanctification in the imagined relation to the state" (2004, 131). The desire to achieve recognition and legitimacy according to the terms set by power represents a pointed caution recalling, for example, the Supreme Court ruling *Gong Lum v. Rice* (1927), which centered on the right of Chinese Americans to attend white schools in Mississippi and enjoy the same "protections" that whites enjoyed under segregation, primarily the protection from social intercourse with African Americans. The rights of this interstitial group acceded to the logic of segregation, leaving it intact.[14]

Transgender rights advocates caution that adding new categories does not necessarily challenge the binary distinctions that the law depends upon. In highlighting court cases that expose a legal system ill-equipped to account for a continuum of legal identities, Laura Colker signals the need for the addition of new categories and asserts that a pluralistic view of the law necessarily calls attention to social injustice:

> Sometimes, breaking down this bipolarity will cause us to add new categories such as bisexual, transsexual, or multiracial. . . . [Y]et at other times, it will cause us to see the stark differences in justice that are accorded to people who lie on one end of the bipolar spectrum (e.g., whites, men, or heterosexuals) and to people who lie on the other end (e.g., blacks, women, or homosexuals). (1996, 233–234)

Colker's call for greater awareness of and accommodations for legal "hybrids" speaks to a more nuanced and inclusive sense of legal identities that can be immediately and practically implemented. Nevertheless, as Paisley Currah has established, transgender rights advocates do not view advocacy merely in terms of amending forms of legal identification but, drawing from Critical Race Theory, in terms of challenging the liberalism underlying the law and its reliance on gender distinction.[15] Nevertheless, it is important to note that race and gender advocacy often come into conflict. For example, race has been echoed in the justification of gender-segregated facilities to ironic effect. Challenging the fact that "[g]ender-segregated bathrooms are a bedrock principle under the law," Colker notes that "In the seminal law review article on the proposed federal Equal Rights Amendment, the authors state that we must permit separate 'toilet facilities' in public buildings where separation carries no implication of 'inferiority'" (Colker 1996, 112). As Currah points out, racial analogies have been invoked by those opposing transgender rights, as if prohibiting discrimination against transgender people "would debase the long and proud history of the civil rights movement" (2006, 15).

Within transgender theory, race analysis becomes the context for warnings against universalism, particularly concerning African American men and the subversive potential of gender play. It has been noted that African American male-to-female transsexuals literalize castration in ways that recall the history of lynching.[16] Bell hooks's challenge to claiming the transgressive potential of drag in the film, *Paris is Burning*, recalls the ways in which subjects are differently positioned; the film, she argues, portrays the ways in which "colonized black people (in this case black gay brothers, some of whom were drag queens) worship at the throne of whiteness" (1992, 149). Judith Halberstam highlights racial differences in the translation of masculinity on the New York cabaret circuit in suggesting that African American drag kings assume a rapper aesthetic out of respect for black men, a tribute rather than a parody (1997). Her discussion represents a serious inquiry into the ways in which race makes a difference in transgender criticism beyond invocations of the American Indian *berdache* or the *hiras* in India as examples of race's entry into transgender analysis.

However, my central concern is not to track the intersection between race and transgender theory but to explore their conceptual parallels. If Loewen's community study and chapter 2's discussion of the Lumbee reveal the untenability of intermediacy, in contrast, in what ways does transgender theory reveal the conceptual promise of interstitial status? How does transgender theory underscore the potential of intermediacy in ways that do not merely call for additive categories or a greater tolerance for gender variation? As Currah establishes, transgender rights advocates are not merely concerned with expanding and amending legal categories of gender, but with dismantling gender as a legal concept (2003).

The promise embedded in drawing analogies of difference is suggested by Stone's "manifesto" on transgenderism before it became known under that rubric.[17] Foregrounding the practice of reading and interpretation occasioned by transsexual subjects, Stone suggests "constituting transsexuals not as a class or problematic 'third gender,' but rather as a genre—a set of embodied texts whose potential for productive disruption of structured sexualities and spectra of desire has yet to be explored" (1991, 296). Early on, she located transsexuality as a site for a deconstructive methodology that, in the words of Christopher Norris, "seeks to undo both a given order of priorities *and* the very system of conceptual opposition that makes that order possible" (1988, 31). Likewise, Marjorie Garber views cross-dressers not as the expression of gender's "third term," but "'the third' as a mode of articulation, a way of describing possibility" (1992, 11). As Stryker similarly reveals, "I began to see transsexuality not as an inauthentic state of being but rather as yet another communicational technology . . . for generating and sustaining the desired reality effects of my gender identifications through the manipulation of bodily surface" (1998, 151). By delinking birth sex from gender, this unruly figure exposes reliance on gendered epistemologies be they systems of etiquette, sports, marriage laws—or "urinary segregation." Whether addressing transsexuals, transgender rights, cross-dressing, or intersexuality, transgender theorists see in the interstitial body a critical methodology with widespread implications: "In the transsexual's erased history," Stone suggests, "we can find a story disruptive to the accepted discourses of gender" (1991, 295). One logical offshoot of this disruption is social reorganization, revised concepts of belonging that challenge sedimented histories that have come to define both community and exile.

In thinking of transgenderism as a genre of interstitiality, a racial parallel emerges: the transracial individual does not so much constitute a "third race" in the South as provide a similar site of cultural disruption that may likewise signal the limitations of existing social organization and our investment in similarly naturalized racial categories. This orientation echoes my previous chapters in its focus on status dissonance, but unlike the first section of this book where the potential challenge of the "partly colored" became contained by segregationist logic, I want to suggest another direction. Transspaces challenge our continued investment in black/white distinction by encoding alternative notions of community, echoing Kandice Chuh's invocation of "transnation" to designate "cross-border collectivities and identity formations" (2003, 62). My mirroring of race and gender continuums also finds resonance in anthropologist Victor Turner's concept of liminality and his belief that new forms of belonging emerge from it. Writing in the late 1960s and early 1970s, Turner highlights the ways in which social structure becomes visible through ritual practices, turning his gaze not only to tribal cultures, but to Western culture as well. Liminality, he writes, is a "midpoint of transition in a status-sequence between two positions" that attends the ritual processes of initiation (1974, 237). Those undergoing new status definition, liminal *personae* or "threshold people," are "necessarily ambiguous, since this condition and these persons elude or slip through the network of classifications that normally locate states and positions in cultural space" (1969, 95). He writes, "A society's secular definitions do not allow for the existence of a not-boy-not-man, which is what a novice in a male puberty rite is (if he can be said to be anything)" (1967, 95). I invoke Turner's discussion of liminality here because it suggestively places subjects "ambiguous" to established social structures within a spatial and temporal abstraction, a place of nebulous signification. The condition of those who "fall in the interstices of social structure" (1969, 125) speaks to the cultural placement of transgender and transracial individuals. While for Turner the liminal "betwixt-and-between period" of ritual process is transient, a temporary state in which an initiate is stripped of rank, he nevertheless engages the concept in order to speak more broadly about moments of cultural flux and potential reorganization (1967, 110). Thus, states of liminality unveil the attributes of societies informed by hierarchy and differentiation, in other words, the attributes that separate "men in terms of 'more' or 'less'" (1969, 96).[18]

It is within the liminal period, Turner suggests, that nonhierarchical forms of social relationships emerge, what he calls forms of communitas. Existing in dialectical relationship to social structure, communitas describes a community-in-equality—what Marxist theorists might deem horizontal comradeship: "It is in liminality that communitas emerges, if not as a spontaneous expression of sociability, at least in a cultural and normative form— stressing equality and comradeship as norms" (1974, 232). In the case of the initiates in male puberty rites, a form of communitas or shared fellowship emerges among those "not-boys-not-men" awaiting an elevation in social status. Nevertheless, communitas "is a fact of everyone's experience": "[I]t becomes visible in tribal rites of passage, in millenarian movements, in monasteries, in the counterculture, and on countless informal occasions" (231).

Turner's work reveals that gender and racial intermediacy might not only perform a kind of status dissonance, but initiate new forms of nonhierarchical community that emerge within and potentially against established social norms.[19] The analogy between forms of interstitiality—both racial and gendered—might suggest ways of conceiving kinship that are not based on identity categories but on shared positionalities. In witnessing the relationship between a Vietnamese exchange student and a white cross-dresser in the

Deep South, *Mai's America* offers one way to rethink identity-based concepts of alliance and community as the subjects of the film—an Asian in the South and a transvestite—model a form of what Victor Turner calls "communitas" based on what they share: "trans" status.[20]

## *'Do I look like boy now?': Race and Gender Liminality in America*

To return to the image suggested by the divided restroom doors and drinking fountains, to what extent does having "no place else to go" expose the continuums that define social norms, whether racial or gendered? In *Mai's America*, liminal *personae* reveal the limitations of cultural organization predicated on communities based on race-, sexuality- and, I would add, nationality-based communities. As they bare the processes of cultural inclusion and exclusion, they ask us to see alternative forms of connection that challenge loyalty to entrenched histories. Through a productive analogy, the documentary's portrayal of Asian transracialism in the South queers the black/white division that has come to frame American race relations.

The documentary narrates a specific story: America's defeat of an intrepid spirit. It represents 72 minutes of what was 150 hours of footage following the exchange student's experiences with two host families as she attends high school, her move to Tulane upon being awarded a half scholarship, and finally, her dropping out of college to work in a nail salon. Mai's vivacity, hope, and belief in the First World as a site of opportunity are gradually eroded. In documenting a Vietnamese woman's transformation from an exuberant and ambitious student to a depressed and defeated foot scrubber, the film exposes two myths: that in the United States, hard work translates into class status, and that the First World is a paragon of modernization and site of enlightened, progressive belief. Along the way, the film unveils the systemic and spiritually deadening forces that enforce the status quo: racial violence, poverty, and homophobia.

Mai's presence within a racially divided town generates the film's suspense, centering not only on her educational quest, but on the degree to which she can be "integrated" into either the black or white community.[21] Moreover, as a central figure, Mai blurs other, nonracial boundaries: while the film does not overtly mark her urban background and class privilege, in the United States she is nonetheless viewed as an inhabitant of the Third World ("What do you eat? Coconuts? Squid?"). As a Vietnamese person among American high school seniors learning about the Vietnam War, she is an ambiguous former adversary: she is on the side of victors who conspicuously lack global leverage in a world system dominated by the United States. Her political views, those of a generation born in Hanoi after the war, clash with those of the marginalized expatriate Vietnamese community and potentially with those of a generation of Americans raised to accept the premises of the Cold War. Choosing a host family is not akin to "choosing" between signs of the segregated fountain's iconography—in the post-1954 era, it is not a "choice" between racial uplift and degradation—but it resonates with the questions posed by the earlier period: what is the Asian's affiliation with communities defined by Jim Crow and its legacy?

The still that introduces the film on its PBS website offers a visual conundrum: it features Mai's smiling face under a Vietnamese peasant's hat as she stands next to a billboard at the state border: "Mississippi Welcomes You."[22] The sign invokes legendary southern hospitality at the same time that it solidifies Mai's alien status, providing a visual cue as to the documentary's fish-out-of-water premise and prefiguring the contingency of that welcome. The film's self-conscious (and continual) juxtaposition between Mai and her environment begins with the stark contrast between her character and that of her first host family of self-described rednecks. The family's prefab house, red velvet cake-making, and continuously running television serve as the backdrop to the film's depiction of Mai as the antithesis of Don, Susan, and their daughter, Kim; her bubbly personality and wonderment in experiencing American culture offset the family's passivity, poverty, physical disability, and clinical depression. Here, the film perhaps too easily feeds northern fantasies of the southern white trash stereotype; nevertheless, the South becomes a stand-in for American parochialism. The film presents Mai's outsider status as a matter of youth vs. age, vivacity vs. melancholy, and ambition vs. complacency rather than as a matter of race, which is rarely commented upon. The documentary relies on Mai's voiceover complemented by Poras's choice of visual to make clear her feelings of alienation in Mississippi. As Mai narrates her homesickness and feelings of being out of place, for example, the film shows her walking through a deserted street in front of a Bible bookstore. On a car ride during which her Vietnamese American friends establish that the Klan targets Asians—"any colored people"—as well as African Americans ("Ooh, don't scare me! Don't say that!"), the camera focuses on a "Dixie Gas" sign illuminating the darkness outside the moving vehicle. When Mai is excluded from graduation ceremonies and watches the action, fittingly, from the sidelines, the camera lingers over the program's inspirational inscription, "In all ways, you acknowledge Him," and witnesses the communal prayer that blesses the proceedings. These scenes establishing Mai's distance from southern communities invoke whiteness only to the extent that, like Christianity, it is always already assumed to be normative, assumed to be an accepted and embedded aspect of southern public life: it does not need to be remarked upon by the white people who inhabit it.

Rather than submit to the potential contagiousness of depression that attends white rural poverty as depicted in the film, Mai requests a host transfer on the advice of a street psychic. The establishing shot of the new African American host family deliberately shifts the tone of the film; the scene opens with Mai's public welcome before an exuberant black congregation. Upon introduction, she takes the microphone to announce how welcome she feels, should the viewer miss that point: "I thank everyone for making me feel great." The youth of Mai's hosts, Justin and Latoya, their gender-enlightened daily practices, and willingness to acknowledge a teenager's needs ("How are you doing? Do you need to go to the mall?") present a stark contrast to the general indifference of her previous hosts. In this, the film readily indulges in a romanticized portrait of African American affect and communalism. Nevertheless, it does not portray the shift in tone and feeling from white to black communities as a result of naturalized alliance or as a seamless erasure of Mai's cultural and racial difference. Her distance is conveyed, as before, as befuddlement; for example, she can't appreciate "You Know You're Black" jokes because she doesn't understand the class implications that attend the black/white division, although she understands the camaraderie they engender. Among her black friends at Tulane, Mai's bewilderment at their attempted philosophizing leads her to express feelings of alienation.

Mai's inability to grasp the full meaning of those around her is a constant theme running across ethnic lines: she fails to appreciate the pun made by a white Mardi Gras reveler with a horned headdress who self-identifies as a "horny beast." She mistakes a Vietnamese American's views on the war when he attempts to inform her that "not all Vietnamese wanted communism." ("All?" she asks. "*Not* all," he corrects her.) While temporarily working as a waitress in a Chinese restaurant, she resists the owner's tutorial in how to read the menu for customers ("You don't need to tell me anymore if it's spicy"). These repeated scenes of failed interpretation underscore her status as an outsider to American culture, its linguistic codes, its class and race associations, its Cold War politics. As the film asks us to evaluate American culture through the perspective of the transracial subject—one "betwixt and between" (Turner 1967, 110) historically sedimented southern communities—it reverses the perspective of my previous focus on southern culture's attempts to read (and resolve) racial ambiguity. Yet here, the outsider provides a disorienting perspective on southern-as-American culture not by hammering home the racial divide that is Jim Crow's legacy, but by engaging differing beliefs about homosexuality.

The film portrays the failure of Mai's integration by highlighting sexual politics. In a pointed scene, Mai contests her African American host mother's view that "God did not, when you were born, make you gay." "God," Latoya emphasizes, "doesn't have anything to do with it." The scene is striking precisely because through religion it introduces a value system that transcends the southern racial divide and bridges the two communities in Meridian, Mississippi: homophobia. Poras intentionally places this scene alongside the moment that Mai's white girlfriends—the "popular" ones who, we are told, normally do not befriend foreign exchange students—express, with typical adolescent eloquence, their hatred of gay men and the "sickness" of homosexuality: "Gay men are so nasty. It's really gross." These scenes of conflict establish another aspect of Mai's segregation from both communities. As the viewer has learned, her best friend is the white male transvestite she meets in a gay bar, Chris aka Christy. Moreover, although she has invited him to the prom, she subsequently reverses herself, aware that her liberal views on sexuality mark her difference from both black and white. In articulating her fear of ostracism, she implicitly recognizes the tenuous status that "foreign exchange student" confers within the hyper-hierarchized atmosphere of American high school: she enters with no peer group, bereft of even a falsely naturalized racial one among Asian Americans. Delinked from community, she is a social nobody; the film is in essence her search for an elusive sense of belonging even as she is marked as alien to the categories that traditionally define group membership in the South—race, religion, political belief. As if to compound that distance, she adds gender to the mix by remaking her body to fit her chosen affiliation, her relationship with a transgendered person.

The film forces an analogy between race and sexuality in two ways: first, as a straightforward account of shared oppression articulated as a lack of place, and second, as a more complex question of desire, belonging, and "trans" status. The parallelism between cultural and sexual marginality derives from Poras's editorial choices and is articulated by Christy herself. However, it is not Mai's placement as Vietnamese in the South that she acknowledges; rather, Mai's status as someone away from "home" reflects her own feelings of displacement. In response to Mai's dissatisfaction with her first host family, Christy confesses,

I don't feel that I'm right here. You know what I'm saying? I feel like I'm out of place. Does that make sense? You know, I know you probably know enough because I bet you feel that you're out of place. Being in Meridian or Stonewall, you just feel that you're out of place. You're not home. You see, that's the way I feel. I feel that I'm not supposed to be here. I feel I'm supposed to be somewhere where people accept me for what I am.

In highlighting Christy's feeling of being "out of place" as a transgendered individual, the film implicitly calls up a conventional narrative: urban spaces as sexually liberated. The film thus relies heavily upon what queer theorists identify as the spatial inflection of coming-out stories discussed in the previous chapter—the migration from rural spaces to urban centers as part of the individual's quest for community.[23] As Kath Weston writes, the imaginary urban (and nonsouthern?) elsewhere is "a symbolic space that configures gayness itself by elaborating an opposition between rural and urban life" (1995, 274). Here, Christy's commentary on being out in the South reflects this traditional narrative, which is partially constitutive of her transgendered identity; nevertheless, her testimony of rural sexual small-mindedness is placed in the service of a dissonant racial commentary. The film compounds a sense of their alliance-in-difference as her voiceover continues over shots of Mai walking alone at night, a visual that grafts Christy's isolation onto Mai's. The fact that neither of them can be seen by the camera as she utters this confession enforces a sense of their mutual invisibility. The scene's darkness erases the very markers of visually inscribed difference and implicitly invokes another scene shot at night, a scene in which Mai's Vietnamese American friends express fear of the KKK; both sequences draw a veiled link between intolerance and the threat of violence.

Christy's inadvertently ambiguous invocation of Stonewall—that is, Stonewall, *Mississippi*—implicates the Stonewall Inn in New York City, the symbol of gay resistance to police repression. Yet this ambiguous reference is intended to evoke Mai's displacement, where she feels "out of place." Ironically, the documentary's location evokes their shared "trans" status: both Mai and Christy are meridian to Meridian itself, part of an imaginary circle passing between two poles. This lens reorients the black/white dichotomy of segregation; they are not exactly "yonder" the scene of African American humiliation in Morrison's novel, a scene that takes place within nature, outside the same southern town. The film thus plays upon gender to express the anomaly of Asian "trans" status in that both subjects are refused incorporation into identity-based communities. Echoing Turner's concept of liminal *personae* who are "structurally, if not physically 'invisible'" (1967, 95), the drag queen (speaking literally from somewhere in the dark) experiences her difference as a lack of place. Feinberg's sense of belonging as a transgendered individual invokes a similar metaphor: "I respect that right of each person who finds their home in man or woman, male or female" (1998, 70). While the film might confirm "metronormativity" in its devaluation of rural spaces, it nonetheless also recasts those spaces as alternative sites of connection beyond what Weston calls the "symbolics of urban/rural" gay migration narratives.

Chris seizes upon Mai's status as foreign exchange student as a vehicle for articulating his own transgender status: it implies a transitional state of not belonging. As in the preceding chapter, "foreignness" is not explicitly racialized, but is also expressive of being outside the (right) place. The conjoining of Chris and Mai suggests one avenue through which the anomaly of Asian racial position in the South becomes mediated by sexuality, however traditionally understood within queer topographies. For an Asian in Mississippi, "integration" lies in the abstract, within meaningful, associative bonds and alternative alliances that are not wholly based on a racial binarism. That is, in their shared "trans" status, they find communitas, fellowship in status equality. Yet a reading of alliance based on political *simpatico*, the recognition of likeness via mutual boundary blurring, ignores an obvious point: that connection is also erotic. Desire remains veiled in the documentary's treatment of Chris's and Mai's relationship. Chris's voiceover introduces the idea of Mai's attraction to him (a point I will return to), only to reassign it to his "attitude," an attraction to exploring "the wild side of herself." The film takes pains to represent the latter precisely because it carries the weight of its critique of American culture. While the United States is often extolled as a site of freedom wherein the self can be remade, *Mai's America* narrates the opposite, the insidious and potentially punitive structures that enforce the status quo.

Moreover, the film produces an analogy between race and gender differences not merely by paralleling forms of outsidedness, but through its portrayal of what I am calling, as a means of reorienting the derogatory term that I take as my title, Mai's transracial status and, I would argue, her own transgenderism. Early in the film, Mai shaves off her hair. Simply put, she looks like a boy through most of the film. Compounding her inability to find a place among communities, she is visually "de-girled." Mai's performative bent, her experimentation with her own appearance, naturalizes her alliance with a drag queen; transvestitism offers a ready visual metaphor for trying on

Still from *Mai's America,* a film by Marlo Poras. Courtesy of Marlo Poras.

alternative identities, an opportunity now opened through her distance from Asian patriarchy.[24] Mai's voiceover before the mirror conveys her awareness of her gender betrayal: "All mothers in Vietnam want their daughters to be charming and gentle. And the typical wife in Vietnam, when her husband comes home, she should take off his jacket and prepare the meal—and never, never talk back. I don't think I'll ever be a typical Vietnamese woman."

The film dramatizes the duality of her gender position: looking as she does, she cannot be mistaken for a traditional Vietnamese woman—or, for that matter, for a woman. Her cropped hair offers a startling contrast to her actual activity in the scene, lavishly applying cosmetics in the manner of a drag queen. The visual succeeds in establishing her penchant for dress-up and play made possible in the United States at the same time that the intensely feminizing action jars with the boyishness of the figure she cuts. The film uses Mai's gender liminality to visually align her with her transgendered friend who, perhaps reflecting a Westerner's inability to perceive gender distinction in Asians, had mistaken her for a boy even prior to her haircut ("I said to myself, 'Oh no, not another little Oriental boy! Not another one!'").

This approximate transgendering prefigures what will be the eventual erosion of Mai's girlishness—her innocence, vivacity, and wonder—that signals America's defeat of its former enemy. Despite the supposed freedom that distance from home confers, in the South she is continually schooled in gender conformity, most notably by the patriarch of her first host family, Grandpa, with whom she shares a sympathetic rapport. Her haircut elicits this exchange:

GRANDPA: You look good, but a girl ain't supposed to cut her hair off.
MAI: (laughing) I'm not a girl anymore.
GRANDPA: What your daddy say about that?
MAI: He doesn't know.

The dialogue dramatizes what is possible outside the range of paternal influence: the ability to renounce one's previous self and challenge a fundamental signifier of social status. But such a message is undercut by the images that follow, scenes that enforce perception of Mai's isolation in the Bible Belt. The film implies that it is not only her racial, cultural, political, urban, and presumably religious differences (her consultations with a street psychic are unironic) that convey her separation, but her gender bending as well.[25] This boundary blurring lends visual support to her alliance with Christy, highlighting the performative bent they share. Mai's ease in front of the camera was one reason she was selected as an ethnographic subject in the first place.[26] By the same token, the very theatricality that surrounded Mai during filming was clearly a reason for Chris's interest in her; as he admitted after wrap-up, "Mai made me feel like a star."[27] Nevertheless, the film's focus on Chris's sexuality as purely theatrical—he is seen in drag at a gay club or getting made up at home while singing gospel, never being intimate with gay men or transmen—neuters the possibility of the gay man's threat to a straight audience. Mai, newly queered, is the only object of his affection.

Yet the film refuses to push the boundaries of the sexual narrative it introduces. It admits erotic attraction ("I wish to be your girlfriend," Mai tells him when they first meet) only to deflate it; it cannot decide whether their relationship is sororial or something else. While it may hint that likeness, their mutual transgenderism, underlies Mai's attachment, it cannot represent what is too complex to be understood within traditionally narrow routes of desire, those firmly fixed on either end of the homosexual/heterosexual continuum. Sexual tension between them is always rendered playfully. After her haircut, conscious of her gender ambiguity, she confronts Christy with the question:

MAI: Do I look like boy now?

CHRISTY: No, you look good with it. You still look like a little girl, but it really looks good on you.

MAI: So now you're more of a girl than me.

CHRISTY: No, you'll always have a little bit on me. You see what I'm saying? Not much, but a little bit more.

The lighthearted exchange is posed as a competition over femininity, but their supposed sorority—they are both "girls" together—is belied by Mai's own transgendering. In effect, she has transformed herself into a boy *for* him, becoming the "little Oriental boy" that he initially thought she was.[28] The very complication of routes of desire here—her transformation into a boy for a man dressed as a woman—like those in David Henry Hwang's play, *M. Butterfly*, cannot be articulated within the simple opposition between gay and straight. Does she love him as her object choice or as a manifestation of a difference in herself? Is the mutual boundary blurring reflective of a desire for him or a desire for a shared likeness? Significantly, this ambiguity of gender and desire serves the film's interest in witnessing an Asian's experiences within a racially polarized landscape. In mirroring racial and sexual discourses, the film redirects questions of communal integration away from issues of identity to locality, the irresolution of not being in the "right" place, a place characterized by racial and sexual fixity.[29] The film's conjoining of Mai and Chris/Christy through both ambiguous appearance and ambiguous erotic attraction thus highlights their mutual segregation. In doing so, it pushes the very definition of segregation and the forms it may take. Nevertheless, their failure to integrate, to find belonging within stratified subcultures, culminates in social death.

The film's analogy between differences is driven home in the fate of its characters; Christy's defeat prefigures Mai's. Near the end of the film, Chris is shown for the first time in men's clothing confessing his change of heart and his "murder" of Christy:

CHRIS: I went to church. I want to be more of a boy now. I want a family. I want the wife and the children and all the stuff like that . . .

MAI: What in the hell get your butt up back to church?

CHRIS: I just wanted to go for some reason.

MAI: Is there anyone wanted you to change?

CHRIS: My mama wanted me to change for a long time, but she wasn't the reason. I changed because I wanted to. It's because I wanted to be dif-

ferent. I wanted to be a different person and I did. I just had a reality
check . . . Does that make sense? I came back to earth . . .

MAI: Came back to earth . . . from a star?

CHRIS: I went from this "Christy" person to Chris. And I'm more happy
with it now. I got rid of her. I buried her behind my house.

MAI: That's dangerous. That's bad thing you bury her behind your house
because she can come back whenever she wants to.

CHRIS: No, I burned her. She ain't going anywhere.

The presumably enlightened viewer is asked to see this exchange as Mai
does, as a capitulation to social norms, as a tragic if predictable consequence
of living in the Bible Belt. In highlighting Christy's death, the film relies upon
what Donna Jo Smith calls the myth of southern queerness, one that assumes
"that queers in the South not only would want to leave home but literally
would be required to leave home, as a matter of survival" (D. Smith 1997,
381). Via proximity, the film likewise poses a question about Mai's "survival"
in the South; the juxtaposition between this confession and the sequence that
follows heightens the film's parallelism between Mai and the dearly departed,
likewise alien Christy, pulled from a star and buried in the backyard. The film
cuts to Mai clinging to Chris's back while roughhousing in a pool; as they
break the surface of the water together she reassures him, "I'm still alive."
Both the image and the dialogue evoke the previous exchange: Mai emerges
from the depths and "comes back" just as she anticipates that Christy will.
(And, of course, Christy is resurrected, albeit not on camera. She cheerfully
informs us on the film's PBS website, "Well, let's just say that I'm a Queen
again.") In Christy's forced disappearance, the film achieves its indictment
of southern-as-American culture where tolerance is driven underground
and given a proper burial. Liminality in the United States suffers a symbolic
death and ambivalent reincorporation.

The impossibility of "trans" spaces is brought home in the film's invocation
of Christy in its final scene. Poras hearkens back to the film's opening images
of destitute Hanoi shoeshine boys in its end in which Mai is visibly depressed
and also working on feet in a Vietnamese-run nail salon in Detroit. While the
move restores her to a naturalized sense of community among those "like"
her, other Vietnamese expatriates, her migration to the North nonetheless
marks her as like African Americans whose exodus out of the South was, as
is hers, filled with hopes largely unmet. Northward migration is thus reso-
nant with the symbolic failure of American promise for both African Americans and new immigrants. Kneeling before a chatty and well-intentioned

but ignorant customer (conveniently adorned in red, white, and blue), her hair now grown out, Mai woodenly remarks in the film's final dialogue: "You remind me of my friend, Christy." In Mai's abjection, we can read the deflation of RuPaul's motto—not "We're all born naked and the rest is drag," but "We're all born naked and the rest is a drag." She does not achieve the desired academic degree, but instead carries away the detritus of American culture symbolized by a suitcase overflowing with crap. The suitcase's bunny slippers and plastic M & M's dolls are the analogue of other junk—racial and sexual attitudes—that cannot be wholly compacted but must nonetheless be taken home. In its portrayal of twinned spiritual deaths one can read a pointed national critique, but, more significantly, the film opens up a space for reconsidering the nature of integration, alliance, and community.

## Beyond the Intersection: The Uses of Analogy

Even as it promises a new look at the nation, *Mai's America* relies on standard tropes of the South, particularly regarding the association between Christian conservatism and sexual and gender oppression. Christy's "death" is represented as the logical outcome of being transgendered in the Bible Belt. Far from being made to signify postmodern futurity and gender flexibility as Halberstam notes about transgendered figures, Chris/Christy is a martyr; as in Williams's recognition that her transgendered student "S" has "no place else to go," he finds ambiguous stability in the death of his other half. Thus, "transspace" is not necessarily liberating, but a site subject to the pressures of normativity enforced by gender expectation and, as Mai's migration reveals, the historical legacy of black/white division. In the end, Mai and Christy find belonging together, if only in the abstract.

Yet the treatment of this somewhat conventional representation of southern queerness provokes an analogy between race and gender in perhaps unconventional ways. Expressive of the neither-nor placement of Asians within the racial economy of the South, a term such as "transracial" then might convey a greater sense of fluidity between what are perceived to be, even after *Brown v. Board of Education*, two fixed communities, black and white. My point is not to argue for a naturalized alliance between the differently gendered and differently raced, nor am I claiming that being transracial is the "same" as being transgendered. Rather, my goal has been to suggest a shared conceptual framework in the present moment that derives from historicity as well as spatialization. Exploring the relationship between a Vietnamese woman and a cross-dressing white man—and its facets that defy representation—signals the need to understand alliances that are not singularly based on ethnic community, nationality, political coalition, or even erotic intimacy. In thinking about friendship as a form of alternative kinship, I am reminded of Lauren Berlant's sense that "attachments are developing that might redirect the different routes taken by history and biography" (1998, 286). "To rethink intimacy," she writes, "is to appraise how we have been and how we live and how we might imagine lives that make more sense than the ones so many are living" (286). Her comment echoes with the disruptive force of Judith Butler's question, "Is Kinship Always Already Heterosexual?"—a question that might be extended to include other nonsanctioned forms of affiliation, not simply those defined by sexual distinction (2004). The film thus depicts alliance and kinship through routes alternative to those naturalized by identity politics and history, opening up the space for social reorganization.

The transracial/transgender analogy, then, becomes the occasion to think about race beyond the terms set by the Civil Rights Movement. For an Asian in Mississippi, for example, "integration" might signal meaningful bonds and connections not based on identitarian concepts of community. The very nature of integration as it is traditionally cast, as the push toward a single, putatively color-blind community based on shared equal rights, becomes reconceived. Its horizon is no longer an illusory form of likeness based on access to rights, but alternative collectivities not aspiring to incorporation or representation in the public sphere.

The structural twinning between doors and fountains highlights the restrictive necessity of establishing legal status within bipolar frameworks. In her work on drag kings, Halberstam counter-intuitively establishes that "[i]t is the very elasticity of the gender binary in particular that allows the biological categories of male and female to hold sway" (2005, 109). My emphasis on Asian Americans here likewise does not discount the primacy of the black/white dialectic but, in fact, affirms its ability to "hold sway" long after the dissolution of de jure segregation, a point that *Mai's America* makes visible. In effect, Asian America is a site of multiple ambiguities against which, I would argue, the complexity of black/white relations—often conflated with "race relations"—stands out in heightened relief. Nevertheless, in highlighting the ways in which subjects are created and disciplined within parallel (and, of course, intersecting) continuums that name normativity and deviance, I want to enrich that framework for comparative race studies through a detour through gender theory.

By foregrounding Asian oscillation between the unstable poles of "like blacks" or "like whites," I do not want to establish a third space between them, but to uncover deep structures associated with beliefs attached to status fixity—a process that underlies the goals of transgender theory. Stryker outlines these goals in broad strokes: "[T]he field of transgender studies," she notes,

> is concerned with anything that disrupts, denaturalizes, rearticulates, and makes visible the normative linkages we generally assume to exist between the biological specificity of the sexually differentiated human body, the social roles and statuses that a particular form of body is expected to occupy, the subjectively experienced relationship between a gendered sense of self and social expectations of gender-role performance, and the cultural mechanisms that work to sustain or thwart specific configurations of gendered personhood. (2006, 3)

In order to explore how gender theory might help illuminate our understanding of race, one might also say, echoing Stryker, that transracial studies should be concerned with anything that disrupts, denaturalizes, rearticulates, and makes visible the normative linkages we generally assume to exist between the biological specificity of the *racially* differentiated human body, the social roles and statuses that a particular form of body is expected to occupy, the subjectively experienced relationship between a *racialized* sense of self and social expectations of *race-role* performance, and the cultural mechanisms that work to sustain or thwart specific configurations of *raced* personhood (emphasis added). My ventriloquism of Stryker here is intended to parallel the ways in which transracialism likewise shifts away from concepts of biology and the visual epistemology of race toward an analysis of social status and its dependence on historically entrenched binarism. The substitution highlights the shared relation to social justice that underlies both theories of racial performativity and gender studies.

In emphasizing analogy, I hearken back to the Women's Movement not to graft oppression onto oppression, but to focus on the potential within comparison. Comparison, a hallmark of social movements, has certainly been displaced within academia by a focus on intersectionality, explorations of the interconnection, and mutually constitutive categories of race, gender, class, and sexuality. I am certainly aware, too, that the palimpsest of continuums that I highlight here find intersection most obviously, for example, in Asian transpeople living in the South who, in distinction to my claims regarding Mai here, identify as transgendered. Nevertheless, I would claim that analogy opens up the space for a critical methodology that renews and expands the exploration of intersecting axes of difference. Affirming the significance of analogy, Eve Sedgwick links the discourses of "fat phobia" and homophobia in asserting that "it's possible to come out of the closet as a fat woman" (1990, 72). Defending her usage against the charge that it may disrespectfully evacuate historical gay specificity, she notes, "I hypothesize that exactly the opposite is true. I think that a whole cluster of the most crucial sites for the contestation of meaning in twentieth-century Western culture are consequentially and quite indelibly marked with the historical specificity of homosocial/homosexual definition" (72). I would second that expansion even at the risk of political dilution; I want to suggest that the male/female dichotomy can initiate a reconsideration of black/white relations. As the film shows, this might occur not via the figure of the interracial intersexual or via an analogy between race passing and sexual closeting, for instance, but through a broad conceptual mirroring: the transracial Asian, the transgendered drag queen.

Meridian is thus not merely a small town in Mississippi; in the context of *Mai's America* and of Asians in the South, it specifies a way of seeing between two poles. Echoing Homi Bhabha's notion of the interstitial wherein culture "produces occasional spaces in which those annihilating norms, those killing ideals of gender and race, are mimed, reworked, resignified" (1994, 124), I affirm the significance of the comparative gesture and its ability to rework and resignify race and gender continuums that define belonging and exclusion. The film's lesson, then, above and beyond its sentimental documentation of the failure of American promise and the disruption of associations between the First and Third Worlds, lies in its potential to reconceptualize the historically saturated terms that we use to talk about race, terms like integration and segregation that cannot help but conjure up the South in all of its supposed perversity.

# Afterword

## *Continuums, Mobility, Places on the Train*

In 2005, the *New York Times Magazine* carried two personal narratives about segregation, one a memoir about South African apartheid in its food section, and the other, a memoir about riding the so-called women's car on the subway in Cairo in its "Lives" section.[1] The essays were not linked in any way other than their pointed address to an American audience and the fact that they appeared in the same issue on the same day. That they are thematically connected by a shared focus on social separation is no doubt a coincidence; moreover, they take opposing views on "segregation." Consistent with post–Civil Rights liberalism, the author of the essay on food condemns the apartheid that was part of his childhood experience in South Africa. In contrast, the author of the personal narrative on gender-segregated public transportation in Egypt implicitly praises the virtues of privacy in a public conveyance, an "amenity" not available to American women. In their differing ethical resonances, their invocations of global cultures, and their near-contiguity, these two essays reveal why Americans might resist drawing analogies between forms of social division in the public sphere.

In the first essay, "American Dreams," food becomes the occasion to recall racial segregation in its global context; as the subtitle attests, "Food may be pleasurable, but in its essence it's political." Author Jon Robin Baitz queries, "How could a cool iceberg salad with Russian dressing served by an elderly waitress at the late, lamented Dolores's Drive Inn on Wilshire Boulevard seem like a perfect refutation of apartheid? Easy. Because at Dolores's, you didn't have to be white like me to get fries and a Coke" (55). The white American's longing for home during his "exile" in a racially divided South Africa is represented as nostalgia for diner food in a multicultural Los Angeles. Baitz's difference from white South Africans lies in his race liberalism, a political orientation that is intrinsic to claiming membership in the collective identity, "American" in the post-1954 moment (Wiegman 1999).

In contrast, the following essay about a western woman's experience in the Middle East is meant to make Americans sit up and question our premises about women's liberation. In "The Comfort of Strangers," as a Muslim American, G. Willow Wilson establishes her solidarity with Egyptian women on the metro. Subtitled, "In Cairo's subway, a Western woman like me can find safe haven," the essay tells the story of her fellow riders' censure of a male teenager who innocently enters the gender-segregated car to hawk tissues. At the moment of the adolescent's rebuke, Wilson notes, "I was grateful to be part of the floating world of the women's car. In that small corner of a culture so different from my own, culture itself ceased to matter. For a few station stops I carried no baggage—no problematic nationality, no suspect political agenda. I was simply a woman among other women" (62). It is not merely a feeling of cultural transcendence in the shared position of "woman" that the author wants to highlight, it is another collective rebuke. American women might be surprised to find that they lack what the author feels is a fundamental right enjoyed by Middle Eastern women: the right to privacy, ironically, on a public conveyance.

Proximity initiates my comparison; the essays are separated by only eight pages. Nevertheless, in the context of American culture, they are also separated by a moral gulf. South Africa's example is meant to confirm what Americans already know about racial segregation; Baitz exudes self-conscious pride in national egalitarianism, however unevenly practiced. Cheap, fast American food is superior to the mushy, bland cuisine of the former European colonies because it is served regardless of race. In contrast, the Egyptian anecdote is meant to level American superiority by asking a presumably biased audience to consider a benefit of gender separation: the erasure of other divisions. The stories are essentially about national affiliation and its ability to comfort as well as divide. That they underline an ethical distinction between forms of social separation reveals the complication involved in drawing conceptual analogies of difference. One example is indefensible as a blatant instance of inequality, yet the other is worthy of consideration precisely on the basis of group rights, in this case, the right to "safety." By and large, we get the gist of the stories: the American is not like the Afrikaaners of the author's boyhood. The American is like her Middle Eastern peers, bonding over the violation of public transportation's *purda*.

I offer these post-1954 examples of global segregations not merely to suggest that the struggle between Afrikaaner and African, between men and women, is mediated through the lens of the West. What interests me is the unspoken in-between of both stories, the subjects who, like those of this book, go unmarked: the "coloureds" under South African apartheid, the "not-boy, not-man" who finds his place on the train suddenly contested. Their presence (or lack thereof) complicates the questions about segregation that both writers think they know: served or refused service? Mobility or restricted movement? Inclusion or exclusion? The interstitial remains on the margins of history's narration of injustice and change, perhaps because it worries lines of moral absolutism, easy dichotomies between privilege and oppression.

Throughout this work, the South has been ironically situated as itself a liminal space, between tradition and modernity, simultaneously a rural backwater and emergent cosmopolite. As regional eccentric, it is a site of national fascination and repulsion. The South figures as a source of cultural anxiety, the unschooled hick cousin who threatens to disrupt the national family reunion. As critic Diane Roberts asserts, "The curse and the blessing of the South is that it functions as a sort of national theater, acting out the subjects—race, history, class—that the rest of the country assumes immunity from. While mainstream America cheerfully dismisses the past as irrelevant, the South is still the designated land of suffering, poverty, prejudice: America's 'old country'" (1998, 12L). That is, the South is often conveniently represented as the Third World within, part of the First World but not quite. One has only to explore media response to Hurricane Katrina in 2005 to witness how this plays out on the national scene. Or responses to Oprah Winfrey's creation of a school for girls in Malawi, Africa: we could use such a school in Winfrey's home state of *Mississippi*, sniped critics. In the words of Jon Smith and Deborah Cohen, as "the uncanny double of both the First and Third Worlds," the U.S. South is betwixt and between, blurring relations between center and periphery (2004, 10). The southern stereotype becomes a convenient scapegoat for affirming progressive attitudes about cultural difference or marking the irony of foreign aid to developing countries. This is not to say that southern culture does not also indulge in its own exceptionalism. For example, John Shelton Reed appreciates Choong Soon Kim's admission that, as a Korean, he finds it difficult to read southerners, noting in what is intended to be a reversal of a cliché, "He finds us, in a word, inscrutable" (2003, 103). Marking pride in southern distinction, the statement gestures to its opposite: southerners are just as apt to trot out the old stereotypes as anyone else.

The archive surrounding the "partly colored" only partially interrupts the history of discrimination that we have granted iconic and infamous status. Shifting from African Americans to Asian Americans or from race to sexuality and gender does not fundamentally challenge our perception of southern history or its investment in black-white distinction. Nevertheless, the interstitial is a potentially productive site for unveiling the work of culture; as Bhabha notes, it is "the in-between space that carries the burden of the meaning of culture" (1994, 38). To draw another parallel to transgender theory, anomaly reveals structure; Susan Stryker notes, "Transgender studies has a deep stake in showing how the seemingly anomalous, minor, exotic, or strange qualities of transgender phenomena are in fact effects of the relationship constructed between those phenomena and sets of norms that are themselves culturally produced and enforced" (2006, 3). These stakes apply to unveiling racial "phenomena" as well.

The issue is not merely one of inclusion or exclusion, integration or segregation, or racial classification as a sign of assimilation or its limits, but how the in-between exposes the complex interplay of multiple axes of social status and normativity—in sometimes surprising ways. In the context of the pre-1954 South and beyond it, I have foregrounded that crucible between "not black" and "not white" within a society where, in Cherríe Moraga's words, "Black is divided from white and the rest of us are required to fall inside that great divide" (2000, 183). Toni Morrison's call for understanding "the ways in which the presence of Afro-Americans has shaped the choices, the language, the structure—the meaning of so much American literature" applies more broadly to culture in general (1989). This "presence," whether materially or metaphorically, has loomed large for those "dark races" whose place became measured by degrees of proximity to the "Negro." A Chinese American merchant in Mississippi once observed, "No matter what we do, we're caught in the middle" (cited in Quan 1982, 90). Being "caught in the middle" takes on a number of connotations as multiple continuums come to inform distinctions between the dominant and the minor, the invisibly universal and the abject—"colored"/white, male/female, able-bodied/disabled, heterosexual/homosexual, vanilla/perverse. What I hope to have shown is not merely that gender and sexuality intersect with or are mutually constitutive of race, but that they indicate alternative fulcrums around which social status turned. The continuum enforced by segregation's racial binarism is not the only one that locates subjects within the space between the normative and the deviant.

Thus, while my engagement begins with a question of racial epistemology, it does not intend to end there or with the claim that restoring anomaly to visibility is historically transformative. While the black-white dialectic is a recognized trope for understanding Asian American experience in particular, I invoke it in order to highlight a broader set of relations: for one, the interplay between disavowal and identification, a dynamic that echoes Butler's theory of gender approximation and can be witnessed in other periods and regions. The cultural pressures are dual and simultaneous—not merely repudiation or desire, but both. Moreover, what I have witnessed here is how these dynamics played out over time in multiple arenas—governmentality and the law, popular and visual culture, ethnography and history—as well as literature. Engaging a number of disciplines, I am aware that like the "not-boy, not-man" in Cairo, I too have presumptively entered disciplinary cars where I do not belong, or claimed a transdisciplinary space that only nebulously exists. Invoking diverse figures canonical to various disciplines—C. Vann Woodward, Georg Simmel, Victor Turner, Richard Wright, Eve Sedgwick, or Judith Butler—I have perhaps assumed too great a mobility between history, sociology, anthropology, literature, and queer and feminist theory. But these figures find unity, I think, in the tools that they offer to critical practice, whether tracing progressive narratives of caste shift or its interruption, or exploring race's latency beyond intended disclosure.

The caste shift of the two interstitial communities that provide case studies here are characterized as successes; both communities refused to allow segregation-era culture to encroach upon their collective senses of self, establishing tenuous "third" spaces. Yet they also represent failures; the communities achieved caste elevation without integration, without contesting the premises on which segregation was based. Of course, I offset both "success" and "failure" in ironic quotation marks; both cases indicate the space between achievement and irresolution, between the celebrated evasion of southern interpellation, and an elusive social equality. While this perspective may be key to claiming coalition with African Americans—American Indians and Asian Americans have been subject to the same forms of discrimination and for the same reasons—I also hope that this work has established a shared history between Asian American and American Indians that is not based simply upon either calls for Third World solidarity reflected in social movements of the 1960s and 1970s, or an essentialist appeal to a common origin. This work does not bridge indigenous sovereignty and land-based claims with immigrant concerns over exclusion and inclusion, but marks the ways in which American Indian and Asian American histories can be seen as parallel responses to the same cultural pressures. To some extent, this cross-racial dynamic is enabled by the very anomaly of Lumbee history in the context of American Indian histories of removal, federal treaties, and the struggle for sovereignty. I place these case studies side-by-side not to argue for Asian American/American Indian comparative studies, but to suggest a shared framework of representation, a generative rubric.[2]

In marking the excess of intermediacy, these case studies disclose a potentially productive failure that bares the pressures of identification and processes of state and cultural recognition. Cultural anxiety reveals a complicating dissonance that underscores the potential in thinking interstitiality. What I have established in this book is a process of reading contradiction and rupture in uneven assignment, particularly in moments in which status is either forcibly reconciled or, just as powerfully, incompletely realized. The promise of interstitiality, then, is the promise of incompletion.

The subtlety of simultaneity that has been my subject here does not intend to devalue the suffering, violence, and dehumanization that are part and parcel of the history of race relations in the United States. And yet I am nonetheless interested in the latency of race, where it signifies even where its influence is disavowed. In looking at subjects who are, as I claim, only partially coherent to culture, I want to explore what it means to be less reviled, less abjected, less *colored*. At one level, this intermediacy grants racialized subjects the illusion of autonomy even as they only imperfectly perform an unmarked, disembodied humanity. While I have highlighted these effects in the first part of this book, I also want to acknowledge interstitiality's double valence, one suggested by transgender activist, writer, and actress, Kate Boorstein. One might say that after his sex change operation Boorstein only imperfectly approximates femininity or "being" a woman. Yet she draws a distinction between her representation in culture and her sense of self in noting that "there are rules to gender, but rules can be broken. . . . [G]ender can have fluidity, which is quite different from ambiguity. If ambiguity is a refusal to fall within a prescribed gender code, then fluidity is the refusal to remain one gender or another" (1995, 52–53). The distinction between gender ambiguity and gender fluidity marks the difference between how one is interpreted within dominant culture, and how one acts upon that awareness. An object of cultural scrutiny, Boorstein nonetheless takes a strategic—and potentially freeing—response to gender in playing with and flouting its conventions. In other words, intermediacy is not merely a social condition to be negotiated, but can offer a strategic positionality. For example, in speaking about the origins of her film, *Mississippi Masala*, Mira Nair cites her experience at Harvard where she is accepted by more than one community: "That story was again this idea of trying to explore the hierarchy of color being an Indian woman undergraduate in a white university with black people who regarded me as their own, and whom I could regard as close. . . . I was like a sister, 'Third World sister.'"[3] Whether or not Nair's interstitial Asianness actually grants unique "accessibility to the white and the black," she nonetheless suggests that it enabled a specific kind of vision that served as the catalyst for thinking about American race relations. Racial intermediacy pushed her to become "aware of invisible and sometimes visible lines that were drawn" (128), the same perspective that I have claimed for writers such as Susan Choi and Abraham Verghese. The perspective is not equivalent to racial objectivity or color blindness, but represents, for "the rest of us" who "fall into that great divide," an ability to affirm collectivities beyond those historically saturated social divisions.

If there are case studies yet to be explored, one has only to turn to the New South as it contends with the influx of new capital that forces these divisions into relief or forces their reconsideration. The representation of Japanese automakers in the South provides one such case; John Egerton's 1983 book, *Nissan in Tennessee*, celebrating the origins of the corporation's plant in Smyrna, for example, overwrites "foreign" ownership and management, incorporating them into the company's preferred narrative: southern homecoming. Far from characterizing the Japanese as alien to a southern landscape, the new owners of capital are represented as the catalysts for racial reconciliation. White, black, and American Indian men and women are, at long last, allowed to staunch their outward migration and come home to Tennessee as a result of new jobs in Japanese auto manufacturing. As one worker profile attests, "Dave Jones left Lewisburg, Tennessee, right out of high school. . . . One day his mother sent him a clipping from a Nashville newspaper, announcing that Nissan was going to build a plant in Smyrna. To Dave Jones, the news was like a one-way ticket home" (Egerton 1983, 120). The anomaly, the Japanese businessman among good ole boys, does not disrupt but sutures race relations in the globalized South, soothing historical antagonism with the promise of collective prosperity. In the photographic documentation of triumphant transnational corporate cooperation, the face of Asian difference undergoes a different kind of inscription alongside the multicultural face of American labor.

The Mississippi Band of Choctaw's economic growth in the state has been acknowledged to be "one of the greatest success stories in Indian country."[4] After resisting removal to "Indian Territory" (Oklahoma) in 1831, the remaining tribal members lived as tenant farmers and sharecroppers amid segregation-era restrictions. Over a decade after federal recognition in 1945, the tribe transformed reservation land into an economic development zone attracting manufacturing to Mississippi by offering tax incentives. Moreover, they

From *Nissan in Tennessee* by John Egerton, 1983.

were able to transform discriminatory separation into financial autonomy in the form of not only tourism and gambling revenues, but diverse business ventures such as shopping centers and nursing homes. The Choctaw have become one of Mississippi's largest private employers.[5] To what extent will the black/white binary influence the racial representation of these new owners of capital in the New South?

Yet if the "partly colored" represent bridge figures, they are imperfect ones In conservative Indian American Bobby Jindal's first, unsuccessful run for governor of Louisiana in 2003, legislators speculated that Jindal was "too dark for the white folks, and not dark enough for the blacks."[6] His status as racial middleman initially refused any ready history through which to infer political bias. And yet, as governor in 2007, the first nonwhite governor in Louisiana since Reconstruction, in what ways does Jindal's race mark him simultaneously as a figure of reconciliation and as someone between constituencies whose loyalties are continually questioned?[7] Historians such as Ariela Gross have affirmed that "[o]ver the course of U.S. history, the possibility of mixed, intermediate, and hybrid identities has narrowed" (2008, 12); I have documented that narrowing as it came to circumscribe meaning, but also what lies in its excess. Interstitiality asks us to read in a dual register, often within the spaces between official histories and in defiance of the stories that we ourselves have chosen to remember. Sun Gay Chow writes that "As a Chinese who grew up in Mississippi, I have as an initial impression that my childhood wasn't that bad":

> I don't remember feeling different. I don't even remember experiencing any prejudice as a child. But then I begin to remember bits and pieces of stories that my father once told me about the way it was for his generation, who came primarily in the 1920s and 1930s to the Mississippi Delta as poor immigrants from a rural part of China. And long forgotten words, images and actions came rushing back. (1986, 96)[8]

What had been repressed were memories of "second-class citizenship" in the South, memories subsumed by his father's preferred narrative, that of immigrant achievement and pride. Yet each generation presides over its own story; the issue is not whose are most accurate, but that the stories exist, side by side, in dialectical tension. One is the official story of the community— we did well, we persevered. The other rushes to the surface against the dam of memory to be recovered in "bits and pieces," in fragments of uncertain meaning.

These "bits and pieces" reveal only partial truths that can likewise be conveniently rewritten to suit the agendas of culture and history—mine included. Bubley's photograph of the segregated tobacco plant is not the only photograph that I have submitted to rereading. While writing this book, I kept a photograph on my desk of my father in college in the 1950s at what was then Southwestern at Memphis. It depicts a sophomoric prank; he and his friends in the "Independent Men's Association" poised to push the plunger that dynamites fraternity row. It was a joke intended to highlight a sports rivalry between men's clubs on campus. But there's a less funny side as well: my father founded the organization because he was barred from membership in white fraternities. In that context, I like to think that the image takes on metaphoric meaning: the Chinese man and his accomplices blowing up the fraternal organization of white men, the exclusive dominion of those scions of Tennessee gentry who exist somewhere just outside the photograph's frame. There are other apt connotations here, of course: blowing up history, blowing out of proportion.

Suffice it to say, my father does not read the photograph as I do—nor does he have to. But like Chow, I know there are multiple ways of living Jim Crow:

"[W]e who came of age in Mississippi in the 1960s and early 1970s know there is more," he writes. "We know there are other stories about the life of the Chinese in Mississippi, stories perhaps a little more painful in the telling. They aren't told with a hint of pride or with a sense of nostalgia. Instead, they're told with less expression, with a lower voice" (1986, 98). I have tried to amplify these stories spoken in a lower voice, or, to echo Ellison, histories broadcast on the lower frequencies. Whether muted or invisible, they are not those represented in the violent panorama of American race relations or its iconography of the South, perhaps because they elude the sure and sometimes necessary distinction between victims and perpetrators. Yet the space of the in-between renders something more complex. Frantz Fanon once wrote, "All I wanted was to be a man among other men" (1991, 112). The "partly colored" reveal how impossible this was—and how hopeful.

# Notes

## INTRODUCTION

1. I will be looking primarily at representations of the "Deep South"—Georgia, Alabama, Mississippi, Louisiana, Arkansas, and South Carolina—as well as the "Upper South"—North Carolina, Tennessee, and Virginia. I also include references to the District of Columbia, Florida, Kentucky, Maryland, and Texas. My focus does not preclude the fact that segregation has taken place outside these boundaries, but in looking at the South as a region—and, as significantly, an idea—I focus not merely on the more pervasive and resistant area of racial separation in terms of the law, but its persistent cultural and historical representation as a region divided along a black-white axis. I am aware of the contentiousness surrounding the homogenizing tendencies of positing a single southern regionalism. There are many ways of defining "the South"; some draw a geographic boundary by including those states south of the Mason-Dixon line, others a political one by including former slave states in 1860 or former Confederate states. The U.S. Census draws other boundaries for statistical purposes. These distinctions and others are depicted in Gunnar Myrdal's *The American Dilemma: The Negro Problem and Modern Democracy* (see in particular table 1 and appendix 4, pp. 1071–1702). For my purposes, I choose to invoke "one South" along the lines suggested by W. J. Cash's *The Mind of the South*, which identifies "a fairly definite social pattern—a complex of established relationships and habits of thought, sentiments, prejudices, standards and values, and associations of ideas" that emerge across the region (viii). I would go further in situating "the South" as yet a microcosm of the nation; this is reflected in Houston Baker's assessment of Cash. In *Turning South Again*, Baker writes, "[O]ne might say Cash got the psycho-cultural commonalities of southern *resentiment* and racism absolutely 'on the mark' not only for the Confederate states, but also for the United States at large. He captured, that is to say, the *mind* of America in providing a comprehensive analysis of what he called the *South*" (22). For an interesting overview of the distinctions between the "Old South," "Confederate South," "New South," and the "Census South," see Jane Kohen Winter, *Culture Shock! USA—The South* (Portland, OR: Graphic Arts Center, 1996).

2. For example, as Mamie Garvin Fields recalls, by tacit agreement whites reserved Saturday for African Americans from the South Carolina countryside to come into town to do their shopping. They frowned on black presence in town on the weekdays because it connoted leisure time. Cited in Edward L. Ayers, *The Promise of a New South* (New York: Oxford University Press, 1992), 132.

3. It is this perception that prompts Laura Lovett to speculate that the African American practice of assuming Native American costumes during Mardi Gras stems from a desire to mimic those who are "outside segregation and [therefore] seen as a symbol of defiance in the face of white domination" (2002, 203).

4. Of course, racial segregation existed outside of the South. For a discussion of Asian American segregation in the military, for example, see K. Scott Wong's *Americans First: Chinese Americans and the Second World War* (2005). For a discussion of Asian American residential segregation in California, see Cindy I-Fen Cheng's "Contesting Chinese/American Identities in the Age of Cold War Politics" (2004).

5. I use the term "people of color" in its contemporary meaning to connote racialized groups in the United States: nonwhite Latinos, American Indians, Asians, and African Americans. I render "colored" in quotation marks in order to connote its historical—and derogatory—usage.

6. Regarding the "whiteness" of Mexican Americans in Texas as adjudicated by the courts, see *Hernandez v. Texas* 347 U.S. 475 (1954) and George Martinez, "Mexican-Americans and Whiteness" (1997).

7. Cited in Egerton (1969), 18. Another of Egerton's informants affirms that racism is intrinsic to Americanization: an Afro-Cuban American teacher notes, "I think most Cubans identify with the white population here—they treat Negroes differently, they take up the white American habits quickly" (21).

8. Morrison's ideas regarding European immigrant "whiteness" as it was secured through the Africanist presence are also reflected in her novels. In *Sula*, for example, Morrison notes about Irish immigrants, "baiting [black people] was the one activity that the white Protestant residents concurred in. In part their place in this world was secured only when they echoed the old residents' attitude toward blacks" (1973, 53). This antagonistic relationship between new immigrants and African Americans is likewise affirmed in Derrick Bell's witnessing the change of demeanor of a white judge in a southern courtroom in 1964 as he moves from adjudicating a case regarding school desegregation to administering the oath of citizenship to white immigrants. Bell remarks,

> [W]hat held me in my seat was the realization that in the moment when these white people became citizens, their skin color made them more acceptable to this country, more a part of it, than my black clients would probably ever be. The presumptions based on their whiteness would make it far easier for them to find employment, lease or purchase homes, obtain bank loans. (2004, 105)

9. Thanks to Grace Hong for this reference.

10. This is not to say that my concerns are wholly distinct from those of social science. Sociologist Barbara Ellen Smith articulates the promise of her demographic inquiry thusly:

> Our interest in the Race and Nation project arose initially from concern for the implications of Latino immigration in Memphis, a majority-black, predominantly working class city, and the Deep South more generally. In this sub-region where African American oppression and resistance and white supremacy have all been visible and longstanding, the arrival of large numbers of people who do not fit within the bipolar black-white paradigm is disrupting conventional understanding of "race" in ways that are potentially volatile as well as promising. (11)

From Barbara Ellen Smith, "The New Latino South: An Introduction," A joint project of The Center for Research on Women, University of Memphis, the Highlander Research and Education Center, and the Southern Regional Council, unpublished paper, 2001.

CHAPTER 1

1. For a discussion of what Chicago sociologists described as the "Oriental Problem" as distinct from the "Negro Problem" in the 1920s and 1930s, see Yu (2001). As Yu notes, Robert Park's conception of the "Oriental Problem" in which race thwarts immigrant assimilation derived from both his experience at the Tuskegee Institute and his knowledge of European immigration to the United States.

2. Harry H. L. Kitano, "Japanese Americans: The Development of a Middleman Minority," *Pacific Historical Review* 42 (1974): 500–519; Eugene F. Wong, "Asian American Middleman Minority Theory: The Framework of an American Myth," *Journal of Ethnic Studies* 13.1 (1985): 51–86; Okihiro (1994); Kim (2000); Dhingra (2003); and Daniel Y. Kim, *Writing Manhood in Black and Yellow: Ralph Ellison, Frank Chin, and the Literary Politics of Identity* (Stanford: Stanford University Press, 2005).

3. For a discussion of such embellishments and omissions in *Black Boy*, see Marcus Klein, *Foreigners: the Making of American Literature, 1900–1940* (Chicago: University of Chicago Press, 1981); and Timothy Dow Adams, "'I Do Believe Him Though I Know He Lies': Lying as Genre and Metaphor in *Black Boy*," in *Richard Wright: Critical Perspectives*, ed. Henry Louis Gates, Jr. and Kwame Anthony Appiah (New York: Amistad, 1993), 302–315.

4. James Dunwoody Brownson, "Miscellany," *DeBow's Review*. A.W. S. II (August 1866): 215–217. Quote appears on page 217.

5. "The Importation of Coolies," *DeBow's Review* IV (1867): 362–364. Quote appears on page 363.

6. "Immigration and Labor," *DeBow's Review* IV (1867): 362–364. Quote appears on page 364.

7. Whitelaw Reid, *After the War: A Tour of the Southern States, 1865–1866* (New York: Harper & Row, 1965 [1866]). Quote appears on page 397.

8. George Benham, *A Year of Wreck: A True Story by a Victim* (New York: Harper and Brothers, 1880). Quote appears on page 28.

9. See Munasinghe (2001); and Brownson (1866).

10. Ralph Keeler, "The 'Heathen Chinese' in the South," *Every Saturday* (1871): 117–118. Quote appears on page 118.

11. L. E. Allason, "Chinese in Arkansas," *The American Missionary* XVI (March 1872): 52–53. Quote appears on page 53; emphasis added.

12. This history is also covered briefly in Eric Foner, *Reconstruction: America's Unfinished Revolution 1863–1877* (New York: Harper & Row, 1988); Ronald Takaki, *Iron Cages: Race and Culture in 19th-century America* (Oxford: Oxford University Press, 1979); and John Kuo Wei Tchen, *New York Before Chinatown: Orientalism and the Shaping of American Culture 1776–1882* (1999).

13. Frederick Douglass, "The Great Question," *Christian Register* (Boston) August 21, 1869. n.p.

14. See Peabody (1967).

15. *New Orleans Times* 5 January 1870. Cited in Peabody (1967), 59.

16. *New Orleans Times* 6 January 1870. Cited in Peabody (1967), 59.

17. "Evangelist," "Chinese Labor," *The American Missionary* 16 (March 1872): 54–55. Quote appears on page 54.

18. Cited in Keeler, 117.

19. "Evangelist," 54.

20. On efforts to attract European immigration to the South during the reconstruction era, see Robert F. Futrell, "Efforts of Mississippians to Encourage Immigration, 1865–1880," *Journal of Mississippi History* 20 (April 1958): 65–79; and Loewenberg (1934).

21. Robert De Courcy Ward, "Immigration and the South," *Atlantic Monthly* 96 (Nov. 1905): 611–17. Quote appears on page 614.

22. From the Jacksonville *Florida Grower*, 27 September 1913. Cited in Pozzetta and Kersey (1976). Quote appears on page 71.

23. As Thomas Gregersen reveals, while alien land law legislation was not passed in Florida, the topic was introduced in the legislature in reference to the Yamato Colony. Settler attrition and crop failure—the pineapple fields were struck by blight in 1908—contributed to the decline of the colony by 1928, and there now remain no traces of it. Nevertheless, George Morikami, the lone Japanese settler remaining in Florida, rose to prominence as a local businessman and deeded land to Delray Beach for what is now Morikami Park, a landmark dedicated to Japanese culture. See Thomas Gregersen, "The Yamato Colony: Pioneering Japanese in Florida." Unpublished manuscript. Delray Beach: The Morikami Museum and Japanese Gardens. See also Pozzetta and Kersey (1976); and Dominick J. Scarangello, "The Yamato Colony and the Japanese Colonization Movement to the Southern United States." M.A. Thesis, Florida State University, 1996.

24. See, for example, Takaki (1979); Lowenberg (1934); Pozzetta (1974); and also Sarah Gualtieri, "Strange Fruit? Syrian Immigrants, Extralegal Violence and Racial Formation in the Jim Crow South," *Arab Studies Quarterly* 26, 3 (2004): 63–85. I thank Juanid Rana for this reference.

25. *Plessy v. Ferguson* 163 U. S. 537 (1896).

26. In an anomalous instance uncovered by historian Victor Jew, in 1910 a Chinese man "suspected of being engaged in assisting Chinese smugglers" purportedly passed as black in order to cross the Canadian border into the United States. In this case, blackface was presumably used to circumvent questions of citizenship. Anxious letters exchanged between Immigration Service inspectors in Sault Ste. Marie and Chicago verify that the "Chinaman was as 'black as the ace of spades' and that it was common knowledge among the passengers on the train that the man blackened like a Negro was a Chinaman." Nevertheless, while daily papers reported that the suspect was arrested en route, the reports went unsubstantiated. Letter from Inspector in Charge, Department of Commerce and Labor, Immigration Service, Sault Ste. Marie, MI to Immigrant Inspector in Charge, Chicago, IL No. 25-B, 16 April 1910.

27. From "Over the Ocean Wave," in *The Best of the Brownies' Book*, ed. Dianne Johnson-Feelings (New York: Oxford University Press, 1996 [1920]), 258–260. Quote appears on page 259.

28. As the editor of the *Atlantic Monthly* noted, "If the stronger and cleverer race, is free to impose its will upon 'new-caught, sullen peoples' on the other side of the globe, why not in South Carolina and Mississippi?" (cited in Woodward 2002, 72).

29. In this sense, Bonacich affirms the intersectionality between race and modes of production at the same time she confounds a developmental narrative that would simply posit a lessening of racial or ethnic antagonism or social vulnerability along with class rise.

30. Asian "settlers" imported as agricultural workers to Hawai'i provide another example of the "middleman minorities," in this case, defined by relations between white planters and indigenous Hawaiians. In addition, for the ways in which Korean Americans became ambiguously placed as simultaneously "part exploiter and part victim," during the 1992 Los Angeles Riots/Rebellion, see Nancy Abelman and John Lie, *Blue Dreams: Korean Americans and the Los Angeles Riots* (Cambridge: Harvard University Press, 1995). David Palumbo-Liu's "Los Angeles, Asians, and Perverse Ventriloquisms: On the Functions of Asian America in the Recent American Imaginary," sharply underscores Korean American positionality between the dominant and the minor in the context of contemporary Los Angeles (*Public Culture* 6 (1994): 365–381).

31. For a discussion of the racial classification of Mexican Americans, see Lopez (2003); Martinez (1997); and Stephen H. Wilson, "Brown over 'Other White': Mexican Americans' Legal Arguments and Litigation Strategy in School Desegregation Lawsuits," *Law and History Review* 21.1 (2003): 109–194. On the link between Mexican American racial status and naturalization rights, see Ngai (2004).

32. For emphasis on the sexual act, see Adams (2001).

33. Eliza Frances Andrews, *The War-Time Journal of a Georgia Girl* (New York: D. Appleton and Co., 1908). Quote appears on page 353.

34. Archie Robertson, "Chang-Eng's American Heritage: Renowned Siamese Twins Founded Large Families Still Flourishing Today," *Life*, 11 Aug. 1952: 70–82. Quote appears on page 79.

35. In the West, the argument contesting anti-miscegenation laws was put forth by the California Supreme Court only four years later. In *Perez v. Sharp* [198 P. 2d 17, 32 Cal. 2d 711 (1948)], the court ruled that the ban on interracial marriage in California violated the equal protection clause of the Constitution, a judgment that prefigured the Supreme Court ruling striking down anti-miscegenation laws by almost 20 years. In his decision, Justice Traynor of the California Supreme Court held marriage to be a "fundamental right of free men," one of man's "basic civil rights." His pre–*Brown v. Board of Education* ruling offered a subtle hierarchy between the degree of offense offered by anti-miscegenation laws and those barring school integration. Implying that the ban on intermarriage could not be defended by the "separate but equal" rationale of *Plessy v. Ferguson*, Traynor wrote, "A member of any of these races may find himself barred by law from marrying the person of his choice and that person to him may be irreplaceable. Human beings are bereft of worth and dignity by a doctrine that would make them as interchangeable as trains." The comparison betrays an implicit rank order between segregation's offenses, echoing that enumerated by Myrdal: while upholding separate public facilities might retain a shred of rational defensibility, interracial marriage statutes could not. Even after the Brown ruling, such statutes remained, in the words of legal historian Randall Kennedy, the "untouchable third rail of racial politics" (2003, 267).

Hannah Arendt's controversial 1959 "Reflections on Little Rock" reflects this hierarchy between arenas of racial separation, foregrounding her sense that the battle over school integration was misguided in part because it was less defensible on legal grounds than the case against anti-miscegenation law. What Myrdal identified as the greatest sore spot in the white southern psyche, "the end for which the other restrictions are arranged as means," Arendt imbued with heightened legal and moral stakes. "[T]he most outrageous law of Southern states," she wrote, is that "which makes mixed marriage a criminal offense. The right to marry whoever one wishes is an elementary human right compared to which 'the right to attend an integrated school, the right to sit where one pleases on a bus, the right to go into any hotel or recreation area or place of amusement, regardless of one's skin or color or race' are minor indeed" (1959, 49). Compelling integration in education was, she believed, a violation of the individual's right to free association, a position that she did not recant despite controversy. Her distinction between the two prohibitions—integrated education and interracial marriage—hinges on an illusory division between public and private, the political and the social. Arendt's objection to Eisenhower's attempt to enforce integrated education ironically formed the basis of her outrage over anti-miscegenation laws; while she believed that the state should not compel association, neither should it outlaw voluntary association. Among her many critics, Arendt only conceded a point to one—Ralph Ellison, acknowledging in a letter to him, "It is precisely this idea of sacrifice which I didn't understand" [cited in Elisabeth Young-Bruehl, *Hannah Arendt: For Love of the World*. 2nd ed. (New Haven, CT: Yale University Press, 2004 [1982]), 316]. Unwittingly echoing the position taken by the California Supreme Court a decade earlier, "Reflections on Little Rock" conceives the right to desire as a "human" right and *more* defensible than the fight for civil rights in the realm of education. If this ranking of levels of segregation's egregiousness was shared among civil rights activists, such a sense of priority was strategically shelved in favor of the work that would culminate in the iconic *Brown* ruling. As activists saw it, challenging anti-miscegenation laws in the "private" realm of sexuality was a cause for greater controversy and potential resistance.

36. Between 1913 and 1948, 30 of 48 states had enacted anti-miscegenation laws. All states excluding six and the District of Columbia enacted such legislation at one time or another; by 1966, the year prior to the Supreme Court ruling *Loving v. Virginia*, which struck down such laws, the 17 remaining states still firm in their anti-miscegenationist allegiance were clustered in the South. (By 1967, the states with intermarriage prohibitions remaining were Alabama, Arkansas, Delaware, Florida, Georgia, Kentucky, Louisiana, Mississippi, Missouri, North Carolina, Oklahoma, South Carolina, Tennessee, Texas, Virginia, and West Virginia. Cited in *Loving v. Virginia* 388 U.S. 1 (1967) fn 5).

37. In the West, anti-miscegenation laws reflected greater specificity in naming Asian ethnicities as ineligible for intermarriage with whites; California's 1872 law, for example, was amended to include "Mongolians" in 1901 and "Malays" in 1933 following the influx of Chinese and Filipino populations to the state. See *Perez v. Sharp*, 198 P.2d 17, California Supreme Court, 1948.

38. As late as 1967, the dissent to *Loving v. Virginia* invokes the language of "equal application," claiming that the law was not a violation of the equal protection clause because it "equally" prevented marriages between blacks and whites. [*Loving v. Virginia* 388 U.S. 1 (1967)]. The two southern states that prohibited marriage between indigenous people and African Americans were Louisiana and North Carolina, neither of which did so with the global import of Oklahoma's, which prohibited marriage between persons of "African descent" with persons *not* of "African descent" (see Fowler 1987, 412). Oklahoma's

blanket depiction of African Americans as taboo subjects for intermarriage (the inverse of Virginia and Georgia's blanket protection against white intermarriage with any people of color) was challenged and upheld in *Maynard v. Hill* (see *Naim v. Naim*, 197 Va. 80, 87 S.E. 2d 749 (1955)). Louisiana prohibited marriage and "concubinage" between "a person of the aboriginal Indian race, known as the red race, and a person of the colored or black race" (*Acts of the State of Louisiana*, Acts 220, 230 (1920) 366, 381).

39. Al. Code Title 14, 360 (1958).

40. *Acts*, State of Louisiana; Act 220, (1920) 366. The 1958 statute includes the caveat, "Statute applies to person who is part Indian.—The contention that a person who is part Indian should be considered as of the Indian race, and therefore not subject to the operation of the miscegenation statue, is without merit."

41. Civil Codes of Louisiana, Art. 94 (1894), *Compiled Edition of the Civil Codes of Louisiana* (Baton Rouge: Louisiana State Law Institute, 1940), 54. See also Fowler (1987), 378.

42. The shift reflected a desire to broaden the definition of blood quantum for those who counted as black in lieu of a previous attempt of the legislature to set a blood quantum level at 1/32 or above, and a court case that found that "octoroons" were not "Negro." See Charles S. Mangum, Jr., *The Legal Status of the Negro* (Chapel Hill: University of North Carolina Press, 1940).

43. Mississippi Code Ann. 2361 (1930) 1158.

44. Mississippi Revised Code sec. 2859 (1892). Cited in Fowler (1987), 677.

45. For a discussion of the name changes, see chapter 2. For the shift in intermarriage statutes, see Fowler (1987), 408–409.

46. Georgia's amended law reads, "All negroes, mulattoes, mestizos, and their descendants, having any ascertainable trace of either Negro or African, West Indian, or Asiatic Indian blood in their veins, and all descendants of any person having either Negro or African, West Indian, or Asiatic blood in his or her veins, shall be known in this State as persons of color." *Georgia Laws* 1927 No. 317, Pt. I–Title VII, pp. 272–273.

47. Virginia Code Ann 4546 (1942), 1732 and 5099a (1942), 1944.

48. See Walter Wadlington, "The Loving Case: Virginia's Antimiscegenation Statute in Historical Perspective," *Virginia Law Review* 52 (1966): n. 1, 1189. Of course, the laws were not universally applied. In regard to Virginia's statute, following the Loving verdict, one local paper asserted that authorities reserved arrest for white-black couples only, while nonetheless withholding marital civil rights such as adoption and inheritance from "other racially mixed couples." *Virginia-Pilot* 13 June 1967, p. 14.

49. In 1958, Mildred Jeter, a black woman, and Richard Loving, a white man, were married in the District of Columbia and returned to settle in their home in Virginia. They were subsequently indicted for violating Virginia's ban on interracial marriage; the judge suspended their sentence on the condition that they leave the state and not return together for 25 years. In 1963, the Loving family brought suit against the state from their exile in the District of Columbia because they wished to return home with their three children. In writing the opinion of the court, Chief Justice Warren affirmed the unconstitutionality of anti-miscegenation laws, noting, "[T]his court has consistently repudiated 'distinctions between citizens solely because of their ancestry' as being 'odious to a free people whose institutions are founded upon the doctrine of equality." *Loving v. Virginia* 388 U.S. 1 (1967).

50. *Naim v. Naim* 350 U.S. 891 (1955).

51. See also Wallenstein (2002); and Tushnet (1993).

52. See also *Naim v. Naim*, 197 Va. 80, 87 S.E. 2d 749 (1955), and *Naim v. Naim*, 350 U.S. 985 (1956).

53. As Mark Tushnet notes, this claim was specious: "The justices knew that they could not uphold the statue without undermining Brown's moral force, yet they knew as well that they could not invalidate the statute, which represented the heart of the white South's emotional commitment to segregation, without exacerbating an already difficult situation. On entirely specious grounds the Court refused to consider the constitutional challenge. The Court invoked technical grounds to explain its refusal, and only an insider could appreciate that on the facts of *Naim*, those grounds were quite ridiculous" (1993, 5).

54. Mildred Loving née Mildred Dolores Jeter "preferred to think of herself as Indian rather than black." Although Mildred Loving had stopped giving interviews, on the 40th anniversary of the Supreme Court ruling she urged that gay men and lesbians be allowed to marry. Douglas Martin, "Mildred Loving, Pioneer, Dies at 68; Battled Ban on Mixed-Race Marriage," *New York Times*, 6 May 2008, p. C13.

55. For a fuller account of *Mendez v. Westminister*, see Gonzalez (1990); and Lopez (2003).

56. See, for example, Delgado (1997); Angelo N. Ancheta, *Race, Rights, and the Asian American Experience* (New Brunswick, NJ: Rutgers University Press, 1998); Robert S. Chang, *Distoriented: Asian-Americans, Law, and the Nation-State* (New York: New York University Press, 1999); and Frank Wu, *Yellow: Race in America Beyond Black and White* (New York, Basic Books, 2002).

CHAPTER 2

1. Cited in Bryce Nelson, "Lost Colony? Lumbee Indians of N.C. Think They Have Answer," *Atlanta Journal and Constitution*, 15 May 1977.

2. David Wilkins notes,

> The Lumbees' name transformations prior to the 1950s had all been imposed by non-Lumbee individuals or official agencies. These impositions legally began in the mid 1880s and included: Croatan (1885), Indians of Robeson County (1911), and Cherokees of Robeson County (1913). Later attempts to change the tribe's name officially to Cheraw Indians (1933) and later to Siouan Indians of Lumber River failed to reach the state or federal legislative arena. Finally, in 1951 the Indians of Robeson County, tired of these paternalistic efforts, held a referendum and by a vote of 2,169 to 35, created their own name: the Lumbee Tribe of North Carolina. (1998, 159)

3. For theories of "tri-racial" isolation, see Berry (1963); and Guy B. Johnson (1939), who invokes the phrase, "Indians by courtesy" to describe mixed-raced peoples.

4. When the Choctaw Indians were subject to removal to Okalahoma territory in 1830, they left behind some 6,000 members of the tribe who refused to leave their homes in Mississippi; those who remained were eventually recognized as the Mississippi Band of Choctaw Indians. See Satz (1986).

5. Dr. Wesley Johnson, Chief. Cited in *Proposed Legislation for the full-blood and identified Choctaws of Mississippi, Louisiana, and Alabama: with Memorial, Evidence, and Brief*, 63rd Congress. Washington, DC: Judd and Detweiler. n.d. (1913): 14.

6. In 1887, the General Assembly of North Carolina established a Normal school for the "training of teachers of the Croatan race" that would become the University of North Carolina at Pembroke (McMillan 1907, 45).

7. See, for example, Lopez (1996); and Ariela Gross's *Double Character: Slavery and Mastery in the Antebellum Southern Courtroom* (Princeton, NJ: Princeton University Press, 2000); and Gross (2008).

8. For a discussion of the visual depiction of Native Americans in the 19th century, see Jeffrey Steele, "Reduced to Images: American Indians in Nineteenth-Century Advertising," in *The Gender and Consumer Reader*, ed. Jennifer Scanlon (New York: New York University Press, 2000); and Gerald Vizenor, *Fugitive Poses: Native American Indian Scenes of Absence and Presence* (Lincoln: University of Nebraska Press, 1998).

9. Contemporary discussions of Lumbee origin include Dial and Eliades (1975); Robert K. Thomas's unpublished manuscript, "A Report on Research on Lumbee Origins" (1980); Blu (1980); Sider (1993); Wilkins (1993, 1998); and Padget (1997).

10. Suffice it to say, in addition to the aforementioned evidence left onsite by the colonists, his text cites a number of sources that testify to the probability of English presence in what is now North Carolina. These include early map legends of the territory called "Virginia" from 1608; Rev. Morgan Jones's 1686 account of experiences among the Tuscaroras, and John Lawson's 1714, *The History of North Carolina*. The anecdotal testimony as to the traces of European influence on the natives cited by McMillan in 1888—Indian houses built in the manner of the English, Indians appareled in European garb, sightings of a powerful, bearded tribe of men—are subsequently enlarged and repeated by others. Turning to the cultural practices of the Indians themselves, McMillan draws upon the oral traditions of the Indians who claim to be descended from Cherokees and Englishmen from "Roanoke in Virginia." Many of the Indians in Robeson County, he notes, still use the surnames that appear in the roster of the Lost Colony; moreover, "every family bearing the name of one of the Lost Colony, point to 'Roanoke' as the country of their white ancestors" (McMillan 1907, 36). In addition, he reports that these Indians use an old English dialect already obsolete in England by 1888, one that evokes "the days of Chaucer."

11. Both Laura Lovett and David Wilkins support Blu's assessment of the political motivations behind McMillan's advocacy. This demographic influence is also cited by Robert Thomas, who accounts for the change in Mary Norment's characterization of the community from "Mulatto" in 1875 to "Portuguese" in 1890 in her book, *The Lowery History*. He writes, "When there is any hint of black blood, she uses the term Portuguese. It is quite common in the South to stress a Latin background where black ancestry is suspected" (n.p.). As significantly, the desire for the community's renaming stemmed from the ways in which "Croatan" assumed negative associations because of its eponymous connection to "Jim Crow."

12. I thank Victor Jew for this reference.

13. On the Internet there is a currently unfunded project that proposes using DNA to prove conclusively that the Lumbee Indians are descendants of Raleigh's colonists, much in the way that Thomas Jefferson's sexual relationship with Sally Hemings was historically validated. The project would use scientific evidence to determine, once and for all, the fate of the colonists and, perhaps inadvertently in the process, validate Lumbee oral history. What was once crudely yet "scientifically" demonstrated by "common sense" visual inspection is now *theoretically* made possible through the advent of technology with

one caveat: as I note in regard to Weeks, such "evidence" does not specify *when* "English" lineage was introduced to a gene pool.

14. Henry Berry Lowrie was accused of killing a Confederate official who had accused Lowrie's father of theft. Moreover, the Lowrie rebellion was in part a response to the Confederate labor conscription of community members alongside slaves. This resistance to the state's presumption of proximity to African Americans is likewise reflected in a funeral speech honoring the slain Lowrie brothers: "In order to be great like the English we took the white man's religion and laws . . . yet white men treated us as Negroes. Here are our young men killed by a white man and we get no justice, and that in a land where we were always free" (cited in Dial and Eliades 1975, 49).

15. The figure of Henry Berry Lowrie nonetheless continues to inspire contradictory impulses. As Dial and Eliades report, while his name "meant lawlessness and terror to the white community," in contemporary times, the Lumbees "annually give the Henry Berry Lowrie Award to the citizen who best exemplifies the highest standard of service to the community" (Dial and Eliades 1975, 86–87).

16. On the ways in which the rise of Jim Crow culture forced "Indian" to become a racial identity rather than a citizenship category reflective of tribal sovereignties, see Gross (2008).

17. "Bad Medicine for the Klan: North Carolina Indians break up Ku Kluxers' anti-Indian Meeting," *Life Magazine*, 27 January 1958, 26–28.

18. "Indians Back at Peace and the Klan at Bay," *Life Magazine,* 3 February 1958, 3–36A. Quote appears on page 36.

19. The *Life* articles give no indication of the tribe's racial intermixing or contested tribal status, nor logically would they: such nuances would signify little in the context of being targets of the Ku Klux Klan. Interestingly, one photograph depicting the community's return to normalcy shows teenage "Indian Boy Scouts" bare-chested and bedecked in homemade feathered headdresses dancing outside a log cabin. The costumes are no doubt inspired by the garb of the Plains Indians, and the drum-beating scout master is himself identified as Cree. The article represents this "traditional" sign of Indianness without apparent irony: the Indians themselves are playing (other) Indians according to a ritual associated with American norms. These Boy Scouts, like any others, are attempting to earn Indian Lore merit badges. The article does not establish this incongruity; rather, the photo succeeds in marking Indian specificity at the same time that it familiarizes difference within the rituals of American life.

20. Theda Perdue, "Native Carolinians: The Indians of North Carolina" (Raleigh: Division of Archives and History, North Carolina Department of Cultural Resources, 1985), 52.

21. William Sturtevant, Smithsonian, letter. Cited in Wilkins (1998), 170.

22. As part of the Federal Indian Relocation Program, blood quantum, notes Limerick, set the stage for the "statistical extermination" of indigenous populations within U.S. borders. Cited in Arlene Hirschfelder and Martha Kreipe de Montano, *The Native American Almanac: A Portrait of Native America Today* (New York: Prentice Hall, 1993), 42.

23. The Lumbee application for tribal enrollment requires petitioners to trace tribal genealogy to any great grandparent.See www.lumbeetribe.com/enrollment/index.htm .

24. See Wilkins (1993, 1998); and Padget (1997). In 1997, Padget noted that the Cherokee, the largest recognized tribe, feared that the Lumbee would stand to absorb $120 million in funds from the BIA (413).

25. As numerous websites attest, Heather Locklear does not disavow her Indian heritage, nor does she claim it. While it is said that "she could get tribal membership if she wanted to" her affiliation to the tribe is based on the fact that Locklear, derived from "Lochlayah," is specific to Robeson County and common among Indian families in the area.

26. *Lumbee Recognition: Hearing before the Committee on Indian Affairs,* U.S. Congress, Senate Committee on Indian Affairs. 108th Con., 1st sess., 17 Sept. 2003.

27. "Croatan" is taken to be a name imposed by the English upon contact; it refers to a geographic place name rather than a tribal self-designation.

28. As of 1998, Wilkins noted that these included the Lumbee Tribe of Cheraw Indians, the Hatteras Tuscarora Tribe, the Cherokees of Robeson and Adjoining Counties, the Tuscarora Indian Tribe of Creek Reservation, the Tuscarora Tribe of North Carolina, the Eastern Carolina Tuscarora Indian Organization, and the Tuscarora nation of North Carolina (1998).

29. Ironically, however, while Thomas came to validate the Lumbee's Hatteras ancestry, he nonetheless theorized that "many Lumbees came to accept McMillan's idea about their origin largely because it gave them a rather high status origin" (1980, 5). Thus, the self-authorized definitions of their collectivity are not necessarily at odds with those that emerged out of dominant discourses reflective of "differing races and ranks."

30. Cited in the documentary film, *Shattering the Silences,* Produced and directed by Stanley Nelson and Gail Pellett, Gail Pellett Productions, Inc., 1997.

## CHAPTER 3

1. Other ethnographies include Kit-Mui Leung Chan, "Assimilation of Chinese-Americans in the Mississippi Delta" (M.A. Thesis, Mississippi State University, 1969); John Jung, *Chopsticks in the Land of Cotton: Lives of Mississippi Delta Chinese Grocers* (Ying and Yang Press, 2008); Pao Yun Liao, "A Case Study of a Chinese Immigrant Community" (M.A. Thesis, University of Chicago, 1951); Sieglinde Lim de Sanchez, "Crafting a Delta Chinese Community: Education and Acculturation in Twentieth-Century Southern Baptist Mission Schools," *History of Education Quarterly* 43, 1 (Spring 2003): 74–90; O'Brien (1941); Quan (1982); Rummel (1966); Mary Jo Schneider and William M. Schneider, "A Structural Analysis of the Chinese Grocery Store in the Mississippi Delta," in *Visions and Revisions: Ethnohistoric Perspectives on Southern Cultures,* ed. George Sabo III and William M. Schneider (Athens: University of Georgia Press, 1987), 83–97; Shih-Shan Henry Tsai, "The Chinese in Arkansas," *Amerasia Journal* 8.1 (1981): 1–18; and *The Chinese in Arkansas: Final Report* (Little Rock: University of Arkansas, 1981). For historical context surrounding this community, see Barth (1964), and Cohen (1984). For a personal narrative and history regarding the Chinese community in Georgia, see John Jung, *Southern Fried Rice: Life in a Chinese Laundry in the Deep South* (Ying and Yang Press, 2005), and Daniel Bronstein, "Formation and Development of Chinese Communities in Atlanta, Augusta, and Savannah: From Sojourners to Settlers, 1880–1965," Ph.D. Diss., Georgia State University, 2008, respectively. For personal narratives about the Chinese in Mississippi, see Chow (1986); and Bobby Joe Moon, "Growing up in Mississippi in the 40's–60's," at www.usadeepsouth.com.

2. Karen Brodkin, *How Jews Became White Folks and What That Says About Race in America* (New Brunswick, NJ: Rutgers University Press, 1999); Noel Ignatiev, *How the Irish*

*Became White* (New York: Routledge, 1996) and *Are Italians White?: How Race Is Made in America,* ed. Jennifer Guglielmo and Salvatore Salerno (New York: Routledge, 2003).

3. Morrison's class analysis in *The Bluest Eye* focuses on the aspirations of African American women who work assiduously to cultivate "thrift, patience, high morals, and good manners" while subduing—however incompletely—the "base" passions that demarcate the working classes: "Whenever it erupts, this Funk, they wipe it away, where it crusts, they dissolve it; wherever it drips, flowers, or clings, they find it and fight it until it dies. They fight this battle all the way to the grave. The laugh that is a little too loud; the enunciation a little too round; the gesture a little too generous" (1970, 68).

4. *Gong Lum v. Rice* 275 U.S. 78 (1927).

5. On the racial classification of the Chinese in the 1870, 1880, and 1900 census records, see Cohen (1984), 167–170. Cohen notes that Chinese in Louisiana were either classified as white, black, or mulatto. Interestingly, the mixed-blood descendants of Chinese who immigrated from Cuba mistakenly believed that their forebears came from Mexico and were classified as Mexican, an identification that ironically allowed them to pass as white (Cohen 1984, 170).

6. In this regard, one could say that the Chinese were ironically more modern than the "feudal" southern context they adopted. This is certainly implicit within Edna Bonacich's analysis of "middleman minority" communities whose ability to abstract themselves from the "status hang-ups of the surrounding society" gave them the freedom "to trade or deal with anyone" (1973, 584). In their devotion to capitalist accumulation, they were, one could say, *uber*-capitalists.

7. Cited in Doris Black, "The Black Chinese," *Sepia* (January 1975): 19–24.

8. Mississippi Code Ann. 2361 (1930), 1158.

9. Ruthanne Lum McCunn's *Chinese American Portraits* (1988) devotes a chapter to Arlee Hen, giving a full page to her portrait and using her family's history, as does the film, as a point of origin for the Chinese community in Mississippi. While *Mississippi Triangle* impresses upon the viewer Hen's distance from the community, McCunn characterizes that relationship as one of qualified integration.

10. Adria Bernardi, "Heat in the Delta: Reactions to the Triangle," *Southern Exposure* (July/Aug. 1984): 22–23. This reaction is confirmed by Ray Lou, who worked as a consultant on the film. Personal communication, April 1999.

11. Georgia: Gerald Chan Sieg (Chung Tai-pan) interview, 20 January 1939, Folder 252 and South Carolina: Ruth D. Henderson interview with Joe Shing, 24 December 1938, Folder 859, both in the Federal Writers' Project Papers # 3709, Southern Historical Collection, Louis Round Wilson Special Collections Library, University of North Carolina at Chapel Hill.

12. Louise Gee, the cheerleader in Yung's book and on my cover, attributes the difference in treatment to region, noting that she "did not feel different" until she moved to Mississippi where she now resides. At the time her picture was taken in 1959, she was fourteen and a cheerleader at Dumas High School in Dumas, Arkansas. A few years earlier, her older brother had not been allowed to attend this public school and had to enroll in a Chinese boarding school in Mississippi. The girl in the other photograph, Nancy Bing Chew, is her husband's niece. Personal communication, 17 July 2009.

13. Contrast this to another depiction of color blindness within *Mississippi Triangle*. Interviewed regarding his marriage to an African American woman, grocery store owner

Henry Goon comments, "You look beneath the surface of a person. Because they say beauty is skin deep and sometimes it's true."

14. One can see a similar shift in the voiceover of an unidentified African American girl, but to opposite effect. In the course of the girl's testimony describing Chinese disassociation from her, free will is both affirmed and subtly questioned:

> Girl's Voiceover: The first time I ever met Chinese friends who live around here was when I went to church. I met them, but sometimes they start getting stuck up. Don't want to talk to me because they hang around white people a lot. They go to private schools and they hang around these white people a lot. So that's why they don't get a chance to hang around black people.

Her voiceover confirms Chinese status transformation as it is enacted on a personal level and from a child's point of view; their increased association with whites inflates their sense of their standing and they "start getting stuck up." But oddly, the girl's choice of phrasing begins to mediate her own testimony: "they don't get a chance to hang around black people" seems to distance them from the choices they themselves have made. In the process of depicting white identification, the statement introduces a peculiar absolution as if Chinese agency in choosing church and school were negated. In its mediation of volition, the distinction between choice and opportunity, the comment seems to call attention to systemic, cultural prohibitions around interracial intimacy even at the moment that it testifies to its freely chosen enactment.

15. In Cheng's view, the over-the-top display of national belonging on the part of the marginalized is a veil for its lack (2001).

16. For example, Susan Koshy takes the Chinese community in the Delta as evidence of an Asian American "aspiration to whiteness" as well as of the influence of white power. "Morphing Race into Ethnicity: Asian Americans and Critical Transformations of Whiteness," *boundary 2* 28 (2002): 153–194. Loewen's 1988 afterword to the second edition of this "book of [his] youth" offers subsequent evidence to support his earlier prophecy on the status rise of the Chinese. This evidence is accompanied by a self-conscious statement on how it might be used against his subjects: "In Mississippi as in most of America, many whites consider them a 'model minority'—studious as children and sober, hard-working, and thrifty as adults. In Mississippi, as in the rest of America, many Asian Americans *are* these things. Asian American intellectuals are wary of stereotypical praise, however, for they know it is overgeneralized, and they suspect that the same shallow 'credit the victim' reasoning might turn into 'blame the victim' prejudice" (1988, 200).

CHAPTER 4

1. See Hannah Arendt, "Reflections on Little Rock" (1959) and in the same volume, "A Reply to Critics" (179–181). See also the responses published with it: David Spitz, "Politics and the Realms of Being," *Dissent* 6:1 (Winter 1959): 56–65; and Melvin Tumin, "Pie in the Sky . . ." *Dissent* 6, 1 (Winter 1959): 65–71.

2. One might also read this as Woodward's attempt to account for Sir Naipaul's identification with a faded southern aristocracy. Of course, Naipaul might himself deny that bias. As he remarked somewhat disingenuously in regard to his ethnographic writing on Islam in India and Africa, "A scholar would look at these people and draw conclusions.

I don't do that. The reader looks at these people and makes a pattern, and the pattern depends on the reader" (Adam Shute, "Literary Criticism," *New York Times Magazine*, 28 October 2001: 19).

3. Mary Church Terrell recounts an incident of passing in Washington, DC. dependent upon African American perception of the Asian foreigner's heightened status in the segregated South. An "East Indian" performer is (re)introduced within a black social circle:

> "Mr. So and So," said his sister, "let me present my brother to you." The eyes of the two men met in instant recognition. "Hello, Bert," said the great East Indian reaching out his hand. "We haven't seen each other since we used to play marbles together when we were boys." This case was all the more remarkable, because the "East Indian" had been born and brought up as a colored boy in that very southern city and some of his relatives were still living there. He visited them almost every night after dark when he removed his costume. (1996, 376)

4. I am not suggesting that there is no concept of "Asianness" that circulated apart from these terms. But I want to establish that the southern context put pressure on that meaning for communities and individuals.

5. Interestingly, Kim finds that affecting a posture of humbleness does not work among the "least educated blacks" who "are likely to look down on" him (1977, 131). Like whites, he finds that they take his behavior to be intrinsically Oriental, but they don't move to accommodate it.

6. Edgar C. McVoy, "Social Processes in the War Relocation Center, *Social Forces* 22, 1–4 (Oct. 1943–May 1944): 188–190. Others have contradicted this view, citing "good" treatment based on Southern manners and its parallel to Japanese conventions of speech. See Russell Bearden, "Life Inside Arkansas's Japanese-American Relocation Centers," *Arkansas Historical Quarterly* 68 (Summer 1989): 169–196.

7. *United States v. Bhagat Singh Thind*, 261 U.S. 204 (1923).

8. Beliefs regarding the institutionalization of the disabled were reflected in the 1882 Immigration Act that prohibited the entry of those deemed "unfit." See Douglas C. Baynton, "Defectives in the Land: Disability and American Immigration Policy, 1882–1924," *Journal of American Ethnic History* (Spring 2005): 31–44.

9. For an interesting depiction of caste and marriage in contemporary India with a focus on women's appearance and other criteria, see Anita Jain, *Marrying Anita* (New York: Bloomsbury, 2008).

10. Elizabeth Eckford's account appears in Will Counts, *A Life is More Than a Moment: The Desegregation of Little Rock's Central High* (Bloomington: Indiana University Press, 1999), and Daisy Bates, *The Long Shadow of Little Rock* (New York: McKay, 1966).

11. Renato Rosaldo writes, "My use of personal experience serves as a vehicle for making the quality and intensity of the rage in Ilongot grief more readily accessible to readers than certain more detached modes of composition. At the same time, by invoking personal experience as an analytical category one risks introduction to an act of mourning or a mere report on my discovery of the anger possible in bereavement" (1989, 11).

12. This lack of distinction between textual and material bodies is surprising given that Behar takes pains to distinguish between herself and the persona she has created in her book: "Since I have put myself in the ethnographic picture, readers feel they have come to know me. They have poured their own feelings into their construction of me and in

that way come to identify with me, or at least their fictional image of who I am. These responses have taught me that when readers take the voyage through anthropology's tunnel it is themselves they must be able to see in the observer who is serving as their guide" (1996, 16).

13. Or, as Sedgwick writes, "In a world where no one need be delusional to find evidence of systemic oppression, to theorize out of anything *but* a paranoid critical stance has come to seem naïve, pious, or complaisant" (1997, 5).

## CHAPTER 5

1. I thank Elena Tajima Creef for this reference.

2. Rubin's focus on the historical instances of social disciplining of sex distinguishes her work from the exploration of a continuum of sexual desire from heterosexual to homosexual inscribed by Havelock Ellis, or gender difference from feminine to masculine, something I explore in the next chapter.

3. Rubin's work is controversial for the same reason that it is powerful: it refuses to place sexual practices within a moral hierarchy. It develops a "pluralistic sexual ethics" wherein one criterion is pleasure, and another is the nebulously defined "presence or absence of coercion" (15). Thus, in her refusal to condemn "cross-generational" sex, pedophilia, or statutory rape, her focus lies in exposing the arbitrary boundaries placed on consensual sex. The practical implications of the theory become murky in cases in which the state intervenes in polygamist sects who practice underage marriage such as, to cite one example, the Fundamentalist Church of Jesus Christ of Latter Day Saints led by Warren Jeffs.

4. See Siobhan B. Somerville, *Queering the Colorline: Race and the Invention of Homosexuality in American Culture* (Durham, NC: Duke University Press, 2000).

5. For an overview of Asian American literature about the South, see Jennifer Ho, "Southern Eruptions in Asian American Narratives," forthcoming in *Improbable Southerners: Asian Americans in the South*, ed. Khyati Joshi and Jigna Desai (Athens: University of Georgia Press).

6. As I have noted in chapter 1, C. Vann Woodward draws a connection between American imperialist endeavors in Asia and the rise of segregation in the 1890s. He has suggested that segregation was *not*, in fact, a logical extension of the separation between blacks and whites that had existed under slavery. For one, he links American imperialism in the Pacific and the Caribbean to the rise of Jim Crow through belief in the White Man's Burden and the superior care-taking abilities of the white race (1951, 72).

7. For a discussion of the division of Korea, see Richard Whelan's *Drawing the Line: The Korean War, 1950–1953* (Boston: Little, Brown, 1990).

8. Cited in Andrew S. Hughes, "Novelist Susan Choi Uses Story of Her Korean-born Father," *South Bend Tribune*, 15 November 1998, p. 12. On the novel's representation of postcolonial politics, Choi notes, "I was concerned that the book would seem critical, but I felt that in light of the actual history of the war, the book is pretty easy on the American presence." Cited in Jun Kim, "From Korea to Faulker Country: Novelist Susan Choi discusses her work," Korean Journal.com [www.koream?journal.com/april2000/artists2. shtml].

9. Don Lee, Review of *The Foreign Student*, *Ploughshares* 25, 1 (Spring 1999): 193.

10. As John Dollard recognized in his admittedly biased field research notes, white southern hospitality was contingent upon his silence regarding race relations: "These white people down here are very charming and really exert themselves to do friendly things once you are accepted, but they seem very much like the psychotics one sometimes meets in a mental hospital. They are sane and charming except on one point, and on this point they are quite unreliable. One has exactly the sense of a whole society with a psychotic spot, an irrational, heavily protected sore through which all manner of venomous hatreds and irrational lusts may pour" (33).

11. The idea of the "North" as a racially freeing space is subtly suggested through the image of water: Chang's impulse in Chicago is to write to Katherine telling her "there is an ocean here." The national promise of American self-fashioning is located in the Midwest metropolis where anonymity promises rebirth and the cancellation of previous identities. However, the novel marks this promise as contingent upon racial embodiment and the political fellowship of other Asians whose past colonial animosities become cancelled by their mutual segregation within an ethnic ghetto. For a discussion of the Great Migration, see Farah Jasmine Griffin's *Who Set You Flowin'?: the African-American Migration Narrative* (New York: Oxford University Press, 1995).

12. For example, none of the reviews of *The Foreign Student* make reference to *Lolita* or pedophilia. Nevertheless, Choi deliberately raises the question of consent not only in the age of her protagonist, but by setting the scene while Katherine is only partially awake.

13. This dynamic reconciles the love story more obviously than an allegorical reading of their relationship. When asked whether or not the reader is meant to see in Katherine and Chuck a parallel to the relationship between the United States and Korea, Choi replied, "I think that's a fair interpretation. I hadn't initially tried to create [characters] that might symbolize the difficult relationship between the two nations. But I actually did after I'd written several of the chapters in which Chuck and Katherine are trying to understand each other; trying to find some way around the recurring difficulty they have communicating. . . . Chuck's almost happier in the end to present a façade to her that's more in line with her world and her expectations" (cited in Jun Kim). While the analogy makes sense in terms of the novel's portrayal of Orientalist projection and the dynamics of repulsion and desire that difference inspires, it would seem that allegory breaks down over the question of power relations. That is, domination and submission are necessarily intrinsic to individual fantasy projection and, more obviously, colonial relations between nations. What Katherine and Chuck share are similar responses to the experience of domination and the trauma of violation, situating them as like objects of occupation; in the context of allegory, she is not the United States, but the South, the occupied Confederacy.

14. See Chang Choi, "On Subgroups of M24. II: The Maximal Subgroups of M24," *Transactions of the American Mathematical Society* 16.7 (May 1972): 29–47.

15. In validation of its literary merits, the *Sewanee Review* noted, "[R]eaders feel sure that Chuck and Katherine will find their way to each other; the suspense is appropriately not in whether they do but in how they do, which is one basic distinction between commercial fiction and serious literature" (xx). Floyd Skloot, "Buried Secrets. Review of *The Foreign Student* by Susan Choi," *Sewanee Review* 107.1 (Winter 1999): xx–xxii.

16. Cited in Tunku Varadarajan, "A Patel Motel Cartel?" *New York Times* 4 July 1999, p. 36.

17. Other reviews place the then 29- year-old, Houston-bred Choi in the company of Flannery O'Conner and Kaye Gibbons (Elizabeth Hass, "Good Country People; Southern

Drama Draws Strength from Enigmatic Pair," *Houston Chronicle*, 20 Sept. 1998, p. 18). Such comparisons are intended to be complimentary as is the attempt of one critic to wrest Choi away from an association with bad ethnic writing. Skloot writes approvingly, "*The Foreign Student* does not feel like another trendy novel by another ethnically hyphenated, overhyped young writer" (Skloot 1999, 3).

18. For an overview of early literature on AIDS, see Edmund White's "Journals of the Plague Years," *Nation* 12 May 1997: 13–18.

19. Posts on January 17, 2000 and July 29, 1999 on www.amazon.com.

20. Enforcing the conceptual mirroring between the doctor and patient, Verghese has noted about his book, "It's my search for a place to call home. It's my patients' search for a place to call home" (12). Farwa Imam Ali, "Abraham Verghese, Doctor-turned-writer," *The Week*, 26 Nov. 2000.

21. For a discussion of the Immigration Act of 1965 and its impact on Asian medical professionals, see Paul Ong and John M. Liu, "U.S. Immigration Policies and Asian Migration," In *The New Asian Immigration in Los Angeles and Global Restructuring*," ed. Paul Ong, Edna Bonacich, and Lucie Cheng (Philadelphia: Temple University Press, 1994), 46–73.

22. Nair's film reinforces the doctor's foreign status by having his name pronounced three different ways. *My Own Country*, Produced and directed by Mira Nair, Showtime Entertainment, Third Row Center Films, 1998.

23. See, for example, Nayan Shah's *Contagious Divides: Epidemics and Race in San Francisco's Chinatown* (Berkeley: University of California Press, 2001); and Priscilla Wald's *Contagious: Cultures, Carriers, and the Outbreak Narrative* (Durham, NC: Duke University Press, 2008).

24. The film heightens the text's depiction of racial alienation by situating Abraham's wife, Rajani, as the symbolic repository of cultural difference, casting an actress trained in classical Indian dance. Nair portrays the couple as the object of community speculation in a scene in which Rajani practices in their living room under the covert surveillance of a (white) child caught peeping through the window. The brief sequence visualizes what in the narrative is conveyed as an increasing paranoia regarding Abraham's sense of racial difference as it becomes written onto the difference of his patients.

25. Verghese joined the faculty of Stanford University's School of Medicine in 2007 and published his first novel, *Cutting for Stone*, in 2009.

26. Cited in Rajini Srikanth, "Identity and Admission into the Political Game: The Indian American Community Signs Up," *Amerasia Journal* 25:3 (1999/2000): 59–80.

27. Victor Jew, "Asian American Studies and Critical Regionalism: the Midwest as the Site of Racialized Governmentalities," paper delivered at the Association for Asian American Studies, Chicago, April 19, 2008.

CHAPTER 6

1. Cited in Patricia Leigh Brown, "A Quest for a Restroom That's Neither Men's Room Nor Women's Room," *New York Times*, 4 March 2005, p. A11. It would take a space longer than this chapter to explore the terrain of other socially accepted forms of gender "segregation" exclusive of public restrooms. The discourses surrounding Title IX and gender-designated sports teams, for example, follow a "separate and equal" logic that is designed

not to enforce hierarchy, but to provide a level playing field. Gender division in sports represents one of many mechanisms in place intended to address fairness; other measures adjust for differences in weight, level, age, etc., among competitors.

2. I am invoking "transgenderism" as a broad term that engages not only intersex individuals and pre- and postoperative transsexuals, but also individuals who represent as male or female distinct from their "bio" assignment or, to invoke Leslie Feinberg's phrase, "birth sex." As Feinberg writes, "What makes me transgendered is that my birth sex— which is female—appears to be in social contradiction to my gender expression—which is read as masculine" (1998, 69). This idea of transgenderism as "social contradiction" also encompasses cross-dressers regardless of sexual orientation. Susan Stryker uses the term "transgender" "not to refer to one particular identity or way of being embodied but rather as an umbrella term for a wide variety of bodily effects that disrupt or denaturalize heteronormatively constructed linkages between an individual's anatomy at birth, a nonconsensually assigned gender category, psychical identifications with sexed body images and/or gendered subject positions, and the performance of specifically gendered social, sexual, or kinship functions" (1998, 149).

3. Williams shifts from "he" to "she" presumably in keeping with the chronology of "S.'s" sex-change operation. In regard to the use of gendered pronouns in reference to transgendered individuals, both Judith Halberstam and Leslie Feinberg take the obvious approach; ask what pronoun people prefer. When dealing with texts, I follow the lead of the author or the pronoun corresponding to the individual's chosen name. In the context of the transvestite character in *Mai's America*, for example, I refer to Christy as "she," Chris as "he." I recognize that this is not consistent usage; I want to retain a sense of fluidity that is essential to transgenderism in defiance of standardization.

4. Ono coined the phrase, "woman is the nigger of the world," in a 1969 interview with the British women's magazine, *Nova*. It became the title of a song co-written with John Lennon and released in 1972.

5. *Goodridge v. Department of Public Health* 440 Mass. 309 (2003).

6. In ironic contrast, antiquated state laws intended to prohibit interracial unions have been called upon in order to render same-sex marriage illegal. In 2004, then Governor of Massachusetts Mitt Romney invoked a 1913 state law barring out-of-state couples from marrying in Massachusetts in order to avoid the marriage laws of their home states. Intended to prevent same-sex marriages, this move was criticized as an effort to resurrect discriminatory law for political purposes. See Scott S. Greenberger, "History suggests race was the basis," 21 May 2004 on www.boston.com/news/specials/gay_marriage/articles/2004/05/21/history_suggests_race_was_the_basis/.

7. Cited in Lynette Clemetson, "Both Sides Court Black Churches in the Battle Over Gay Marriage," *New York Times*, 1 March 2004, pp. A1,14.

8. Paisley Currah notes that in contrast to the frequent invocation of African American oppression in gay rights rhetoric, this comparison in transgender rights advocacy is rare. Nevertheless, Currah finds that the litigation strategies used by transgendered rights advocates have been informed by those of the Civil Rights Movement (2006).

9. In drawing a contrast between domestic transracial (read as black-white) adoption and international (read as Chinese-white) adoption, Sara K. Dorow reveals the ways in which Asian interstitiality takes on transnational resonance. Chinese children are viewed as being between the "abject (black, older, special-needs) and unattainable (white, young,

healthy) children at home" (55). Moreover, she also notes that Chinese adoptees were presumed to be "less burdened by a volatile history of intractable black-white relations" by prospective adoptive parents (55). Sara K. Dorow, *Transnational Adoption: A Cultural Economy of Race, Gender, and Kinship*" (New York: New York University Press, 2006).

10. See Michael Awkward, *Negotiating Difference: Race, Gender, and the Politics of Positionality* (Chicago: University of Chicago Press, 1995); Susan Gubar, *RaceChanges: White Skin, Black Face in American Culture* (Oxford: Oxford University Press, 1997); and Andrea K. Newlyn, "Undergoing Racial 'Reassignment': the Politics of Transracial Crossing in Sinclair Lewis's *Kingsblood Royal*," *Modern Fiction Studies* 48, 4 (Winter 2002): 1041–1074.

11. Cited on the PBS website publicizing the film, www.pbs.org/itvs/globalvoices/maisamerica.html.

12. Harun Karim Thomas, personal communication 15 April 2007.

13. Anne Fausto-Sterling, "How Many Sexes Are There?" *New York Times*, 12 March 1993, p. A29.

14. On the limitations of adding new categories under the law without addressing the necessity of such classifications, one might turn to racial court cases to consider how attempts to rectify racial injustice on behalf of the individual fail to ameliorate systemic racism within the law. Cases in which individuals contested their nonwhite status to gain naturalization rights in the 1920s, for example, clearly uphold the tenets of white supremacy. Both Ozawa and Thind claimed white status in order to petition for the right of naturalization denied them as Asians. Their arguments in defense did not contest the cultural system upon which exclusions were based as much as they declared individual fitness for incorporation and claimed inclusion based on broader definitions of whiteness—i.e., skin color and Aryan descent. See *Ozawa v. United States*, 260 U.S. 178 (1922), and *United States v. Bhagat Singh Thind*, 261 U.S. 204 (1923).

15. In questioning whether the goal to dismantle gender as a legal category is separate from the goal to amend those categories to include transgendered or gender-variant people, Currah's view is that transgender rights advocates do both, meeting the legal needs of transgender people while acknowledging "the larger political imaginary of the transgender rights movement" (2003, 707). Similarly, drawing upon an analogy between racial rights and transgender rights, Richard Juang argues that legal advocacy should not simply hinge upon the politics of recognition. Richard M. Juang, "Transgendering the Politics of Recognition," in *Transgender Rights*, ed. Paisley Currah, Richard M. Juang, and Shannon Price Minter (Minneapolis: University of Minnesota Press, 2006), 242–261.

16. See, for example, Gordene Olga MacKenzie, *Transgender Nation* (Bowling Green, OH: Bowling Green State University Popular Press, 1994).

17. In regard to her title, Stone has since noted that "'[p]osttranssexual' was an ironic term, since when this essay was first published [in 1991] everything in theory was post-something-or-other. I was looking for a way forward. 'Transgender' is way better." Cited on www.actlab.utexas.edu/~sandy/empire-strikes-back.

18. Robert Crouch finds Turner's concept of liminality useful for understanding the medical discourses surrounding intersexed children. The surgeon, he suggests, "sculpts the genitals of the intersexed person not because there is a medical dysfunction . . . but rather because the physician cannot fit the intersexed child into one of two available sex and gender categories" (39). Thus, Crouch invokes Turner in order to understand the medical establishment's intervention into intersexuality; doctors see themselves as aiding

an individual's transition rather than correcting pathology. Robert A. Crouch, "Betwixt and Between: The Past and Future of Intersexuality," in *Intersex in the Age of Ethics*, ed. Alice Domurat Dreger (Hagerstown, MD: University Publishing Group, 1999), 29–49.

19. In linking Turner's work to the work of transgender theory, I do not intend to imply that all trans people are "liminal" in the sense that they are merely in suspension, waiting to achieve gender fixity. By the same token, I do not mean to imply that all Asian Americans are white-identified.

20. *Mai's America* aired on PBS on August 6, 2002.

21. The film initially intended to follow the experiences of a number of Vietnamese exchange students across the United States. For comments on the origins of the film, see www.pbs.org/itvs/globalvoices/maisamerica.html. Background on the film's history can be found on the POV link, "Behind the Lens" in the Director's Interview.

22. The publicity image appears on the PBS website publicizing the film, www.pbs.org/itvs/globalvoices/maisamerica.html.

23. Inscribing an expanded notion of gay culture in the South, John Howard both confirms and redirects the idea that the South is the site of greater sexual oppression than other regions in the United States: "In Mississippi, spatial configurations—the unique characteristics of a rural landscape—forged distinct human interactions, movements, and sites. Gay community, thus, is not simply a *phenomenon* lacking at this place and time. Rather, it is a concept lacking in explanatory power, a notion that incompletely and inadequately gets at the shape and scope of queer life. Gay culture certainly existed, increasingly flowed into and out of this region" (15). John Howard, *Men Like That: A Southern Queer History* (Chicago: University of Chicago Press, 1999). Drawing from the work of David Bell, Halberstram similarly contests the privileging of urban spaces in gay and lesbian regionalism, noting that a "metronormative" migration narrative is confounded in the case of Teena Brandon, the transgendered teenager who passed as male in rural Nebraska. "Metronormativity," Halberstram writes, "reveals the rural to be the devalued term in the urban/rural binary governing the spatialization of modern U.S. sexual identities" (2005, 37).

24. While my reading highlights the gender-subversive nature of Chris's cross-dressing, I am aware that drag performance does not inherently deauthorize social norms. In this, I would echo Judith Butler's point that, "drag may well be used in the service of both the denaturalization and reidealization of hyperbolic heterosexual gender norms. At best, it seems, drag is a site of a certain ambivalence, one which reflects the more general situation of being implicated in the regimes of power that one opposes" (1993, 125). Nevertheless, it is clear that the film locates gay subculture as beyond the pale of normative community in more ways than one. The bar in which Mai first meets Christy is both theoretically and literally beyond the law: Mai is initially taken there by her host sister because it caters to underage drinking.

25. This recognition is tempered by the awareness that for a woman, being sexual in a small southern town may be as subject to censure as representing as sexually ambiguous. Witnessing the one instance of Mai's display of feminine sexuality—she models a form-fitting mini-dress for her white host sister, Kim—merely elicits the bland comment, "It would look better if you had matching shoes."

26. Mai's theatrical bent is validated by the filmmaker, who notes that during two-and-a half years of filming, Mai "never once asked me [to] turn off the camera. That's

why she was such a perfect subject" [Cited in Wendy Mitchell, "Coming to America with a Few Surprises: Marlo Poras on *Mai's America*," *IndieWIRE* 6 Aug. 2002. www.indiewire.com/article/interview_coming_to_america_with_a_few_surprises_marlo_poras_on_mais_americ/]. Moreover, when Mai was in New Orleans, she auditioned for MTV's *RealWorld*. Cited in Walter Chaw, "Marlo's 'America': Film Freak Central Interviews Director Marlo Poras," *Film Freak Central*, 2 June 2002. http://filmfreakcentral.net/notes/mporasinterview.htm.

27. Cited on the PBS website for *Mai's America* at http://www.pbs.org/pov/pov2002/maisamerica/index.html.

28. I am not arguing that the film presents Mai as lesbian. In effect, she is portrayed as having no sexual desire. While forming cross-racial friendships with black and white girls, she seems to attract no heterosexual interest in the small, southern town. Her one "date" stands in marked contrast to the easy physical intimacy she shares with Chris. The sequence depicting her eventual prom substitute, a Spanish exchange student, is characterized by awkwardness: they dance stiffly and have to be ordered to embrace for the obligatory photo. Nevertheless, the film presumes her heterosexuality precisely in its refusal to mark her sexual orientation. Some years after the film's completion, Mai confessed that the biggest pressure she faces in Vietnam is the pressure to get married, a statement that reveals nothing about her sexual orientation, but much about her awareness of being subject to the pressures of social conformity. Personal communication with Mai Nguyen, March 2007.

29. Contrast this portrayal to the 1996 film by Ira Sachs, *The Delta*, about a straight-identified, white teenager's experimentation with gay subculture in Memphis. According to the filmmaker, the "find" of black, Vietnamese nonprofessional actor Thang Chan took over the film, whose center was initially intended to be the southern, white boy and his tenuous coming of age. While *The Delta* is also about racialized routes of desire in its portrayal of a biracial Vietnamese prostitute's encounters with black and white cultures in the South, the film ends up pathologizing both its Amerasian subject and gay culture as well. After seducing the white protagonist and being rejected by him, the mixed-race Vietnamese character ends up murdering a black man he picks up at a bar. *The Delta* can only conceive of the gay, black Asian's racial and cultural status as an indication of alienation so intense that its only outlet is violence. Rejected by whites, he must murder the blackness within himself—or so the film suggests. *The Delta*. Produced by Margot Bridger, written and directed by Ira Sachs. Strand Home Video, Santa Monica, CA, 1998.

AFTERWORD

1. Jon Robin Baitz, "American Dreams: Food May Be Pleasurable, but in Its Essence, It's Political," *New York Times Magazine*, 29 May 2005: 55–56. G. Willow Wilson, "The Comfort of Strangers: In Cairo's Subway, a Western woman Like Me Can Find Safe Haven," *New York Times Magazine*, 29 May 2005: 62.

2. In parallel, Mae Ngai's *Impossible Subjects* looks at the racialization of the category "illegal alien," establishing a framework in regard to the state and to public policy by both Asians and Mexicans in the United States. Her work cannot be located merely within either Asian American or Latino/a Studies; rather, she names the narratives that link them, productively eroding the ethnic particularism of disciplinary inquiry.

3. Cited in Sunaina Maira and Rajini Srikanth, "Visualizing Three Continents: An Interview with Filmmaker Mira Nair, June 3, 1996," In *Contours of the Heart: South Asians Map North America*, ed. Sunaina Maira and Rajini Srikanth (New York: Asian American Writers' Workshop, 1996) 125–139.Quote appears on pages 127–128.

4. Cited in Barbara Hagenbaugh, "Mississippi Choctaws Find Opportunity," *Canku Ota* 60. 4 May 2002, www.turtletrack.org.

5. See Hagenbaugh (2002) and Mississippi Band of Choctaw Indians, Tribal Profile, www.choctaw.org.

6. Cited in Adam Cohen, "A New Kind of Minority Is Challenging Louisiana's Racial Conventions," *New York Times*, 12 October 2003.

7. This dynamic is somewhat different from the politics of multiracialism that arose during Barack Obama's presidential campaign in 2008. Obama's biracial heritage was not only a screen for reconciliation, but a cause for suspicion. One southern voter complained, "He's neither-nor. . . . He's other. It's in the Bible. Come as one. Don't create other breeds." In the context of the candidate's interracialism, another noted that Obama was the type of person "you can't really hate, but you don't really trust." Cited in Adam Nossiter, "For Some, Uncertainty Starts at Racial Identity, *New York Times*, 15 October 2008, p. A21.

8. I am indebted to Bobby Moon for this reference.

# Works Cited

Aarim-Heriot, Najia. 2003. *Chinese Immigrants, African Americans, and Racial Anxiety in the United States, 1848–82.* Urbana: University of Illinois Press.

Abel, Elizabeth. 1999. "Bathroom Doors and Drinking Fountains: Jim Crow's Racial Symbolic." *Critical Inquiry* 25, 3 (Spring): 435–481.

Adams, Rachel. 2001. *Sideshow U.S.A.: Freaks and the American Cultural Imagination.* Chicago: University of Chicago Press.

Anzaldúa, Gloria. 1987. *Borderlands/La Frontera: The New Mestiza.* San Francisco: Spinsters/Aunt Lute.

Arendt, Hannah. 1959. "Reflections on Little Rock." *Dissent* 6, 1 (Winter): 45–56.

Baker, Houston A., Jr. 2001. *Turning South Again: Re-thinking Modernism/Re-reading Booker T.* Durham, NC: Duke University Press.

Baker, Houston A., Jr., and Dana D. Nelson. 2001. "Preface: Violence, the Body and 'The South.'" *American Literature* 73, 2 (June): 231–244.

Baker, Ray Stannard. 1964 [1908]. *Following the Color Line: American Negro Citizenship in the Progressive Era.* New York: Harper & Row.

Baldwin, James. 1961. *Nobody Knows My Name: More Notes of a Native Son.* New York: Dial Press.

———.1955. *Notes of a Native Son.* Boston: Beacon.

Barth, Gunther. 1964. *Bitter Strength: A History of the Chinese in the United States 1850–1870.* Cambridge, MA: Harvard University Press.

Behar, Ruth. 1996. *The Vulnerable Observer: Anthropology that Breaks Your Heart.* Boston: Beacon Press.

Bell, Derrick. 2004. *Silent Covenants: Brown v. Board of Education and the Unfulfilled Hopes for Racial Reform.* Oxford: Oxford University Press.

Berlant, Lauren. 1998. "Introduction: Intimacy: A Special Issue." *Critical Inquiry* 24, 2: 281–288.

Berry, Brewton. 1963. *Almost White.* New York: Macmillan.

Bhabha, Homi. 1997. "Halfway House." *Art Forum* (May): 11–12, 125.

———.1994. *The Location of Culture.* London: Routledge.

Blalock, Jr., Hubert. 1967. *Toward A Theory of Minority-Group Relations.* New York: Wiley.

Blu, Karen. 1979. *The Lumbee Problem: The Making of an American Indian People.* New York: Cambridge University Press.

Bonacich, Edna. 1973. "A Theory of Middleman Minorities." *American Sociological Review* 38 (October): 583–594.

Boorstein, Kate. 1995 [1994]. *Gender Outlaw: On Men, Women, and the Rest of Us.* New York: Random House.

Boswell, Maia. 1999. "'Ladies,' 'Gentlemen,' and 'Colored': 'The Agency of (Lacan's Black) Letter' in the Outhouse." *Cultural Critique* 41 (Winter): 108–137.

Bow, Leslie. 2007. "Meditations of the 'Partly Colored.'" *Southern Review* 43, 1 (Winter): 89–95.

———.2001. *Betrayal and Other Acts of Subversion: Feminism, Sexual Politics, Asian American Women's Literature*. Princeton, NJ: Princeton University Press.

Brah, Avtar. 1996. *Cartographies of Diaspora: Contesting Identities*. London: Routledge.

Butler, George Edwin. 1916. *The Croatan Indians of Sampson County, North Carolina: their Origin and Racial Status, A Plea for Separate Schools*. Durham, NC: Seeman Printery, Electronic Edition, University of North Carolina, Chapel Hill.

Butler, Judith. 2004. "Is Kinship Always Already Heterosexual?" In *Going Public: Feminism and the Shifting Boundaries of the Private Sphere*, ed. Joan W. Scott and Debra Keates. Urbana: University of Illinois Press. 123–150.

———.1993. *Bodies That Matter: on the Discursive Limits of 'Sex.'* New York: Routledge.

Caldwell, Dan. 1971. "The Negroization of the Chinese Stereotype in California." *Historical Society of Southern California* 53: 123–131.

Cameron, D. 1999. "Caught Between: An Essay on Intersexuality." In *Intersex in the Age of Ethics*, ed. Alice Domurat Dreger. Hagerstown, MD: University Publishing Group. 91–96.

Carr, Brian. 2004. "Paranoid Interpretation, Desire's Nonobject, and Nella Larsen's *Passing*." *PMLA* 119.2: 282–295.

Cash, W. J. 1941. *The Mind of the South*. Garden City, NY: Doubleday.

Cavafy, Constantine. 1995. *The Essential Cavafy*, ed. and trans. Edmund Keeley. Hopewell, NJ: Ecco Press.

Cell, John W. 1982. *The Highest Stage of White Supremacy: The Origins of Segregation in South Africa and the American South*. Cambridge: Cambridge University Press.

Chen, Tina. 2005. *Double Agency: Acts of Impersonation in Asian American Literature and Culture*. Palo Alto: Stanford University Press.

Cheng, Anne Anlin. 2001. *The Melancholy of Race: Psychoanalysis, Assimilation, and Hidden Grief*. Oxford: Oxford University Press.

Cheng, Cindy I-Fen. 2004. "Contesting Chinese/American Identities in the Age of the Cold War Politics." PhD Diss., University of California, Irvine.

Chesnutt, Charles W. 2003 [1901]. *The Marrow of Tradition*. Mineola, NY: Dover.

———.1999. *Essays and Speeches*, ed. Joseph R. McElrath, Jr., Robert C. Leitz, III, and Jesse S. Crisler. Palo Alto: Stanford University Press.

Chin, Frank, and Jeffrey Paul Chan. 1972. "Racist Love." In *Seeing Through Shuck*, ed. Richard Kostelanetz. New York: Ballantine. 65–79.

Choi, Susan. 1998. *The Foreign Student*. New York: HarperCollins.

Chow, Sun Gay. 1986. "A Personal View of the Mississippi Chinese." In *Mississippi Writers: Reflections of Childhood and Youth*, Vol. 2, ed. Dorothy Abbott. Jackson: University Press of Mississippi. 96–102.

Chuh, Kandice. 2003. *Imagine Otherwise: On Asian Americanist Critique*. Durham, NC: Duke University Press.

Clark, William Bedford. 2006. "Robert Penn Warren's Band of Angels at Fifty." *Southern Quarterly* 43, 2 (Winter): 176–185.

Clifford, James. 1986. "Introduction: Partial Truths." In *Writing Culture: the Poetics and Politics of Ethnography*, ed. James Clifford and George E. Marcus. Berkeley: University of California Press. 1–26.

Clifton, James A. 1989. *Being and Becoming Indian: Biographical Studies of North American Frontiers.* Chicago: Dorsey Press.

Cobb, Joseph B. 1970 [1851]. "Mississippi Scenes; or Sketches of Southern and Western Life and Adventure, Humorous, Satirical, and Descriptive." Gregg Press.

Cohen, Lucy M. 1984. *Chinese in the Post-Civil War South: A People Without a History.* Baton Rouge: Louisiana State University Press.

Cohn, David L. 1948. *Where I was Born and Raised [And God Shakes Creation, 1935].* Boston: Houghton Mifflin.

Colker, Laura. 1996. *Hybrid: Bisexuals, Multiracials, and Other Misfits under American Law.* New York: New York University Press.

Creef, Elena Tajima. 2005. "Trying to Find My Way Back Home to East Lake, North Carolina." *North Carolina Literary Review* 14: 75–82.

Currah, Paisley. 2006. "Gender Pluralisms under the Transgender Umbrella." In *Transgender Rights*, ed. Paisley Currah, Richard M. Juang, and Shannon Price Minter. Minneapolis: University of Minnesota Press. 3–31.

———.2003. "The Transgender Rights Imaginary." *Georgetown Journal of Gender and the Law* IV.2 (Spring): 705–720.

Daniels, Jonathan. 1938. *A Southerner Discovers the South.* New York: Macmillan.

Delgado, Richard. 1997. "Rodrigo's Fifteenth Chronicle: Racial Mixture, Latino-Critical Scholarship, and the Black-White Binary." *Texas Law Review* 75, 5 (April): 1181–1201.

Dhingra, Pawan H. 2003. "Being American Between Black and White: Second-Generation Asian American Professionals' Racial Identities." *Journal of Asian American Studies* 6, 2 (June): 117–147.

Dial, Adolph L., and David K. Eliades. 1975. *The Only Land I Know: A History of the Lumbee Indians.* San Francisco: Indian Historian Press.

Diehl Elias, Veronica. 1994. "AIDS and HIV Infection." In *Human Sexuality: An Encyclopedia*, ed. Vern L. Bullough and Bonnie Bullough. New York: Garland. 15–22.

Dittus, Erick. 1985. "Mississippi Triangle: An Interview with Christine Choy, Worth Long and Allan Siegel." *Cineaste* 14, 2: 38–40.

Dollard, John. 1937. *Caste and Class in a Southern Town.* New York: Doubleday.

Du Bois, W. E. B. 2007 [1935]. *Black Reconstruction.* Oxford: Oxford University Press.

———.1965 [1903]. "The Souls of Black Folk." In *Three Negro Classics.* New York: Avon. 213–389.

Dudziak, Mary. 2000. *Cold War Civil Rights: Race and the Image of American Democracy.* Princeton, NJ: Princeton University Press.

Duncan, Patti. 2001. "Claiming Space in the South: A Conversation Among Members of Asian/Pacific Islander Lesbian, Bisexual, Transgendered Network of Atlanta." In *Out in the South*, ed. Carlos L. Dews and Carolyn Leste Law. Philadelphia: Temple University Press. 26–55.

Dykeman, Wilma, and James Stokely. 1957. *Neither Black Nor White.* New York: Rinehart & Company.

Egerton, John. 1983. *Nissan in Tennessee.* Smyrna, TN: Nissan Motor Manufacturing Corporation, U.S.A.

———.1969. *Cubans in Miami: A Third Dimension in Racial and Cultural Relations*. Nashville, TN: Race Relations Information Center.

Ellison, Ralph. 1989 [1947]. *Invisible Man*. New York: Vintage.

———.1964 [1953]. *Shadow and Act*. New York: Vintage.

Erdrich, Louise. 1984. *Love Medicine*. New York: Bantam.

Fanon, Frantz. 1991. *Black Skin, White Masks*, trans. Charles Lam Markmann. New York: Grove Weidenfeld.

Faulkner, William. 1984 [1929]. *The Sound and the Fury*. New York: Random House.

Feinberg, Leslie. 1998. *Transliberation: Beyond Pink or Blue*. Boston: Beacon Press.

Fisher, Maxine P. 1980. *The Indians of New York City: A Study of Immigrants from India*. Columbia, MO: South Asia Books.

Foley, Neil. 1997. *The White Scourge: Mexicans, Blacks, and Poor Whites in Texas Cotton Culture*. Berkeley: University of California Press.

Forbes, Jack D. 1990. "Undercounting Native Americans: The 1980 Census and the Manipulation of Racial Identity in the United States." *Wicazo sa Review* 6: 2–26.

Foucault, Michel. 2003. *Society Must be Defended: Lectures at the College de France, 1975–76*. New York: Picador.

Fowler, David. 1987. *Northern Attitudes Towards Interracial Marriage: Legislation and Public Opinion in the Middle Atlantic and the States of the Old Northwest, 1780–1930*. New York: Garland.

Frankenberg, Ruth. 1993. *White Women, Race Matters: the Social Construction of Whiteness*. Minneapolis: University of Minnesota Press.

Friedman, Susan Stanford. 1998. *Mappings: Feminism and the Cultural Geographies of Encounter*. Princeton, NJ: Princeton University Press.

Gallop, Jane. 1985. *Reading Lacan*. Ithaca, NY: Cornell University Press.

———.1982. *The Daughter's Seduction: Feminism and Psychoanalysis*. Ithaca, NY: Cornell University Press.

Garber, Marjorie. 1992. *Vested Interests: Cross-dressing and Cultural Anxiety*. New York: Routledge.

Gonzalez, Gilbert G. 1990. *Chicano Education in the Era of Segregation*. Philadelphia: Associated University Presses.

Gould, Janice. 1992. "The Problem of Being 'Indian': One Mixed-Blood's Dilemma." In *Decolonizing the Subject: The Politics of Gender in Women's Autobiography*, ed. Sidonie Smith and Julia Watson. Minneapolis: University of Minnesota Press. 81–87.

Gray, Richard. 2000. *Southern Aberrations: Writers of the American South and the Problems of Regionalism*. Baton Rouge: Louisiana State University Press.

Gross, Ariela. 2008. *What Blood Won't Tell: A History of Race on Trial in America*. Cambridge, MA: Harvard University Press.

———.1998. "Litigating Whiteness: Trials of Racial Determination in the Nineteenth-Century South." *Yale Law Journal* (October): 111–185.

Gualtieri, Sarah. "Strange Fruit? Syrian Immigrants, Extralegal Violence and Racial Formation in the Jim Crow South." *Arab Studies Quarterly* 26, 3 (2004): 63–85.

Halberstam, Judith. 2005. *In a Queer Time and Place: Transgender Bodies, Subcultural Lives*. New York: New York University Press.

———.1997. "Mackdaddy, Superfly, Rapper: Gender, Race, and Masculinity in the Drag King Scene." *Social Text* 52–53 (Fall/Winter): 104–131.

Hale, Grace Elizabeth. 2000. "'For Colored'" and 'For White': Segregating Consumption in the South." In *Jumpin' Jim Crow: Southern Politics from Civil War to Civil Rights*, ed. Jane Dailey, Glenda Elizabeth Gilmore, and Bryant Simon. Princeton, NJ: Princeton University Press. 162–182.

Handman, Max Sylvius. 1930. "Economic Reasons for the Coming of the Mexican Immigrant." *American Journal of Sociology* 35, 4 (January): 601–611.

Himes, Chester. 1973. *If He Hollers Let Him Go*. New Jersey: Chatham.

hooks, bell. 1992. *Black Looks: Race and Representation*. Boston: South End Press.

Hosokawa, Bill. 1969. *Nisei: The Quiet Americans*. New York: William Morrow.

Hughes, Langston. 1995. *The Collected Poems of Langston Hughes*, ed. Arnold Rampersad. New York: Vintage.

Hurston, Zora Neale. 1978 [1935]. *Mules and Men*. Bloomington: University of Indiana Press.

Isaacs, Harold R. 1962 [1958]. *Images of Asia: American Views of China and India*. New York: Capricorn Books.

Iyer, Pico. 1994. Review of *My Own Country*. *Time*, June 6, p. 70.

Jacobson, Matthew Frye. 1998. *Whiteness of a Different Color: European Immigrants and the Alchemy of Race*. Cambridge, MA: Harvard University Press.

Johnson, Charles S. 1943. *Patterns of Negro Segregation*. New York: Harper.

Johnson, Guy B. 1939. "Personality in a White-Indian-Negro Community." *American Sociological Review* 4: 516–523.

Kadohata, Cynthia. 2004. *kira-kira*. New York: Atheneum.

Kennedy, Randall. 2003. *Interracial Intimacies: Sex, Marriage, Identity, and Adoption*. New York: Pantheon.

Kim, Choong Soon. 1998. "Asian Adaptations in the American South." In *Cultural Diversity in the U.S. South: Anthropological Contributions to a Region in Transition*, ed. Carole E. Hill and Patricia D. Beaver. Athens: University of Georgia Press. 129–143.

———.1977. *An Asian Anthropologist in the South: Field Experiences with Blacks, Indians, and Whites*. Knoxville: University of Tennessee Press.

Kim, Claire Jean. 2000. *Bitter Fruit: the Politics of Black-Korean Conflict in New York City*. New Haven, CT: Yale University Press.

Kincaid, Jamaica. 1997. "The Little Revenge from the Periphery." *Transition* 73: 68–73.

Kingston, Maxine Hong. 1989. *Tripmaster Monkey: His Fake Book*. New York: Knopf.

Kreyling, Michael. 2001. "The South in Perspective." *Mississippi Quarterly* 54:3 (Summer): 383–391.

Kristeva, Julia. 1991. *Strangers to Ourselves*, trans. Leon Roudiez. New York: Columbia University Press.

Lacan, Jacques. 1977 [1966]. *Écrits*, trans. Alan Sheridan. New York: Norton.

Lawson, John. 1718. "The History of Carolina." London: T. Warner.

Lee, Josephine. 1997. *Performing Asian America: Race and Ethnicity on the Contemporary Stage*. Philadelphia: Temple University Press.

Lerch, Patricia. 1992. "State-Recognized Indians of North Carolina, Including a History of the Waccamaw Sioux." In *Indians of the Southeastern United States in the Late 20th Century*, ed. J. Anthony Paredes. Tuscaloosa: University of Alabama Press. 244–208.

Lipsitz, George. 1998. *The Possessive Investment in Whiteness: How White People Benefit from Identity Politics*. Philadelphia: Temple University Press.

Liu, Eric. 1998. *The Accidental Asian*. New York: Random House.

Loewen, James W. 1988 [1972]. *The Mississippi Chinese: Between Black and White*. 2nd ed. Prospect Heights, IL: Waveland Press.

Loewenberg, Bert James. 1934. "Efforts of the South to Encourage Immigration, 1865–1900." *South Atlantic Quarterly* 33: 363–85.

Lopez, Ian F. Haney. 2003. *Racism on Trial: the Chicano Fight for Justice*. Cambridge, MA: Harvard University Press.

———.1996. *White by Law: the Legal Construction of Race*. New York: New York University Press.

Lovett, Laura L. 2002. "'African and Cherokee by Choice': Race and Resistance under Legalized Segregation." In *Confounding the Color Line: The Indian-Black Experience in North America*, ed. James F. Brooks. Lincoln: University of Nebraska. 192–221.

Lowe, Lisa. 1996. *Immigrant Acts: On Asian American Cultural Politics*. Durham, NC: Duke University Press.

———.1994. "Unfaithful to the Original: The Subject of Dictée." In *Writing Self/Writing Nation: A Collection of Essays on Dictée by Theresa Hak Kyung Cha*, ed. Elaine Kim and Norma Alarcón. Berkeley: Third Woman Press. 35–69.

*Mai's America*. 2002. Directed by Marlo Poras. Independent Television Service and the Corporation for Public Broadcasting. 72 minutes, DVD.

Martin, Biddy, and Chandra Talpade Mohanty. 1986. "Feminist Politics, What's Home Got to Do with It?" In *Feminist Studies/Critical Studies*, ed. Teresa de Lauretis. Bloomington: Indiana University Press. 191–212.

Martinez, George. 1997. "Mexican-Americans and Whiteness." In *Critical White Studies: Looking Behind the Mirror*, ed. Richard Delgado and Jean Stefancic. Philadelphia: Temple University Press. 210–213.

Mazumdar, Sucheta. 1989. "Racist Responses to Racism: The Aryan Myth and South Asians in the United States." *South Asia Bulletin* 9, 1:47–55.

McCunn, Ruthanne Lum. 1988. *Chinese American Portraits: Personal Histories 1828–1988*. San Francisco: Chronicle Books.

McLean, Angus W. n.d. "Historical Sketch of the Indians of Robeson County." McLean Collection, Robeson County Public Library, Lumberton, NC.

McMillan, Hamilton. 1907 [1888]. *Sir Walter Raleigh's Lost Colony: Historical Sketch of the Attempts Made by Sir Walter Raleigh to Establish a Colony in Virginia, with Traditions of an Indian Tribe in North Carolina, Indicating the Fate of the Colony of Englishmen Left on Roanoke Island in 1587*. Raleigh, NC: Edwards & Broughton, rev. ed.

McPherson, O. M. 1915. *Indians of North Carolina. Letter from the Secretary of the Interior, transmitting, in Response to a Senate Resolution of June 30, 1914, a Report on Condition and Tribal Rights of the Indians of Robeson and Adjoining Counties of North Carolina*. Senate Documents, v. 4. Washington, DC: Government Print Office. 63rd Congress.

Mehta, Ved. 1985. *Sound-Shadows of the New World*. New York: Norton.

———.1957. *Face to Face: An Autobiography*. New York: Little, Brown.

*Mississippi Masala*. 1991. Directed by Mira Nair. Columbia TriStar Home Video, VHS.

*Mississippi Triangle*. 1984. Produced and directed by Christine Choy, Worth Long, Allan Siegel. New York: Third World Newsreel, VHS.

Moraga, Cherríe. 2000 [1983]. *Loving in the War Years*, Expanded Edition. Cambridge, MA: South End Press.

Morrison, Toni. 1994. "On the Backs of Blacks." In *Arguing Immigration: Are New Immigrants a Wealth of Diversity or a Crushing Burden?* ed. Nicolaus Mills. New York: Simon & Schuster. 97–100.

————.1992. *Playing in the Dark: Whiteness and the Literary Imagination*. Cambridge, MA: Harvard University Press.

————.1989. "Unspeakable Things Unspoken: The Afro-American Presence in American Literature." *Michigan Quarterly Review* 28:1 (Winter): 1–34.

————.1982 [1973]. *Sula*. New York: Plume.

————.1970. *The Bluest Eye*. New York: Simon & Schuster.

Mukherjee, Bharati. 1989. *Jasmine*. New York: Ballantine.

————.1988. *The Middleman and Other Stories*. New York: Ballantine.

Munasinghe, Viranjini. 2001. "Redefining the Nation: The East Indian Struggle to Inclusion in Trinidad." *Journal of Asian American Studies* 4, 1 (February): 1–34.

Mura, David. 1995. "The Internment of Desire." In *Under Western Eyes: Personal Essays from Asian America*, ed. Garrett Hongo. New York: Doubleday. 224–240.

*My America . . . Or Honk if You Love Buddha*. 1997. Directed by Renee Tajima-Peña. Produced by Quynh Thai. Independent Television Service. 87 min., VHS.

Myrdal, Gunnar. 1962 [1944]. *The American Dilemma: The Negro Problem and Modern Democracy*. New York: Harper & Row.

Naipaul, V. S. 1989. *A Turn in the South*. New York: Vintage.

Nathan, Joan. 2003. "East Meets South at a Delta Table: Chinese-Americans Bring the Tastes of Their Ancestors Down Home." *New York Times,* 4 June: D1–D 5.

Ngai, Mae M. 2004. *Impossible Subjects: Illegal Aliens and the Making of Modern America*. Princeton, NJ: Princeton University Press.

Nishio, Alan. 1969. "The Oriental as a 'Middleman Minority.'" *Gidra* (May) n.p.

Norris, Christopher. 1988 [1982]. *Deconstruction: Theory and Practice*. New York: Metheun.

O'Brien, Robert W. 1941. "Status of Chinese in the Mississippi Delta." *Social Forces* (March): 386–390.

Okihiro, Gary Y. 1994. *Margins and Mainstreams: Asians in American History and Culture*. Seattle: University of Washington Press.

Olmsted, Frederick Law. 1970 [1860]. *A Journey in Back Country*. New York: Schocken.

Padget, Cindy D. 1997. "The Lost Indians of the Lost Colony: A Critical Legal Study of the Lumbee Indians of North Carolina." *American Indian Law Review* 21: 391.

Park, Robert E. 1928. "Human Migration and the Marginal Man." *American Journal of Sociology* 33, 6: 881–893.

Pascoe, Peggy. 1991. "Race, Gender, and Intercultural Relations: The Case of Interracial Marriage." *Frontiers: A Journal of Women Studies* 12, 1: 5–18.

Pateman, Carole. 1988. *The Sexual Contract*. Palo Alto: Stanford University Press.

Peabody, Etta. 1967. "Effort of the South to Import Chinese Coolies 1865–1870." MA Thesis, Baylor University.

Peck, John G. 1972. "Urban Station—Migration of the Lumbee Indians." PhD Diss., University of North Carolina.

Perea, Juan F. 1997. "The Black/White Binary Paradigm of Race: The 'Normal Science' of American Racial Thought." *California Law Review* 85, 5: 1213–1258.

Peterson, John H., Jr. 1971. "The Indian in the Old South." In *Red, White, and Black: Symposium on Indians in the Old South*, ed. Charles M. Hudson. Athens: Southern Anthropology Society and University of Georgia Press. 116–132.

Powell, Clayton. 1969 [1915]. *The Aftermath of the Civil War in Arkansas*. New York: Negro University Press.

Pozzetta, George. 1974. "Foreigners in Florida: A Study of Immigration Promotion, 1865–1910." *Florida Historical Quarterly* 53: 164–180.

Pozzetta, George, and Harry A. Kersey, Jr. 1976. "Yamato Colony: A Japanese Presence in South Florida." *Tequesta* 36: 66–77.

Pratt, Minnie Bruce. 1984. "Identity: Skin, Blood, Heart." In *Yours in Struggle: Three Feminist Perspectives on Anti-Semitism and Racism*, ed. Barbara Smith, Elly Bulkin, and Minnie Bruce Pratt. Ithaca, NY: Firebrand Books. 11–63.

Quan, Robert Seto. 1982. *Lotus Among the Magnolias: The Mississippi Chinese*. Jackson: University Press of Mississippi.

*Real Indian*. 1996. Produced and directed by Malinda Maynor. Women Make Movies, VHS.

Reed, John Shelton. 2003. *Minding the South*. Columbia: University of Missouri Press.

Rhoads, Edward J. M. 1977. "The Chinese in Texas." *Southwestern Historical Quarterly* 81: 1–17.

Roberts, Diane. 1998. "'Student' Artfully Reveals Past's Hold on Present." *Atlanta Journal and Constitution*, October 25, p. 12L.

Roediger, David. 2002. *Colored White: Transcending the Racial Past*. Berkeley: University of California Press.

———.1991. *The Wages of Whiteness: Race and the Making of the American Working Class*. London: Verso.

Rogoff, Irit. 2000. *Terra Infirma: Geography's Visual Culture*. London: Routledge.

Rosaldo, Renato. 1989. *Culture and Truth: The Remaking of Social Analysis*. Boston: Beacon.

Rubin, Gayle S. 1993 [1984]. "Thinking Sex: Notes for a Radical Theory of the Politics of Sexuality." In *The Lesbian and Gay Studies Reader*, ed. Henry Abelove, Michele Aina Barale, and David M. Halperin. New York: Routledge. 3–44.

Rummel, George, III. 1966. "The Delta Chinese: An Exploratory Study in Assimilation." MA Thesis, University of Mississippi.

Said, Edward W. 1978. *Orientalism*. New York: Random House.

Satz, Ronald N. 1986. "The Mississippi Choctaw: From the Removal Treaty to the Federal Agency." In *After Removal: The Choctaw in Mississippi*, ed. Samuel J. Wells and Roseanna Tubby, 112–120. Jackson: University Press of Mississippi.

Saxton, Alexander. 1990. *The Rise and Fall of the White Republic: Class Politics and Mass Culture in Nineteenth-century America*. London: Verso.

Sedgwick, Eve Kosofsky. 1997. "Paranoid Reading and Reparative Reading; or You're So Paranoid, You Probably Think This Introduction Is about You." In *Navel Gazing: Queer Readings in Fiction*, ed. Eve Kosofsky Sedgwick. Durham, NC: Duke University Press. 1–37.

———.1990. *Epistemology of the Closet*. Berkeley: University of California Press.

Shankman, Arnold. 1982. *Ambivalent Friends: Afro-Americans View the Immigrant*. Westport, CT: Greenwood Press.

Sider, Gerald M. 1993. *Lumbee Indian Histories: Race, Ethnicity and Indian Identity in the Southern United States*. New York: Cambridge University Press.

Simmel, Georg. 1950. *The Sociology of Georg Simmel*, trans. Kurt H. Wolff Glencoe, IL: Free Press.

Smith, Donna Jo. 1997. "Queering the South: Constructions of Southern/Queer Identity." In *Carryin' On in the Lesbian and Gay South*, ed. John Howard. New York: New York University Press. 370–385.

Smith, Jon, and Deborah Cohn, eds. 2004. *Look Away!: The U.S. South in New World Studies*. Durham, NC: Duke University Press.

Spivak, Gayatri. 1990. *The Post-colonial Critic: Interviews, Strategies, Dialogues*, ed. Sarah Harasym. New York: Routledge.

Spurlin, William J. 2000. "Remapping Same-Sex Desire: Queer Writing and Culture in the American Heartland." In *De-centering Sexualities: Politics and Representations Beyond the Metropolis*, ed. Richard Phillips, Diane Watt, and David Shuttleton. London: Routledge. 182–198.

Srikanth, Rajini. 2004. "Ethnic Outsider as the Ultimate Insider: The Paradox of Verghese's *My Own Country*." *MELUS* 29: 3/4 (Fall/Winter): 433–450.

Staples, Brent. 2003. "Interracialism Among the Jeffersons Went Well Beyond the Bedroom." *New York Times*, July 16.

Stone, Sandy. 1991. "The 'Empire' Strikes Back: A Posttranssexual Manifesto." In *Body Guards: The Cultural Politics of Gender Ambiguity*, ed. Julia Epstein and Kristina Straub. New York: Routledge. 280–304.

Strum, Circe. 2002. "Blood Politics, Racial Classification, and Cherokee National Identity: The Trials and Tribulations of the Cherokee Freedmen." In *Confounding the Color Line: The Indian-Black Experience in North America*, ed. James F. Brooks. Lincoln: University of Nebraska Press. 223–257.

Stryker, Susan. 2006. "(De)Subjugated Knowledges: An Introduction to Transgender Studies." In *The Transgender Studies Reader*, ed. Susan Stryker and Stephen White. New York: Routledge. 1–17.

———.1998. "The Transgender Issue: An Introduction." *GLQ* 4, 2: 145–158.

Swanton, John R. 1933. *Probable Identity of the 'Croatan' Indians*. Washington, DC: U.S. Department of the Interior, Office of Indian Affairs. #73619.

Talmadge, Herman E. 1955. *You and Segregation*. Birmingham, AL: Vulcan Press.

Taylor, Charles. 1994. *Multiculturalism: Examining the Politics of Recognition*. Princeton, NJ: Princeton University Press.

Tchen, John Kuo Wei. 1999. *New York Before Chinatown: Orientalism and the Shaping of American Culture 1776–1882*. Baltimore: Johns Hopkins University Press.

Terrell, Mary Church. 1968 [1940]. *A Colored Woman in a White World*. National Association of Colored Women's Clubs, Inc., Washington DC.

Thomas, Robert K. 1980. "A Report on Research of Lumbee Origins." Unpublished manuscript prepared for the Lumbee Regional Development Association.

Thompson, Vernon Ray. 1973. "A History of the Education of the Lumbee Indians of Robeson County, North Carolina from 1885 to 1970." Ed.D Diss., University of Miami.

Tien, Chang-Lin. 1996. "Affirming Affirmative Action." *Perspectives on Affirmative Action and Its Impact on Asian Pacific Americans*. LEAP: Asian Pacific Americans Public Policy Institute, ed. Gena A. Lew. 19–20.

Torres, Hector A. 2003. "'I don't think I exist': Interview with Richard Rodriguez." *MELUS* 28, 2 (Summer): 165–202.

Tsiang, H. T. 1937. *And China Has Hands*. New York: Robert Speller.

Tsukamoto, Mary, and Elizabeth Pinkerton. 1987. *We the People: A Story of Internment in America*. Elk Grove, CA: Laguna Publishers.

Turner, Victor. 1974. *Dramas, Fields, and Metaphors: Symbolic Action in Human Society*. Ithaca, NY: Cornell University Press.

———.1969. *The Ritual Process: Structure and Anti-Structure*. Chicago: Albine Publishing.

———.1967. *The Forest of Symbols: Aspects of Ndembu Ritual*. Ithaca, NY: Cornell University Press.

Tushnet, Mark. 1993. "The Warren Court as History: An Interpretation." In *The Warren Court in Historical and Political Perspective*, ed. Mark Tushnet. Charlottesville: University of Virginia Press. 1–34.

Twain, Mark. 1992. *Collected Tales, Sketches, Speeches, and Essays, 1852–1890*. New York: Library of America.

Verghese, Abraham. 1997. "The Cowpath to America." *New Yorker* (June 23 and 30): 70–88.

———.1996. "Untitled." In *Contours of the Heart: South Asians Map North America*, ed. Sunaina Maira and Rajini Srikanth. New York: Asian American Writers' Workshop. 251–252.

———.1994. *My Own Country: A Doctor's Story of a Town and Its People in the Age of AIDS*. New York: Vintage.

———.1994. "A Child's Book of Death and Dying." *Granta* 48: 229–237.

Verghese, Abraham, Steven L. Berk, and Felix Sarubbi. 1989. "*Urbs in Rure*: Human Immunodeficiency Virus Infection in Rural Tennessee." *Journal of Infectious Diseases* 160, 6 (December): 1051–1055.

Walker, Alice. 1983. *In Search of Our Mothers' Gardens: Womanist Prose*. New York: Harcourt Brace Jovanovich.

Wallenstein, Peter. 2002. *Tell the Court I Love My Wife: Race, Marriage, and Law—An American History*. New York: Palgrave Macmillan.

Wallerstein, Immanuel, and Etienne Balibar. 1991. *Race, Nation, Class: Ambiguous Identities*, trans. Chris Turner. London: Verso.

Warren, Robert Penn. 1957. *Segregation: The Inner Conflict in the South*. London: Eyre and Spottiswoode.

Weeks, Stephen B. 1891. *The Lost Colony of Roanoke: Its Fate and Survival*. New York: Knickerbocker Press.

Weston, Kath. 1995. "Get Thee to a Big City: Sexual Imaginary and the Great Gay Migration." *GLQ* 2, 3: 253–277.

White, Edmund. 1997. "Journals of the Plague Years." *Nation*, May 12, pp. 13–18.

Wiegman, Robyn. 1999. "Whiteness Studies and the Paradox of Particularity." *boundary 2* 26: 115–150.

Wilkins, David E. 1998. "The Lumbee Tribe and Its Quest for Federal Recognition: Lumbee Centurions on the Trail of Many Years." In *A Good Cherokee, A Good Anthropologist: Papers in Honor of Robert K. Thomas*, ed. Steve Pavlik, Publications of the American Indian Studies Center, no. 8. Los Angeles: University of California, Los Angeles.

———.1993. "Breaking Into the Intergovernmental Matrix: The Lumbee Tribe's Efforts to Secure Federal Acknowledgement." *Publius: The Journal of Federalism* 23: 123–142.

Williams, Patricia J. 1991. *The Alchemy of Race and Rights: Diary of a Law Professor.* Cambridge, MA: Harvard University Press.

Wittig, Monique. 1992 [1981]. *The Straight Mind and Other Essays.* Boston: Beacon Press.

Wong, K. Scott. 2005. *Americans First: Chinese Americans and the Second World War.* Cambridge, MA: Harvard University Press.

Woodward, C. Vann. 2002 [1955]. *The Strange Career of Jim Crow.* Oxford: Oxford University Press.

———.1989. "Rednecks, Millionaires and Catfish Farms: *A Turn in the South.*" *New York Times*, February 5.

———.1951. *Origins of the New South: 1877–1913.* Baton Rouge: Louisiana State University Press.

Wright, Richard. 1993 [1945]. *Black Boy (American Hunger).* New York: HarperCollins.

Wu, Cindy. 2008. "The Siamese Twins in Late-Nineteenth-Century Narratives of Conflict and Reconciliation." *American Literature* 80, 1 (March): 29–55.

Yochelson, Bonnie with Tracy A. Schmid. 2005. *Esther Bubley on Assignment.* New York: Aperture Foundation.

Yu, Henry. 2001. *Thinking Orientals: Migration, Contact, and Exoticism in Modern America.* Oxford: Oxford University Press.

Yung, Judy. 1986. *Chinese Women of America: A Pictorial History,* edited by Crystal K. D. Huie. Seattle: University of Washington Press.

# Index

A *Journey in Back Country* (Olmsted), 32
A *Southerner Discovers the South* (Daniels), 101–102
A *Turn in the South* (Naipaul), 124
Abel, Elizabeth, 13, 23–24, 204–205, 206
African Americans: Asian Americans, adversarial relationship with, 35, 41; blood quantum as criterion of blackness, 48, 245n42; Chinese-black intimacy, 15, 96, 97, 102–103, 107, 117; Chinese disassociation from, 21, 95, 104–105, 116–117, 251n14; Chinese service-oriented labor addressed to, 98, 101; coalition with, 233; drag queens, 211; immigrants and, 9–10, 240n8; male-to-female transsexuals, 211; marriage to indigenous people, 244n38; passing, 39, 124, 252n3; segregation, role in, 30–31; as subjects of grievance, 13; in whiteface, 119
"Agency of the Letter in the Unconscious" (Lacan), 201, 202
AIDS (Acquired Immunodeficiency Syndrome), 179–180
Alabama, anti-miscegenation laws in, 48
Allison, Dorothy, 174
*Almost White* (Berry), 31, 156
American Civil Liberties Union, 52
American Indians: Asian Americans, shared history with, 233; blood quantum as criterion of Indian authenticity, 83–85; Choctaw Indians in the South, 59, 235–236; discrimination suffered by, 233; Indianness as a set of physical features, 67; Lumbee Tribe of North Carolina (*see* Lumbee Tribe of North Carolina); native authenticity, 63, 83–84; racial status

under segregation, 3–4; as socio-cultural isolates, 3–4; as a third caste within a caste system, 3–4
Amin, Idi, 41, 178
*An American Dilemma* (Myrdal), 123–124
*An Asian Anthropologist in the South* (Kim), 125–138; denial of southern segregation against Asians, 134–135; distancing from black-white relations in the South, 125–126; effect of Kim's Asianness on his fieldwork, 125, 129–131; marginalization of migrants, 136; performative duplicity, 128, 131–138, 136–137, 162; southern paternalism, 171
*And God Shakes Creation* (Cohn), 6–7
Andrews, Eliza Frances, 43
anti-miscegenation laws, 46–54; in Alabama, 48; Arendt on, Hannah, 243n35; blood quantum as criterion of blackness, 48, 245n42; blood quantum as criterion of Indian authenticity, 83–85; in California, 52, 243n35, 244n37; creation of "colored" subjects, 26–27; defenders of, 48; in Georgia, 46, 49–50, 51; Kennedy on, Randall, 243n35; in Louisiana, 48; *Loving v. Virginia*, 51, 52, 244n38, 245n49; *Maynard v. Hill*, 244n38; in Mississippi, 46, 48–49, 51, 104; Myrdal on, Gunnar, 46–47, 52, 243n35; *Naim v. Naim*, 51–53; in North Carolina, 46, 48, 51; *Perez v. Sharpe*, 52, 243n35; states enacting, 244n36; in Tennessee, 172; in Virginia, 46, 49, 50, 51–52, 73; Warren on, Earl, 245n49; in Western states, 46, 47–48, 244n37; white-Chinese intermarriage, 48–49

apartheid in South Africa, 2, 3, 229
*Are Italians White?* (Guglielmo and Salerno), 93
Arendt, Hannah, 123, 243n35
Arkansas: Chinese in, 112; Japanese interned in, 130–131, 172; Little Rock Central High School, integration of, 149, 166; Negro School for the Deaf and Blind (Little Rock), 149
*Arkansas Democrat* (newspaper), 149
Arkansas River Valley Immigration Company, 34
Arkansas School for the Blind, 138, 142
assimilation: acculturation as learned racism, 10–11; belief in unassimilability of "Orientals," 161–162; disassociation from African Americans, 120

Baitz, Jon Robin, 229, 230
Baker, Houston A., Jr., 20–21, 54, 239n1
Baker, Ray Stannard, 28–29
Baldwin, James: on being controlled by others, 193; on the etiquette of segregation, 29–30; on the French, 173; on the spirit of segregation, 29–30, 50–51; "Stranger in the Village," 161
*Band of Angels* (Warren), 176
Barth, Gunther, 34
*Bastard Out of Carolina* (Allison), 174
Behar, Ruth, 129, 154, 252n12
Bell, Derrick, 26
Berry, Brewton, 3, 7, 31, 156
Bhabha, Homi: on "in-between" spaces, 15–16, 21; on the interstitial, 4, 194, 227, 232; places of estrangement and engagement, 190
*Bitter Fruit* (Kim), 18
*Black Boy* (Wright), 29–30, 132
blackface, 242n26
Blalock, Hubert, 40, 98
blood quantum, 48, 83–85, 245n42
Blu, Karen, 57, 59, 73
*The Bluest Eye* (Morrison), 250n3
Bonacich, Edna, 18, 40–41, 123, 243n29
Boorstein, Kate, 234
Brandon, Teena, 258n23

Brass Ankles, 3
"Brief Sketch of a Few Prominent Indian Families of Sampson County" (Emanuel and Brewington), 67–68
*Brown v. Board of Education*: in context of white oligarchic power, 99; continuity surrounding, 20; era following, 13, 16; Harlan's dissent in *Plessy v. Ferguson*, 114; *Naim v. Naim* and, 52; precursor to, 54; as symbol, 1
*Brownies' Book* (NAACP), 39–40
Bubley, Esther, 22, 23–24, 55, 237
Bunker, Chang and Eng, 26–27, 42–45
Butler, George: "The Croatan Indians of Sampson County, North Carolina," 61–62, 64–69, 78–79, 88, 89; on Lumbee Tribe's black disavowal, 74, 82
Butler, Judith: on drag, 258n24; gender as approximation, 9, 208, 209, 233; identification with a gender, 208; kinship and heterosexuality, 225; state recognition of gay and lesbian marriage, 210

Cash, W. J., 239n1
Certificate of Degree of Indian Blood, 84
Cheraw Indians, 59. *See also* Lumbee Tribe of North Carolina
Cherokees of Robeson County, 59, 85, 86. *See also* Lumbee Tribe of North Carolina
Chesnutt, Charles, 24–25, 37
Chinese, 91–122; African Americans, disassociation from, 21, 95, 104–105, 116–117, 251n14; in Arkansas, 112; black-Chinese, ostracism of, 104–107; caste shift from "colored" to white, 11, 14–15; Chinese-black intimacy, 15, 96, 97, 102–103, 107, 117; Civil Rights Movement, 114–115, 117–119, 121; as "colored," 11, 92, 96–97 (see also *Gong Lum v. Rice*); coolie system, 32–36; laundry owners, WPA interviews of, 110–112; in Louisiana, 35–36, 250n5; as middleman minority, 18; in Mississippi, 6–7, 18, 57, 91–92, 112, 114–115, 232, 237–238 (see also *Mississippi Chinese*); as "model minority," 251n16; passing, 242n26; the South, out-

migration from, 120–121; status elevation from "colored" to white, 11, 14, 92–93, 94–95, 98–101, 103–114, 117–118, 120–122, 209–210, 233–234, 251n16; in Tennessee, 237; white, middle-class identification as, 106, 108; white-Chinese intermarriage, 48–49

*Chinese American Portraits* (Lum McCunn), 106, 250n9

Chinese Exclusion laws, 104, 161–162

Chinese Labor Convention, 34

*Chinese Women of America* (Yung), 112–114, 250n12

Choctaw Indians in the South, 59, 235–236. *See also* Mississippi Band of Choctaw

Choi, Chang, 177

Choi, Susan, 20, 164, 235. See also *Foreign Student*

Chow, Sun Gay, 237–238

Choy, Christine, 98, 105–106. See also *Mississippi Triangle*

Civil Rights Movement: Chinese in Mississippi, 114–115, 117–119, 121; racial representation since, 92; transgendered rights advocates, 256n3

Clifford, James, 129, 137–138

Cohen, Deborah, 231

Cohen, Lucy M., 34

Cohn, David, 6–7

Cohn, Deborah, 21

color line: and Asian Americans, 30; as metaphor, 2–3; status elevation through upholding, 96, 100; uneven application of, 37–38

"colored": anti-miscegenation laws in creation of, 26–27; Chinese as, 11, 92, 96–97 (see also *Gong Lum v. Rice*); conflation between "black" and, 1, 25; usage of, 13, 24–25, 39, 50, 240n5

*Colored White* (Roediger), 10

communitas, 213–214

coolie system, 32–36

"Coolies as a Substitute for Negroes" (*DeBow's Review*), 32–33

Counts, Will, 149

Creef, Elena Tajima, 30, 164

Critical White Studies: degrees of whiteness in, 38; foundational works, 93–94; *The Mississippi Chinese* (Loewen), 11, 94; *Mississippi Triangle* (film), 117; precursor to, 11, 94

Croatan Indians, 59, 62–63, 71, 72–73. *See also* Lumbee Tribe of North Carolina

"The Croatan Indians of Sampson County, North Carolina" (Butler), 61–62, 64–69

Cuban American, 10, 240n7

Currah, Paisley, 210–211, 256n8, 257n15

Daniels, Jonathan, 101–102

Dare, Virginia, 70

*Dark Princess* (Du Bois), 40

*Daughter from Danang* (film), 164–165

Dawes Act (1887), 77

"Deep South" (definition), 239n1

Delgado, Richard, 54

Deloria, Vine, 129

*The Delta* (film), 164–165, 259n29

Dial, Adolph L., 62, 82, 89

Dollard, John, 254n10

double consciousness, 136

Douglass, Frederick, 34

drag, 219, 220, 224, 258n24

"Drinking Fountains in a Tobacco Warehouse" (Bubley), 22, 23–24, 55, 237

Du Bois, W.E.B., 2, 40, 136

Dudziak, Mary L., 25, 166

Dunbar, Paul Laurence, 136

Duncan, Patti, 159–160, 164, 173

Eckford, Elizabeth, 149

Egerton, John, 235, 236, 240n7

Eliades, David K., 62, 82, 89

Ellison, Ralph: Arendt and, Hannah, 243n35; on Gunnar Myrdal, 123–124; on race prejudice, 144, 166; on racial consciousness, 157

"The 'Empire' Strikes Back" (Stone), 209–210

*Face to Face* (Mehta), 125, 138, 146

Fanon, Franz, 30–31, 127, 238

Faubus, Orval, 149
Faulkner, William, 27, 178
Federal Writers' Project interviews of
   Chinese laundry owners, 110–112
Feinberg, Leslie, 197–198, 219, 256n3
Filipinos, 39, 97–98
Florida, Yamato Colony in, 36–37, 242n23
Foley, Neil, 18, 41
"Foreign Medical Graduate" (FMG),
   181–182
*The Foreign Student* (Choi), 165–179
foreignness: applicability to sexuality, 164;
   of Asians, 137, 179, 182, 194
*The Forest of Symbols* (Turner), 197
Foucault, Michel, 19
Fourteenth Amendment, 7–8
Frank, Leo, 10
Frankenberg, Ruth, 93
Freud, Sigmund, 19, 155, 156

Gallop, Jane, 19, 203
gender: ambiguity in, 202, 220–222, 234;
   analogy between race and, 198–199,
   202–214, 219; as approximation, 9, 208,
   209, 233; dissolution as a legal category, 197–198; fluidity in, 234; gender
   advocacy and race advocacy, 211; gender
   difference as "separate but equal," 207;
   gender-divided restrooms, 197–198,
   202–206, 225; identifying with a, 208;
   "Ladies" and "Gentlemen," division
   between, 201–202; as legacy of segregation, 201–202; in reproduction of status
   hierarchies, 12
Georgia: anti-miscegenation laws in, 46,
   49–50, 51; intermarriage in, 245n46
*Gong Lum v. Rice*: Chinese as "colored," 11,
   96; "colored" status of Chinese established, 92; in context of white oligarchic
   power, 99; events leading to, 96–97;
   origin of, 49
Gross, Ariela: legal determination of
   racial identity, 53, 63; performance of
   whiteness in litigation over racial status,
   76–77; on possibility of hybrid identities,
   236; "race by association," 102

Halberstam, Judith: on African American
   drag queens, 211; on futurity of trans-
   gendered figures, 224; on gay metronormativity, 258n23; on gender, 225; on
   pronouns for transgendered individuals,
   256n3
Hale, Grace Elizabeth, 23–24
Handman, Max, 5
Harlan, John Marshall, 38, 114
Hen, Arlee, 105–107, 250n9
hermeneutics of suspicion, 128, 150
*Hernandez v. Texas*, 7–8
heterosexism, analogy between racism
   and, 199, 205–207
Himes, Chester, 124
"Historical Sketch of the Indians of
   Robeson County" (McLean), 71
*The History of North Carolina* (Lawson),
   247n10
HIV (Human Immunodeficiency Virus),
   179–180
Honda, Nobuo, 152–153
hooks, bell, 211
Hosokawa, Bill, 130–131
*How Jews Became White Folk* (Brodkin), 93
*How the Irish Became White* (Ignatiev), 93
Howard, John, 258n23
Hughes, Langston, 23, 29
"Human Migration and the Marginal Man"
   (Park), 136
Hurricane Katrina (2005), 231
Hurston, Zora Neale, 137

*If He Hollers Let Him Go* (Himes), 124
*Impossible Subjects* (Ngai), 259n2
Indian Reorganization Act (1934), 63
Indians. *See* American Indians
*Indians of North Carolina* (McPherson),
   61–62, 71, 86
Indians of Robeson County, 59, 71. *See also*
   Lumbee Tribe of North Carolina
intermarriage: blood quantum for, 48,
   83–85, 245n42; Chinese disavowal of,
   95–96, 99–100, 103–104; in Georgia,
   245n46; integrated education compared to, 243n35; in Louisiana, 244n38,

245n40; in North Carolina, 244n38; in
Oklahoma, 244n38; in Virginia, 245n48;
white-Chinese intermarriage, 48–49
intersexuality, medical intervention into,
257n18
interstitiality, 8–10; ambiguity of, 39;
Bhabha on, Homi, 4, 227, 232; cultural
anxiety and, 21; displaced hostility and,
40; incompletion as a function of, 156;
interstitial populations, 4–5, 11–12; racial
(*see* racial interstitiality); sexual interstitiality, 175; thinking interstitially, 5, 234;
transgenderism as genre of, 212
Iyer, Pico, 189

Jackson, Helen Hunt, 73
Jackson, Jesse, 199
*Jackson v. Alabama*, 52
Jacobs, Harriet, 174
Jacobson, Matthew Frye, 10, 46, 93
Japanese American Citizen's League, 52
Japanese Americans: in Florida's Yamato
Colony, 36–37, 242n23; as honorary
whites, 2; interned in Arkansas, 130–131,
172; in the South, 38, 150–152
Japanese automakers, 235
*Jasmine* (Mukherjee), 192
Jeter, Mildred (later Mildred Loving). *See*
Loving, Mildred
Jew, Victor, 192, 242n26
Jim Crow: Asians' place in, 94–95; cer-
emonial requirements for living under,
27–28; contradictions of, 28–29; creation
of other "colored" people, 8; incon-
sistent accommodation of ambiguity,
6–7; interpretation and negotiation of,
necessity for, 7–8, 29–30, 55; "one drop"
rule of hypodescent, 29, 49; racial status
as something to be earned, 78; uneven
application of, 25, 28–29, 55, 150–151
Jindal, Bobby, 236
Joe, Shing, 111–112
Johnson, Charles S., 28, 123, 156, 160

Kadohata, Cynthia, 30, 124, 164
Kennedy, Randall, 51–52, 243n35

Kim, Choong Soon: on Asians and "south-
ern hospitality," 109–110; on being the
object of scrutiny, 30, 31; First World
smugness experienced by, 192; as read by
John Shelton Reed, 231; as a "southern"
writer, 164. *See also An Asian Anthro-
pologist in the South*
Kim, Claire Jean, 18, 26, 41
Kincaid, Jamaica, 9, 150
Kingston, Maxine Hong, 43–44
*kira-kira* (Kadohata), 30, 124
Koopmanschap, Cornelius, 34, 35
Korean Americans, 41, 153, 243n30. *See also*
Kim, Choong Soon
Koshy, Susan, 251n16
Kristeva, Julia, 161
Ku Klux Klan, 62, 79–82, 172, 218

Lacan, Jacques, 19, 201, 202–206
"Ladies" and "Gentlemen," division
between, 201–202
"'Ladies,' 'Gentlemen,' and 'Colored'"
(Boswell), 204–205
Lamberth, Ruby Elaine (later Ruby Naim),
51
Latin America, creolization in, 47
Lawson, John, 247n10
liberalism: deracinated liberalism, 114,
116–117; post-Civil Rights liberalism,
229; post-segregation era, 115
*Life* (magazine), 62, 79–82, 248n19
Limerick, Patricia Nelson, 85
liminality: attributes of, 11–12; in *Mai's
America* (film), 220; medical interven-
tion into intersexuality, 257n18; the
South as a liminal space, 231; Turner
on, Victor, 11–12, 212–213, 218–219,
257n18
Little Rock Central High School, Arkansas,
149, 166
Loewen, James. See *Mississippi Chinese*
*Look Away* (Smith and Cohn), 21
Lopez, Ian Haney, 8, 63, 93
Los Angeles, Korean Americans in, 243n30
Lost Colony of Roanoke: amalgamation
with friendly Indians, theory of, 71;

Lost Colony of Roanoke (*continued*):
"legend of" as product of segregation-
era southern culture, 72; *The Lost Colony
of Roanoke* (Weeks), 61–62, 71, 74–77;
Lumbee Tribe's descent from, 24, 60,
61–62, 70–73, 75–76, 85–86, 89, 247n10,
247n13; *Sir Walter Raleigh's Lost Colony*
(McMillan), 61, 70–74, 85–86
*The Lost Colony of Roanoke* (Weeks), 61–62,
71, 74–77
Louisiana: anti-miscegenation laws in, 48;
Chinese in, 35–36, 250n5; intermarriage
in, 244n38, 245n40
Loving, Mildred (nee Mildred Jeter): gay
marriage, support for, 246n54; marriage,
51, 52, 54, 245n49; self-identification,
preferred, 52, 246n54
Loving, Richard, 51, 245n49
*Loving v. Virginia*, 51, 52, 244n38, 248n49
Lowe, Lisa, 18, 161–162, 168
*The Lowery History* (Norment), 247n11
Lowrie (also Lowery), Henry Berry, 75, 79,
82, 248n14, 248n15
Lum, Gong, 96
Lum, Martha, 96
*The Lumbee Problem* (Blu), 57
Lumbee Tribe of North Carolina, 58–89;
absence of forced migration, 60, 84;
authenticity as a tribe, 14, 58, 84–85, 87;
Butler on, George, 64–69, 74, 78–79, 82;
caste flexibility in, 209; collective sense of
selfhood, 59, 82–83, 87–88; Emanuel and
Brewington on, Enoch and C. D., 67–68;
English influences on, 75–76, 247n10;
factionalization of, 86; family names, 88;
as "free persons of color," 60–61; intermarriage, racial status for purposes of,
49; *Life* magazine article about, 62, 79–82,
248n19; lifestyle of, 74–77; Lost Colony
of Roanoke, descent from, 24, 60, 61–62,
70–73, 75–76, 85–86, 89, 247n10, 247n13;
McMillan and, Hamilton, 61, 70–74, 77,
249n29; McPherson on, O. M., 61–63, 77;
as middleman minority, 18; name transformations, 58–59, 246n2; post-segregation portrayals of, 83; "Probable Identity

of the 'Croatan' Indians (Swanton), 71;
property ownership by, 77; public education, racial status for purposes of, 49;
racialization of, 76; recognition, quest for
federal, 84; recognition by State of North
Carolina, 59, 61, 72; school segregation,
24; schools for, 64–69, 71, 72–73, 82,
85–86; status elevation from "mulatto"
to Indian, 57–58, 63–67, 77–78, 233–234;
tribal membership, 85; visual evidence of
Indian blood, 63–67, 69, 89; voting rights,
60–61; Weeks on, Stephen B., 61–62, 71,
74–77; whiteness, claims to, 24, 67–73, 89
lynching, 28–29, 172

*Mai's America* (film), 202, 214–224; analogy
between race and gender, 219; analogy
between race and sexuality, 217; gender
ambiguity in, 202, 220–222; gender
conformity in, 221; gender liminality,
220; homophobia in, 217; integration in,
failure of, 217; migration, 223–224; myth
of gay metronormativity in, 218–219;
origins, 258n21; southern race relations
in, 200–202; southern tropes in, 224;
still from, 220; twinning of transgenderism and transracial, 201–202
Manteo, 70–71
marginal man theory, 136
*The Marrow of Tradition* (Chesnutt), 37
Marshall, Margaret H., 199
Marshall, Thurgood, 52
Martinez, George, 42
*Maynard v. Hill*, 244n38
Maynor, Malinda, 58, 87–88
Mazumdar, Sucheta, 139
McKoy, Millie and Christine, 44
McMillan, Hamilton: Lumbee Tribe,
advocacy for, 73–74, 77; Lumbee Tribe,
origin of, 61, 70–74, 249n29; McPherson
and, O. M., 74; political motivations,
247n11; *Sir Walter Raleigh's Lost Colony*,
61, 70–74, 85–86
McPherson, O. M.: *Indians of North Caro-
lina*, 61–63, 71, 77, 86; McMillan and,
Hamilton, 74

"Meditations of the 'Partly Colored'"
(Bow), 153
Mehta, Ved, 125–128, 138–156; Arkansas
School for the Blind, 138, 142; Disability Studies, contributions to, 138;
*Face to Face,* 125, 138, 146; MacArthur
Fellowship, 139; photograph of, *147;
Sound-Shadows of the New World* (see
*Sound-Shadows of the New World*); as a
"southern" writer, 164
Melungeons, 3
Memphis Convention, 34
*Mendez v. Westminister School District,* 54
*mestizos,* 3–4
metronormativity, gay, 187–189, 218–219,
258n23
Mexican Americans: civil rights litigation,
absence from, 53–54; public schooling in
California, 53–54; as white, 7–8, 32, 42
middleman minorities: Bonacich on, 18,
40–41, 123, 243n29, 250n6; Chinese as,
18; economic position of, 40–41; function of, 40–41
migration, 123, 136, 187–189, 218, 258n23
*The Mind of the South* (Cash), 239n1
*Miss India Georgia* (film), 164–165
Mississippi: anti-miscegenation laws in, 46,
48–49, 51, 104; Chinese in, 6–7, 18, 57,
91–92, 112, 114–115, 232, 237–238 (see also
*Mississippi Chinese*)
Mississippi Band of Choctaw: economic
growth, 235–236; petition for relief,
59–60; recognition of, 246n4; sociocultural isolation, assumed, 3
*The Mississippi Chinese* (Loewen), 92–109,
117–118, 120–122, 233–234; Critical White
Studies, precursor to, 11, 94; disassociation from African Americans, 95; disavowal of intermarriage, 95–96, 99–100,
103–104; ostracism of black-Chinese,
105–106; out-migration from the South,
120–121
*Mississippi Masala* (film), 164–165, 178,
184–185
*Mississippi Triangle* (film), 104–108,
114–120

Mississippi Valley Immigration Company,
34
Morikami, George, 241n23
Morrison, Toni: on African American
women, 250n3; on "Africanist presence" in American culture, 18–19, 68,
150, 232; on assimilation, 10, 120; *The
Bluest Eye,* 250n3; *Sula,* 204–205, 218,
240n8
Mukherjee, Bharati, 160, 192
*My America (... or honk if you love Buddha)*
(film), 97–98
*My Own Country* (film), 184–185, 255n24
*My Own Country* (Verghese), 179–192;
AIDS advocacy in, 165, 179–180, 185,
191; association between race and
sexuality, 190; gay migration stories,
187–189; identification with AIDS
patients, 181–182, 185–186; myth of
gay metronormativity in, 187–189;
outsider status in, 182–183; racial
latency in, 180; racism against Asian
Americans in the South, 187; regional
belonging in, 181, 186; reviews of, 189;
rural homecoming, 188–189; stigma
from association with AIDS patients,
186–187
Myrdal, Gunnar: *An American Dilemma,*
123–124; on anti-miscegenation laws,
46–47, 52, 243n35; on race hierarchy, 27,
49; on segregation, 46

NAACP, 52
Naim, Ham Say, 51
Naim, Ruby (nee Ruby Elaine Lamberth),
51
*Naim v. Naim,* 51–53, 246n53
Naipaul, V. S.: identification with southern
aristocracy, 251n2; on manners in the
South, 170; as a "southern" writer, 164; *A
Turn in the South,* 124
Nair, Mira: acceptance by multiple communities, 234–235; *Mississippi Masala*
(film), 164–165, 178, 184–185; *My Own
Country* (film), 184–185, 255n24
Naturalization Law (1790), 161

Negro School for the Deaf and Blind (Little Rock), 149
*New Orleans Times* (newspaper), 35
New Southern Studies, 16, 20
*New York Times* (newspaper), *90*, 91–92
*New York Times Magazine,* 229
*New Yorker* cartoon, 144, *145*
Ngai, Mae, 5, 53, 259n2
*Nissan in Tennessee* (Egerton), 235, *236*
North Carolina: anti-miscegenation laws in, 46, 48, 51; intermarriage in, 244n38; Lumbee Tribe (*see* Lumbee Tribe of North Carolina); Robeson County, 24, 25; white-Indian marriages in, 49

O'Brien, Robert, 97
Okihiro, Gary, 19, 26, 120
Oklahoma, intermarriage in, 244n38
Olmsted, Frederick Law, 32
*The Only Land I Know* (Dial and Eliades), 62, 82, 89
Ono, Yoko, 199, 256n4
"The Oriental as a 'Middleman Minority'" (Nishio), 26
the "Oriental Problem," 241n1
Orr, Tye Kim, 34
*Ozawa v. United States,* 257n14

Page Act (1875), 104
*Paris is Burning* (film), 211
Park, Robert E.: "Human Migration and the Marginal Man," 136; on migration, 123; the "Oriental Problem," 241n1; on the stranger, 131, 160
"partly colored" people: in civil rights litigation, 53–54; Kim's disconnection from "partly colored" Asians, 135–136; "Meditations of the 'Partly Colored'" (Bow), 153
Pascoe, Peggy, 46, 47
passing: by African Americans as Asians, 39, 124; analogy to transracialism, 227; by Chinese as black, 242n26; incidents as sites for cultural critiques, 29; in Washington, DC, 252n3

Pateman, Carole, 175
*Patterns of Negro Segregation* (Johnson), 28, 123, 156
Peabody, Etta B., 34
Peña, Rene Tajima, 97–98
peoplehood, internally derived notions of, 88
Perea, Juan, 53
*Perez v. Sharpe,* 52, 243n35
"The Personal Habits of the Siamese Twins" (Twain), 42
*Plessy v. Ferguson:* Harlan's dissent, 114; *Perez v. Sharp* and, 243n35; "separate but equal" doctrine, 97, 243n35; use of Asian Americans to affirm "separate but equal," 97; visual evidence of racial identity, 63
Pocahontas, 50, 73
Poras, Marlo. See *Mai's America*
*The Possessive Investment in Whiteness* (Lipsitz), 93
Powell, Clayton, 35
Pratt, Minnie Bruce, 117, 157, 175
"Probable Identity of the 'Croatan' Indians" (Swanton), 71

Quan, Robert Seto, 108
queerness, southern, 159–160, 224

race: adjudication by white oligarchy, 99; American focus on black-white axis, 25–26; analogy between disability and, 140–144; analogy between gender and, 198–199, 202–214, 219; analogy between sexuality and, 217; discourse of equal opportunity and, 115–116; legal determinations of racial identity, 53, 63; passing, 29, 39, 124, 200, 227, 252n3; performance of whiteness in litigation over racial status, 76–77; physiological signs of, 64–65; primacy of the black-white dialectic after desegregation, 225; race advocacy and gender advocacy, 211; in reproduction of status hierarchies, 12; social class, link to, 31, 38, 41
racial binarism, 232

racial intermediacy: affirmation of normative class values, 76; Asian American literature and, 162; convenience of, 42; Nair and, Mira, 234–235

racial interstitiality: Asian racialization, 126; economic function, 98; identification with power, 122

racial latency, 127, 154–155, 180, 234

racism: acculturation as learned racism against African Americans, 10; analogy between criminalization of sexual behavior and, 199; analogy between heterosexism and, 199, 205–207; against Asian Americans, 121, 187; latency of southern racism, 154–155, 193

"Racist Love" (Chin and Chin), 170–171

Raleigh, Sir Walter, 24, 61, 70

*Ramona* (Jackson), 73

*Real Indian* (film), 58, 87–88

Red Apple Boycott, 41

Reed, John Shelton, 171, 231

"Reflections on Little Rock" (Arendt), 123, 243n35

restrooms, gender-divided, 197–198, 202–206, 225

Ricoeur, Paul, 150

*The Rise and Fall of the White Republic* (Saxton), 93

Roberts, Diane: on *The Foreign Student* by Choi, 166–167, 169, 171, 178; on South as national theater, 231

Robeson County, North Carolina, 24–25

Rodriguez, Richard, 20

Roediger, David, 10, 25, 93

Rogoff, Irit, 188, 191

Rolfe, John, 50, 73

Roosevelt, Eleanor, 144

Rosaldo, Renato, 154, 193, 252n11

Rosedale Consolidated High School, Mississippi, 96

Rubin, Gayle: continuum of erotic practices, notion of, 17, 184; criminalization of sexual behavior, 199; hierarchical system of sexual value, 163–164, 175, 179, 193; pedophilia, 174; pluralistic sexual ethics of, 253n3; "Thinking Sex," 162–164

Rummel, George, III, 97, 103

RuPaul, 224

Said, Edward, 161

Saxton, Alexander, 93

Sedgwick, Eve Kosofsky: linkage of fat phobia and homophobia, 227; "paranoid" interpretation, critical stances, 128, 155, 253n13

segregation: African Americans' role in, 30–31; as an etiquette, 27–30; Baldwin on, 30, 50; creation of a caste system, 27; creation of racial identity, 27; as a cultural system, 29; economic exploitation, 32–33; educational opportunity and, 82; gender as legacy of, 201–202; images of, 23; imperialism and, 39–40; interpretation of, 28, 55; legacy of, 1, 201–202; Myrdal on, Gunnar, 46; psychic violence from, 110; sexual caste system within, 193; sexually defined (see *Foreign Student* (Choi); *My Own Country* (Verghese))

sexuality: analogy between race and, 217; foreignness applicable to, 164; hierarchical system of sexual value, 163–164; interstitiality and, 175; parallelism between cultural and sexual marginality, 217–218; sexual caste system within segregation, 193; southern, 159–160

Sieg, Gerald Chan (Chung Tai-pan), 110–111

Simmel, Georg, 123, 128, 170, 233

Siouan Indians of Lumber River, 59. *See also* Lumbee Tribe of North Carolina

*Sir Walter Raleigh's Lost Colony* (McMillan), 61, 70–74, 85–86

Smith, Donna Jo, 159, 188, 223

Smith, Jon, 21, 231

social class: race, link to, 31, 38, 41; in reproduction of status hierarchies, 12

social status: alternative fulcrums around which it turns, 232; dependence on historically entrenched binaries, 226; erotic practices and, 163, 175; racial identification in consolidating group status, 94 social status, elevation in: acceptance of racial subordination as condition of, 101; ambivalence and incompletion in narratives of, 122; of Chinese in Mississippi from "colored" to white, 11, 14–15, 92–93, 94–95, 98–101, 103–114, 117–118, 120–122, 209–210, 233–234, 251n16; disruptions of, 96, 103–114, 118; economic stability as precondition of, 98; of European immigrants, 93–94; of Lumbee Tribe from "mulatto" to Indian, 57–58, 63–67, 77–78, 233–234; upholding of the color line, 96, 100

*Sound-Shadows of the New World* (Mehta), 138–150; absence of African Americans in, 148, 149; acceptance of the dominant culture, 142–143; analogy of race and disability, 140–144; cultural differences depicted in, 148–149; disavowal in, 126, 139; distancing from black-white relations in the South, 125–126; India, description of caste system in, 144; India, marriage prospects in, 146; integration of the blind, 126; interracial dating, 144–148; racial liberalism, 126; separatism, 141–142

South Africa, apartheid in, 2, 3, 229

South Asians in the South, 7, 139, 192. *See also* Mehta, Ved; Verghese, Abraham

southern Asian American literature, 162–195; integration in, 194–195; latency of southern racism in, 193; racial intermediacy and, 162; racial interstitiality, resistance to, 157; recognition of, 164–165; southern Asian American film compared to, 164–165. See also *Foreign Student* (Choi); *My Own Country* (Verghese)

southern culture, flexibility of, 45

southern hospitality, 109–110, 254n10

southern queerness, 101–102, 159–160, 221–224, 258n23

Spivak, Gayatri Chakravorty, 166, 167

status. *See* social status; social status, elevation in

Stone, Sandy, 209–210, 211–212

Stonewall, Mississippi, 218

Stonewall Inn, New York City, 218

*The Strange Career of Jim Crow* (Woodward), 40

"The Stranger" (Simmel), 123, 128, 131

"Stranger in the Village" (Baldwin), 161

Stryker, Susan: on transgender phenomena, 207–208; on transgender studies, 226, 232; transgenderism, definition of, 256n2; transsexuality as a communicational technology, 212

*Sula* (Morrison), 204–205, 218, 240n8

Swanton, John, 63, 71

Taft, William Howard, 96–97

Talmadge, Herman, 47

Tennessee, Asian-white intermarriage in, 172

Terrell, Mary Church, 38–39, 252n3

Thind, Bhagat, 139, 257n14

"Thinking Sex" (Rubin), 162–164

Thomas, Robert K.: on authenticity of Lumbees as a tribe, 14, 58, 87; Lumbee perceptions of persecution, 82; Lumbee tribal origins, 72, 86

"Towards a Theory of Middleman Minorities" (Bonacich), 40–41

transgender studies, 226, 232

transgendered individuals: cross-dressers, 212; futurity and gender flexibility of, 224; legal accommodation of, 210–211; pronouns referring to, 256n3

transgendered rights advocates, litigation strategies of, 256n3

transgenderism: definition, 256n2; as genre of interstitiality, 212; legal accommodation, 210; in *Mai's America* (film), 201–202; twinning with transracial, 18, 199–200, 201, 224–225

transracial in *Mai's America* (film), 201–202

transracial studies, 226

transspaces, 212–213, 224

Trinidad, Indian agricultural workers in, 33

Tsiang, H. T., 164

Tsukamoto, Mary, 2, 19

Turner, Victor: communitas, 213–214; on cultural institutions, 16; *The Forest of Symbols*, 197; on liminality, 11–12, 212–213, 218–219, 257n18; on social expectation, 197, 201; visibility of social structure through ritual practices, 212–213

Twain, Mark, 42, 43

*United States v. Thind*, 139

"Upper South" (definition), 239n1

Uppuluri, Ram, 192, 193

van Gennep, Arnold, 11

Verghese, Abraham, 179–193; in El Paso, Texas, 190–191; at Johnson City Medical Center, 179; in *Journal of Infectious Diseases*, 187; *My Own Country* (see *My Own Country*); in *New Yorker* magazine, 182; racial perspective of, 235; as southern author, 20, 164

Virginia: anti-miscegenation laws in, 46, 49, 50, 51–52, 73; intermarriage in, 245n48

*The Vulnerable Observer* (Behar), 129

*The Wages of Whiteness* (Roediger), 25, 93

"Waiting for the Barbarians" (Cavafy), 161

Walker, Alice, 164

Wallerstein, Immanuel, 41, 161

Ward, Robert De Courcey, 36

Warren, Earl, 245n49

Warren, Robert Penn, 47, 176

Weeks, Stephen B. See *Lost Colony of Roanoke*

Weston, Kath, 187, 218, 219

White, Edmund, 190

*White by Law* (Lopez), 93

white privilege in post-segregation era, 116

*The White Scourge* (Foley), 18

white supremacy: ambiguity and nuance of, 27; within deracinated liberalism, 114; irrational nature, 7–8; nuances of, 150; sexual morality and, 175

*White Women, Race Matters* (Frankenberg), 93

Whitelaw, Reid, 33

whiteness: American Indians and, 57; class solidarity school of, 94; Lumbee Tribes' claims to, 24, 67–73, 89; of Mexican Americans, 7–8, 32, 42; "near-whiteness," 115, 150–151; as normative, 216; performance of whiteness in litigation over racial status, 76–77; "race traitor school" of, 93; "white trash school" of, 93–94

*Whiteness of a Different Color* (Jacobson), 93

Whiteness Studies, 93–94

whites: as arbiters of the color line, 116; Asians as "honorary whites," 92; Chang and Eng Bunker functioning as, 43, 45; Chinese "acting" as, 119–120; Chinese association with, 250n14; Cubans' identification with, 10, 240n7; Filipinos as, 97–98; Japanese Americans as "honorary whites," 2; Lumbee Tribe performing as, 76–77; white-Chinese intermarriage, 48–49

Wiegman, Robyn, 93–94, 115, 116

Wilkins, David E.: factionalization among Lumbee Tribe, 86; on Lumbee quest for federal recognition, 84; on Lumbees' name transformations, 246n2; McMillan's motivations, 247n11; self-identification as Lumbee, 88

Williams, Patricia, 198–199

Wittig, Monique, 199

Wong, K. Scott, 151

Woodward, C. Vann: on Naipaul, 124; segregation and imperialism, 253n6; on the South, 159; *The Strange Career of Jim Crow*, 40

Wright, Richard: *Black Boy*, 29–30, 132; Ellison on, Ralph, 157

*Writing Culture* (Clifford), 129

Wu, Cindy, 26, 45

Yamato Colony, Florida, 36–37, 242n23

Yates, Sarah and Adelaide, 42

Yu, Henry, 136

Yung, Judy, 112–114, 151, 250n12

# About the Author

LESLIE BOW is Professor of English and Asian American Studies at the University of Wisconsin, Madison. She is the author of *Betrayal and Other Acts of Subversion: Feminism, Sexual Politics, Asian American Women's Literature,* editor of a scholarly reissue of Fiona Cheong's novel, *The Scent of the Gods* (University of Illinois Press), and is editing *Asian American Feminisms* (Routledge). She is a contributor to the *Progressive* and the Progressive Media Project.